D0031486

The Gilded Age

The Gilded Age

Joel Shrock

West Hills College Lemoore
LRC/Library
One College Avenue
Lemoore CA 9324

American Popular Culture Through History
Ray B. Browne, Series Editor

GREENWOOD PRESS
Westport, Connecticut • London

Library of Congress Cataloging-in-Publication Data

Shrock, Joel.
    The Gilded Age / Joel Shrock.
       p. cm.—(American popular culture through history)
    Includes bibliographical references and index.
    ISBN 0–313–32204–X (alk. paper)
    1. United States—Civilization—1865–1918. 2. Popular culture—United States—
History—19th century. I. Title. II. Series.
    E169.1.S5585 2004
    306'.0973'09034—dc22   2003057120

British Library Cataloguing in Publication Data is available.

Copyright © 2004 by Joel Shrock

All rights reserved. No portion of this book may be
reproduced, by any process or technique, without the
express written consent of the publisher.

Library of Congress Catalog Card Number: 2003057120
ISBN: 0–313–32204–X

First published in 2004

Greenwood Press, 88 Post Road West, Westport, CT 06881
An imprint of Greenwood Publishing Group, Inc.
www.greenwood.com

Printed in the United States of America

The paper used in this book complies with the
Permanent Paper Standard issued by the National
Information Standards Organization (Z39.48–1984).

10 9 8 7 6 5 4 3 2 1

For
Kelly, Owen, J.D., and Brenton

Contents

Contents

Series Foreword

Popular culture is the system of attitudes, behaviors, beliefs, customs, and tastes that define the people of any society. It is the entertainments, diversions, icons, rituals, and actions that shape the everyday world. It is what we do while we are awake and what we dream about while we are asleep. It is the way of life we inherit, practice, change, and then pass on to our descendants.

Popular culture is an extension of folk culture, the culture of the people. With the rise of electronic media and the increase in communication in American culture, folk culture expanded into popular culture—the daily way of life as shaped by the *popular majority* of society. Especially in a democracy like the United States, popular culture has become both the voice of the people and the force that shapes the nation. In 1782, the French commentator Hector St. Jean de Crèvecoeur asked in his *Letters from an American Farmer*, "What is an American?" He answered that such a person is the creation of America and is in turn the creator of the country's culture. Indeed, notions of the American Dream have long been grounded in the dream of democracy—that is, government by the people, or popular rule. Thus, popular culture is tied fundamentally to America and the dreams of its people.

Historically, culture analysts have tried to fine-tune culture into two categories: "elite"—the elements of culture (fine art, *literature*, classical music, gourmet food, etc.) that supposedly define the best of society—and "popular"—the elements of culture (comic strips, bestsellers, pop music, fast food, etc.) that appeal to society's lowest common denominator. The so-called "educated" person approved of elite culture and scoffed at popular culture. This schism first began to develop in Western

Europe in the fifteenth century when the privileged classes tried to discover and develop differences in societies based on class, money, privilege, and lifestyles. Like many aspects of European society, the debate between elite and popular cultures came to the United States. The upper class in America, for example, supported museums and galleries that would exhibit "the finer things in life," that would "elevate" people. As the twenty-first century emerges, however, the distinctions between popular culture and elitist culture have blurred. The blues songs (once denigrated as "race music") of Robert Johnson are now revered by musicologists; architectural students study buildings in Las Vegas as examples of what Robert Venturi called the "kitsch of high capitalism"; sportswriter Gay Talese and heavyweight boxing champ Floyd Patterson were co-panelists at a 1992 SUNY–New Paltz symposium on Literature and Sport. The examples go on and on, but the one commonality that emerges is the role of popular culture as a model for the American Dream, the dream to pursue happiness and a better, more interesting life.

To trace the numerous ways in which popular culture has evolved throughout American history, we have divided the volumes in this series into chronological periods—historical eras until the twentieth century, decades between 1900 and 2000. In each volume, the author explores the specific details of popular culture that reflect and inform the general undercurrents of the time. Our purpose, then, is to present historical and analytical panoramas that reach both backward into America's past and forward to her collective future. In viewing these panoramas, we can trace a very fundamental part of American society. The "American Popular Culture Through History" series presents the multifaceted parts of a popular culture in a nation that is both grown and still growing.

Ray B. Browne
Secretary-Treasurer
Popular Culture Association
American Culture Association

Acknowledgments

This book grows out of the pioneering work of scholars like Ray Browne and Russel Nye, who seemed to discover before other historians that "popular" did not necessarily mean inferior. The "American Popular Culture through History" series and this book on the Gilded Age perform a much-needed service. It is time to synthesize all of the wonderful popular culture work that scholars have produced in the last 30 years. By producing one volume on the popular culture of the entire Gilded Age it allows readers to see the themes that run so strongly through this era of American history and to make connections.

This book would never have happened without the kind recommendation of Thomas Winter, and to him I must give my sincere thanks. Rhonda Enloe, Joy Sweeney, Bobbi Claytor, Chris Mitchell, Lynne Owens, and Sally Knowles all played an important role in this project. My sincere thanks also go to my colleagues Jim Fuller, Richard Adkins, and Eric Henderson for their encouragement and conversation on the project. The people at Greenwood Press, Rob Kirkpatrick and Liz Kincaid, have been extremely understanding and helpful. This project never could have been completed without the massive commitment of my family. Owen graciously did without his dad on too many weekends. J.D. and Brenton went from wee babes in intensive care to great crawling boys over the course of this project. My spouse, Kelly Kirby Shrock, through illness, bed rest, premature delivery, and shouldering the incredible burden of the home front alone for the last eight months, never wavered in her support for this project. If this book has any merit it is due to the efforts of those who trained me—Mary Cayton, Drew Cayton, Allan Winkler, and Mary Frederickson—and if there are faults it is because I did not listen well enough.

Introduction

This is a book about popular culture in the Gilded Age. It is important to start with this simple statement because it clearly identifies what this book is not about. There are numerous studies that chart the rise of industrial output, the growth of railroad corporations, the rise of the robber barons, the creation of the steel and oil industries, political battles, the output of mechanized agriculture, and the intellectual history of the era. This book is not primarily concerned with these changes in the Gilded Age. Instead, it focuses on how the vast changes of the Gilded Age influenced the lives of average Americans, from the way they ate and dressed to their entertainment and vacations.

The lives of average Americans did undergo enormous changes in the Gilded Age as the country was transformed by the forces of immigration, industrialization, corporatization, urbanization, mechanization, and a revolution in transportation. Indeed, the United States witnessed the creation of modern, mass urban society, interconnected by new transportation and communication networks. These forces altered the country from a predominantly rural nation based primarily on agriculture and dedicated to the Protestant work ethic into an industrial, urban-dominated society that embraced leisure as one of the best things in life. The effects of these large changes on Americans were dramatic.

Youth were particularly affected. Middle-class youth found themselves largely kept free from the labor force and put into years of education, which allowed them to pioneer the creation of a new youth culture. The idea of adolescence gained greater acceptance in this period. Even as middle-class writers and thinkers were transforming their own children into romanticized innocents, working-class and immigrant youth seemed to pose a real threat to the nation. While middle-class youth were creating a distinctive culture focused around school, working-class youth were also forming their own distinctive urban culture that focused on new urban entertainments, sexuality, and sometimes crime. The case of the teen serial killer Jesse Pomeroy seemed to exemplify the problems of urban youth gone wild.

Advertising was a key force in the creation of the new leisure culture. At its heart, Gilded Age advertising promoted desires for greater status, better looks, cleaner teeth, a closer shave, and dapper clothes. Advertising sought to convince Americans that buying goods and services that made their lives easier or more meaningful was a good thing. This took a great deal of effort, because unlike the twentieth century, which would be characterized by an abundance of goods, the United States before industrialization and mechanized agriculture was dominated by scarcity. It took great effort for advertising to overcome the ingrained and historically necessary economic conservatism of Americans. Advertising had a strong influence over the development of a new leisure culture that stressed fulfillment of desire.

Modern mass society also transformed where and how people lived and worked. Most studies of Gilded Age architecture focus on elite mansions, public architecture, and the new skyscraper. All of these were important innovations, but perhaps more significant was the mass production of standardized building materials which revolutionized house building—house construction went from an enterprise that manufactured all the pieces of the home on-site and built it, to an activity where construction crews simply assembled the house from existing, standardized materials. And while there is no doubt that the skyscraper and elevators transformed the work world, perhaps a more important change was the introduction of amenities into residential housing. The introduction of gas lights, electricity, hot water heaters, indoor plumbing, and even indoor toilets on a limited scale certainly had a wider and more personal impact.

The emergence of the fashion industry was important because of its significant influence on everyday clothing styles. Mechanized factories produced ready-made clothes that, due to improved transportation networks and mail order catalogs, were suddenly available virtually everywhere. Before the Civil War the United States was a country where women purchased cloth and made clothing for the entire family, but by the 1890s ready-made clothing with standardized sizes was available for the entire family.

The transformative forces of the Gilded Age also dramatically altered what people ate. Dining out became more common and restaurants of all levels flourished. Most Anglo-Americans tended to stay within their own culinary traditions, but technological innovations such as the refrigerated rail car and factory and the expansion of railroads allowed for the efficient and inexpensive transportation of foods to markets everywhere in the nation. For the first time beef and out-of-season and exotic fruits and vegetables became widely available and affordable. Before the Civil War the meat Americans ate most frequently in every part of the country was pork, but in the Gilded Age that preference changed to beef. National brand-name processed foods also hit the market. Modern Americans commonly believe people in the past ate much better than we do today, but in reality Gilded Age Americans ate very heavy, starch-laden meals that focused on meat, skimped on green vegetables, grossly increased the intake of sugar, and averaged roughly 4,000 calories per day.

The new urban leisure culture also transformed the way Americans thought of and participated in leisure activities. Games, which had been viewed with some suspicion early in the century, became an integral part of American society. Not only boys and girls but also grown men and women participated in games! As the culture adjusted from one of scarcity, leisure activities no longer had to focus around work as they did previously with things like the quilting bee, barn raising, or corn husking. In the Gilded Age young people and adults were encouraged to participate in athletics and a number of modern sports appeared: football, basketball, and volleyball. Hobbies also gained in prominence as leisure and not work increasingly came to dominate American ideology.

The new leisure culture also encouraged people to vacation and travel more. Resorts, cottages, campgrounds, boardwalks, baseball games, and fairs all relied on railroads and electric trolleys to transport millions of Americans to their gates. To Gilded Age Americans, vacations and day trips seemed more important than ever due to the complexity and stress of modern life.

The Gilded Age also saw incredible changes in music, theater, and art. Many historians have noted the bifurcation of culture in the Gilded Age, as cultural elites sought to promote a "high" culture that centered around painting, European opera, classical orchestral music, and "legitimate" theater. There is no doubt that the elite saw this narrow collection of arts and performance as real "culture," and its restricted nature provided them with the prestige that they sought. "High" culture cannot be left out of this study, however, because in reality the exchange and flow between popular and high culture was significant. Indeed, the story of American culture in the Gilded Age is the story of the conflicts, borrowings, and compromises between popular and elite culture. The lines between the two look clear from a distance, but when examined closely they blur. For example, the famous illustrators Charles Dana Gibson, Frederic Remington, and Howard Pyle studied under the famous painters Adolph van der Wielen, Julien Alden Weir, Kenyon Cox, William Merritt Chase, and Thomas Eakins. Gibson, Remington, and Pyle all produced critically acclaimed paintings late in their careers and Remington is renowned for his bronze sculptures. Winslow Homer was a famous illustrator before gaining fame with his painting. Vaudeville and Broadway frequently traded stars; for example, vaudeville star May Irwin went on to become a Broadway star and legitimate theater star Ethel Barrymore performed in vaudeville. The result of this ambiguous mixing was a truly popular culture that was heavily influenced by elite culture and an elite culture that was just as heavily influenced by popular culture.

This book deals with these questions of how Gilded Age Americans responded to the vast changes transforming the nation in their everyday lives. The Gilded Age suffers under the weight of the term "Gilded Age," which was coined by Charles Dudley Warner and Mark Twain in their book of the same name that satirized the acquisitiveness of business in this age. What I hope the present book makes apparent is that the lives of average Americans were beginning to look strikingly similar to our own and that they were not so gilded after all.

Timeline of Popular Culture, 1875–1900

1875

The U.S. Patent Office has 1,138 brand names and trademarks registered.

Macy's department store opens the nation's first Toy Department.

Thomas Eakins finishes painting *The Gross Clinic*.

Heinz reorganizes after a bankruptcy with Heinz tomato ketchup as its major product.

Dime novel publishers produce cheap libraries consisting of short pamphlets for $.05 each. (Cheap libraries were low-cost books sold in a packaged series, and they were the inexpensive counterparts of the middle class–oriented Home Library Series.)

Daniel Chester French finishes the sculpture *The Minuteman*.

1876

The hay loader is invented.

National League baseball plays its first official game between Boston and Philadelphia, and Jim O'Rourke slaps the first hit.

Fred Harvey opens his first railroad depot restaurant in Topeka, Kansas.

Alexander Graham Bell invents the telephone.

The Centennial Exposition in Philadelphia begins in May and the 2,500 horsepower Corliss engine becomes a big attraction for the nearly 10 million people who attend.

Successful merchant John Wanamaker opens his Philadelphia "Grand Depot" which would produce the full-fledged retail department store by the 1890s.

General Armstrong Custer is defeated at the Battle of Little Bighorn.

Teenage serial killer Jesse Pomeroy is convicted and sentenced to life in solitary confinement.

The American Library Association (ALA) is formed.

Ira Sankey publishes the first gospel music in *Gospel Hymns*.

1877

The Great Railroad Strike.

Richard Kyle Fox purchases the *National Police Gazette*.

1878

Harrigan and Hart's musical comedy *The Mulligan Guard Picnic* appears on Broadway.

Gilbert and Sullivan's *H.M.S. Pinafore* sweeps the United States in pirated versions of the operetta.

Thomas Edison forms the Edison Electric Light Company, which later becomes General Electric.

Thomas Edison patents the phonograph.

James Bland hits it big with his song "Carry Me Back to Old Virginny."

The American Cereal Company introduces Quaker Oats as the first national brand-name breakfast cereal.

Terence Powderly is chosen as the leader of the Knights of Labor.

J. Walter Thompson buys his first advertising agency.

The Chautauqua Literary and Scientific Circle (a book club) is formed.

The cord binder is invented.

1879

Procter & Gamble names Ivory Soap.

The National Croquet Association is founded.

Department store pioneer John Wanamaker places the first full-page advertisement.

Jerome Secor of Ives, Blakeslee, & Secor creates the first cast iron vehicle toy, a locomotive.

The dumbbell tenement is introduced.

1880

P. T. Barnum merges with James Bailey to create the Barnum & Bailey circus.

The U.S. population is 50,100,000, with 6,600,000 immigrants.

Roughly 80 percent of New Yorkers are foreign-born or of foreign-born parentage, and the city has twice as many Irish as Dublin and over double the Jewish population of Warsaw.

Joel Chandler Harris publishes *Uncle Remus.*

John Wanamaker hires a full-time advertising writer, John E. Powers, who creates a new style of honest advertising.

Walter Camp leads rule changes that would create modern football.

Lew Wallace publishes *Ben Hur: A Tale of the Christ.*

1881

The United States National Lawn Tennis Association is formed.

American-born opera singer Adeline Patti makes her first U.S. tour.

Charles Guiteau assassinates President James Garfield.

Frederick Eugene Ives invents the halftone process, which allows original illustrations to be printed in magazines.

George Pullman opens his company town, Pullman, Illinois, to house the workers in his famous railroad sleeping car business.

Henry Lee Higginson creates the Boston Symphony Orchestra, which was the nation's first standing orchestra.

1882

John D. Rockefeller creates his Standard Oil Trust in order to avoid monopoly laws.

The Chinese Exclusion Act is passed, which excludes Chinese immigration to the United States.

Van Camp Packing Company Incorporated manufactures 6 million cans of pork and beans.

Thomas Edison's Pearl Street steam-powered central station begins to supply commercial electricity to New York City.

The *Montgomery Ward Catalogue* offers 282 pages of mail order goods.

1883

Buffalo Bill Cody begins his Wild West Show.

Illustrator Palmer Cox introduces his cartoon Brownies in *St. Nicholas.*

The Brooklyn Bridge opens after 14 years of construction.

The Novelty Electric Company of Philadelphia introduces the first electric toy—a train.

Robert Louis Stevenson publishes *Treasure Island*.

Joseph Pulitzer purchases the *New York World*.

Illustrator and author Howard Pyle publishes *The Merry Adventures of Robin Hood*.

1884

William Dean Howells publishes *The Rise of Silas Lapham*.

John Singer Sargent paints *Madame X*.

The linotype machine, which dramatically improves the ability to reproduce color, is invented.

Frank Julian Sprague invents the electric trolley.

Lake Chautauqua resort constructs the Athenaeum Hotel.

Winslow Homer finishes painting *The Life Line*.

1885

A box camera, with the film sealed inside, is sold for the first time.

Mark Twain's *Hucklebery Finn* appears.

Benjamin F. Keith introduces a shortened, pirated version of *The Mikado* in 1885 in his vaudeville theater for $.25 and attracts massive crowds.

The Haymarket Square Riot.

William L. Jenney's Home Insurance Company Building in Chicago is the first true metal-frame skyscraper.

The genteel magazine *Century* hits height of circulation, 250,000, and literary significance.

Witmark Brothers is formed, which would become one of the major Tin Pan Alley music firms.

1886

The American Federation of Labor is organized and led by Samuel Gompers.

Geronimo surrenders.

1887

Congress passes the Dawes Severalty Act.

John Reid establishes St. Andrews Club in Yonkers, New York, the oldest surviving golf club in the nation.

The Quaker Mill Company creates first cereal registered trademark for Quaker Oats.

William Randolph Hearst takes control of the *San Francisco Examiner*.

1888

Parker Brothers game manufacturers is founded.

Edward Bellamy publishes *Looking Backward*.

The Daisy BB gun appears.

George Eastman invents the first roll film camera which he names the Kodak.

"Drill, Ye Tarriers, Drill" is a hit song.

1889

Street and Smith dime novel publishers is formed.

Industrialist Andrew Carnegie donates money to build a library, starting a trend until he had donated $56 million to build 2,509 libraries.

The Columbian Reading Union (a Catholic book club) is formed.

1890

Twelve major circuses are using the railroad, including Barnum & Bailey and Ringling Brothers.

A Trip to Chinatown is one of the biggest Broadway hits of the decade.

Jacob Riis publishes *How the Other Half Lives*.

Anna Sewell publishes *Black Beauty* in the United States.

Reporter Nellie Bly travels around the world like the fictional Phineas Fogg and the board game *Round the World with Nellie Bly* comes out the same year.

Mississippi introduces the poll tax and literacy test to restrict African-American voting.

Safety bicycle is introduced in the United States.

Roughly 80 percent of New Yorkers are foreign-born or of foreign-born parentage.

1891

Thomas Edison patents his motion picture camera and a primitive radio.

Hamlin Garland publishes *Main-Traveled Roads*.

James Naismith invents basketball.

The Chicago Symphony Orchestra is formed, with Theodore Thomas hired to conduct.

Nathan Fowler recommends that advertisers direct their ads to women because they do most of the household shopping.

The American Express Traveler's Cheque is copyrighted.

First annual convention of the American Numismatic Association (stamp collectors).

Leopold Vincent produces the *Alliance and Labor Songster*.

The United States is a signatory of the International Copyright Law.

Louis Comfort Tiffany finishes his famous stained glass piece *Peacock Mosaic*.

1892

The Metropolitan Opera burns down and the new Met is built with the famous "Diamond Horseshoe" of box seats.

Harry Dacre's "Daisy Bell," better known as "A Bicycle Built for Two," is a popular song.

Ellis Island is opened.

John Philip Sousa forms his military band.

The Homestead Strike.

Ladies' Home Journal bans patent medicine advertising.

Gentleman Jim Corbett defeats John Sullivan in a gloved prizefight under Queensbury rules.

The International Cyclist Association is created.

The Populist (or People's) Party is founded.

"After the Ball" by Charles K. Harris is a massive hit, selling 2 million copies of sheet music and marking the start of the Tin Pan Alley's song factories.

1893

Coca-Cola is established as a registered trademark by pharmacist Asa Briggs Chandler.

The Columbian Exposition (World's Fair) in Chicago attracts 27 million visitors.

S. S. McClure creates *McClure's* mass-market magazine.

Frank Munsey cuts the price of his *Munsey's* magazine to $.10 per issue and $1 per year.

Duryea motorized buggy is invented.

Sears, Roebuck and Company introduces its mail order catalog.

1894

Entrepreneurs open parlors to show short films on Edison's kinetoscope.

By this date, 261 YMCA gyms have been founded across the country.

R. C. Maxwell agency, which specializes in outdoor advertising, is founded.

Mary Cassatt finishes painting *The Boating Party*.

Pullman Strike.

1895

Stephen Crane publishes *The Red Badge of Courage*.

The United States Open, United States Amateur, and U.S. Women's Amateur golf tournaments are held.

Ben Harney publishes the first ragtime song, "You've Been a Good Old Wagon but You've Done Broke Down."

By this date, 850 trolley lines are operating in U.S. cities.

William G. Morgan invents volleyball at the Holyoke, Massachusetts, YMCA.

The Supreme Court decision *In re Debs* allows use of court injunctions to halt strikes.

Gilbert Patten (Burt L. Standish) publishes the first of 208 Frank Merriwell books.

The Socialist newspaper *Appeal to Reason* begins publication, soon becoming the largest radical publication in the country.

Frederic Remington finishes his bronze sculpture *The Bronco Buster*.

1896

Benjamin Franklin Keith first uses a film in a vaudeville theater.

Sam Nixon, Fred Zimmerman, Charles Frohman, Al Hayman, Marc Klaw, and Abraham Erlanger create the Theatrical Syndicate which soon dominates legitimate theater.

The Monarch Bicycle Company spends $125,000 for advertising and sponsors a touring bicycle racing crew; total bicycle industry sales top $60 million.

Ivory Soap provides chromolithographic advertising prints to magazines, which rarely spent the money for full-color ads, so Ivory could guarantee they would have quality color ads.

Tootsie Roll candy is introduced.

John Wanamaker and Siegel-Cooper's department stores open in New York City.

May Irwin has a musical hit with a coon song known as the "Bully Song."

The Supreme Court issues the *Plessy v. Ferguson* decision, which creates the "separate but equal" doctrine.

Color comics are introduced into newspapers, first Richard Outcault's "The Yellow Kid," followed shortly by Rudolph Dirks' "Katzenjammer Kids."

Isabella Stewart Gardner purchases Titian's famous painting, *The Rape of Europa*.

1897

John T. Dorrence invents condensed soup for the Joseph A. Campbell Preserve Company.

Bob Cole and Billy Johnson produce *A Trip to Coontown*, the first all-black musical.

L. Frank Baum founds *The Show Window* journal for the people involved in the new occupation of department store window decorator.

Augustus Saint-Gaudens finishes the Robert Gould Shaw Memorial in Boston.

George Tilyou creates the first amusement park at Coney Island.

Field and Stream magazine is published.

Emma Gray's *Fun for the Household: A Book of Games* is published.

Munsey's magazine hits circulation of 700,000.

Pearl B. Wait introduces Jell-O.

1898

The National Biscuit Company hires N. W. Ayer & Son advertising agency to promote its new cracker, and Ayer devises the very successful Uneeda Biscuit campaign.

The Spanish-American War.

Caleb D. Bradham introduces Pepsi-Cola.

L. Frank Baum founds the National Association of Window Trimmers.

Orison Swett Marden publishes one of his many success books, *The Secret of Achievement*.

1899

Kate Chopin publishes *The Awakening*.

Thorstein Veblen publishes *A Theory of the Leisure Class*, which coined the phrase "conspicuous consumption."

"On the Banks of the Wabash" is a huge musical hit for Paul Dresser.

Byron Bancroft Johnson creates professional baseball's American League.

The St. Nicholas League is started by *St. Nicholas Magazine* so its young readers can contribute stories, games, puzzles, illustrations, and photographs to the magazine.

Scott Joplin's "Maple Leaf Rag" becomes a huge ragtime hit.

Edward Stratemeyer publishes the first three Rover Boys books, starting the syndicate that would later produce Tom Swift, the Hardy Boys, and Nancy Drew.

1900

Frank Baum publishes *The Wizard of Oz*.

Ayer & Son is the largest advertising agency in the nation, employing 160 people and handling accounts for Hires' Root Beer, J. I. Case threshing machines, Procter & Gamble soaps, the National Biscuit Company, Mellin's Baby Food, and Standard Oil.

Hard liquor consumption hits a low of 1.2 gallons per capita but beer consumption rises to 15.5 gallons per capita.

Theodore Dreiser publishes *Sister Carrie*.

Railroads carry 576,831,000 passengers.

The *Montgomery Ward Catalogue* offers 1,000 pages of mail order goods.

The Gilded Age

1

Everyday America

BACKGROUND

The Gilded Age was a period of incredible change, and the United States looked very different by the 1890s than it had in the 1870s. Urbanization was transforming American culture as urban residents and values came to dominate American discourse. Even rural America underwent its own metamorphosis as the forces of industrialization mass produced agricultural machines that dramatically increased yields. The very nature of American democracy was tested as millions of immigrants streamed into the nation, the U.S. government won the last of the Indian wars, and American society had to come to grips with the legacy of the Civil War and Reconstruction regarding the place of African Americans. Through all of these contentious changes the federal government accomplished important tasks including Reconstruction, civil service reform, and the beginnings of industrial regulation.

CITIES

Explosive urban growth was one of the most revolutionary forces in Gilded Age America. At the beginning of the Civil War the United States was largely rural and agriculture dominated the economy, but by the turn of the twentieth century the nation was an industrial giant with a massive urban network. Vast demographic, cultural, and geographical changes altered not only the physical layout of cities but also the very mores and values of the American people. The Gilded Age gave birth to the metropolis in the United States, and these great urban centers began to exert increasing influence over the nation.

Urbanization

Massive population growth was one of the most easily recognizable changes in American cities. The nation's urban population stood at 6.2 million in 1860, but grew exponentially to 30 million by the end of the century. Although 46 million people still lived in rural America in 1900, the rate of urban growth astounded and sometimes frightened Gilded Age Americans. New York City, for example, took over 200 years to reach a population of roughly 515,000 by 1850, but by 1900 counted over 3.4 million residents! Although urban areas in the Gilded Age were defined rather broadly as any city over 2,500 people, the sheer number of urban areas swelled remarkably. In 1860 there were only 400 towns with more than 2,500 residents, 58 cities with 10,000–25,000 residents, and just nine cities with more than 100,000 residents. By 1900 there were 1,737 towns of 2,500 or more, 280 cities of 10,000–25,000, 38 cities of more than 100,000, and three cities (New York, Chicago, and Philadelphia) with more than 1 million residents.[1] It is difficult to overestimate the impact of these demographic changes in the last three decades of the nineteenth century.

Migrants and Immigrants

The migrants pouring into these urban areas, new and old, were mainly coming from rural backgrounds. Roughly half of the new city dwellers were from the American countryside, making their way to urban areas as a result of a confluence of events: the growing industrial job base, large rural populations, falling farm prices, and the increased mechanization of farming which now needed far less full-time human labor. The other half of the new city residents were immigrants leaving largely rural, peasant villages for the new American metropolis. Between 1866 and 1900, 13.25 million immigrants would pour into the United States and most of these new arrivals stayed in large cities, creating massive foreign populations in these giant urban centers. On the East Coast New York City, in the interior Chicago, and on the West Coast San Francisco all boasted foreign populations of over 40 percent in 1890. Even cities like Cleveland and Minneapolis possessed immigrant populations of 37 percent. Even more telling is the fact that roughly 80 percent of New Yorkers in 1890 were foreign born or of foreign-born parentage. Any visitor to New York City would have noticed the polyglot population; after all, this was a city that in 1890 had twice as many Irish as Dublin and more than double the Jewish population of Warsaw.[2]

African-American Migration

African Americans from the rural South were also pushing into American cities in unprecedented numbers, a small foreshadowing of the Great Migration that would come in the second decade of the next century. In the 1870s, 68,000 African Americans left the rural South and this number increased every decade of the Gilded Age, culminating in the 1890s when 185,000 left their homes. In this era most African-American urban movement was not to Northern industrial cities but instead to the cities of the South. Black populations in Atlanta, Savannah, and Nashville all doubled while Memphis experienced a 235 percent increase. Although numbers of African Americans remained small in most Northern cities at the turn of the century, roughly 60 percent of Northern blacks lived in cities and sizeable populations were beginning to develop in New York, Chicago, and Philadelphia.[3]

Regional Metropolitan Growth

The spectacular metropolitan growth during the Gilded Age completed a large urban network in the United States. A truly urban society had emerged and nearly every city that would reach even medium size in the twentieth century was established during the Gilded Age. Industrialization and the massive proliferation of railroads in the Gilded Age stimulated the founding of new municipalities. City boosterism created an atmosphere of intense competition among cities to attract commerce and people.[4]

It is important to note, however, that though this urban growth was widespread, encompassing cities from New York to St. Louis, Tacoma to San Francisco, it was far from evenly distributed in every state or region. The Northeast was by far the most urbanized section of the nation, boasting an urban population of 66.1 percent in 1900. Even this generalization has to be tempered because there was incredible variation even among the Northeastern states. For example, in 1880 Vermont's rural population outnumbered its urban population 9 to 1, whereas Rhode Island had 82 percent urban dwellers. The Northcentral and Western sections of the country possessed urban populations of close to 40 percent in 1900, with substantial variation again from state to state. The South followed far behind the other regions of the country with an urban population of only 18 percent. Of the 20 largest cities in the country in 1900 none were in the old Confederate states. And though certain regions had high percentages of urban residents, the bulk of the urban population in total numbers still resided in the old Union and border states from the Civil War that spanned an arc from the Midwest through the Northeast.[5]

Form of the Modern City

The spatial increase of American cities coincided with the massive population growth. The old walking cities of colonial America disappeared over the course of the nineteenth century and faded ever more rapidly during the frenzied expansion of the Gilded Age. Horse-cars, horse railways, elevated railroads, and electric trolleys vastly expanded the reach of American commuters (see Chapter 11).

As cities spread geographically, the modern radial city appeared and separated commercial, industrial, and residential land. As geographic mobility increased and land costs exploded, city financial districts developed. Real estate values in downtown Chicago increased by a whopping 700 percent from 1887 to 1891. As a result of the increase in land prices and the geographic expansion of the city, greater differentiation of residential areas by social class occurred. Encircling the financial district with its prosperous retail stores and office buildings were slums where the poorest city residents lived, packed tightly together in tenements, shacks, and sometimes cellars. Outside of the ring of slums were rings of the upper-working-class and lower-middle-class neighborhoods. On the fringe of the cities were middle-class suburban residents living in new apartments or private homes and commuting into the city to work and shop.[6]

Urban Values versus Rural Values

Perhaps the most important change wrought by urbanization in the Gilded Age was a dramatic shift from the predominance of rural values to urban values. A substantial shift in power occurred in the late nineteenth century as cities came to dominate the nation economically, politically, and culturally. Cities became centers of transportation and industrial hubs, huge voting blocs for any potential political candidate, and they developed a vibrant new urban culture which included bastions of high culture such as opera, symphony orchestras, and museums to popular public recreations like ballparks, amusement parks, dance halls, and vaudeville theaters. All of these factors combined during the Gilded Age to lay the foundation of modern, secular culture which was dedicated to consumption, leisure, and pleasure. One prime example where cities led the way in changing cultural values was in the area of sexuality, which was highly contested terrain. Under the influence of Victorian middle-class mores, premarital sex rates fell to a century low of roughly 10 percent by 1850. The massive growth of urban centers in the Gilded Age and the resulting urban culture began a rebellion against Victorian sexual morality. Premarital sex rates from 1880 to 1910 rose to 23 percent, signaling a sexual revolution that would culminate in the 1920s.[7] The great cities became the dominant force in Gilded Age America and spear-headed culture change.

COUNTRY

Even though industrialization and urbanization were twin forces of change altering American society dramatically and permanently, the countryside still possessed the majority of the population in 1900—46 million people—and was itself going through radical changes during the Gilded Age. Miners, ranchers, and farmers pushed west in a tidal wave of settlement. The mechanization of farming brought industrial life and even some of its work patterns into the country. And in spite of common experiences and widespread protest movements, like the Farmer's Alliance and Populism, rural life in the different regions of the nation had different textures and experiences.

Settlement

Gilded Age America witnessed successive waves of settlement into the American West that rapidly transformed the region. Whereas it took European Americans from 1607 to 1870 to settle 409 million acres and cultivate 189 million acres of land, a massive wave of settlement in the West from 1870 to 1900 brought another 430 million acres settled and 225 million acres cultivated. Ironically, the railroad, a harbinger of industrialization, penetrated the uninhabited West and made the rapid invasion of this region possible. By 1890 the U.S. Census declared the frontier officially closed—there was an average of two non-Indian people per square mile. The Western half of the nation was settled and came into statehood from 1859 to 1900. The only exceptions out of the 17 Western states were Texas (1845), California (1850), Oklahoma (1907), Arizona (1912), and New Mexico (1912). In fact, Washington, Montana, Wyoming, Idaho, North Dakota, and South Dakota all became states within one frenetic two-year period of state building from 1889 to 1890.

Sale of Public Land

The federal government sponsored most of this dramatic growth by passing a number of laws that provided for the orderly transference and sale of almost half of the 1 billion acres of public lands. The famous Homestead Act of 1862 provided 160 acres of land for settlers willing to pay the $10 fee, improve it, and reside on it for five years. Homesteaders could purchase the land after six months of residence for $1.25 per acre if they chose not to fulfill the residency requirement. From the time of the law's passage until 1900 the federal government gave away almost

48 million acres of land to nearly 400,000 homesteaders. Railroads also sold large amounts of land to settlers for one-fourth of the total cost down and payments extended over a period of 10 years. Additional acts, such as the Timber Culture Act of 1873, Desert Land Act of 1877, and Timber and Stone Act of 1878 all sold land cheaply for farming or natural resource extraction. By 1900 the federal government had given away nearly 500 million acres of land, but the vast majority of it went to corporations and land speculators. And though it is important to observe that the common farmer did not receive as much proportionally as large businesses and wealthy speculators, historian Gilbert Fite has noted that many small farmers were also speculators seeking to profit from purchasing land cheaply and selling when land prices rose, rather than developing a successful farm through hard work. The fact that two-thirds of all homesteaders failed before 1890 starkly illustrates the difficulties confronting settlers in their attempts to create successful farms in the West. In spite of the hurdles, the total number of U.S. farms grew from just over 2 million in 1860 to over 5.7 million in 1900.[8]

Mining and Ranching

Mining and ranching also brought European-American settlers into the West. The great mining boom brought a transient population of white Americans as well as a host of international miners from as far away as Chile and China into the West. Silver and gold mines in Washington, Nevada, Montana, Arizona, Idaho, Colorado, and South Dakota kept a steady stream of miners pouring into the West. The Gilded Age West was also notable for its creation of cattle culture. After the Civil War, Texas rancher Joseph McCoy pioneered driving herds of cattle from Texas ranches to railroad centers in Kansas. Abilene, for example, became one center of long cattle drives and received 700,000 cattle in 1871. By the mid-1880s the invention of barbed wire was beginning to carve up the open range into separate ranches and farmer homesteads throughout Kansas and Nebraska. The era of the open range ended almost entirely with the terrible winter of 1887 that killed tens of thousands of cattle. Ranchers survived by fencing in their land, trimming herd numbers, concentrating on quality, and using crude irrigation to grow hay to feed their livestock in the winter. Less well-known but equally as important was the sheep industry in the West, which produced both meat and wool. By 1900, Montana, New Mexico, and Wyoming were the three largest sheep producers in the country and the West possessed 38 million sheep.[9]

Mechanization of Agriculture

One of the most revolutionary events in the countryside during the Gilded Age was the mechanization of farming. A host of new inventions flooded the market and soon farm implements were used by all but the smallest farms. Western farmers needed the chilled-iron plow to break up the heavy prairie grass. The grain drill (1874) planted grains from a hopper at an incredible rate and allowed farmers to plant more land much faster than hand planting. The lister (1880) was a double mold-board plow that could till and plant crops at the same time. The hay loader (1876) cut labor by using the turning of its wheels to drive a conveyor of wooden slats that picked hay off the ground, which had already been cut and raked into neat rows, and deposited it on a hay wagon. Another important invention was the cord binder (1878), which cut and tied crops into bundles with twine to allow them to dry. The wheat industry was propelled to new heights of production by the self-binding reaper, header, steam-powered threshers, and by the 1890s large steam-powered combines. Farm production as a whole increased three fold from 1865 to 1900. Wheat production provides a stark example of how mechanization revolutionized farming. The United States produced 211 million bushels of wheat in 1867, but through mechanization this number grew to a staggering 599 million bushels in 1900. In the same era U.S. exports of wheat grew from 6 million to 102 million bushels per year.

Bonanza Farms

Mechanization encouraged the growth of bonanza farms, particularly those in the Red River Valley in North Dakota and Minnesota. Managers began to view farming as big business and looked to the model of in-dustry. Strict business principles were applied to these large farms: large economy of scale, heavy investment in the latest mechanized farm im-plements, specialized production, absentee ownership, and professional management. By 1874 bonanza farms were appearing in the Red River Valley and in the Central Valley in California, to be followed by the central Plains states. Famous bonanza farmer Oliver Dalrymple pio-neered the bonanza farm in the Red River Valley. He would eventually manage a 61,000-acre farm that employed an army of workers and lit-erally hundreds of machines to cultivate 600,000 bushels of wheat in 1881. Although the bonanza farm boom stalled by the late 1880s (the inability to control production and price made the techniques of industry difficult to reproduce in agriculture), the pattern of large-scale farms sur-vived and continued to dominate agriculture. Ironically, mechanization and increased yields created the need for massive amounts of itinerant laborers to work the wheat harvests in the Gilded Age and early twen-tieth century. Large numbers of seasonal workers from urban and rural America were attracted by high wages.[10]

The farming boom in the Plains states during the unusually wet 1880s, particularly in Kansas and Nebraska, came to a screeching halt in the drought of 1887. Over half the population of Kansas fled the state between 1888 and 1892. New farming techniques, particularly dry farming, elements of which had been in use in California and Utah since the 1860s, came to be widely adopted in the Plains states. Farmers also began to plant Turkey Red wheat from Russia, which was hardier and better able to handle the tough conditions of the Great Plains.[11]

Rise of Farm Protest

Perhaps more significantly, farmers found themselves increasingly marginalized in a nation that in prior decades had staked its very survival on the independent, yeoman farmer. As industry moved into a position of dominance in the American economy, agriculture became a secondary industry. Relative to the other sectors of the economy farming fell, generating only 24 percent of the gross domestic product in the 1890s compared to 38 percent in the 1870s. International competition in wheat production and increasing tariff barriers by the 1880s hurt U.S. wheat producers. Farm tenancy rates rose alarmingly from 25 percent of the farm population in 1880 to 36 percent in 1900. The mechanization and expansion of agriculture in the 1870s encouraged farmers to use credit to acquire implements and land. But in the lean times after the 1880s farmers found credit increasingly difficult to obtain. Unfair railroad shipping rates, tight credit policies after the United States re-adopted the gold standard, cyclical economic recessions, falling wheat and cotton prices, and the sharecropping system of the South would spark an unprecedented agrarian revolt that generated successive waves of reform movements.

The Grange

Oliver Kelley, a Department of Agriculture clerk, founded the National Grange of the Patrons of Husbandry in 1867. The Grange grew rapidly with the Panic of 1873. Grange leaders encouraged the founding of farmers' cooperatives to provide cheaper equipment and seed for their members as well as the formation of their own insurance companies, grain elevators, and banks. Grangers aggressively attacked the system of railroad rates and scored several successes in states like Illinois, which passed Granger laws regulating railroad freight costs.

The Farmer's Alliance

The Grange declined in the late 1870s to be replaced by a larger, more aggressive organization, the Farmer's Alliance. Describing this movement as a single organization is difficult since it actually consisted of several state and regional units like the Kansas Farmer's Alliance, the Southern Farmer's Alliance, as well as the Colored Farmer's National Alliance. The Southern Farmer's Alliance combined with the state Alliances in Kansas, North Dakota, and South Dakota in 1889 and renamed itself the National Farmer's Alliance and Industrial Union. The new National Farmer's Alliance dominated the Alliance movement thereafter, though regional conflicts within the organization were commonplace.

The Populist Party

Motivated by their moderate successes in the elections of 1890, the Alliances formed a new third political party, the Populist (or People's) Party in 1892 in order for the organization to achieve its reform goals. Agrarian radicals consciously sought to ally themselves with organized labor and industrial workers against the monopolies and corporate interests dominating the economy and government. The U.S. government increased tariff rates fairly consistently in the Gilded Age, which helped most American industries but hurt farmers. Farmers had to purchase their manufactured goods at inflated prices while U.S. agricultural commodities were hurt by the retaliatory tariffs erected by other nations. Populists demanded an end to the corporate domination of the government and for the federal government to work aggressively to mitigate the effects of industrial capitalism for the benefit of the people. These reformers sought greater government control of the money supply, a combined gold and silver standard set at 16 to 1 to ease credit problems, government control of railroads and telegraphs, postal savings banks, a graduated income tax, initiative, referendum, recall, the direct election of the president and senators, and an end to the voting restrictions in the South. People like Tom Watson (Georgia), Jeremiah Simpson (Kansas), and Mary Lease (Kansas) provided dynamic leadership for the cause.

In the elections of 1892 and 1894 the Populists had some measure of success nationally and in Kansas they won the governorship and the Senate. In the South widespread fraud and violence against African-American voters in these elections insured Democratic victories in all but North Carolina, where a fusion of Republicans-Populists carried the state. Populist-held offices actually declined in 1894, but they scored 41 percent more votes in congressional elections than they had in 1892. More impressively, while Republicans controlled the Senate, Populists held the balance of power. By 1894 the Populist Party was one of the two major parties in the South and West. The election of 1896 proved to be disastrous, however, as the Democrats took the free silver platform that was central to Populist support. The Populists supported Democrat William Jennings Bryan in a campaign that saw the Republicans win the presidency and control of both houses of Congress. Although the People's Party sent 31 people to Congress in 1897, they accomplished little. By 1900, Populists had been turned back even in Kansas. Urban industrial laborers never supported Populists, but stayed wedded to the Democratic political machines that catered to their needs. Also, by the turn of the century widespread violence and the effective manipulation of racial fears destroyed the interracial coalition of Populists in the South. While the Populist Party died in the late nineteenth century, its commitment to an egalitarian society managed for the benefit of the people, not corporations, resonated powerfully in the United States. Many Populist measures would become law under the Progressive movement in the early twentieth century. But more significantly, Populists would set a pattern for future reform movements, particularly the Progressives, by organizing a political party and using governmental might to effect reform in the face of incredible corporate power.[12]

SELF-PROTECTION

Gilded Age America witnessed the massive expansion of gun culture. *Arming America* by Michael Bellesiles clearly illustrates how the U.S. government consistently tried to arm the American public from the Revolutionary to the Civil War, and largely failed. As industrial gun making emerged during the Civil War, however, widespread gun ownership became a reality in the United States. Union and even Confederate soldiers often returned home with their firearms and the federal government sold 2.5 million surplus rifled muskets. Firearm prices plummeted in a gun market already saturated by gun makers. An entire generation had easy access to inexpensive firearms and viewed gun ownership and use as a patriotic necessity.

National Rifle Association

With subsidies from the U.S. government, the National Rifle Association, founded by Civil War veterans William Conant Church and George Wood Wingate, launched a campaign to make Americans comfortable with gun ownership. As cheap, mass-produced firearms spread rapidly throughout the nation, the NRA developed into a popular organization which promoted firearm use among American men. The widespread gun culture that emerged in the Gilded Age was so ubiquitous that a religious magazine in 1879 gave away a gun with every new subscription.

Advertising

Gun makers consistently geared their advertising toward self-protection, playing on fears of dangerous Indians, brigands, tramps, and immigrant hordes. Even before the Civil War, Samuel Colt marketed his weapons as necessities for the defense of every man and referred to his pistols as "peacemakers." By 1872, Colt's company introduced its "peacemaker" pistol, which employed self-contained metal cartridges. Guns not only brought manly security but also peace. The Western Gun Works of Chicago advertised a $3 pistol called the "Tramps Terror" and urged every man to arm himself against the hordes of thieves and tramps roaming the country. Colt continued to play up Americans' fears with an ad that pictured a revolver and one word, "Protection." By the early twentieth century Colt ads carried the slogan "the arm of law and order." Fears of immigrants and increasingly violent confrontations between management and organized labor in places like Homestead, Pennsylvania, where 16 men were killed in a day-long gun battle in 1892, added to the perceived need of a firearm for self-protection.[13]

CRIME

Crime is a socially defined construct that determines what behaviors a society will and will not tolerate. In the Gilded Age the reconstructed nation's white elites defined, regulated, and politically controlled crime to fit their needs and vision of the nation. Crime took on new guises in the Gilded Age as the nature and style of crimes changed with massive immigration, the emergence of a mass urban society, and the ready availability of firearms. In addition, corporations and government entities used injunctions to halt strikes, and this strategy was upheld in 1895 by the Supreme Court decision *In re Debs*. The Comstock Law represented Victorian efforts to criminalize the growing sex industry by attacking pornographic and obscene materials (which included birth control information) sent through the mail. Many states built modern penitentiaries and cities further professionalized their police forces. In 1880 census data indicates the United States had 13,700 police serving in varying capacities.[14] The white elite criminalized behaviors in an attempt to suppress vice, contain the militancy of organized labor, and to control immigrant populations and newly freed African Americans.

Guns and Violent Crime

The massive expansion of inexpensive firearms in the United States in the Gilded Age made violent crime, particularly murders using guns, increase dramatically. With small, relatively cheap revolvers readily available, homicide levels grew alarmingly in cities as well as frontier areas, sparking fears of a national murder crisis. Just after the end of the Civil War in 1865 violent crimes rose by 60 percent. Yet, for all the fears of the homicide crisis, most murders still occurred where large numbers of single men gathered in dangerous and physically demanding occupations. Western miners and cowboys as well as the "floating army" of men who tramped around the country, hopping from industrial jobs to wheat harvests, lived in highly volatile bachelor subcultures filled with alcohol and guns. Mining towns were murderous places. Bodie, California, boasted a homicide rate of 116 per 100,000 people between 1878 and 1882 and Leadville, Colorado (1880) was nearly as high with 105. Cattle towns frequented by cowboys fresh off the long cattle drives from Texas were nearly as deadly. The Kansas cattle towns of Abilene, Ellsworth, Wichita, and Caldwell averaged 1.5 homicides per year, but given their small populations this was 50 murders per 100,000 people. Dodge City may have boasted the highest murder rate, somewhere close to 116 per 100,000. Fort Griffin, Texas, had to be one of the deadliest places in the United States, claiming a murder rate of 229 per 100,000 in the 1870s. Eastern cities like Boston and Philadelphia paled in comparison to the frontier regions with 5.8 and 3.2 homicides per 100,000 people, respectively, from 1860 to 1880.[15]

Even though crime rates leveled off by the 1870s criminal behavior appeared more public and troublesome than ever. Crimes seemed to be more daring and intelligent as demonstrated by thieves who stole $1.2 million from the Wall Street offices of Lord Bond. Butch Cassidy and the Sundance Kid and numerous others like the James, Dalton, and Younger families robbed trains and banks throughout the West. Lawlessness seemed rampant as industrial workers engaged in large-scale strikes such as the Great Railroad Strike of 1877, Haymarket Riot in 1886, Homestead Strike in 1892, and the Pullman Strike of 1896 where strikers fought with hired strikebreakers and even troops.

Immigrants and Crime

Of course many native-born Americans blamed crime on the new immigrants pouring into the United States. Even the sympathetic reformer Jacob Riis, in his famous book *How the Other Half Lives* (1890), seemed to blame the immigrants themselves for the crime and poverty in their neighborhoods. And while there is clear evidence that crime was rampant in poor immigrant neighborhoods, American nativism and racism clearly accounts for some of the arrests in these areas. In 1860 over half of New York City's population were foreign born but this group made up 80 percent of convicted criminals that year. African Americans comprised 90 percent of the convicts in Southern prisons and were subject to the convict leasing system. Southern prisons leased prisoners out on chain gangs where they labored in horrendous conditions. Similarly, Asians were disproportionately incarcerated at a rate 3.8 times that of whites. The first drug to be criminalized in the Gilded Age was opium, which was the drug of choice of the Chinese. White populations in the West used the law punitively against Chinese immigrants in a blatant effort to drive them out of the territory.

Gangs

There were men among all of these immigrant communities that looked to crime as a way out of the misery and squalor of urban slums to prestige and power. Gangs of native-born and immigrant toughs populated the slums of New York City, Philadelphia, Baltimore, Buffalo, and Cincinnati (see Chapter 2). Criminal gangs also emerged in the Gilded Age among many immigrant groups. Chinese men, for example, had strong criminal gangs, known as tongs, that fought for control of criminal activities in America's Chinatowns.[16]

News Media

Americans were also more intimately apprised of crime than ever before. Metropolitan daily newspapers reported lurid tales of crime and sex. Specializing in selling sex with illustrations of scantily clad women and prurient crime stories, *The National Police Gazette* roared into prominence after Richard Kyle Fox purchased it in 1877. "Homicide Harvest," and "Murder Mania" headed the *Police Gazette*'s crime columns, bringing to Americans the vivid details of love, betrayal, and murder (see Chapter 8). Although totally different in its goals, Victorian middle-class reform efforts to banish prostitution also had the unintended effect of broadcasting the problem throughout America in newspapers and pamphlets. Reformers did have some successes as they attempted to spread the news that prostitution was so ubiquitous, but in the end they added to the feeling in the nation that crime was rampant.

Science of Crime

Ultimately, the new science of criminal anthropology justified white middle-class nativism and racism by safely limiting crime to the biologically inferior. Using Darwinian evolutionary theory and recapitulation theory, mainstream anthropology explained that criminal behavior could always be expected from Negroes, Asians, and the lower white races (southern and eastern Europeans). Recapitulation theory neatly explained how native-born criminals of the higher white races (northern and western European) were in fact part of a subspecies of man, frozen in a lower evolutionary developmental level than other members of the higher white races. Crime always came from those "other" people.[17]

DEMOCRACY

Although difficult to define and even harder to gauge during the Gilded Age, the idea of democracy had a powerful hold on the United

States. Over 13.4 million immigrants poured into a nation that only had a population of 76 million in 1900. The United States, which already boasted a more heterogeneous population than many European nations, suddenly found itself a much more ethnically, culturally, and religiously diverse country. Democracy appears to have been at least part of the lure that brought the millions from Africa, Central and South America, Europe, Canada, and Asia. But what exactly was democracy to these new Americans? Did democracy mean different things to the native born? Was democracy equality of economic opportunity, the ability to participate in the political process, or was it both? These are difficult questions to answer, but what we know for certain is that democracy was defined differently by the various groups in the country and that tensions between all of these groups rose as they competed to have a voice in the meaning of American democracy. The vast number of industrial worker strikes, over 23,000 between 1880 and 1900, the farmers' revolt in the form of Populism, women's increasing activism, and the creation of African-American organizations to stop institutionalized racism all demonstrate the contentious nature of American democracy in the Gilded Age.

Political Machines

The rise of urban political machines represents a fascinating glimpse into these struggles to participate in and define democracy in the United States. Although Progressive era reformers and early historians interpreted political machines as innately corrupt and "the shame of the cities," they can also be seen as based primarily on the widespread, democratic support of the urban, working-class Americans. Both native-born and immigrant working-class city dwellers often found themselves working in dangerous manufacturing enterprises, living in slums, and outside of an American culture dominated by the Victorian middle class.

Machine Social Services

In the home wards and precincts of the urban poor, however, the local alderman, ward bosses, precinct captains, and assemblymen catered to their needs and provided much-needed social services. In an era when federal, state, and local governments did little in the way of providing social services to the poor, the efforts of urban political machines to offer essential services to their needy constituents earned the machines loyalty and votes. The infamous Boss Tweed, for example, provided $50,000 for the poor families in New York's seventh ward during the harsh winter of 1870. Political machines in cities throughout the country often furnished food, legal assistance, jobs, entertainment, assistance after fires, and help for immigrants to earn their citizenship quickly. By the early twentieth century many machines endorsed reforms aimed at helping their main constituents, such as housing reform, worker's compensation, workplace safety regulations, and regulation of utilities and banks. Machine politicians had intimate and personal contact with their supporters in every neighborhood in homes, bars, clubs, churches, and on the streets. Large-scale immigration, which started in the 1840s, created the foundation for the rise of ethnic politics in American cities in the Gilded Age and provided these new Americans with the opportunity to significantly participate in city-wide politics.

The Machine Boss

Political machines rose in many major American cities in the Gilded Age as city governments proved incapable of dealing with the massive urban growth and subsequent problems. The most well-known and infamous of the nineteenth-century bosses is without a doubt Boss William Tweed. Tweed and his supporters controlled the Democratic Tammany Hall machine in New York City from 1866 to 1871 until their excesses brought their downfall. Powerful Democratic machines also were built by Alexander Shepherd in Washington, D.C. (1871), Isaac Freeman Rasin in Baltimore (1870s–1895), and Robert Speer in Denver (1890s–1920s). Political machines had wildly varying degrees of centralization of power and not all catered to immigrant votes. George Cox in Cincinnati and James McManes in Philadelphia built powerful Republican machines that did not rely on the votes of the urban working class.

Machine Corruption

In spite of some positive services they provided to working people in cities, most machines brought with them varying levels of graft, contract peddling, and bribery. The Tweed machine bilked the city out of an estimated $200 million. One method of this corruption was Tweed's control of an office supply company, the Manufacturing Stationers' Company, which won the city's office supply contract. In 1870 the Manufacturing Stationers' Company provided the city of New York with some ink bottles, rubber bands, and six reams of paper for which it was paid $3 million. Tweed's ring would collapse under legal pressure and he died in prison in 1878. The incredible excesses of the Tweed ring would be scaled back by later Tammany politicians who continued to operate their political machine in New York City, but they looked mainly for "honest graft."[18]

Political machines which relied on the votes of foreign-born Americans, however, continued to hold power in spite of middle-class reformers' attacks throughout the Gilded Age. Whether these machines actually helped the working classes is a matter of great debate among historians, but what can be clearly stated is that these political rings did provide some services to the urban poor and did perform some positive functions for Gilded Age cities. Urban immigrants primarily chose to support these politicians who catered to them and thereby came to participate in American democratic government.

Reconstruction

African Americans also enjoyed political participation, at least to a small degree, during the early years of the Gilded Age. The future seemed promising for African Americans at the end of the Civil War with the victory of Northern Republican forces and the abolition of slavery. Republicans in Congress committed themselves to black suffrage when confronted with continued resistance in ex-Confederate states and from President Andrew Johnson. One Northern Republican congressman stated, "party expediency and exact justice coincide for once."[19] As radical Reconstruction wiped out President Johnson's attempts at quickly restoring the Southern states and imposed military rule throughout the defeated Confederacy, African Americans became the lynchpin of the Republican Party in the South, constituting 80 percent of Southern Republican voters.

African-American Office Holding

In the state conventions held to write new constitutions in line with congressional Reconstruction during the late 1860s, blacks had a strong minority voice, holding on average 30 percent of the seats in the Republican delegations. From 1868 through 1876, African-American voters in the South sent two African-American senators and 14 African-American representatives to Congress. Black influence, however, was limited. Although blacks were 80 percent of Republican voters in the South, they never held more than 15 to 20 percent of the offices during Reconstruction. Only in South Carolina did African Americans hold the majority of state and federal offices, 52 percent, from 1868 to 1876. African-American political participation endured well into the 1890s with hundreds of blacks holding state office, thousands winning local offices, and from 1881 to 1901 at least one Southern black man held office in Congress.[20]

Importance of Voting

Even when confronted with violence and intimidation, black Southerners continued to bravely exercise their democratic rights and participate in local, state, and federal government (see "Restrictions on Democracy"). American democracy did not mean freedom from want, wealth, or an easy life for most urban immigrants or former slaves, but it did mean the right to participate in choosing politicians that at least made the attempt to address their concerns and problems. Both of these groups confronted the hostility of the dominant white culture and yet persisted in their efforts at political participation. The symbolic importance of former slaves, naturalized immigrants, and the children of both groups participating in the most important democratic ritual in the United States, voting, cannot be overstated.

RESTRICTIONS ON DEMOCRACY

Gilded Age restrictions on democracy are unfortunately all too apparent to any modern observer. While the protection of minorities' civil liberties appeared to have been won through the Fourteenth and Fifteenth Amendments to the Constitution, this democratic promise was in reality very limited. While European immigrants from southern and eastern Europe undoubtedly faced nativist hostility and women of all races confronted economic and political restrictions, ironically, two nonwhite groups of native-born Americans—African Americans and American Indians—became particular targets of white violence inside the democratic United States.

Hostility toward African Americans

African Americans sought inclusion into the democratic system of the United States, but widespread white Southern violence attempted to topple the Reconstruction governments and deny blacks the ballot. In 1866 a white mob killed 46 blacks in a vicious riot in Memphis and a New Orleans mob, which included police, attacked a black suffrage convention, killing 37 black and 3 white delegates. Ultra-violent groups like the Ku Klux Klan and the Knights of the White Camellia terrorized the white and black supporters of the Republican Party. In the election year of 1868 white Southern opponents of Reconstruction in Louisiana alone murdered over 1,000 Republicans, most of them black.[21] In spite of these concerted efforts to destroy active support of the Republican Party, African-American voter participation was protected by the ratification of the Fifteenth Amendment in 1870. African-American political participation continued well into the 1890s.

Waning Republican Commitment

The white Northern commitment to Reconstruction principles of black equality and voting proved short-lived. Although there were small numbers of radical Republicans deeply committed to racial equality, the bulk of Northerners and Republican politicians were ambiguous at best concerning African Americans. Before the ratification of the Fifteenth Amendment, 11 of the 21 Northern states and all five border states still denied black men suffrage. By the elections of 1876 the North was tired; four years of war and eleven years of turmoil in the South were enough. One Republican politician vehemently declared, "The truth is our people are tired out with this worn out cry of 'Southern outrages'!!! Hard times & heavy taxes make them wish the 'nigger,' 'everlasting nigger,' were in hell or Africa."[22] Northern will waned. White Democrats increased their control of Southern states and increased their violence against black voters. In the disputed presidential election of 1876, Democrats and Republicans both participated in widespread voter fraud in several Southern states, notably South Carolina, Louisiana, and Florida. Ultimately, an electoral commission comprised of five senators, five representatives, and five Supreme Court justices awarded the disputed votes and the election to Republican candidate Rutherford B. Hayes. Democrat Samuel Tilden had won the popular vote and needed only one electoral vote for victory, but behind the scenes a deal between Republicans and Democrats, called the Compromise of 1877, gave Republicans the election in return for the withdrawal of remaining federal troops from the South. Reconstruction and a strong Republican commitment to African-American voters was over.

Disenfranchisement

White Southerners would begin to more completely disenfranchise African Americans in the 1890s. In 1890, Mississippi established a literacy test and it was soon followed by other Southern states. These efforts were soon modified by "understanding" clauses which gave local voter registrars power to determine if the voter applicant understood part of the state constitution, essentially guaranteeing whites could vote and blacks could not. Poll taxes and grandfather clauses were added on top of the literacy tests and by 1908 every ex-Confederate state had some or all of these methods of limiting black voting. Black voter participation fell by 62 percent from 1890 to 1900. White elites were certainly concerned over the cooperation of the black and white farmers in their Farmer's Alliance organizations and later in the Populist Party, whose 1896 platform attacked voting restrictions in the South. The crushing defeat of the Populists in 1896 ensured the Democrats' dominance of the South, and the subsequent disenfranchisement of blacks and some poor whites ensured the Southern white elite their power would be unopposed. The Supreme Court upheld the voting restrictions in its 1898 *Williams v. Mississippi* decision.

Jim Crow Segregation

In addition to destroying black voting, Southern states also segregated nearly every part of life. By the 1880s, Southern states had started the process of creating the Jim Crow system of segregation which would ultimately lead to the separation of the races in virtually all public venues: schools, restaurants, hospitals, hotels, public transportation, restrooms, and even drinking fountains. The Supreme Court announced the "separate but equal" doctrine in its 1896 *Plessy v. Ferguson* decision, which found separate train cars for blacks and whites legal as long as they were equal. Future high court rulings would allow Southern states to extend the separate but equal doctrine to virtually all parts of society.

Violence and Terror

Voting disenfranchisement, Jim Crow, and the overall subordination of African Americans in the South was bolstered by a campaign of terror and violence that was explicitly sanctioned by Southern society and its leaders. Between 1882 and 1899 over 2,500 blacks were lynched, 98 percent of whom were men. Lynching was by no means a problem only in the South, but 88 percent of these horrifying events occurred in the former Confederate states. Black men who defied local white norms, became too economically successful, or were accused of crimes could easily become targets of mob violence. Entire towns would turn out, including children, in the carnivalesque atmosphere to watch or participate in the torture, maiming, murder, and further mutilation of the corpse of the black victim. False accusations of attacks on white women routinely accompanied these orgies of sadism.[23] Democracy indeed had its limits for African Americans in the Gilded Age.

Native Americans

Native Americans also found themselves outside of the promise of American democracy. The old Manifest Destiny and the new scientific racism based on Darwinian evolutionary theory bolstered the claims of white America that the Indian savages had to be subdued to make way for economic, cultural, spiritual, and even evolutionary progress. Although the era would start with some promise, by the turn of the twentieth century the United States had subdued the remaining independent tribal groups. The old way of life of the First Nation people was ending and a new one was forming.

Donehogawa/Ely Parker

The post–Civil War era opened with some promise for Native Americans when President Ulysses S. Grant (1828–1895) appointed his friend and fellow army officer Brigadier General Ely Parker, also known by his Indian name Donehogawa, to be Commissioner of Indian Affairs in 1869. Parker was a Seneca who had grown up on a reservation in New York and knew firsthand the prejudice toward Indians. The new commissioner took his post seriously; he appointed a host of new Indian agents to replace the corrupt bureaucrats in the Indian Office and worked diligently to create fair policies for Native Americans. Powerful enemies in Congress and among mining companies interested in opening the Black Hills to gold mining began to mercilessly hound Parker. Donehogawa resigned in 1871 in part to protect his close friend, President U.S. Grant, from the increasing pressure and criticism. For the most part, white America did not want Native Americans protected, but rather wanted them removed to make way for white settlement and exploitation of resources in the West.

Military Conquest

By 1890 the U.S. Army had crushed Native American armed resistance. Under the leadership of General Phil Sheridan, the man credited with saying "The only good Indians I ever saw were dead," the Army defeated the Southern Cheyenne, Arapaho, Kiowa, and Comanche on the southern plains. On the northern plains the Sioux and Northern Cheyenne lost the War for the Black Hills and became reservation bound by 1877, in spite of impressive victories at the Battle of the Rosebud and the Battle of Little Bighorn (1876). Also in that year, the Nez Percé under Chief Joseph fled Oregon only to be hunted for 1,700 miles. The Army finally captured the Nez Percé 30 miles from the Canadian border. Even the legendary Geronimo finally surrendered in 1886, marking the end of Apache resistance in the Southwest. The Indian Wars ended sadly in 1890 when the Seventh Cavalry massacred a band of unarmed Sioux (estimates of the dead range from 150 to 400) at Wounded Knee, South Dakota.

Dawes Severalty Act

Congress now confronted the dilemma of what to do with Native Americans in the face of mounting white pressure for Indian lands. In 1871, Congress declared that no treaties would be signed with tribal groups, only agreements. Also, as early as 1883 a group of activists, calling themselves "the Friends of the Indian," began to lobby Congress to abolish the communal, tribal holdings on the reservations, because this blocked Indians from developing civilized manhood and trapped them in savagery. Congress obliged with the 1887 Dawes General Allotment Act (also called the Dawes Severalty Act), which divided land into 160-acre allotments for families with excess land to be sold. In 1887, Native American reservation lands amounted to 138 million acres, but by 1900 these holdings had shrunk to 78 million acres. Indian agents and Indian boarding schools, such as Haskell in Kansas and Chilocco in Oklahoma, relentlessly sought to destroy Indian culture.[24] Native Americans persevered throughout this challenging time as they struggled to adapt to a new way of life under the government that declared all men were created equal.

WAR

The rapid industrialization of the United States catapulted the nation into international prominence and the United States responded by building a modern navy. In 1889 the U.S. Navy was the twelfth largest in the world, but by 1900 it was the third largest in the world. The new power of the United States led it to use military force in support of its foreign policy and economic and domestic goals. Unlike the eras before and after the Gilded Age, however, there were no major wars, just relatively small-scale conflicts against vastly inferior military forces.

Imperialism

American global economic expansion, the closing of the frontier in 1890, Social Darwinism, scientific racism, the rise of the United States to great power status, as well as a new, more belligerent vision for American manhood pushed the United States into imperialist ventures in the Gilded Age. U.S. policy toward the military defeat and dominance of Native Americans in the country reflected U.S. imperialistic ventures abroad. The imperialist enterprises of the 1890s, however, were not isolated events out of step with earlier decades, but were instead the logical culmination of U.S. imperial policies.

Hawaii

Hawaii offers a vivid example of state and nonstate actors working toward American suzerainty. In the 1820s, Americans began to move in increasing numbers to Hawaii, bringing U.S. investment dollars as well as Christian missionaries. U.S. cultural and economic imperialism were so successful that in 1840, Hawaii declared itself a Christian nation and English became the main language of business and government, soon replacing Hawaiian in public schools. By 1893, though amounting to only 5 percent of the population, white American and European businessmen controlled 65 percent of Hawaiian land and dominated the economy. When the Hawaiian Queen Liliuokalani began to reassert Polynesian power, the business-missionary ruling clique initiated a successful coup that was reinforced by Marines from a U.S. warship at the behest of the U.S. minister to Hawaii.

Spanish-American War

The Spanish-American War started as sympathy for Cuba but eventually turned into a rather imperialist land grab. Sympathy welled up in the United States for the poor Cuban revolutionaries fighting for their independence from Spanish colonial rule, fanned by the popular press to such an extent that the 1896 Populist Party platform called for the government to support Cuban independence. The extent of American support for Cuba was clearly illustrated by the fact that western, mid-western, and southern farmers, suffering from terrible economic misfortunes of their own, felt so moved by the revolution that they wrote a demand for U.S. support of Cuban independence into their radical third-party platform. Altruism aside, the United States had realpolitik reasons for desiring an end to the war. U.S. companies had roughly $50 million invested in Cuban sugar, mining, and utilities. Furthermore, the $100 million per year trade with the island had fallen by two-thirds because of the war. In addition, the United States wanted to ensure its continued domination of the Caribbean. President William McKinley (1843–1901) carefully and without great jingoism guided the nation toward war with Spain. This feat was even more impressive given the incredible popular pressure caused by the intense anti-Spanish jingoism of the yellow journalism produced by Joseph Pulitzer's *New York World* and William Randolph Hearst's *New York Journal* (see Chapter 8). In February 1898, the *New York Journal* published a letter written by the Spanish minister to the United States that excoriated President McKinley, and enraged Americans. Six days later the battleship *Maine* exploded in Havana harbor, killing 250 U.S. sailors. By April the United States had declared war on Spain, President McKinley called for 100,000 volunteers, and 1 million men responded.

The Spanish-American War lasted a mere 100 days and consisted of little more than two disastrous naval battles for the Spanish and small land battles at Guantanamo Bay, El Caney, and San Juan Hill. The war proved to be a relatively easy victory for the United States and one where fatalities from disease far outnumbered those caused by Spanish attacks. Significantly, Congress annexed Hawaii in July, partially due to its increased importance as a staging area for war with the Spanish Pacific fleet. The war also brought Theodore Roosevelt and his Rough Riders national acclaim, and his war hero status would launch his bid for national political office. With victory the United States gained a far-flung empire from Spain which included Guam, Puerto Rico, the Philippines, and ironically, Cuba. Although Congress passed the Teller Amendment in April, before the war broke out, stating that Cuba would not be annexed, the United States ignored Cuba in the fighting and the peacemaking. After the war the United States forced Cuba to write a constitution that recognized and ensured U.S. economic interests and suzerainty.

Filipino-American War

Ironically, the Spanish-American War would lead the United States into a much longer and more costly war with the Philippines. Even though Filipinos under the able leadership of Emilio Aguinaldo aided the United States in its fight against Spain and quickly formed a government in the power vacuum that followed the Spanish defeat, they were virtually ignored by McKinley and Congress after the war. The conflict soon deteriorated into a vicious guerrilla campaign where the U.S. Army found itself trying to fight a hostile population and guerrilla fighters who struck and quickly disappeared into the jungle. American racism played a prominent role in the attempt to control the Philippines in the first place and played out in the very ugly treatment of Filipinos. White U.S. soldiers soon nicknamed the Filipinos "Goo Goos" or simply used a more familiar term, "Niggers." A scorched earth policy that included the movement of people into concentration camps and the burning of their villages and crops in areas where rebels were active would eventually destroy the Filipino rebellion. The United States used more than 126,000 soldiers, sustained 4,200 casualties, and spent $400 million. Filipinos lost 18,000 in battle and an estimated 100,000 to 200,000 from disease and famine. Although President Roosevelt officially declared the Philippine Insurrection over in July 1902, in fact Filipino Muslims would continue to fight U.S. forces well into the 1910s. American domination of the main island quickly followed, however, along with U.S. business and culture. The Philippine experience was the culmination of U.S. imperialist policies in the Gilded Age.[25]

POLITICS AND POLITICAL FIGURES

In spite of strong and thoughtful studies on Gilded Age politics by historians of the era, there are many who continue to focus on it as only a time of outrageous spoilsmanship, naked partisanship, and corruption. The reality of Gilded Age politics is far more complex. The federal government managed to reconstruct the nation, begin regulation of industry, and start civil service reform in spite of tremendous obstacles.

Split Government

This was an age when partisan loyalty was high, the two major parties were remarkably evenly balanced, and the major parties generally split control of the government. In all but the four years from 1874 through 1894, the Democrats dominated the House of Representatives and the

Republicans controlled the Senate. Although the Democrats only managed to win two presidential elections in this era, both by Grover Cleveland (1837–1908) in 1884 and 1892, no presidential winner took over 48.5 percent of the popular vote from 1876 through 1892 with the exception of Democratic candidate Samuel Tilden in 1876, and he lost by one electoral vote! The closeness of elections made it difficult for either major political party to stray too far from the expectations of the generally conservative American electorate, or they would pay the price at the polls. In addition, the Democrats often controlled the House and were committed to a neutral, small government and states' rights, which often led them to obstruct legislation, while Republicans desired an activist federal government that guided industrial development.

U.S. Government Accomplishments

What is truly amazing is that the government accomplished so many important tasks given these very real limitations, and all while confronted with the dizzying changes of the Gilded Age such as the massive growth of industry, urbanization, immigration, labor unrest, and the challenge of Populism. To their credit, federal governmental officials reunited the nation with Reconstruction, guided industrial development, and passed the first national business regulatory laws: the Interstate Commerce Act (1887) and the Sherman Antitrust Act (1890). The federal government also started the professional civil service with the 1883 Pendleton Civil Service Act after the mentally disturbed Charles Guiteau shot President Garfield. Only with the massive Republican victories in 1896 would the political balance of the two parties be broken and a Republican majority be established that would last until 1932.

Political Figures

It is difficult to find dominant politicians in the Gilded Age but several figures were very influential. From 1876 to 1900 only two presidents served two terms and Grover Cleveland's were the only split terms in U.S. history. Several of these presidents provided strong leadership and deftly handled delicate issues, particularly Republican William McKinley, setting the pattern for strong presidential leadership that would emerge in the twentieth century. Republican Senator James G. Blaine from Maine exercised considerable influence in the battles with the Democrats and within his own party, losing the very hotly contested presidential election of 1884 to Democrat Grover Cleveland. Charismatic speaker William Jennings Bryan burst onto the political scene as the Democratic candidate for the presidency in 1896. Although he had been a former congressman from Nebraska and he had been a speaker in the free silver camp for two years, this 36-year-old firebrand seemed to come from nowhere to win the Democratic nomination in 1896. One should also not overlook Grover Cleveland's success: winning the only two presidential contests for the Democrats in the Gilded Age (1884, 1892) and their first since 1856.

CONCLUSION

Gilded Age Americans did indeed live in interesting times. The very composition of American society was changing, which made questions of democratic inclusiveness vital. Native-born Americans feared hordes of poverty-stricken immigrants entering the country, which made questions of criminality and democracy pressing issues. Industrialization made manufacturing the dominant part of the economy and also revolutionized agriculture through mechanization. This was also an age of contradictions, where the federal government achieved important accomplishments but its commitment to democracy for minorities was small indeed. By the 1890s the country was obviously in the process of becoming a modern mass society dominated by huge cities which were united through advanced transportation and communication networks.

2

World of Youth

BACKGROUND

Youth became a focus of attention in Gilded Age America, and was both idolized and feared. Middle-class adults, mired in the staid, controlled world of work and domesticity, celebrated the freedom and innocence of "youth." Of course, the youth celebrated was that of white, middle-class young people. From some ideologues like Theodore Roosevelt and psychologist G. Stanley Hall, the celebration of youthfulness came across as the veneration of essential characteristics necessary for all red-blooded American men and women. Gone were the Calvinist views of innately depraved and sinful children, replaced by a more benign vision of youthful innocents waiting to be molded by appropriate didactic lessons. Ideology and practice, however, often diverged, and traditional physical punishments like spanking appear to have been common in all social classes, though perhaps less than half of all families used spanking frequently.[1]

At the same time new scientific definitions of the different stages of youth appeared, particularly the term "adolescence." Adolescence entered popular speech in the late nineteenth century, defining the turbulent period starting with puberty and ending in the late teens. Directing and controlling the urges of young people during this period of "storm and stress," as G. Stanley Hall called adolescence, became a major focus of the numerous youth organizations that emerged in the late Gilded Age. Christianity, sports, paramilitarism, and camping all came together in the adult-sponsored youth organizations of the late nineteenth century. As the Gilded Age progressed, adults increasingly controlled the free time of young people through organizations. Equally important was that at least middle-class youth were freed from the world of work and able to carve out a distinctive space. Also, during these decades the connections between young people and popular culture became much stronger as they emerged as a distinctive consumer group, spending money in the new mass society on goods marketed to them.

EDUCATION

Ideas on education for youth in the Gilded Age indicated strongly that conceptions of young people were undergoing change. The idea that young people went through adolescence around the onset of puberty and that this treacherous period needed supervision was widely supported by educators and youth counselors. Underlying this was a general belief among educators and youth commentators that life in the Gilded Age was too frenzied and there was too much pressure put on youth. To mitigate this pressure young people were to be protected in schools during their adolescence. The concerns over young people reflected many of the tensions middle-class Americans had with the rapid changes altering the nation, such as massive urbanization and immigration, blended with a romantic vision of childhood and fears of over-civilization. By the 1870s communities began to put more emphasis on schools than they had in the early part of the century, as many more communities established schools and approached the educational curriculum more systematically. Higher education was also taking on more importance and college attendance grew accordingly.

Common Schools

Common schooling continued to be the major part of the American public education system in the Gilded Age. One-room school houses across the nation educated the bulk of the population. These schools reached 64.7 percent of young Americans from ages 5 to 18 in 1869, and this number increased steadily to 71.9 percent by 1900. The days attended per pupil (78 to 99) and the overall length of the school year (132 to 144) increased steadily from 1869 to 1900 as well, indicating more systematic emphasis on pedagogy, curriculum, and attendance. There were some regional differences, which were the greatest for African-American children in the South. Roughly 78 percent of white children ages 10 to 14 attended school while only 51 percent of African-American children of the same age made it to school at any time during the year. There were more specialized schools, like kindergartens, slowly spreading throughout the nation, but a very small percentage of children at-

Interior view of a schoolroom in Wetmore, Custer County, Colorado, 1886. © Denver Public Library, Western History Collection.

tended them. As late as 1902 only 5 percent of four- and five-year-olds attended kindergartens.[2]

Common schools relied on one-room schools in rural America and most commonly taught children ages 6 to 14. The curriculum focused primarily on reading, writing, spelling, and arithmetic in the beginning phase. Intermediate study continued with the former disciplines and added geography and nature study. Finally, advanced study continued all of the former subjects and added history and grammar. The ubiquitous *McGuffey Reader* was the mainstay of the common school curriculum in 37 states and sold 122 million copies from 1836 until 1922. The *McGuffey Reader*'s content reflected the concerns and morality of the Victorian middle class.[3] The need for further education and the spread of new ideas on adolescence led to the creation of more elaborate age gradations and eventually the high school.

High Schools

High school attendance, however, continued to be a luxury of elite working-class and middle-class families. Industrialization created a strange situation for youth. In order to get into higher-paying jobs young people had to stay out of the labor force long enough to get an education, but at the same time industry aggressively sought to hire child labor. For most working-class youth their teenage years were not spent in schools, but in factories and mines working long hours in dangerous conditions. Only the upper echelon of working-class and middle-class families could afford to keep their children out of the labor force long enough to get them an education. This also accounts for the higher number of girls in American high schools in this period, who were about 60 percent of high school graduates. For urban families that did not need their girls to work, or did not need them for for domestic labor, the high school was the perfect solution. The high school student population doubled in the decade of the 1890s, though still only 3.3 percent of the eligible population attended.[4]

Focus of Youth Culture

These schools developed to be an all-encompassing cultural, social, and educational experience for young people. A host of extracurricular activities emerged, centering around a massive outpouring of sports, student government, and all manner of clubs. High school administrators destroyed fraternities and sororities, which were very popular at universities and colleges, and established strict controls over their young students. High schools also profited from the fact that many universities and professional schools increasingly required a four-year high school diploma for entrance. High schools were creating something that would not come to full fruition until the early twentieth century: a virtually universal and distinctive youth culture that centered around school. Ironically, even as the society at large promoted independence, particularly for young men, high schools were creating an institutionalized education that emphasized the dependence and subordination of youth.[5]

Colleges and Universities

The massive growth in professional schools, universities, and colleges in the Gilded Age illustrates the growing importance of education for upward mobility in the industrial capitalist economy. Colleges and universities increased in number from 563 in 1869 to 977 by 1900. The great millionaires of the Gilded Age poured tens of millions of dollars into new universities like Duke, Stanford, and Vanderbilt. Also important was the Morrill Federal Land Grant Act of 1862, which provided each state with land to establish state universities. In addition, the number of professional schools established in the Gilded Age more than doubled that of those founded in the preceding 25 years. The founding of the American Medical Association in 1847 and the Association of American Law Schools in 1900 exemplified this growth of professional schools. The expense of college meant that a very small portion of Americans attended, though the figures did increase throughout the era from 1 percent of college-age Americans in 1870 to 5 percent by 1910.

College Curriculum

Colleges and universities continued to rely on traditional classical curricula in the nineteenth century, but with important changes. There was particular emphasis on oral recitation and rhetoric. This was an era of the spoken word and oratory far more than today, though the Gilded Age marked the beginning of a decline. Student recitation and explication of texts, while still widespread, were slowly replaced by lectures. While Greek, Latin, French, German, mathematics, history, philosophy, physics, and chemistry were still a major part of the traditional curriculum, the emergence of professional schools caused the multiplication of new courses in a myriad of disciplines like sociology, anthropology, and engineering. Harvard President Charles Eliot introduced an elective system that allowed students much greater choice in their college classes. Other signs of higher education's attempt to become more systematized was the introduction of the college entrance exams and the creation of the College Entrance Examination Board to standardize the admissions process.[6]

Higher Education Diversity

Opportunities were also growing for those outside of the dominant white, Anglo-Saxon, Protestant male circles. Women began to move forcefully into higher education. There were almost five times as many coeducational institutions of higher education in 1900 than the paltry 22 that existed in 1867. Women comprised only 21 percent of college students in 1870 but were nearly 36 percent by 1900. In addition to most state universities opening their doors to women, a host of new women's colleges were founded after Vassar's 1861 example: Wellesley (1875), Smith (1875), Bryn Mawr (1884), Mount Holyoke (1888), Barnard (1889), and Radcliffe (1894).[7] African American students also embraced new educational opportunities at institutions developed for them because of their exclusion from the largely all-white university systems. Universities like Fisk, Atlanta, and Howard provided new opportunities to African Americans seeking higher education. Likewise, Fordham and Notre Dame provided opportunities for American Catholics just as the City College of New York and New York University availed Jews of higher education.

College Culture

By the 1890s an extremely well-developed college culture had appeared which was organized largely around classes and extracurricular activities. Literary societies, social fraternities and sororities, debating societies, drama clubs, and student government were a small part of the explosion of extracurricular activities that were increasingly sanctioned and regulated by the faculty, administration, or alumni.

SPORTS

Sports for youth also took on incredibly heightened importance in the Gilded Age, as physical prowess became associated closely with middle-class manhood and fears of immigrant hordes sparked the desire for socializing institutions (see Chapter 7). Many of these sporting activities were connected with public schools but there were also large organizations separate from the school systems. Youth, however, increasingly lost control of their own sporting events, surrendering control to adults who supervised these "character-building" activities. These sporting events appealed to adults as methods of spreading manly virtues and socializing youth in the competitive and aggressive values of capitalist society.

Sports Ideology

The equation of physical and moral force was widespread in the late nineteenth century, and can be seen most noticeably outside of sports in the arena of success writing. Literally thousands of success manuals and advice books for boys and young men poured off the presses in the late nineteenth century, and most advocated physical force as a necessity for success in life. Success writer Orison Marden clearly connected physical vigor and success to true manhood in 1898:

As a rule physical vigor is the condition of a great character. The weak, chestless, calfless, forceless, languid, hesitating, vacillating young man may manage to live a respectable sort of life; but he seldom climbs, is not a leader, rarely gets at the head of anything important.

In his book *Choosing a Career* (1905), Marden elaborated on the connection between physical force and success: " 'Mentally able, but physically weak,' would make a good epitaph on the tomb of many a failure." As early as 1873, William Mathews exclaimed to his readers, "Ridiculous as this may seem, it is certain that the brain is often credited with achievements that belong to the digestion." Intestinal fortitude and raw physical power were necessary to carry a man to success. Only physical toughness would give men the fortitude to last in the rough-and-tumble world of business.[8]

Roosevelt, Hall, and Muscular Christianity

These values neatly coincided with fears of effeminization and over-civilization shared by men like Theodore Roosevelt (1858–1919) and psy-

Elko (Nevada) boys' baseball team, 1897.

chologist G. Stanley Hall (1844–1924). Boys in particular needed rough play to develop the manly qualities of courage, aggressiveness, violence, competitiveness, and the desire to win, which ideologues like Hall and Roosevelt believed were necessary for American manhood. These drives neatly coincided as well with the movement known as Muscular Christianity, which witnessed old-stock Protestants' push for institutions to save modern youth from the sins of city life and to provide socialization for immigrant youth. Leaders of this movement were particularly concerned with developing rural values in children reared in the city. Regardless of who sponsored these youthful sports activities, what occurred was an unprecedented creation of massive youth organizations controlled by adults.

YMCA and Others

Undoubtedly, the premier Muscular Christianity organization was the Young Men's Christian Association. Muscular Christianity sought to convince young men that Christianity was not weak and effeminate, but strong and manly. In spite of intense opposition, the YMCA switched its orientation from gymnastics to competitive team sports in the 1890s. By 1892 almost 250,000 young men belonged to the YMCA, and near the end of the decade the organization could field teams of near-professional quality in football, basketball, and track and field. Other religious groups soon followed the YMCA's lead. Exponents of sports formed Protestant Sunday School leagues in Brooklyn in 1904, which quickly spread to cities across the country. Catholics followed soon after with the Boy's Brigade.[9] Competitive sport invaded organized Christianity and used it as a vehicle for spreading the ideals of aggressive competitivism to boys throughout the nation under the moral authority of Christianity.

Luther Gulick

Luther Gulick, one of the leaders most responsible for the changing orientation of the YMCA, was not content with staying only in a religious setting, since his ideology had a strong secular streak. Gulick left the YMCA and became instrumental in the playground movement in public schools. In 1903, the public schools of Greater New York City hired Gulick as the director of physical training, and with the aid of the schools and wealthy benefactors created the Public Schools Athletic League in 1903. In a very short time thousands of fans were turning out to see championship basketball and baseball games in the New York City League. Duty, thoroughness, patriotism, honor, and obedience were the mottoes of the league as it sought to be an agency not only for creating vigorous men but also for Americanizing and controlling immigrants pouring into the city.

High School and College

Even as Gulick went on his athletics crusade, high schools and colleges were finally bringing sports under the control of the administration. In the early and middle decades of the nineteenth century, sporting teams had been informal, often impromptu, affairs, and their games had been under the control and management of the students. After the 1890s, however, sports grew so popular and attracted such large crowds that administrators felt they had little choice but to step in and take control of the games. In New York City, for example, the annual Thanksgiving Day football game between the two best college teams, often Yale and Princeton, drew crowds of 40,000 fans and generated $10,000 for each team. Yale, one of the most successful football teams of the period, took in $106,000 from football. Football's popularity permeated the youth culture. For colleges and universities, successful football teams brought in new students and kept alumni donating money to the university. All of these things made it essential that administrations take over the running of not only collegiate football but all other sports as well. High schools also began to control athletics that started to dominate so many of their students' lives. By 1902, Wisconsin and Illinois and the elite boarding schools of the Northeast controlled their high school sports and by 1922 all but three states boasted statewide high school athletic programs. Men institutionalized athletics and took over the leadership of the sports for the young, seeking to give these activities greater legitimacy in the culture of the era, and ultimately made athletics one of the cornerstones of respectable American manhood.[10]

Women's Sports

Youth athletics were not completely male-dominated. Although men were most commonly associated with sports, women's colleges were also important institutions for spreading competitive sports, at least among elite women. Elite colleges like Smith, Vassar, and Berkeley all adopted baseball and basketball for their female students by the late 1890s. Young women poured into competitive team sports to the detriment of the established gymnastics activities, often against the wishes of college administrators. In spite of an active opposition to women's participation in athletics, there were new voices encouraging women to be physically active and the women themselves energetically moved into new sporting events.[11]

WORKING-CLASS AND IMMIGRANT YOUTH

Working-class youth often had little time for sports or schooling and offered by far the greatest challenge to the control and values of middle-class America. Working-class youth normally worked like adults by the time they were in their mid-teen years. Unlike middle- and upper-class youth, however, these working-class young people enjoyed leisure activities outside of the control of adults. The combination of jobs and new urban amusements created a certain independence in working-class youth. Young men and women of the working classes, particularly those congregating in the great cities, openly rebelled against Victorian norms and created their own subcultures with their own values. Crime and new urban amusements were the mediums used to rebel against Victorian control and expectations.

Work

The reality for most working-class children was work. American industry consciously sought the cheap labor of children. The 1900 Census counted 1.75 million children ages 10 to 15 "gainfully" employed in the United States. Most of the child labor, 62 percent, was agricultural while 16 percent was in industry. The children employed by industry worked in coal mines, textile mills, garment industry sweatshops, factories of all kinds, and also worked as bootblacks, scrap collectors, and newsboys. In the 1870s a survey of working-class families in Massachusetts demonstrated the importance of child labor for working-class families. Children between the ages of 10 and 19 provided a quarter of family income, which jumped to an astounding 30 percent in families where the parents were unskilled workers. As apprenticeships declined and the skilled trades no longer sought youthful helpers, young people, particularly immigrant youth, found themselves stuck in low-paying, unskilled positions that held little chance for upward mobility. Rural poor youth faced equally dismal prospects, working long hours with their parents as tenant farmers and sharecroppers or hiring out as seasonal hands on large farms.[12]

Youth Crime

The lawlessness of the Gilded Age often stemmed from the violence and criminal behavior of young men (see Chapter 1). Ironically, even as middle-class thinkers were reconstructing children into innocents who should be allowed to play, they increasingly came to fear the violence and crimes of working-class youth. There seemed to be no controls over these young criminals gone wild.

Jesse Pomeroy

One of the most famous youthful criminals of the 1870s was Jesse Pomeroy, known as the "Boston boy fiend." When only 12 years old Pomeroy tortured six young boys in 1872, slashing their faces and genitals with a knife. After a brief stint in reform school, Pomeroy, a model inmate, was allowed to return to live with his seamstress mother in 1874. Within six weeks of his release, the budding serial killer murdered two young children, sadistically torturing them with a knife. Several children reported during that time that a teenage boy had tried to lure them away from their south Boston neighborhood, and with the discovery of the bodies a full-fledged panic hit the city. Exhibiting the major characteristics of modern serial killers, Pomeroy never showed remorse or any concern for his victims, appeared normal and intelligent, felt persecuted, and could not explain what drove him to his acts of sexually sadistic torture. Police immediately turned toward Pomeroy as the main suspect and wrangled a confession from the 14-year-old boy. Pomeroy's conviction and his sentence of solitary confinement for life ended the boy fiend's crimes, though he maintained his fame throughout the Gilded Age for his repeated and ingenious escape attempts. Forty-one years in solitary confinement did not cow Pomeroy, but he never escaped his long confinement (1876–1929). Parents frightened children with threats of Pomeroy until the early twentieth century.

Pomeroy's shocking crimes gripped the nation. Newspapers fed on the media frenzy surrounding the killer and printed wild speculations on how the boy could commit such malicious acts of violence. A *New York Times* editorial on July 26, 1874, clearly illustrated America's fascination and fear of a boy "who kills other boys and girls for no other reason than the love of inflicting torture and death, and a curiosity to see how they will act while he cuts their throats and stabs them." While certainly exceptional, to many middle-class observers the Pomeroy case was symptomatic of crime in America's great cities among the hordes of ill-supervised youth.[13] What greater example of the dangers of working-class youth could there be than the boy fiend, Jesse Pomeroy? (See "Sensational Literature.")

Street Gangs

Pomeroy's shocking crimes were part of the perceived overall law-lessness of working-class youth in the great cities of the United States, which was also brazenly exhibited by street-corner gangs. Reformer Jacob Riis reported on the prevalence and misdeeds of these gangs in his famous *How the Other Half Lives* (1890). "Every corner has its gangs," claimed Riis, and they were made up of "the American-born sons of English, Irish, and German parents." The Alley Gang, Rag Gang, Wyho Gang, Rock Gang, Dead Rabbits, Paradise Park Gang, Stable Gang, Short Tail Gang, Gophers, Dutch Mob, Battle Row Gang, Gas House Gang, and many others populated the street corners of urban neighborhoods. Gang members sported distinctive hats, shirts, and pants. These gangs of young ruffians thrived on bravado, impressing their peers, and robbery. Gang members abused the common forms of alcohol as well as drugs like morphine, the opiate laudanum, and cocaine. The Hudson Dusters were notorious for their cocaine use and feared for their violence when high on the drug. Riis reported that in New York City just over one-eighth of those arrested for crimes in 1889 were under the age of 20. The casual violence of these gangs was well known and feared. Within 30 minutes of a visit to the infamous Montgomery Guards, Riis found two gang members in police headquarters accused of robbing a peddler and trying to saw off his head "just for fun." Gang members recruited easily from the poverty-stricken inhabitants of America's slums and as Riis acerbically notes, "The product is our own."[14]

Urban Amusements, Youth, and Sex

In the great cities of America a new urban amusement culture developed in the last half of the century which provided young people with amusements that were outside the control of parents or neighborhood eyes (see Chapter 7). While most middle-class and rural youth attended entertainment activities largely sponsored by their communities and under the watchful eyes of community moral guardians, working-class

The Short Tail Gang under a pier at the foot of Jackson Street (now Corlears Hook Park, Lower East Side, New York), ca. 1889. © Library of Congress.

youth in cities were now able to experience leisure activities on their own. Cheap theaters, concert saloons, and dime museums paved the way at mid-century, followed in the 1880s by the emergence of vaudeville as entertainments where patrons could enjoy hours of amusement for a dime. George Tilyou created the first true amusement park at Coney Island in 1897, but there were boardwalks crammed with amusements decades before. There were also the World's Fairs that appeared regularly in the United States in the Gilded Age and early twentieth century with their wondrous midways.[15] Young working-class urbanites had unprecedented access to public amusements.

Treating

Added to this leisure time was the increasing availability of decent employment for young, working-class women in factories, offices, and retail stores, which provided them with greater autonomy. With more independence and money, young working-class women were able to exercise more control over their activities than their middle-class sisters. By the 1890s there developed a system of "treating" that had wide-ranging implications. Often young women could not afford the urban amusements because they still earned less than young men, so men would "treat" women to shows, dances, vaudeville, and amusement parks. Young men frequently had expectations of sexual exchange for their money. Yet, young women were not simply passive victims, as many middle-class reformers claimed, but active agents in negotiating "treats" and sex. Premarital sexual activity rose substantially among this subculture. After hitting a low of 10 percent at mid-century, premarital pregnancies soared to 23 percent by the 1880s.[16] Keep in mind that this was an era when doctors and scientists considered masturbation one of the greatest evils afflicting youth and a source of serious moral decay. Premarital sex was infinitely worse. So, without a doubt, one of the most serious rebellions from middle-class values was this youthful working-class flouting of Victorian sexual boundaries. Middle-class ideologues feared urban working-class youth not just for their gangs and violence, but also for their moral decadence. These youngsters were a far cry from the visions of playful innocence that middle-class parents conjured up about their own children.

POPULAR LITERATURE

Nothing illustrates how the middle class felt about their own children and the children of the "dangerous classes" better than popular literature. During the Gilded Age popular literature designed specifically for middle-class "young folks" poured out of publishing houses, and these sources reflected and helped to shape the debates and ideas on youth. Respectable middle-class editors and writers defined what young people should be like in their magazines and books and virulently attacked literature that strayed from their ideals. Meanwhile, other writers catered to working-class values and desires by producing a flood of "sensationalistic" literature (see Chapter 8).

Sensational Literature

Popular literature, however, was not only controlled by the gentry elite of the Northeast; it also included less respectable literature that the agents of gentility called "sensational." Indeed, *St. Nicholas* editor Mary Mapes Dodge aggressively attacked this type of literature from her "Jack-in-the-Pulpit" column in 1875: "Bad reading is a dangerous poison; and I, for one, would like to see the poisoners—that is, men who furnish it—punished like any other murderers."[17] The "murderers" that Dodge railed against were in fact pioneers in producing cheap fiction—primarily story papers, dime novels, and cheap libraries—for the masses in the last half of the nineteenth century. These incredibly popular forms of literature appealed widely to working-class audiences.

CONCLUSION

The views of youth in the Gilded Age depended entirely on who was doing the viewing and was heavily influenced by the social class of the observer. While middle-class ideologues and writers developed models of their own children that saw them as innocents waiting to be molded by the appropriate hand, they at the same time viewed working-class youth as a source of danger and immorality. Whereas middle-class young people largely accepted the values and worldview of their parents, working-class youth were pioneering new behaviors and values that challenged middle-class morality and the moral values of their own parents. Clearly, great changes were on the horizon as the forces of modern America were transforming education and leisure activities for young people.

3

Advertising

BACKGROUND

By 1900 advertising had already assumed its modern appearance and purpose, having been radically transformed by the development of industrial capitalism and advertising agents. Indeed, by the turn of the twentieth century modern advertising would appear in forms easily recognizable by modern audiences: color photographs or illustrations, large headlines, easily read copy, and copious amounts of white space surrounding the advertisement. The place of advertising in American business grew somewhat unsteadily as the frequent economic depressions of the Gilded Age wreaked havoc on advertising budgets. Nonetheless, advertising spending rose dramatically by 1900 to somewhere between $256 million and $542 million.[1] By 1900 advertisements saturated American society not only in newspapers, magazines, catalogs, and broadsides, but also on billboards, houses, rock faces, wagons of all kinds, and barns. Outdoor advertising had become so ubiquitous and often obnoxious that municipalities were already regulating this business by the turn of the century, and R. C. Maxwell, an agency which specialized in outdoor advertising, was founded in 1894.

Advertising was integral in the creation of a new American culture during the Gilded Age, which fostered new values that began to take hold and transform the nation. Advertising taught Americans that consumption, leisure, and pleasure were desirable ends and part of the "American Dream." This was a transitional era where the old and new worlds overlapped. As industrial capitalism matured, scarcity, the normal state of the preindustrial economy, gave way to abundance. Older values of production, thrift, hard work, and self-denial had been formed in a world where almost everyone had labored for the economic support of the family by producing something, and scarcity ruled the day. Advertising was one essential element in the process that transformed American values to a consumer-oriented ethic seeking self-fulfillment, leisure, and pleasure. The good life could be had by all, for a price. As real wages rose in the late nineteenth century, access to the plenty of mass-produced consumer items came to define America and define the values of consumerism.

Large businesses invested heavily in advertising in the Gilded Age for several reasons. The enormous companies that formed in this era created large economies of scale so that their businesses could make vast profits, ride out downturns in the economy, and neutralize competition. Such massive enterprises could no longer rely only on orders that they had in hand for their product, because they had so much money invested in structures, equipment, and labor costs. Advertising helped in a variety of ways. First, it helped a business to capture or retain market share where demand for its product already existed. Second, advertising could lead to consumer demand which would force retailers to stock certain products. Third, advertising could help to control costs. For example, if a national company could convince the public that its $50 name-brand piano was far superior to the $30 pianos sold by local makers, then it captured not only market share but also helped to set somewhat predictable prices. Finally, most advertising campaigns after 1890 would try to create new demand for products instead of simply trying to capture existing markets.

Early Advertising Agents

Advertising agents developed well before the Gilded Age. The introduction of chlorine to the paper making process in the 1830s made paper cheaper and the space for advertisements grew. As more ads began to appear, the profession of advertising agents emerged. Volney B. Palmer is generally credited with opening the first advertising agency in Philadelphia in 1841, and is believed to be the first person to use the term "Advertising Agency" in one of his own advertisements (1849). His operations were so successful that he took on partners (John E. Joy, W. W. Sharpe, and J. E. Coe) and opened offices in New York and Boston. Palmer's agency soon had plenty of competition from other agencies as businesses began to invest more in advertising; New York alone boasted 20 agencies in 1861.

Advertising, though aspiring to the status of a reputable profession, was often considered part of the hokum and hucksterism of patent medicines (one of the early advertising agents' largest customers) and P. T.

Barnum. Part of the problem lay in how the agents operated. Volney Palmer represented thousands of newspapers, selling their space to advertisers and in effect representing the media. By the 1850s other agents broke from the newspapers and acted as independent brokers, which was known as space-jobbing. All agents in this early period worked in a gray area representing newspapers while claiming to act in the best interest of the advertisers they solicited. Many agents acted with few scruples, trying to purchase space as cheaply as possible from the publisher and sell it as high as possible to the advertiser with both clients ignorant of the price schedules. Although indulging in hyperbole, Daniel Lord, of the famous Lord and Taylor Agency, recollected that the early ad industry was filled with so many shady deals that early ad men survived due "to the fact that there was a law against killing them." Inhabiting that ethical hinterland that seemed to characterize much of the business world in the Gilded Age, advertising agents garnered little trust.[2] Advertising needed to be transformed to meet the demands of the explosion of Gilded Age manufacturing firms even as paper became cheaper with the introduction of wood pulp techniques devised during the Civil War. By 1870 there were 5,091 newspapers in circulation, all with advertising space (see Chapter 8). Two agents would revolutionize the business and move it into a more profitable and publicly esteemed direction.

Rowell and Dodd

George P. Rowell and Horace Dodd opened their Boston-based advertising agency in 1865, forever changing the business with their "list system." Rowell purchased large amounts of space from New England weekly papers at wholesale prices and then sold it in small segments to advertisers. Dodd and Rowell moved to New York City in 1867 and soon became the largest agency in the city. What made Rowell different was that he compiled a list of 5,000 U.S. and 300 Canadian newspapers with their circulation figures for advertisers to see in *Rowell's American Newspaper Directory*. Advertisers could now see more concretely what they were getting for their advertising dollars and newspapers were guaranteed up-front payment for their ads. Rowell would continue as a giant in the field throughout the Gilded Age.

Francis Wayland Ayer

The second major innovator to help bring more solid ethics and professionalism to the field of advertising was Francis Wayland Ayer. Twenty-one-year-old Ayer founded N. W. Ayer & Son agency in 1869, naming it after his father (who did work with him) to convince clients that the agency had the experience and wisdom of two generations of Ayers. Ayer introduced the concept of the open contract (1875) where he openly informed both the publisher and the advertiser of the prices and he received his payment as a set commission. Ayer represented the advertiser though he received his commission from the publisher. Eventually, this open-contract-plus-commission would become the standard of the profession and helped to transform the advertising business into a more respected profession. N. W. Ayer & Son also introduced the concept of the market survey in 1879.

Even as Rowell and Ayer were remaking the profession into its more modern form their agencies were still fairly small and their functions limited. Indeed, most agencies in the 1870s were one-room offices where the owner-operator employed an estimator who figured rates and expenses, a bookkeeper, a checking clerk, and an office boy. Only the largest advertising agencies employed more than five in an office in the 1870s. What these agents did not do was design the ads or give any advice on style. When Daniel Lord started to give design advice to a client in the 1870s the man replied, "you may know a lot about advertising, but you know very little about the furniture business."[3]

By the last 20 years of the century the size and function of advertising agencies changed. N. W. Ayer & Son illustrated this trend toward large agencies. By 1900, Ayer & Son was the largest agency in the nation, employing 160 people and handling accounts for Hires' Root Beer, J. I. Case threshing machines, Procter & Gamble soaps, Mellin's Baby Food, and Standard Oil. In 1899 the company launched the largest advertising campaign of the Gilded Age for the National Biscuit Company and its new prepackaged crackers, devising the clever product name Uneeda Biscuit (see "Large Campaigns").[4]

P. T. Barnum and Advertising

Phineas Taylor Barnum (1810–1891) would pioneer advertising style and design creativity beginning in the late 1820s and continuing until his death in 1891. Barnum, however, did not make a name for himself through newspaper advertising. Although newspaper advertising was a very important medium in the Gilded Age it had serious limitations for advertisers early in the era. By the 1870s ads boasted large type, breaking from the earlier tradition of six point agate type that dominated the first half of the century, and white space, though pictures were still uncommon. Ads remained largely confined to columns, and they were relatively small. This left other modes of advertisement to develop more creative and visually stimulating styles. P. T. Barnum developed an aggressive promotional style that extensively used handbills, banners, posters, and billboards. In these mediums Barnum employed color, intricate borders, incredible typographic displays that varied font style and size, testimonials, endorsements, and a great deal of exaggeration. Barnum was also the master of other forms of promotion and advertisement such as the use of gas lights, brass bands, large panel paintings, baby shows, and beauty contests. Some historians claim Barnum created the first advertising campaigns that used a wide variety of advertising mediums to entice the public.[5]

While Barnum is probably most well known today for his promotions dealing with his various circuses, he was also very successful in his other promotions. Perhaps his most infamous investment was in the American Museum (1841), which boasted natural and unnatural curiosities. He ceaselessly and some say unscrupulously advertised his "curiosities" to bring in an urban public starved for entertainment. He also mounted extremely economically successful tours which he advertised and promoted. His first efforts involved the 25-inch-tall midget Charles Stratton, promoted as General Tom Thumb. Although Stratton was only 5 years old in the first tour, Barnum assured the public that this small boy was in fact 11. In 13 months nearly 100,000 people paid to see General Tom Thumb. Barnum then mounted a successful European tour where he dressed Stratton like Napoleon and had him arrive in a tiny, highly decorated carriage pulled by Shetland ponies. The tour went on for three years where Tom Thumb entertained most of the royalty of Europe, was kissed by four queens, drew roughly 5 million paying customers, and generated tour profits over $1 million. Barnum similarly promoted and advertised the opera singer Jenny Lind, who was called the "Swedish Nightingale." Although virtually unknown in the United States before her tour in 1850, Barnum's spectacular advertising campaign drew 30,000 people to her arrival and drew tens of thousands to her tour. Barnum then took his skills and used them to promote his traveling circus, which he first purchased in 1870 and which would become the famous Barnum & Bailey Circus that he promoted as "The Greatest Show on Earth" (see Chapter 10). Barnum helped to create promotional advertising using his own aggressive style, which often relied on embellishment. But, astute students of the Gilded Age should not simply throw out Barnum's contributions as hokum and hucksterism. His accomplishments in advertising and promotion were substantial and the product he provided, such as the exceptionally talented Jenny Lind, was often quite real. P. T. Barnum never said "a sucker is born every minute," but he did say, "I thoroughly understood the art of advertising."[6]

Trademarks and Brand-Name Marketing

Companies that wished to sell their products in the new national marketplace, which was growing more interconnected as railroad mileage dramatically expanded in the Gilded Age (see Chapter 11), had to make their products distinctive from locally produced goods. One meaningful way to distinguish national brands from local products was to use a registered brand name or trademark. In 1870 there were a handful of registered trademarks in the U.S. Patent Office, but this number grew to 121 by the end of 1871 and to an impressive 1,138 by 1875. Federal legislation in 1881, which protected trademarks, increased this trend so that by 1906 there were 10,500 registered trademarks and brand names in the United States. Nationally recognizable products began to appear in stores all over the country as early as the 1840s: John Deere (1847), Borden's Eagle Brand Condensed Milk (1866), Campbell's Soup (1869), Levi Strauss' work clothing (1873), Eagle Pencils (1877), Quaker Oats (1897), Ivory Soap (1879), Black Jack Chewing Gum (1884), Coca-Cola (1887), Heinz (1893), the National Biscuit Company's Uneeda Biscuit (1898), and Cream of Wheat (1900). Many of these brand names, however, did not officially have their products registered until the last part of the century: Coca-Cola (1893), Quaker Oats (1897), Ivory Soap (1905), Heinz (1897), and John Deere (1897).[7] Brand names and trademarks helped to distinguish a product from similar products and promoted themselves over locally produced goods through claims that they were cleaner, safer, higher quality, worked better, or were guaranteed. Americans in radically different geographic locations in the United States could be united through what scholars call consumption communities by purchasing and using the same brand-name goods.

Uneeda Biscuit and Heinz

Brand-name goods also had a different appearance from traditional dry goods which were usually sold in bulk: peanut butter in crocks, crackers in barrels, bacon in slabs, and flour in bins. Unique and attractive packaging with prominent logos and names sought to catch consumers' attention with their eye appeal as well as by making claims to greater quality. The National Biscuit Company produced Uneeda Biscuits, for example, and marketed these crackers in flashy cardboard cartons lined with wax paper. Uneeda Biscuits could logically make a claim that its crackers were fresher and of higher quality than those sold in bulk out of a barrel. These crackers started a revolution in product packaging (see "Large Campaigns"). Henry J. Heinz was another pioneer in name-brand advertising. He started with horseradish in 1869 but his company sold almost 200 different canned and prepackaged food products by 1900. By the turn of the twentieth century Americans could purchase foods that had never been part of their diet as companies introduced new and exotic foods prepackaged and heavily advertised (see Chapter 6).[8]

Only a few pioneering industries began the trend of using trademarks and aggressive advertising to differentiate themselves from their local and national competitors, and these industries set the standards of promotional campaigns and brand-name use that most other businesses would follow in the 1890s. Patent medicine, soap, sewing machine, and farm equipment companies all experimented with these new marketing techniques and pioneered advertising and attempts to distinguish their products.

Patent Medicines

Patent medicines were the first industry to turn toward advertising to create markets and differentiate their products, and they were the largest clients of the early advertising agencies, which almost certainly did not do much good for the reputation of early agents. These medicines were rarely actually patented and often did not really do much for one's health. Many of these oils, tonics, bitters, and balms relied on herbal and folk remedies juiced up with liberal doses of alcohol, sometimes as much as 44 percent, or doses of the narcotics morphine or opium (usually the derivatives codeine, paregoric, and laudanum) that were sometimes high enough to be addictive. Some historians have suggested these medicines were particularly popular for women in regions heavily influenced by temperance movements. But there is little doubt about their popularity and sales. Indeed, during the Civil War the U.S. government prescribed liberal doses of Hostetter's Bitters and Peruna, which contained enough alcohol to make it stronger than wine, and tens of thousands of men returned home having experienced patent medicines. Drake's Plantation Bitters was advertised liberally on barns, rocks, and houses along the railroad route between Philadelphia and New York. Lydia Pinkham's Vegetable Compound, a folk remedy she brewed for "female complaints," started to be sold in 1875 and quickly turned to extensive advertising. This patent medicine made the family a fortune well after Lydia's death in 1883.[9] Patent medicines of all stripes often had such little money invested in their business that they sought to use the new medium of advertising and brand names to create demand for their product.

Soap

Soap manufacturers were also quick to turn to advertising campaigns and the use of brand names. Enoch Morgan's Sons spent $15,000 to advertise Sapolio soap in 1871. That amount increased to $28,000 in 1884, $69,000 in 1885, and $400,000 in 1896. The Sapolio advertising campaigns, which normally pictured a young man gazing at his reflection in the radiant sheen of a pan, increased sales to 16.5 million by 1905, which converted to almost one bar purchased by every American family. Competitors quickly mimicked the Sapolio campaign and Ivory Soap, Pears' Soap, and Bon Ami soon became major advertisers.

Sewing Machine Companies

Singer, Willcox and Gibbs, and Wheeler and Wilson all intensely competed for a national and international market in sewing machines, which drove them to magazine and newspaper advertising quite early. Willcox and Gibbs had the great good fortune to hire John Powers to advertise for them in Great Britain and he purchased a full-page ad on the back cover of the *Golden Hours*, an English magazine with good circulation. Powers' imaginative advertisement, which promoted the quality of the machine but also offered clear installment purchasing and a free trial period, took Great Britain by storm and created a demand for sewing machines in Great Britain that Willcox and Gibbs could not meet. Powers would play a major role in transforming American advertising in a few short years.

Farm Equipment Makers

Farm equipment manufacturers also turned very early to magazine advertising; *Southern Planter* advertised an Improved Patent Seed Sower as early as 1855. Again, the intense competition among farm machinery manufacturers led the industry to rely on advertising to attract customers. For all of these products advertising would play a major role and they pioneered the use of advertising and brand names to sell their products and create demand.[10]

Montgomery Ward, Sears, Roebuck and Company, and Mail Order Catalogs

Advertising also took a major leap forward when Aaron Montgomery Ward published the nation's first catalog in 1872. Ward directed his brilliant advertising to farmers angry over falling crop prices and railroad monopolies (see Chapter 1). Ward created an entirely new industry and form of advertising with his first catalog, which was 100 pages long and filled with listings of several hundred goods, descriptions, and prices. Ward's association with the Grange proved instrumental to his success. His catalog offered much lower prices to beleaguered farmers suffering from an economic depression, and in fact followed the efforts of grocer Z. M. Hall & Company who supplied many Granges. Rural Americans were eager to tap into a consumer market that could provide them with less expensive goods. The first Ward catalog in 1874 consisted of one sheet, grew to 238 pages in 1882, and ballooned to in excess of 1,000 pages by 1900. Ward was so successful in aiming his advertising at rural Americans that soon other mail order companies published their own catalogs, which became increasingly specialized in the 1890s. Sears, Roebuck and Company started its catalog business in 1893, joining the other large mail order houses like Spiegel, May, and Stern. By 1900 there were 1,200 mail order companies enticing 6 million rural customers.[11]

The visual appeal and success of advertising became increasingly important as competition increased among the large houses and as rural storekeepers tried to smear catalog companies by claiming they offered substandard goods. Sears and Ward both employed trains that steamed throughout the rural United States advertising to rural Americans and giving them the opportunity to see firsthand the products that they considered ordering sight unseen. These tours were vital to overcome the opposition of local storekeepers and assure farmers that the claims of quality by the mail order companies were indeed true. Catalogs were increasingly ornate as visual appeal became an important advertising tool to attract orders. Both Sears and Ward guaranteed their products and offered full cash refunds, though Sears initiated more aggressive advertising techniques in the appearance, copy, and attempts at eliciting emotional connections to products.

The Catalogs

By the 1890s both the Sears' and Ward's catalogs were over 500 pages and boasted a diversity of products that must have been mind-boggling to rural Americans, particularly those who lived on isolated farms and ranches. The 1895 *Montgomery Ward Spring and Summer Catalog* ran 624 pages, claiming on the cover that it contained "Supplies For Every Trade And Calling On Earth." Remarkably, these giant catalogs came out biannually in March and September, and Ward, like the other giant mail order houses, also printed specialty catalogs. The catalog provided detailed information on orders, returns, cash discounts, and bulk club orders that were discounted. The list of the 38 different departments in the catalog illustrates the incredible multiplicity of goods: dry goods, ladies' and children's suits, books, trimmings and notions, accessories, sanitary supplies, stationery, notions, millinery, watches and jewelry, silverware, clocks, optical goods, photographic and printing equipment, toys and games, musical instruments, artists' supplies, toiletries and drugs, sewing machines, clothing, harnesses and saddlery, wallpaper/carpets/curtains, hardware, stoves, tinware and cutlery, guns and sporting goods, boots and shoes, crockery and glassware, lamps, bicycles/baby carriages/wheel toys, trunks, dairy supplies, woodenware, laundry equipment, buggies and wagons, agriculture implements, carriage hardware and supplies, and furniture.

The range of goods available was stunning. Even the most remote ranch women in Nevada's northern high desert could choose from 31 pages of cloth that offered a wide variety of silk, linen, wool, flannel, corduroy, cotton, sateen, lace, satin, mohair, and cashmere in a wide number of prints and colors for clothing, tablecloths, towels, doilies, or napkins. The catalog contained 59 pages of guns and sporting goods. Firearms alone took up 30 pages: 53 different shotguns ranging in price from $5 for a simple model to $95 for the ornate Colt Hammerless 12 gauge, 4 old muzzle loaders, 26 different rifles, and at least 43 different pistols, though caliber, grip, and ornamentation differences made the actual number of variations much higher. Indeed, only the state of Illinois legally forbade minors to purchase firearms and even required adults to send in a letter signed by two witnesses before they could purchase a firearm. But the catalog made it very clear that "This law does not apply to any state except Illinois." A seven-shot pistol could be purchased for as little as $.74. Baseball gloves, over 20 different patterns of china, traveling trunks, bookcases, every imaginable tool, cameras, baby carriages, watches, books, and 31 choices in horse harnesses as well as a harness for goats appeared in the 1895 catalog.[12] It is little wonder that farmers often called these wondrous catalogs the "Farmer's Bible."

The Post Office

Postmaster General John A. Wanamaker, the famous department store owner (see "Department Stores"), endorsed several changes in U.S. mail policy that led to even greater catalog use in rural America. Parcel post, bulk mail rates, rural free delivery, and postal money orders all helped to make catalog purchases easier. Rural free delivery, championed by Wanamaker, made it possible for rural residents to receive delivery straight to their homes.

Consumer Culture

For farm and ranch families who led relatively isolated lives, particularly on the Great Plains and in the West, these catalogs were an important connection to the larger culture and to the growing movement toward a consumer ethic within the nation as a whole. The reach of America's great mail order houses was so great that when ex-President Theodore Roosevelt went on an African safari in 1909–1910, he found a mission in the Sudan within "the domains of savagery" totally outfitted with tables, beds, furniture, bedding, and other items from the Montgomery Ward catalog. The reach of these mail order houses seemed limitless. Incredible economic changes were transforming rural America led by the mail order houses and their catalogs, which helped to bring consumer culture, installment buying, and often a cash economy to even the most remote parts of the countryside.[13]

Department Stores

Department stores, like their rural counterpart, mail order catalog companies, were harbingers of economic transformation and the dawn

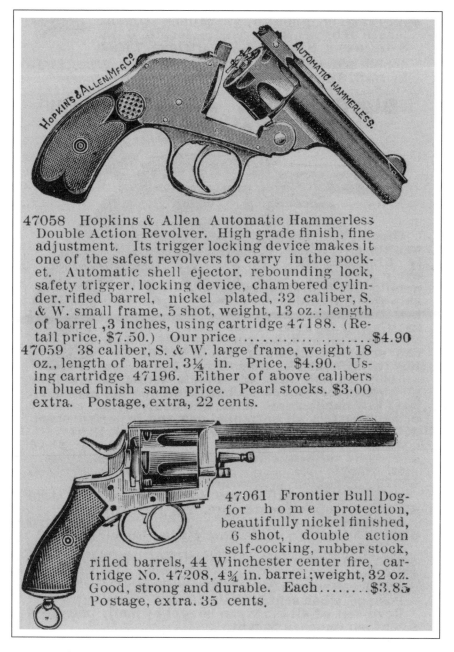

47058 Hopkins & Allen Automatic Hammerless Double Action Revolver. High grade finish, fine adjustment. Its trigger locking device makes it one of the safest revolvers to carry in the pocket. Automatic shell ejector, rebounding lock, safety trigger, locking device, chambered cylinder, rifled barrel, nickel plated, 32 caliber, S. & W. small frame, 5 shot, weight, 13 oz.; length of barrel ,3 inches, using cartridge 47188. (Retail price, $7.50.) Our price $4.90
47059 38 caliber, S. & W. large frame, weight 18 oz., length of barrel, 3¼ in. Price, $4.90. Using cartridge 47196. Either of above calibers in blued finish same price. Pearl stocks. $3.00 extra. Postage, extra, 22 cents.

47061 Frontier Bull Dog- for home protection, beautifully nickel finished, 6 shot, double action self-cocking, rubber stock, rifled barrels, 44 Winchester center fire, cartridge No. 47208, 4¾ in. barrel;weight, 32 oz. Good, strong and durable. Each........$3.85 Postage, extra. 35 cents.

An advertisement for various guns from the 1895 *Montgomery Ward Catalogue*.

of a new consumer culture. The Civil War helped consolidate dry goods merchants and produced some very large establishments, such as A. T. Stewart's in Philadelphia. Stewart and his competitors were primarily wholesalers. Slowly, over the 1870s, large retailers like John Wanamaker, who made his fortune first in war uniforms then in men's and boy's clothing, began the process of creating department stores. Wanamaker purchased the abandoned Pennsylvania Freight Station in Philadelphia in 1876 and opened a "New Kind of Store." Within a year the Grand Depot employed 1,200 and introduced shoppers to electrical lighting in 1878. During the same period other concerns such as Lord and Taylor, Siegel-Cooper, and R. H. Macy of New York, Marshall Field in Chicago, F. and R. Lazarus in Columbus, and the Gimbels in Milwaukee were experimenting with the department store model that dictated the buying of goods directly from the producer, and organizing goods into departments and selling them retail.

By the late 1880s and 1890s massive department stores appeared in particular districts in the great cities of the United States, challenging the wholesalers and small retail dry goods stores. In the 1880s most department stores were still small by modern standards, but they would grow to the massive size of today and proliferated as many as 125 departments by 1910. By 1881, for example, Wanamaker's Grand Depot employed more than 2,000 people, boasted 46 departments, and had nearly three acres of retail space on a single floor. Like their catalog counterparts, department stores offered a dizzying array of products. Siegel-Cooper's department store in the 1890s "sold staples, yard goods, notions, ready-made clothing, machine-made furnishings, and hundreds of name-brand pianos but also photographic equipment in the largest photographic gallery anywhere, and monkeys, dogs, cats, birds, lion and panther cubs, and tropical fish in its huge pet department."[14] Department stores were a magical place where shoppers could see an amazing array of goods on display that would have been beyond the wildest dreams of their counterparts 20 years earlier.

Department stores led the way in advertising as well, adopting some of the strategies employed by P. T. Barnum. Wanamaker gained fame for letting advertising balloons loose and offering a free suit to everyone who returned one to his store in Philadelphia. He also organized large parades (a tradition which continues today with Macy's Thanksgiving Day Parade) to promote his store. All of the department stores promoted holidays, new and old, to boost spending and entice consumers to shop.

John Wanamaker

John Wanamaker (1838–1922) stands out as one of the most innovative advertisers. As early as 1865 he initiated a money-back guarantee, a revolutionary step in advertising retail goods that had never been offered.

Direct appeals to female shoppers were part of the Wanamaker innovations in advertising; ads declared one set price for every customer and guaranteed exchanges and cash refunds. Wanamaker is reputedly the first retailer to place a half-page newspaper advertisement in 1874, the first full-page advertisement in 1879, and would be emulated by virtually the entire retail industry when he placed ads on consecutive pages, several on the same page, and eventually consecutive full-page ads. Philadelphia newspapers gained tremendous advertising business from Wanamaker. He often wrote his own copy in the early days and focused initially on an advertising philosophy that emphasized low cost and high saturation. House magazines proved an equally successful Wanamaker ploy, and he filled them with pithy anecdotes, articles, and shopping advice as well as advertisements. But perhaps Wanamaker's greatest advertising coup was the 1880 hiring of the first full-time copywriter, John Powers, to direct the store's advertising campaigns.[15]

Window Trimmers

Show windows became one of the premier methods for advertising goods in department stores, enticing spectators to enter stores and spawning an entirely new pastime, window shopping. It was not until the 1890s, though, that retailers began to turn significantly toward displaying their goods behind massive windows of plate glass. One of the pioneers in the art of show window display was Frank L. Baum (who would become famous later as the author of *The Wizard of Oz*). In 1898 he founded the National Association of Window Trimmers, which soon had 200 members. Baum also published a journal, packed with advertising to offset the cost, devoted to the art of window display, *The Show Window*. Circulation grew rapidly and it was hailed by Marshall-Fields executive H. Gordon Selfridge as "an indispensable organ." Baum and his journal pioneered window display techniques and psychology to try to entice passersby to desire the items artistically displayed behind the plate glass. By 1900 there were over 1,500 professional window trimmers.[16]

John Powers and New-Style Advertising Agents

Another revolution occurred in the advertising agency business in 1880 when John Wanamaker hired John E. Powers, who is often referred to as the "father of honest advertising." Powers was the first person hired as a full-time ad writer and he invented a style that would develop into one of the two most prominent advertising styles in the last 20 years of the nineteenth century. Less was more in Powers' mind as he pointedly rejected the over-the-top hyperbole of the P. T. Barnum and patent medicine school of advertising. Barnum, for example, promoted his circus as "the greatest show on earth." The genius of the Powers style was that he realized that by 1880 the American public was already savvy about exaggerated advertisements and wise to the way of promotion. Instead, Powers presented advertisements in a straightforward manner, with a plain roman font, few frills, and direct appeals in a colloquial English that a child could understand. The advertising language he used was patterned after spoken rather than written English. Powers himself described his approach as "Print the news of the store. No catchy headings, no catches, no headings, no smartness, no brag, no fine writing, no fooling, no foolery, no attempt at advertising, no mercenary admiration; hang up the goods in the papers, one at a time, a few today, tomorrow the same or others."[17] Powers valued integrity in advertising and his copy focused on "style, elegance, comfort, and even luxury, not price and durability." In a Powers ad for a fly fan, which was designed to keep flies away from people as they ate or slept, he used a simple font with one headline, "A Luxury." In the body of the text Powers used simple language to describe the product, again stating "it IS a luxury" and ending with the claim "It is worth a hundred dollars; send it back if it isn't." While many readers today might see the Powers style as staid, it is important to remember that he was trying to gain the trust of a public inundated with Barnum-style advertising embellishment. Within a few years the profits at Wanamaker's department store doubled from $4 million to $8 million per year. As a person Powers was difficult, always something of an enigma to his employers and to others in the advertising world. His cynicism and cold wit kept most people at arm's length. But there is no doubt that he transformed advertising fundamentally with his factual content, forthright statements, and straightforward, uncomplicated style. Powers became an important role model for new advertising men who would transform advertising agencies from simple brokers buying space for advertisers to full-service agencies that procured space and designed advertising campaigns for their business clients.[18]

Artemus Ward

Enoch Morgan's Sons soon followed Wanamaker's example and hired Artemus Ward to manage their advertising campaign for Sapolio soap in 1884. Ward dramatically increased spending on advertising for Sapolio from $28,000 (1884) to $69,000 (1885) to a staggering $400,000 (1896). Sales soared to match the increased expenditures. Ward brilliantly used the attention surrounding the 400-year anniversary of Columbus' voyage to the Americas to advertise Sapolio. He agreed to sponsor Captain Andrews as he attempted to sail a 14-foot sailboat across the Atlantic to Spain to celebrate the 400-year anniversary if the boat was named *Sapolio*. Ward's sponsorship of the trip proved wise as Andrews' exploits riveted the attention of the American press and public for three months as he battled across the Atlantic in his tiny sailboat and procured tremendous advertising for Sapolio soap. Although Ward did not think much of professional copywriters, his career illustrated the growing professionalization of advertising.[19]

Ad Men

By the 1890s, hundreds of people were employed by advertising agencies and businesses to write advertising copy and direct large campaigns. By 1904, these people were numerous and organized enough to found the Advertising Federation of America. Manly Gillam took over from Powers after Wanamaker fired the difficult ad man for the last time in 1886. But, there is no doubt that the need for good writers of advertising and the incredible $10,000 per year salary that Powers was paid by Wanamaker drew many to the new field. Others soon followed, like Nathaniel C. Fowler, Jr., who jumped into the copywriting field. Perhaps his most well-known advertising achievement that is still with us today was his co-creation of the rock of Gibraltar trademark for Prudential Insurance. Fowler would publish manuals and found a school on advertising. He also recommended in *Advertising Age* (1891) that advertisers direct their ads to women because they did most of the household shopping. Charles Austin Bates and Wolstand Dixey in New York and E. A. Wheatley in Chicago also helped to pave the way for freelance copywriters.

Other Ad Styles

The direct, no-frills advertising of John Powers, often referred to as the Powers style, was not the only type of advertising in the Gilded Age, though its influence was tremendous up to the 1890s. Another style of advertising focused instead on jingles and memorable figures that were associated with a particular product. Advertisers and businesses hoped that short, catchy songs and trademarked figures would become associated with a product and would remain in the minds of consumers. Artemus Ward employed jingles to sell Sapolio, and in 1900 James K. Fraser wrote what would become a famous jingle for the soap company:

> This is the maid of fair renown
> Who scrubs the floors of Spotless Town.
> To find a speck when she is through
> Would take a pair of specs or two,
> And her employ isn't slow,
> For she employs SAPOLIO.[20]

By the late 1890s the Lasker style would promote "reason why" copy that attempted to show consumers why they should purchase a particular product. But the true impact of Albert Lasker of Lord & Taylor's would have to wait for the twentieth century when new types of impressionistic copy directed toward psychological appeals would gain popularity.[21]

Large Ad Campaigns

Truly massive advertising campaigns and the attempt to use advertising to create consumer demand became standard by the 1890s among most businesses. Kodak introduced the slogan "You press the button; we do the rest" in a large campaign promoting its new $5 pocket camera. In 1900, Kodak introduced the Brownie, the first inexpensive camera, retailing for $1, aimed at an audience of "school boys and school girls," and launched a massive advertising campaign connecting the camera to illustrator Palmer Cox's Brownie creation (see Chapter 7). Van Camp pork and beans, Cream of Wheat, Campbell's Soup, and Coca-Cola all launched major campaigns in the 1890s, but none surpassed the National Biscuit Company's Uneeda Biscuit campaign in 1899. N. W. Ayer & Son managed the massive advertising campaign, the largest of its day, for the National Biscuit Company using outdoor, magazine, and newspaper ads. The National Biscuit Company had the new idea of selling crackers in airtight packaging within an attractive tin container, claiming that the new crackers were of much higher quality than crackers sold in bulk from barrels. H. N. McKinney, who worked on the project for Ayer, coined the name "Uneeda" and helped to develop the nation's first million-dollar advertising campaign, which promoted the trademarked figure of a boy in slickers and the slogan "Lest you forget, we say it yet, Uneeda biscuit." The campaign was so successful that the National Biscuit Company was overwhelmed with orders, which forced it to switch to cheaper cardboard containers and more importantly set the precedent for massive, successful advertising campaigns.[22]

Visual Appeal, Louis Prang, and Color

As advertising matured in the Gilded Age the visual appeal of ads took on increasing importance and this was aided tremendously by the introduction of color. The introduction of chromolithography technology in the United States is credited to Louis Prang (1824–1909) and this provided a reliable method for introducing color onto paper (see Chapter 12). Bright, vibrant colors were available to artists and advertisers in excess of one thousand shades after 1880, according to Prang. In 1875, Prang would gain fame by introducing his colors in greeting cards, and is known as the "father of the American Christmas card." Not surprisingly, advertising agents turned to color to spark aesthetic appeal in ads.

Chromolithographic prints, known as chromos, were changing the way Americans saw their world.

Trade Cards

One of the first advertising methods to take advantage of the color possible with chromolithography were trade cards. In the 1870s, businesses of all kinds passed out small, often brilliantly colored cards advertising their products. By the 1880s a trade card mania swept through the nation and Americans of all ages began to collect the novel, highly colored cards and paste them into albums (see Chapter 7). The trade card craze provided businesses with an important method of advertising their goods and services and indicated the incredible impact that color, which was still fairly novel, could have on the public. Color quickly made its way into other types of advertising like broadsides and handbills.

Color Goes Mainstream

Color, however, did not begin to make inroads in newspaper or magazine advertising until the 1890s. Ivory Soap pioneered the use of color in its advertisements by having high-quality chromolithographic prints made and shipped directly to publishers for inclusion in their magazines in 1896. Ivory showed advertisers how to skirt the reluctance of magazine publishers to go to the expense of having to produce chromos for their magazines by providing the more expensive prints. Other businesses soon adopted the Ivory pattern and were supplying chromos to magazines.[23] By 1900 color was everywhere in advertising.

Maxfield Parrish

The revolution in color and the growing importance of the visual attractiveness in advertising brought artists into the advertising world. Maxfield Parrish (1870–1966) was already making a name for himself as an artist in the late 1890s, but his profound influence on advertising would take place in the early twentieth century (see Chapter 12). Astounding brilliant colors, particularly blues, and the connection of a product to the spirit and the emotion of his vibrant art helped Parrish to leave an indelible mark on advertising.

Photography

Equally important regarding visual appeal were developments in photography that allowed photographs to be reproduced in magazines by the end of the century. Life no longer had to be approximated in illustrations but could be reproduced exactly by photographs. The extraordinary ability of advertising to employ brilliant color as well as photographs would forever change the ways in which Americans had

CHAS·H·GETZIN,
PITCHER – DETROIT.

1888 baseball card. © Library of Congress.

the world represented to them in their media. Posters, broadsides, billboards, and magazines virtually assaulted Americans with dazzling color and sharp photographic images by the twentieth century.

Magazine Advertising

Advertising also played a special role in the history of American magazines. The emergence of mass-market magazines in the late Gilded Age was made possible only with revenues generated by advertising (see Chapter 8). Before the 1880s relatively little advertising ran in magazines. The development of a national consumer culture was just beginning and most shopping was still done locally; therefore, most advertising dollars went to newspapers. By the 1880s, a national consumer culture was in the process of being established and Americans were being united by consumption communities of similar products. In addition, Congress lowered postage rates to one cent per pound for second-class mail in 1885, setting the stage for a dramatic increase in magazine sales. The combination of these factors with the rapid expansion of the population that enjoyed greater literacy and more free time and disposable income than in the past would create an unprecedented boom in magazine sales and advertising.[24] The genteel magazines of the Gilded Age—most notably *Harper's*, *Atlantic Monthly*, *Century*, and *Scribner's Monthly*—were standoffish at best to advertising in the 1870s and seriously limited it in their pages. A look at *Harper's* illustrates how this position rather rapidly changed in the 1880s. Businesses that produced luxury items that were clearly not necessities had to try to create a demand for their products and what better place to do this than the genteel literary magazines, like *Harper's*, that boasted a relatively small but affluent sector of middle- and upper-class readers. By 1891, *Harper's* gradually expanded its advertising to 113 pages of advertising from 6 to 7 pages in the early 1870s.

Even more telling was the development of new, low-cost mass-market magazines that were created specifically with advertising revenue in mind. *Ladies' Home Journal*, *Munsey's*, *Cosmopolitan*, and *McClure's* burst onto the American magazine scene in the 1890s selling for 10 cents, far less than the 25 to 35 cents charged by the genteel magazines like *Harper's*. These "10-cent monthly" magazines caused a revolution in the publishing industry and in American reading habits as millions of new magazines flooded into American homes, which readily absorbed them. These magazines provided excellent literature and employed many of the same writers as their more genteel counterparts, such as Rudyard Kipling, Arthur Conan Doyle, Robert Louis Stevenson, and Edward Everett Hale. Indeed, Samuel McClure, founder of *McClure's Magazine*, had formerly worked for the Century Company and used recycled stories from its *St. Nicholas Magazine* in *McClure's*. The number of magazines in the United States grew from 3,300 in 1885 to over 5,500 in 1900 and along with this growth came greater emphasis on advertising. Indeed, the great 10-cent monthlies thrived because advertising revenues came to be more important than cover price. By 1900 the circulation figures of *each* of the new 10-cent monthlies (*Ladies' Home Journal*, *McClure's*, *Munsey's*, and *Cosmopolitan*) individually exceeded the combined circulation figures of *Harper's*, *Atlantic Monthly*, and *Century*. The new mass-market magazines thrived through advertising which often surpassed 100 pages an issue.[25]

CONCLUSION

The Gilded Age witnessed the emergence of the foundations of modern advertising. Businesses turned to advertising increasingly through the last three decades of the century in an effort to maximize profits and to generate national markets for their goods. The number of businesses engaged in advertising to create demand expanded rapidly from the pioneer industries of patent medicines, farm machinery, sewing machines, and soap in the 1870s to include virtually every national company in the late 1890s. Professional advertising agencies transformed themselves from simple brokers into multifaceted businesses that arranged advertising space and oversaw major ad campaigns which included writing copy and creating visually appealing images. By 1900 advertising had taken its modern form and function, and already saturated American streets, trains, magazines, and newspapers.

4

Architecture

BACKGROUND

Architecture also changed during the Gilded Age as modern building techniques and amenities transformed American buildings, both public and private. The American Renaissance movement, which influenced art and sculpture, also profoundly affected architecture, and was heavily influenced by the French Ecole des Beaux-Arts training methodology and style. Massive public statements like the Columbia Exposition's White City as well as the emergence of the modern skyscraper equally influenced the growing scale and grandeur of architecture. On the popular side, architecture changed American homes as new styles, often collectively labeled as Victorian, and important new amenities appeared in homes. At the most personal level the creation of the modern bathroom with its sink, tub, and toilet is as significant as the invention of the skyscraper.

PUBLIC ARCHITECTURE

The dramatic urban expansion of the United States in the Gilded Age created an almost insatiable demand for massive public buildings. Opera houses, theaters, capitols, university buildings, mansions, libraries, government buildings, and most significantly business office buildings all exploded in number. As cities became more concentrated and land prices sky-rocketed the need to build vertically pushed architects to develop innovations that would lead to the modern city. American cities would never be the same.

Professional Architects and Richard Morris Hunt

Mid-nineteenth-century America witnessed the rise and professionalization of architecture as a distinct, highly trained occupation. In 1857 architects founded the American Institute of Architecture, providing legitimacy for this young profession which sought to differentiate itself from draftspersons, builders, and contractors. One of the most influential early architects was Richard Morris Hunt. Hunt trained in France at the Ecole des Beaux-Arts and established a studio in New York City in 1858, where he trained a new generation of architects who would influence Gilded Age architecture: William Henry Ware, George B. Post, Henry Van Brunt, and Stanford White. In turn, these architects would train a new generation from the 1870s through the 1890s. Perhaps the most influential of this group was William Ware, who established the nation's first school of architecture in 1865 at the Massachusetts Institute of Technology (MIT) and another at Columbia University in 1881. Rival architecture schools appeared at Cornell (1871), Michigan (1876), Pennsylvania (1890), Armour Institute (1895), and Harvard (1895). All of these schools were heavily influenced by the Ecole des Beaux-Arts training method and style, which emphasized large projects that would be viewed as works of art.

The Skyscraper

Perhaps the most important technical innovation during the Gilded Age was the skyscraper, which soon came to represent the new urban metropolis in the machine age. The very geography of cities changed as towers soared above city streets, dramatically altering skylines. Capitalizing on techniques for using iron columns, which began in the 1850s, to replace thick, load-bearing masonry walls, William LeBaron Jenney's Home Insurance Company Building (1885) in Chicago was the first true metal-frame skyscraper. Much like the innovative balloon-frame house, skyscrapers relied on a metal skeleton. Skyscrapers would have been impractical without the development of central heating which used radiators (perfected in 1874 by William Baldwin) and advancements made in elevators in the 1870s and 1880s.

The Chicago School

The Chicago School of architects, led by such notables as John Root and Louis Sullivan, developed their style rebuilding Chicago after the disastrous 1871 fire. Sullivan believed "form must follow function." He trained at MIT and the Ecole des Beaux-Arts, and became famous for reconciling aesthetics with functional needs in his large public buildings and skyscrapers. Sullivan's talented disciple, Frank Lloyd Wright, would

Home Insurance Company Building, Chicago, Illinois, 1884. Courtesy of The Francis Loeb Library, Harvard Design School.

absorb these lessons and carry them to even greater heights in the twentieth century.

Neoclassical Eclecticism and the Columbian Exposition

In public buildings the highly eclectic, romantic style of the 1870s and 1880s gave way to more focused Neoclassical designs (though the style was still eclectic) around 1886. The White City at the Columbian Exposition in Chicago (1893) epitomized these ideas on classical grandeur imbued with nationalistic symbolism (see Chapters 7, 10, and 11). The Exposition, celebrating the 400-year anniversary of Columbus' voyage, was a grand statement by the United States that illustrated the nation's new-found economic, technological, and military power. The Neoclassical designs certainly played strongly on the metaphors of empire, power, and culture of imperial Rome. Louis Sullivan and others in the Chicago School were horrified with this return to ostentatious Neoclassical design. Other famous architects, however, like Daniel Burnham, Richard Morris Hunt, and the nation's most prestigious architectural firm McKim, Mead, and White (Charles Follen McKim, William Rutherford Mead, and Stanford White) all worked to create the awe-inspiring White City. Burnham would become a major figure in classicism of the American Renaissance and an influential city planner; he spawned the City Beautiful movement.

Courthouses and Capitols

Perhaps the most visible public buildings to the average American, however, was not skyscrapers or the White City but county courthouses and state capitols. Influenced by Greek Revival, Romanesque Revival, and Neoclassical styles, county courthouses, and on a larger scale state capitols, capped with domes or impressive towers, were the massive monuments to the power of the United States as it conquered Native Americans and asserted its power and influence throughout the world.[1]

RESIDENTIAL ARCHITECTURE

The United States experienced a dramatic need for housing during the Gilded Age as the population exploded with massive immigration and migration from the countryside to cities. A wide array of architects and builders responded with new types of residential living from company towns to tenements to new apartments. As the new leisure culture expanded in this era, more Americans also sought the amenities in their homes that made their lives easier or more pleasant. Middle-class Americans in particular imbued their homes with special philosophical significance as a refuge from the turmoil of the world and as signs of their class status.

Company Towns

As the population of the United States grew so dramatically in the Gilded Age new forms of residential housing developed based on older models. The mill villages of the early nineteenth century, particularly the well-planned town of Lowell, Massachusetts, provided tempting models. In order to attract workers in an age when labor was scarce, towns like Lowell built nice dormitories with house matrons, a hospital, bank, and a lending library. From these models companies in the Gilded Age developed the ideal of a model company town. These new towns were to be well-planned, sanitary, and free from the vices that populated most poor quarters like saloons and brothels. George M. Pullman developed the company town of Pullman, Illinois, in 1881 to separate his workers from the vices of Chicago, exercise greater control over his labor force, and provide them with better housing. Healthy, happy workers would theoretically make a better, more efficient workforce. To save costs and promote the appearance of efficiency, the houses were exactly alike, built in rows, supplied with running water and sewers (which were very rare in 1881), and connected with new macadamized roads. Pullman provided a library, post office, hotel, theater, and bank. The company town encompassed 4,000 acres and cost $8 million to construct. Pullman, though, administered the town in a dictatorial fashion and charged high rents for worker housing. Workers also complained about dictatorial bank policies as well as the high prices charged at the company town store. Pullman's efforts at patriarchal control over his employees, wage cuts, and the exorbitant rents and fees led to a series of workers' strikes in 1882, 1884, 1886, 1888, 1891, and peaked in severity with the massive Pullman Strike in 1894. The Pullman Strike caused so much damage that the Illinois Supreme Court ordered the Pullman company to divest itself of its rental properties in 1898 and the town was soon absorbed into ever-expanding Chicago. Other notable company towns were more successful than Pullman, particularly the Apollo Iron and Steel Company's efforts in Vandergrift, Pennsylvania, the N. O. Nelson Company in Leclaire, Illinois, and the National Cash Register Company's company section of Dayton, Ohio. While these towns did not meet with the same fate as Pullman, they too experienced labor problems and sought, to a degree, to control their workers and profit from them through housing and high prices at company stores. These examples were just a foreshadowing of the large-scale building of company towns in the twentieth century as corporations sought greater efficiency and attempted to lessen conflict with workers.[2]

Tenements

Only the skilled workers enjoyed the benefits of the nicer rental homes, even in company towns, while unskilled European immigrant workers were crowded into tenements or were lodgers in homes. In the poorest quarters of the large metropolitan centers of the U.S. population densities were enormous; 25 percent of the wards in seven of the ten largest cities contained populations of over 100 people per acre in 1890. New York's Tenth Ward boasted an incredible population density of 747 people per acre in 1898. To accommodate such astronomical numbers of people, cities relied on tenements and rental housing. In 1890, 77 percent of residents in cities larger than 100,000 lived in rental housing. Cities differed in their rental housing. For example, Philadelphia and Baltimore relied more heavily on row houses and boarders. Tenements, though, appeared in virtually every city and were built in New York City in great numbers. The term "tenement" came to signify any multifamily structure built in poor neighborhoods. As early as 1850, New York City averaged 65 people per tenement. By 1893, 70 percent of New Yorkers lived in multifamily dwellings and the vast majority of these lived in tenements.

Tenement Qualities

The typical tenement was between three and six stories tall and possessed communal water sources and toilets. Because of tremendous urban crowding the railroad tenement appeared in the 1850s, a 90-foot-long, 25-foot-wide rectangle that contained 12 to 16 rooms per floor. Apartments ran in straight lines, so that the four apartments per floor were a string of four or five rooms (two or three bedrooms, kitchen, and parlor) in a string, and to traverse the apartment one had to go through each room. Stacked next to each other, railroad tenements only opened to an alley on the back and to a road at the front, so only the very end rooms, usually the parlor, had windows. Disease and squalor among these urban tenements prompted reformers to attack tenement design. One reformer, Jacob Riis, tirelessly attacked tenements in a series of famous books: *How the Other Half Lives* (1890), *The Children of the Poor* (1892), *A Ten Years War* (1900), *The Battle with the Slum* (1902), and *Children of the Tenements* (1903).

Dumbbell Tenements

The famous dumbbell tenement was the product of a contest by the New York *Plumber and Sanitary Engineer* in 1879, seeking a solution to the problems of the railroad tenement. This tenement was shaped like a dumbbell. Like the railroad tenement this effort was a 90-foot-long rectangle but with narrow shafts cut out of the center of the building to provide light and ventilation to all of the bedrooms. Generally, dumbbells contained four apartments, a communal sink, and a common toilet per floor. Theoretically, these tenements were intended to alleviate part of the major problem of getting fresh air and sunshine into the interior rooms, but they failed miserably because the shafts were usually so filled with rotting garbage that windows could not be opened. There were model tenements built by philanthropists that possessed better sanitation and brought in more fresh air and sunlight; however, these experiments in reality did little to alleviate the incredibly squalid and taxing living conditions of the vast majority of urban poor.[3]

Middle-Class Apartments

Apartments for middle-class Americans in the Gilded Age differed greatly from the tenements of the poor, even though legally both were defined as multifamily units that housed more than three families. Apartments grew out of the boarding houses where many young men lived when they took jobs in the city. As urban land prices skyrocketed with the tremendous growth of the cities, building tall residential units made sense. Multifamily housing was desperately needed after the catastrophic 1871 Chicago fire, and 1,142 apartments were built in one year. These investments yielded significant returns to investors, usually 10 to 30 percent, and were in demand by urbanites. Occupants were lured by state-of-the-art technology and amenities that even wealthy Americans rarely had in the 1870s and 1880s. Elevators, hot water heaters, fully equipped bathrooms, gas lighting, telephone switchboards, central dining facilities, and even servants were provided by the more luxurious apartment buildings. A wealthy family could rent an apartment of six to ten rooms while middle-class families generally rented more modest apartments with four to five rooms. Apartments did suffer from frequent complaints about noise and the small size of the rooms, as well as attacks by critics and moralists that charged apartments were responsible for increasing immorality, destroying the female domestic ideal, and warping children. In spite of all this, apartment construction continued unabated, attracting tenants by offering a life free from the responsibilities of home ownership and boasting the latest technological innovations.[4]

House Construction

Americans of all social classes sought to purchase their own homes in the Gilded Age, seeking that elusive American Dream even then. Close to 20 percent of Americans owned their own homes in 1870 and residential housing construction was between 50 and 65 percent of total construction in the United States in most years during the nineteenth century.[5] Builders and contractors built homes on order and on speculation, often erecting three or four homes in a neighborhood. Large-scale subdivision development also appeared in the Gilded Age, pioneered by entrepreneurs like Aaron Kaplan in Brooklyn, S. E. Gross in Chicago, and Fernando Nelson on the West Coast in San Francisco. These men planned, built, and sold entire neighborhoods. Building and Loan associations (B&Ls), which had existed in the United States since 1831, provided most housing loans to Americans in the nineteenth century and made home ownership possible for tens of thousands of people. By 1893 the government counted 5,838 B&Ls in the country. Interest rates also either held or fell throughout the last three decades of the nineteenth century and mortgages began to offer longer amortization on new construction, both of which helped buyers to get lower payments and encouraged home ownership. Remarkably, the cost per square foot of house construction actually fell from 1875 to 1900. Inexpensive housing cost roughly $1.20 per square foot in 1875 and only $1 in 1900 while expensive housing could be built for $2 per square foot in 1875 and $1.50 in 1900.[6]

Industrialization and Homebuilding

By the Gilded Age, balloon-frame houses made with light studs cut in standardized sizes; factory-made, mass-produced trim, brackets, architectural parts, and joists; and roof rafters all joined by using mass-produced nails were the order of the day. Factories produced standardized, ready-made cornices, chair rails, latticework screens, wainscoting, an incredible array of wallpaper, and beveled and stained glass. Steam-powered machines mass-produced a dizzying array of building materials and revolutionized house building by making it much more an industry that assembled houses rather than one where skilled carpenters both produced and assembled all the parts of a home. For example, hand-made 3-inch oak flooring cost $21 per 1,000 feet in 1858 but fell to $.54 per 1,000 feet in 1896 when mass produced by machine. Machine-made bricks were also introduced on a large scale in the 1870s and 1880s. The wholesale cost of 1,000 bricks fell from $8.40 in 1870 to $5.31 in 1895. Plastering also changed dramatically. Contractors began to replace wood laths with wire mesh that required only two coats of plaster instead of the traditional three. Augustine Sackett also perfected the creation of gypsum-based drywall in the 1890s, which over the next 50 years would revolutionize house building, though its impact in the Gilded Age was minimal. All of these innovations lowered the cost of homes by an estimated 40 percent from the old mortice-and-tenon construction method.[7]

Middle-Class Homes

Gilded Age middle-class homes were a reflection of this group's romantic ideology; yet, such elaborate and ornate homes were only possible due to industrialization. As middle-class Americans began to place so much importance on the nuclear family and the private home, the house became a more important symbol of the family. As immigrants poured into American cities and public life came to be much more diverse and heterogeneous, the middle-class tendency to turn away from the public to the private intensified as did the middle-class abandonment of cities for suburbs. Beginning in the 1870s and continuing for the rest of the century, middle-class Americans left the cities and sought the peace, order, natural beauty, and social-class exclusiveness of the suburb. Middle-class women, the bastions of morality and civilization in the minds of most middle-class commentators, and their children, who were viewed very romantically as innocents by the middle class (see Chapter 2), both had to be protected from the immorality of the city. The home was to be "a haven in a heartless world," separated from work and the marketplace as thoroughly as it was connected to middle-class morality and refinement. Prices for middle-class homes rose accordingly as their size grew and modern amenities, such as bathrooms and furnaces, multiplied, and ranged from roughly $2,000 up to $5,000. The median sales price for a new home in 1890 was $3,250.

Entry Hall

The typical interior of middle-class homes during the Gilded Age was divided into distinctive zones: formal spaces to receive visitors, kitchen, and the private rooms upstairs. Victorian middle-class homes were designed specifically to keep outsiders away from the private living spaces of the family and the front hall provided this public space. The main entrance of most middle-class residences almost always opened into a neutral space separated from the family's living space; an entry hall which ranged from very elaborate, including a fireplace in large homes, to a simple hallway in more modest homes. Georgian architecture introduced this type of interior room organization extending from a main hallway in the eighteenth century, and most Victorian homes continued to use this pattern. A staircase to the left often led to the upper story of bedrooms. The hall preserved privacy and clearly demarcated the different zones by allowing access to every downstairs room from the hallway, which gave homeowners the ability to also limit access to rooms. Only those the family wished to let into the private parts of their home would ever pass the front hall. Deliverymen, for example, would see only the front hall or enter through the back door into the kitchen.

The front hall would be tastefully decorated to reflect the respectability and refinement of the family and no middle-class home during the Gilded Age was complete without a hallstand. The hallstand served several utilitarian functions—such as providing hat and coat hooks, an umbrella holder, a mirror, and often a table—as well as functioning as a symbol of conspicuous consumption that clearly illustrated wealth and status. Indeed, the sheer size of the hallstands, measuring anywhere from six to ten feet tall, made them very prominent features in the hall entry. These massive structures often sported marble table tops, intricate designs, and a considerable amount of mirrors, all of which added to the fairly high price of these pieces and illustrated their importance as a symbol of respectability and status. Card trays often flanked the hallstand and functioned as receptacles for the calling cards of refined middle-class callers who wished to visit the lady of the home. Both the card tray and the hallstand demarcated the public zone and illustrated the boundary which the outside world and social inferiors could not pass.[8]

Kitchen

The kitchen was another interior zone which was normally located in the back of the residence and connected to the outside world through a back door. Here the woman of the house and servants worked apart from the hall zone and social zones of the house to ensure that the household functioned. Most middle-class women did without servants, roughly 20 to 25 percent of households hired servants in 1880, and were confronted with a considerable amount of sheer physical labor to keep a Gilded Age middle-class home running. The large size of the kitchen, which often had an adjoining pantry, illustrated the importance and amount of work that was done there. Clothes had to be washed with water heated on a stove and then scrubbed vigorously by hand in a tin wash tub or in a new hand-cranked washing machine. Even though industrialization was transforming the food industry, there were few processed foods in the Gilded Age relative to today and women were entirely in charge of food preparation. In addition to meal preparation, bread, pastries, and pies had to be baked frequently to supply family needs. All cooking was performed on an iron stove which required wood or coal fuel, constant adjustment of dampers to achieve the correct temperature, removal of ashes, and frequent rubbing down with a thick wax to prevent rusting. Although canned foods were becoming more popular, many middle-class women continued to can their own vegetables and fruits and to make their own jams and jellies. Items that had to be cooled could be stored in the icebox or ice chest, for which large blocks of ice were delivered by the ice man. The kitchen zone was the primary place of labor in the household.[9]

Social Zones

There were also the social zones of the home. A formal dining room was ubiquitous and served not only as a place for family meals, but also as a signifier of social status due to the Victorian penchant for dinner parties (see Chapter 6). The parlor, however, was the most quintessential room of the era. Before 1850 and after 1900 the parlor would not serve as the defining room for American culture as it did in the last half of the nineteenth century. The parlor functioned to define the household and the people in it. Louise Stevenson brilliantly describes the centrality of the room, "every parlor entertainment and every decoration had the potential to remind people of the ultimate world to which they belonged."[10] Parlors were the center of socializing with friends and family. Wealthier homes would often have several rooms that divided the functions of the parlor into a family parlor and formal parlor, or on an even grander scale might possess a sitting room, game room, music room, or library. In more modest middle-class homes all of these functions would be found in one parlor or "sitting room." Victorian Americans met here to entertain each other with stereoscopic images, singing, playing games, conversation, and reading. Parlors were decorated to illustrate the refinement of the family and contained their most prized possessions: a dizzying array of embroidered, sewn, or crocheted items (see Chapter 7), photographs, the "right" type of books, items from their vacations that edified onlookers (see Chapter 8), paintings or chromolithographs of famous paintings artistically displayed often on easels (see Chapter 12), stereoscopes, busts of famous authors, carte-de-viste albums (see Chapter 7), Bibles, a piano or parlor organ (see Chapter 9), and a great deal of artistic bric-a-brac that often manifested itself in displays of the natural world such as terrariums or aquariums. Parlors also contained special parlor furniture that usually consisted of a table surrounded by a sofa and chairs. Women's chairs were smaller and lacked arms to accommodate their flowing dresses while men's chairs possessed high backs and arms. The focal point of the room was often a fireplace with a highly decorated mantle.[11]

Bedrooms

Bedrooms were the most private zone in the house and were usually located on the second story in larger middle-class homes. Most bedrooms did not contain much furniture beyond dressers, chests, a chair or two, and the bed, so many people preferred to decorate with fancifully patterned and colored wallpaper. Most Victorian couples shared a bedroom, though the wealthy might have separate bedrooms for husband and wife, and same-sex children often shared a bedroom. Servants who lived in, which was increasingly rare, often had the smaller bedroom closest to the back stairs that led down to the kitchen.

Bathrooms

Bathrooms were just beginning to develop in the Gilded Age as the locus of the sink, bathtub, and the toilet. The system that today seems so logical and universal was in fact quite foreign to most Americans in the late nineteenth century. The idea that the bathtub and the toilet facilities would be located next to each other disgusted many Americans. Most people still used the ever-present chamber pot during inclement weather and the outdoor privy in warmer months. Chamber pots, lidded ceramic pots used as toilets, were usually located in bedrooms or in closets. Earth closets were also used and cost less than a water closet because they required no pipes. They relied only on throwing a layer of soil over the waste and were portable enough to move to any room or closet. Part of the problem in introducing water closets to America was the fact that before the 1860s only Chicago had a significant underground sewer system that made the flush toilet, which relied upon water to carry waste, feasible. By the 1880s as more cities were forced to install larger underground sewers to cope with their massive growth, flush toilets began to become more common, particularly after the introduction of the siphon tank. Still, at the turn of the century only new homes of the middle class or wealthy would have boasted an indoor flush toilet, which was still quite expensive for the average American. The washstand served the basic function of today's bathtub and sink and was usually located in bedrooms. Only when piped water became more common in the 1880s did it even become feasible to think of a bathtub and sink. Soap also made its appearance in the late 1870s and by the 1880s knowledge of germs was widespread. As builders tried to cope with the new demands of middle-class cleanliness it made sense to put the toilet, tub, and sink together in one room on the second floor so that all of the pipes went to the same place and gravity helped the pipes drain. By 1910 many suburban middle-class homes boasted a modern bathroom complete with a flush toilet, bathtub, and sink.[12]

Other Amenities

Other new comforts also marked the middle-class home as different from working-class homes and more "modern." For those that could afford the expense, basement furnaces that burned coal and later natural gas became popular, and could heat an entire house with the use of floor registers that allowed the hot air to rise throughout the home, though by modern standards register heat often left the upper floors quite cold in the winter. Those on a more limited budget relied on heating stoves spread throughout the home. Hot water heaters also made their appearance in the homes of the well-to-do in the 1880s. Galvanized iron boilers could be attached to the stove to provide hot water, but water heaters and furnaces powered by natural gas also appeared. Natural gas also was used for lamps, changing the way Americans lit their homes, after its introduction in the United States as early as 1820 in Fredonia, New York. A great natural gas boom would occur after 1850 and last into the 1890s. Middle-class town and suburban dwellers switched from kerosene to gas lights, which had little competition until the introduction of commercial electricity in 1882. Gas lights, however, remained in all likelihood the dominant form of suburban and city lighting in the late nineteenth century and proved more reliable than electricity. Many of the relatively few homes that were wired for electricity in the 1880s and 1890s were also gas capable. Dual gas/electric construction would remain common roughly until World War I.[13] The enormous importance of the history of natural gas use in heating and lighting is often shamefully overlooked because of the introduction of electricity and the dominance of that form of power in the twentieth century.

Exterior Decoration

The eclectic exteriors of middle-class homes in the Gilded Age also reflected the values of the day as the bourgeoisie searched for individuality in small towns and suburbs. Middle-class Americans favored an approach to their homes that they viewed as organic, springing from utilitarian family use and aesthetic beauty. There were a variety of styles in the Gilded Age but most were highly ornamented, irregular in shape, and often boasted four to five colors of paint on their homes. Indeed, these Victorian homes combined a wide variety of color tones that mimicked the natural world's plants, wood, and autumnal leaves in virtually unlimited shades: greens, yellows, golds, browns, reds, grays, and black. These homeowners embraced dark colors that rarely appear on homes today.[14]

Eclecticism and Gothic Revival

Describing the architectural style of Victorian homes can be very difficult because of the great diversity in style. Builders and carpenters often combined elements from the many different styles of the era to produce an incredible eclecticism. But, there were distinctive styles popularized by architects that appeared in homes designed for the upper middle class and the wealthy. What is amazing is that middle-class homes differed from those of the very wealthy in size and amenities but often not so much in style. The style that influenced the very early years of the Gilded Age actually started well before this era. Gothic Revival started in the 1830s and had tremendous influence on middle-class homes before it lost its hold on the Victorian architect's imagination in the 1870s, though it continued to be important in vernacular architecture. The romantic mood in the United States harkened back to the Middle Ages, with visions of maidens and knights inspiring this fairytale-like form. Gothic Revival houses employed steeply pitched roofs, windows and doors in pointed arch form, and ornate vergeboard trim along the rooftop.

Italianate

Italianate emerged in the 1840s and retained some popularity until the 1890s. This style sought to bring the Italian country villas to the United States in a fairly symmetrical (for the era) rectangular house with rectangular masses attached to it as it sought to mimic the rambling nature of the villa. These homes possessed low, virtually flat roofs and heavily ornamented windows. This style often included a cupola or square tower. Italianate homes spread widely through the American East, Midwest, and West and achieved particular expression in the brownstone row houses of New York City.

Second Empire

Second Empire emerged during the 1860s, though its popularity waned much more quickly than Italianate, and it appeared mainly in the Northeast and some Midwestern cities while almost entirely absent in the South and the West. This style is one of the most easily recognizable Victorian styles because of its mansard roof heavily laden with hexagonal or diamond-shaped slate shingles and rounded dormer windows. The upper slope of the Second Empire four-sided hipped roof was almost vertical and appeared to form the upper story of the structure. Ornate cast-iron cresting often topped the roof.

Queen Anne

By far the most influential and widespread of the architectural styles was Queen Anne, introduced into the United States from England and promoted by prominent architects like Henry Hobson Richardson, Charles Follen McKim, and William Rutherford Mead. This design represented an incredible eclecticism that combined stylistic elements of a wide variety of architectural styles ranging from gothic to medieval and classical to colonial. Queen Anne style is the best example of the eclecticism and extreme ornamentation of Victorian residential architecture. The asymmetrical Queen Anne homes could possess a number of projecting bay windows, turrets or towers, balconies, massive arrays of decorative spindle work, ornamental masonry, patterned shingles in what appeared to be a fish-scale pattern, intricate roofs with gables, ornate stained glass, roof finials, and massive porches. These homes normally contained a large entry hall with a highly ornamented fireplace and all kinds of odd, small, out-of-the-way spaces. Modern homeowners have tried to classify existing Queen Anne homes into categories (Spindled, Free Classic, Half-Timbered, and Patterned Masonry) but strictly defining this style has confounded architects and historians for over 100 years.[15]

Stick

The Eastlake or Stick style has few unified architectural details that define this form except for the fact that small wooden boards were used to elaborately decorate the home in complex patterns that were often horizontal, diagonal, and vertical on the same home in an attempt to mimic cross timbers. These decorative cross timbers were also called stickwork and it was this term from which the style took its name by the middle of the twentieth century. Architect Richard Morris Hunt was particularly important in developing this style in Newport, Rhode Island. There is some debate about whether or not this is simply a variation of Queen Anne, but the use of large amounts of decorative board designs makes this form distinctive.[16]

Romanesque Revival

Romanesque Revival appeared in the 1880s primarily due to the efforts of architect Henry Hobson Richardson, who employed this massive stone style in public buildings. This style did, however, make its way into some homes of the upper middle class and the mansions of the very wealthy. While it employed many of the same elements as the Queen Anne, such as the turrets, towers, and multiple gables, it has distinctive elements such as deeply set, rounded-arched windows. But the most distinctive element was the use of rough-hewn stone that gave buildings a heavy, castle-like appearance, which contrasted dramatically with the airy, delicate-looking Queen Anne. Romanesque Revival was an expensive style to build in and aside from public architecture appeared mainly in mansions of the wealthy, well-to-do row houses, and larger homes of the upper middle class.[17]

Shingle and Colonial Revival

There were reactions against the extremely ornamented styles and a return to more simple forms starting in the 1880s, and this movement gained a great boost from the resurgence of neoclassicism in the Columbian Exposition in 1893. Shingle style and Colonial Revival were two of the most important new styles. Shingle style emerged in the 1880s and was one of the more original architectural forms of the Gilded Age, free from European influences. Architects of that day combined the simpler elements of Queen Anne style with eighteenth-century colonial architecture. Noted architects Stanford White and Henry Hobson Richardson designed several Shingle homes for wealthy clients in New York, and both helped to popularize the style. Although Shingle style homes had little in common when it came to shape or even size, they were united by the fact that they were covered completely in shingles, possessed little

Oakhurst, home of George A. Ball, built in 1885. Courtesy of The
Minnetrista Heritage Collection, Muncie, Indiana.

ornamentation, and often boasted large porches. Architects originally
created this fashion for the summer homes of the very rich as they attempted to produce oceanside dwellings that looked like simple rustic
cottages but on a massive scale. Shingle style certainly influenced the
young Frank Lloyd Wright when he built his Oak Park Home and Studio
in 1889. Eventually this style would filter down to more modest middle-
class homes. At about the same time a Colonial Revival became popular
based on the relatively austere Federalist architecture. Although the rectangular, symmetrical exterior looked very different from the highly decorated Queen Anne, like the Shingle style the Colonial Revival's interior
followed traditional Victorian patterns. Other revival styles came out of
the Neoclassical impulse that began to appear in the homes of the very
wealthy in the late 1890s but would not filter down to middle-class
homes until the twentieth century: Italian Renaissance, Tudor, Beaux-
Arts, Chateauesque, and French Revival. The largest private residence in
the United States came out of these elite styles. George W. Vanderbilt's
French Revival style Biltmore House in Asheville, North Carolina,
boasted 255 rooms and was designed by the famous architect Richard
Morris Hunt.[18]

Folk Victorian

Homes built for middle-class and upper-working-class folks, however, were not designed by professional architects but instead by local builders and carpenters who freely adapted elements of all of the popular styles into a blend of vernacular architecture that is referred to today as Folk Victorian or sometimes as Folk Queen Anne. What separated these homes from Queen Anne style was that Folk Victorians were normally symmetrical square or rectangular buildings that lacked the asymmetry, excessive ornamentation, multiple bay windows, turrets, and towers of the Queen Anne. Folk Victorian homes possessed more spare adornment and might have spindles, scrolled brackets, gingerbread, or Gothic Revival details decorating the porch or roof line. Mass-produced ornamental trim gave Folk Victorian homes the flair of their more elaborate cousins but at their core were plain, pragmatic homes.[19] The revolutionary introduction of the foursquare, bungalows, and Prairie School houses influenced by Frank Lloyd Wright's open floor plan were already percolating in the late nineteenth century as middle-class Americans began to reject the ornamentation of the Gilded Age, but would have to wait until the early years of the next century to achieve their full expression.

Working-Class and Rural Homes

Working-class and rural homes were often Folk Victorians or Gothic style cottages that remained very popular throughout the Gilded Age. The generic term "worker's cottage" was often used to describe virtually all of these small, simple rectangular or square homes with Gothic, Stick, or Queen Anne trim and ornamentation. One common style of home was the cross house, which became known as the homestead house when it appeared in towns and cities. This house had two stories and often had a large porch added, which was in step with Victorian fashions. Such a home sold for roughly $1,200 in 1878. Shotgun style homes also appeared in both single- and two-story models. These simple homes were rectangular with a narrow front and the majority of the house extending deep. Shotgun houses spread across the nation in rural and urban areas, selling for approximately $600 for a single story and $1,200 for a two-story home. Also common in rural areas was the I-house, so named because of the style's popularity in the I states of Indiana, Illinois, and Iowa. These simple homes were holdovers from colonial America, featuring a two-story home that was one room deep, two rooms wide, and two rooms high. Sod homes (soddies) were the unique feature of houses built on the Great Plains. Constructed out of the resilient prairie sod, over a million of these homes dotted the plains by 1890. Their appeal was certainly the ease of finding construction material and the low cost and not the earthen materials and dirt floors.

Farmhouses

It would be a mistake to think that all rural homes were small and inexpensive. Indeed, many well-to-do farmers built massive farmhouses that rivaled their suburban counterparts in size, grandeur, and expense. It was not uncommon to see a large Italianate farmhouse. Indeed, in 1870 the farmer's magazine *Moore's* solicited its subscribers to send in architectural plans for a $6,000 farmhouse, quite a palatial residence indeed in 1870! Rural Americans also did not simply accept unfiltered the expectations and fashions of urban and suburban America. Discussions over the appropriate uses of work space and utilitarian functions of the home appeared in farm journals as early as the 1830s and continued throughout the century. But as mechanization increased in the late nineteenth century, farmhouses did begin to conform more to their urban counterparts after 1880 by separating work and living spaces and creating distinct zones. Rural life, however, never made the very sharp gender distinctions that the urban middle-class made and rural people generally were more casual in their homes, particularly the parlor.[20]

CONCLUSION

Skyscrapers and large public architecture were changed in important ways that altered the cityscape of America, but the architectural changes that most influenced the average American were in their homes. Although the introduction of new architectural styles was important, perhaps the most significant change during the Gilded Age was the widespread introduction of elevators, central heating, heated water, and indoor bathrooms. Styles always come and go like all fashions, but the introduction of such modern amenities as indoor toilets and hot and cold running water endured. What had been novelties in the 1870s—indoor toilets, hot running water, bathtubs, and central heating—were commonplace by the early twentieth century, forever altering the most private activities of the vast majority of Americans. Standards of cleanliness rose as did expectations of privacy as Americans segregated and secluded what we think of today as bathroom activities, but what were once activities performed throughout the home and often in view of family members.

5

Fashion

BACKGROUND

In Gilded Age America fashion became increasingly tied to the consumer economy by the mass production and marketing of ready-made clothing. European style continued to have a tremendous influence on the fashion-conscious in the United States. But any discussion of fashion must first define what "fashion" means. Fashion, for our purposes, is most usefully thought of as "a formal arrangement of male and female clothing that expresses the aesthetics and customs of a cultural period. Fashion includes widespread social norms that may be modified by individual self-expression."[1] It is vital to note that fashion and what is fashionable is (and was) a social construct that changes over time, is differentiated by sex, and is always mediated by an individual's subculture and personal choices. These concepts are in reality quite easy to understand. First, what is "popular" in clothing style changes from decade to decade. Second, men and women wear sex-specific clothing in most cases. And finally, personal style influences dress, like the feminist bloomer fad of the 1840s, as much as membership in a specific religious group, say the Amish. Gilded Age Americans adopted clothing styles based on sex, region, social class, occupation, and age.

Before 1870 most women still made the clothes for their families, but by the late Gilded Age standardized sizes and mass production revolutionized the ready-made clothing industry. The Civil War spurred the development of ready-made clothing for men, which blossomed into a billion-dollar-a-year industry by 1890. By 1900 most American men were wearing ready-made clothes and women, though encouraged to make their own dresses, could also fulfill all of their clothing needs from stores and catalogs.

American fashions generally followed the fashion industry in Paris. Important American fashion designers in New York, Philadelphia, and Chicago closely followed the French fashions and included notables such as Madame Harris and Sons, James Gray and Company, Mrs. Cripp, Clark & McLoghan, and Madame Demorest. Although the influence of Paris was tremendous, English designs began to gain acceptance in the 1890s. English style tailored suits became very popular as a number of American women rejected the "tight-laced, exaggerated female curves" of the French haute couture in favor of the comfortable and neat look of the tailored suit.[2]

Perhaps the most revolutionary force in clothing styles, however, was the invention of the paper pattern. Sewing machines had been available for decades but sales skyrocketed after the 1860s, which certainly was a major factor in the explosion of the pattern industry. By the 1860s standardized paper patterns were widely available throughout the nation and provided women with the ability to recreate complicated, fashionable styles. Dress patterns appeared as early as 1855 in *Godey's Ladies Book* and later in *Demorest's Quarterly Mirror of Fashion*, though these were only cutting guides. The entrepreneur Ellen Curtis Demorest was a driving force in the early pattern industry. She transformed herself into Madame Demorest in the French fashion world to appeal to the fashion-conscious in both the United States and Europe. Ellen and Ebenezer Butterick introduced the revolutionary concept of patterns made to fit standardized sizes in 1863. By 1871, Butterick had sold 6 million patterns, costing from $.10 to $.40 each, and provided the public with a far wider range of clothing modeled after the latest Paris fashions. Butterick increased the appeal of its patterns and marketed them through a variety of house publications, the most successful being *The Delineator* (1873). The availability of a wide variety of dress patterns increased in the 1880s and 1890s, and had as dramatic an impact on clothing styles as the ready-made industry.[3]

MEN'S FASHIONS

Industrialization and mechanization produced affordable ready-made clothing for all men, but did nothing to diminish the status associated with particular clothing styles.

Middle-Class Fashions

The Dark Suit

There is little doubt that men's fashions in the Gilded Age were more subdued and predictable than women's fashions as the dark business suit became dominant for middle-class businessmen. A sober middle-class businessman would sport a dark business suit, white shirt with detachable collar and cuffs, vest, and depending on the occasion, a top hat, bowler, or straw hat, all set off with a large, burly moustache or beard. Although businessmen generally stayed with white shirts and plain vests, splashes of color were seen by the 1870s. Colored shirts with a variety of stripes and plaids were available in such exotic colors as blue, red, black, or gray, as were brightly colored jacquard silk vests. The only splashes of color in the suits were plaids, checks, and tweeds. These bright colors and rich patterns were worn mainly by dandies. By the 1880s, plain, casual sack suits replaced the highly ornate suits of the prewar era, though formal attire still sported the long Prince Albert coat. These business suits dropped the ornate frock coat in favor of a shorter, plain jacket that reached just below the waist and had narrow lapels. Styles became even more tailored and fitted in the 1890s, and suit jackets were generally made to be buttoned all the way to the top. Although men could opt for brightly colored ties, vests, and shirts as well as plaid and tweed suits, the universal costume for respectable men in the 1890s was the black wool three-piece suit with a white shirt.

Although the suit was worn by a wide variety of men, there is little doubt that for the middle class it certainly represented an important social marker that defined the wearer's refinement and social distinction. The suit was certainly not appropriate for hard physical labor, but instead denoted the man's genteel occupation. Elite male attire had been shifting since the eighteenth century toward darker fabrics. The English gentry began to move from silk to wool for their sporting clothing and middle-class men continued this trend in the nineteenth century. The coat, waistcoat or vest, and white shirt with detachable stiff collar and cuffs could hardly be called functional in a physical sense. The suit's only function was to illustrate the power and social status of the wearer.

The 1895 *Montgomery Ward Catalogue* illustrated how many different styles and price ranges were available even to rural Americans by the end of the Gilded Age. Montgomery Ward boasted many different styles of suits: round corner sack suit, single-breasted square-cut sack suits, double-breasted square-cut sack suit, old men's frock suit, three-button cutaway frock suits, double-breasted Prince Albert suits, and full evening dress suits that included tails. Suits could be purchased in cotton, varying quality wool, flannel, and corduroy. A superfine wool Prince Albert suit cost a whopping $28 while a cotton round-cornered sack suit could be purchased for the more modest sum of $3. Montgomery Ward particularly pushed its own line of "celebrated" $10 suits over higher-priced competitors. Montgomery Ward suits "far surpass in quality, fit and workmanship any ready-made suits ever before offered for a like sum. They are, in fact, far superior to many suits heretofore sold for a much higher price." The mail order catalog also carried a wide sampling of

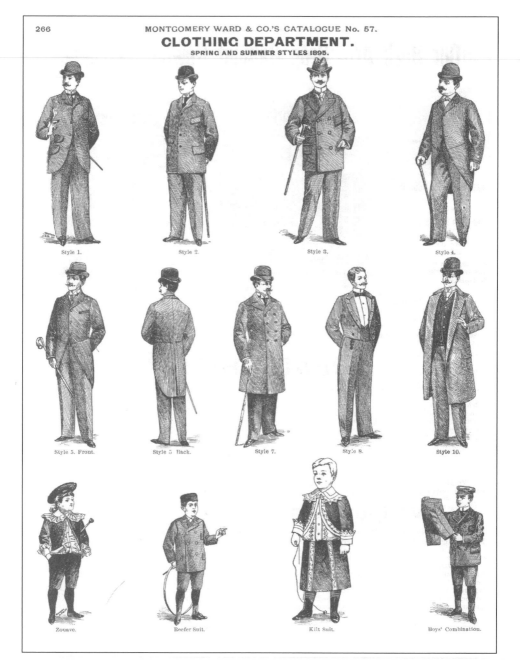

An advertisement for men's suits from the 1895 *Montgomery Ward Catalogue*.

shirts, over 100 different hats, wool pants, vests, overcoats, socks, and dress shoes.[4] One can imagine the variety of suits available at the massive urban department stores like Wanamaker's.

Shirt Collars

Detachable shirt collars were also an essential part of middle-class attire by the 1840s and became emblems of status. Collars normally were made of linen or extremely starched cotton and the styles varied dramatically over the decades. By the 1890s men preferred very high collars, often two and a quarter inches. These starched, white collars were so ubiquitous that the term became a common reference for middle-class occupations and "white collar" still is associated with middle-class managerial employment.[5]

Working-Class Fashions

Working-class men's clothing was often a motley collection of mismatched vests, trousers, and jackets. Those men who could afford it purchased the wide variety of ready-made clothing. Rarely did working men wear the plain white shirt with detachable cuffs and collar, but instead wore a wide variety of colored shirts, blue being a popular color, with attached collars. These shirts normally were pullover and buttoned partway down the front. Distinctive garb of course depended on occupation and region. Cowboys in the West wore the distinctive Stetson, cowboy boots, wild rag (as the neckerchief was called on the northern plains), and a standard town suit when not working. Loggers in the upper Midwest or Northwest might wear flannel shirts, woolen trousers or denim pants, and wool jackets.[6]

Levi's

Perhaps the most important invention for work clothing in the Gilded Age was a product that developed out of the California Gold Rush. In 1853, Leob Strauss traveled to California hoping to sell heavy canvas for tents as the representative of the Strauss brothers wholesale business from New York. He found there was only a small market for canvas tents but there was a massive, untapped demand for rugged, canvas work pants. Legend has it that a miner told Strauss, who soon changed his name to Levi, that what miners really needed was a tough pair of pants that would not wear out so quickly as they worked in their rugged occupation. Levi Strauss took the tough tent canvas and began to make pants. These rugged pants soon caught on throughout the mining frontier and within a few decades became the common costume of working men across the United States. Strauss ordered massive amounts of the tough cotton material which took its name from a French town, Nimes.

Serge de Nimes (material from Nimes) would be anglicized to denim. Working men across the country purchased denim "Levi's." The distinctive copper rivets were added to Levi's after Nevada tailor Jacob Davis convinced Strauss that the only thing his pants lacked were strong fasteners to keep the pockets from ripping away. Levi's denim jeans were distinctive for their copper rivets, orange stitched double arc on the back pockets, and the leather patch on the back waistband. Soon other brands of "waist overalls" appeared and became the characteristic garb of working men across the country.[7]

Home-Produced Clothes

While ready-made clothing certainly played a dominant role in clothing for men in the Gilded Age, men on the frontier who could not afford mail order clothes often made due with what was at hand. Women often used whatever cloth they had to make pants. Pioneer families often reused grain sacks to make shirts and pants and linsey-woolsey homespun continued to appear throughout the century.[8]

Ready-Made Work Clothes

The *Montgomery Ward Catalogue* also provided a variety of working clothing for men. Overalls in blue, brown, and white denim appeared, ranging from $.35 to $1 for 10-ounce reinforced "Cavalry Cowboy Overalls." Ward's also offered Kentucky jean pants for a dollar. Heavy indigo work shorts of cotton and wool ranged from $.40 each for a plain cotton shirt to $2.30 for blue wool flannel with pearl buttons. Leather coats, pants, and vests were available, many of them flannel lined, ranging from $4 to $11. Heavy and durable cotton duck lined suits were also available in brown and gray. A duck coat went for $1.25 while a complete brown duck suit lined with plaid Mackinaw flannel sold for $8.50. Twelve different styles of cowboy hats sold for anywhere from $1 to $6. By the 1890s a variety of heavy, durable work boots were also available for American working men: mining boots ($2), grain plow shoes ($1.30), and cowboy boots ($2.40-$4.75). Men of all classes had a wide range of underwear available in cotton and wool.[9]

Specialized Leisure Clothing

With the advent of the massive ready-made clothing industry in the Gilded Age, specialty leisure clothing appeared. Hunting clothing, which had for centuries been produced for the wealthy, was made affordable for many Americans by the mass-produced ready-made industry. The 1895 *Montgomery Ward Catalogue* sold a wide array of shooting jackets, hunting vests, heavy waterproof hunting pants, sweaters, shirts, leggings, and hats. Specialized sports clothing also appeared and was mass marketed. Ward's offered fencing masks and gloves, athletic sweaters and shirts, tights, athletic supporters, baseball hats and gloves, football uniforms, as well as bicycling sweaters, knickers, and coats. Appropriate wear for a popular sport such as football included a long-sleeved pull-over shirt or turtleneck sweater, padded knickers, and long socks (see Chapters 2 and 7). Baseball teams had pioneered the knickers as the choice of athletic wear when the Cincinnati Red Stockings appeared in 1867, not in the traditional long pants but in knickers and bright red stockings. By the late nineteenth century some male athletes wore sparse uniforms, such as track runners who by this time sported only shorts and sleeveless shirts. By the late 1890s swimming suits had shrunk to positively scandalous proportions, wool short sleeve or tank shirts with shorts that stopped just above the knee. On the other side of the spectrum were more genteel sports like tennis, which continued to demand more clothing. Men often played in tennis suits that look to modern eyes more like casual suits than sporting wear. Men wearing shorts to play tennis would not appear for another 30 years.[10]

WOMEN'S FASHIONS

Fashion Dresses

Clothing for elite and middle-class women was certainly the most physically restrictive dress for anyone in the Gilded Age. Yards of cloth were draped in long, flowing dresses covering multiple layers of petticoats and bone or steel corsets. Genteel women wore costumes that severely restricted their movement. Unlike their working-class sisters, middle- and upper-class women had no economically productive role for the family; they did not produce anything for the family's economic support, like farm women, for example. The restrictive clothing of these genteel women symbolically illustrated that women of this social station did not have to work and ought not work according to genteel convention. Cultural critic Thorstein Veblen noted that the fashionably dressed wife was her husband's "chief ornament."[11]

1870s

Women's fashions were much more ornate and were subject to cyclical changes in aesthetic sensibilities. Women who were trying to dress according to the dictates of fashion would start with a corset designed to force the body into an hourglass shape, though even corset styles changed. In the 1870s women would also have donned five to seven layers of petticoats and a bustle to complement their ornate, layered dresses. Petticoats were generally made of white cotton, though the fashion-conscious could purchase silk petticoats that matched their dresses. Bustles were wire cages worn under the dress that held the voluminous gathers of Victorian dresses behind women. Dresses of the 1870s presented a radically different silhouette than the antebellum and Civil War years, departing from the full hoops which presented a rounded figure to a bustle which pulled the dress material tightly at the sides and gathered it in the back. Women's figures were to look narrow from the front, while from behind the dresses were gathered and pro-truded over the bustle. The bustle as well as the entire underskirt were often ornately decorated with bows, lace, fir, fringes, and braids. Bodices fit tightly, flaring down past the hips, and ornate overskirts covered the underskirt, which was ankle-length. Internal ties constricted the knees in many of these styles causing women to walk in short, mincing steps. These dresses boasted high necklines with finely decorated collars and wrist-length sleeves. Different clothing materials were often used in the same dress; overskirts and sleeves of one material and pattern while the underskirt and sash might be of another material and pattern. A virtually universal accessory in the 1870s was a quarter- to half-inch black velvet neck ribbon, tightly tied in a bow at the back of the neck with ends dangling down. Brooches or cameos decorated the front of the ribbon. Shoes varied widely from heeled slippers to ornate high-heeled shoes to heeled black kid boots. Hairstyles were generally ornate and piled on top of the head or pulled back. A parasol or fan would have completed the outfit.[12]

1880s

Dresses in the 1880s continued to be heavily layered and cold weather fabrics were so heavy that they were like upholstery fabric. Knees were less constricted by the mid-1880s, but larger bustles appeared until they shrank again in 1887. High fashion continued to produce incredibly or-nate dresses with elaborate overskirts and ornamentation. Straight dresses flared below the knee and swept the ground in small trains (later shortened to ankle-length). Bodices were tightly fitted and with tight sleeves often cut at the forearm. Popular dress colors in the 1880s tended toward the darker spectrum, deep purple, claret, copper, or gold. Corsets and bustles were still demanded, though women were beginning to wear only one petticoat as early as 1878. A wide profusion of hats and bonnets were stylish in this era and were heavily decorated with ribbons, flowers, plumes, and even small, stuffed birds. Hat decorations tended to be in brilliant blazing colors like bronze, gold, garnet, and peacock blue. Women often carried fans and parasols as their primary accessory. Large Japanese and ostrich-feather fans as well as parasols covered in lace or satin were very popular. Ankle-high heeled kid boots were the most popular footwear of the 1880s. Although Paris continued to exert tremendous influence over fashions in the United States, American fashion magazines began to multiply. *Harper's Bazaar, Godey's Lady's Book*, and the various Demorest periodicals (*Mirror of Fashions, Quarterly Illustrated Journal, What to Wear, Portfolio of Fashion*) all carried French fashions.[13]

Wash Dresses

The spread of French fashion into U.S. magazines did not herald a turn to the ornate styles of high fashion for average American women. Indeed, the growing ready-made clothing industry and pattern industry responded to average women's demands for more simplified styles that were based on the latest fashion in the 1880s. In essence, work dresses were now patterned after fashion styles and gained a measure of social acceptability. Middle- and upper-class women now added to their wardrobes not only the high fashion, ornate dresses but also the simpler dresses worn for more casual occasions. It is doubtful that everyday dresses sported bustles since most photographs of women in everyday wear could not accommodate the voluminous 1880s bustle. Common dresses made for middle-class women were sometimes still made in the three-piece style with bodice, underskirt, and overskirt. These "wash dresses," so-called because they were easily laundered, also came in very popular, simple, one- or two-piece styles made of cotton and were worn by women of almost all social classes. Wash dresses were widely available in stores and catalogs by the 1880s. These dresses tended to be fairly simple relative to high-fashion models, with bishop sleeves, lightly gathered high on the shoulder, plain necks, and with minimal trim. Middle-class women possessed a variety of dresses for different occasions from formal to wash day. Women who were not so well off economically pressed a wide variety of dresses into service, but mainly relied on fairly simple styles made of calico, gingham, denim, wagon canvas, and even converted flour sacks. Old dresses were never thrown out but simply made into work dresses which were pressed into service as aprons when they grew too worn to continue as dresses. For many rural women, particularly those in the West, the plain Mother Hubbard dress served as their main work dress. This rather shapeless, long-sleeved, full-length gown had no waist to speak of and a yoke. The style became very popular for girls in an ankle-length. Compared to the Mother Hubbard the wash dress was a stylish garment indeed.[14]

1890s

Over the course of the 1890s the bustle would disappear but designers continued to go to great lengths to achieve the hourglass figure. Great, gathered skirts came into vogue along with "leg-of-mutton" sleeve blouses that emphasized the small waist. Blouse sleeves grew until about 1897, culminating in the massive leg-of-mutton look so typical of the

The Drown family, ca. 1880s. Courtesy of the Northeastern Nevada Historical Society.

1890s, but then began to be replaced with a more tight-fitting sleeve topped by a puff and gathering of material on the shoulder much like an epaulet. Gone were the complex underskirt and overskirt styles of the previous decades with their elaborate ornamentation. Although simple in construction compared to the complex, ornate styles of the 1880s, the popular skirts of the 1890s had numerous gathers and could consist of as much as 24 yards of material. These skirts were tulip or vase shaped and boasted satin, lace, velvet, or braid trim. Cynical commentators called these dresses street-sweeper fashions. Velvet, silk, and wool continued to be popular fabrics in expensive clothing and there was a trend to have dark dress colors (dark blue, black, and dark green) trimmed in lighter contrasting colors (turquoise, rose, and baby blue). Oriental fans, gloves (which changed according to the occasion), and feather boas for formal events all maintained their popularity as accessories. Kid boots that buttoned on the side continued to be popular, usually with a high curved heel and sharply pointed toe, but new colors appeared besides black, like champagne, bronze, and brown.

Active Wear

Women demanded and popularized more active wear, for either work or athletics, and the English style tailored suit swept the country in the 1890s. A ready-made shirt for women, called the shirtwaist, became available and was soon the standard garment for working women of all classes. Patterns offered the shirtwaist in a wide variety of styles. The shirtwaist had a neat, form-fitting look with high collars and full sleeves. By 1895 the *Montgomery Ward Catalogue* carried a wide variety of shirtwaists running from calico blouses for $.37 to silk for $4. The catalog also carried the coordinating skirts ($.75–$2), fitted jackets ($3–$6), and sharply pointed boots ($1.35–$4.25). When the shirtwaist was worn with the fluted skirt and tightly laced corset it produced the desired hourglass look. Illustrator Charles Dana Gibson made this style famous in his popular illustrations, and it was soon dubbed the "Gibson Girl" (see Chapter 12). Even the *Ladies Home Journal* in 1893 declared that women should be able to choose their clothes based on comfort. There is little doubt the skirt and shirtwaist of the 1890s represented a remarkable departure for active women from the heavy, ornamented, layered styles of the 1870s and 1880s. These were the beginnings of a dress revolution for women that would culminate in the 1920s.[15]

Undergarments

Undergarments were also ready-made by the 1890s. Corsets were the most distinctive undergarment of the nineteenth century and forced women's bodies into the ideal shape—small waist and uplifted breasts. This maternal, full-figured look dominated fashion after the Civil War

Waists—Continued.

seams, large sleeves, plain belt, stiff laund-collar and cuffs, pointed shirt yoke in back, full front.
Each......$0.69
Per dozen. 8.00

5824 Ladies' Shirt Waists, faultlessly made of fine percale, in a great variety of new patterns and colors; some styles as follows: Stripes in tan and white covered.

with a small black dot; indigo blue and white; light blue and white, pink and white; black and white; assorted small figures on blue, pink or heliotrope; plain solid pink, blue, white or fast black; made with large sleeves, felled French seams, perfect fitting stiff laundered collar and cuffs, re-enforced pointed shirt yoke in back, full front, belt. Each.......$0.85
Per dozen..... .. .. 9 75

An advertisement for a blouse from the 1895 *Montgomery Ward Catalogue*.

and the corset sought to fulfill this style for every woman. Corset styles did change from the 1870s through the 1890s, longer in the earlier decades and gradually becoming shorter, but they were always worn by proper ladies. Corsets grew to be decorated lingerie and appeared in satin of a variety of colors; the most popular color was black but they also came in scarlet, red, gray, drab, and white. The rural-oriented 1895 *Montgomery Ward Catalogue* offered at least 38 different corsets in white, drab, ecru, and black. Stockings came in a variety of colors and fabrics (cotton, silk, wool, and cashmere) and normally matched the outfit. In the summer women wore cotton underwear that ended above the knee. Some women continued to wear a chemise under their corsets while others abandoned the chemise and wore only the corset cover. In cold weather women would don the wool or jersey union suit.[16]

Women's Specialty Clothing

The greater freedoms of the New Woman were often associated with physical activity. Charles Dana Gibson often portrayed his young women in some sort of physical activity such as playing golf. The 1890s hastened efforts that had been underway since the 1870s to provide women with clothing that adequately allowed for exercise and sports. Swimming, walking, bicycling, and gymnastics all became increasingly popular for young women as the Gilded Age progressed, and the clothing they wore for these activities starkly illustrated how women disputed conventional views of femininity. Pattern companies, particularly the giant Butterick, promoted physical culture by selling patterns for gymnastic outfits, bathing suits, and riding skirts, but attempted to mediate these activities with mainstream views of womanhood by making them pretty. Athletic clothing for women was adorned by functionally useless frills like bows, silk trim, and sailor collars that clearly marked them as feminine.

Swimming Suits

Sports clothing for women emerged in the Gilded Age as a normal part of their wardrobe. Commentators noted the most serious concerns were with swimming suits, because unlike gymnastics this was a public activity. Swimming suits commonly consisted of a calf-length dress with long sleeves and ankle-length bloomers in the early 1870s, covering the entire body. Butterick patterns offered a variety of choices, in dress and sleeve length, so that the maker herself could choose according to her own inclinations and local opinion. By the end of the century, bathing suits commonly consisted of short sleeves, dresses that reached just below the knee, bloomers slightly longer than the dress, and dark stockings. While the 1895 *Montgomery Ward Catalogue* sold only men's bathing

Margaret Russell (Newman) and Minnie Johnson. Courtesy of the
Northeastern Nevada Historical Society.

suits, the 1902 *Sears, Roebuck Catalogue* offered blue women's suits like
those described above for $2.50 to $3.50.

Gymnastic, Bicycling, and Tennis Outfits

Gymnastic uniforms were less of a concern because they were generally worn in all-female settings in schools and particularly colleges.
Mount Holyoke, a women's college in Massachusetts, required in 1883
a uniform that was a dress that reached seven inches above the floor
over bloomers. By 1898, Butterick's gymnastic outfit rejected the dress
entirely, and instead featured a long- or short-sleeve yoke blouse with
voluminous bloomers over tights. Walking, tennis, and bicycling outfits
were also made to have more freedom, but these costumes stayed much
closer to typical Victorian dress. Cyclists could wear large gathered skirts
that appeared split or split skirts that were so full they appeared whole.
Tennis, still a bastion of the elite, proved less amenable to change than
gymnastics. Fashionable tennis attire in the 1880s showed women in full
underskirt and overskirt complete with bustle. In the 1890s the typical
tennis costume consisted of the fluted skirt and shirtwaist so popular for
the day—still restrictive but not nearly so mach as the heavily ornamented, petticoated, and bustled fashions of the previous decades. Can
any modern woman imagine playing tennis in a corset, 15 pounds of

dress and petticoats, and a wire bustle nestled in the small of their back? Women of the Gilded Age certainly helped to shape not only societal expectations of them but also influenced the shift in their clothing toward freer, more athletically suitable attire.[17]

CHILDREN'S FASHIONS

Children's fashions also followed the styles and trends coming from Europe and by the Gilded Age appeared in fashion plates like their adult counterparts. Fashion for young people, however, was primarily determined by age; fully adult fashions were not worn until the early teens. Boys and girls both wore gowns as infants and toddlers, but there the similarity ended. Boys graduated from gowns to knee-pants (knickers) and then trousers. Girls' dresses grew longer with age and at puberty middle-class girls had to don the corset and ankle- or toe-length gown. Fashion illustrations for children's clothing often declared the age for which the creation was intended because the age of the wearer determined the boy's pant and the girl's skirt length. The ready-made, mail order, and pattern industries significantly influenced children's clothing as well, allowing Americans with even modest incomes to produce or purchase stylish clothing for their children.

Boys' Fashions

Infant and toddler boys of the Gilded Age would have been virtually indistinguishable from their sisters to modern spectators. While Victorians might have been able to spot the subtleties of more eyelet or lace on the toddler girl's gown, young boys and girls were dressed in remarkably unisex clothing. Infants were dressed in very long gowns, sometimes reaching three or four feet in length. As toddlers, boys often appeared in dresses. Boy toddlers from fashion-conscious families might also have been dressed in kilts with knickers underneath. The 1895 *Montgomery Ward Catalogue* advertised kilt suits ranging from $1.50 to $4.25 for children "2 to 4 years only."[18] Early in the Gilded Age boys might have stayed in gowns until they were 5 or 6 years old, but by the 1890s generally most boys were dressed in gendered clothing by the age of 2 or 3. The move to breech boys at a younger age was probably made possible by the introduction of rubber pants at the turn of the century, which would have allowed boys who were not yet toilet trained to move to knickers or trousers. It made perfect sense to keep boy toddlers who were not toilet trained in gowns and dresses to ease diaper changing and accidents. The invention of the rubber diaper cover suddenly opened up new fashion alternatives for parents with small boys.[19]

Elko (Nevada) children. Courtesy of the Northeastern Nevada
Historical Society.

Popular Styles

After gowns and kilts boys graduated to knickers between 3 and 6 years old, which became the preferred active wear of boys in the 1890s. Knickers would be worn even by men engaged in sports or riding bicycles. Toddlers might also wear Brownie suits (overalls) which were introduced in the 1890s. The 1895 *Montgomery Ward Catalogue* advertised suits sporting knickers for boys "4 to 14 years," ranging in price from $1.90 to $5, and in a wide variety of styles: Windsor suits, Reefer suits, Sailor suits, and Zouave suits. The more ornate styles, such as the Reefer, Zouave, and Sailor suits, were normally reserved for smaller boys "3 to 8" years old. Boys of this era were often dressed in these very frilly suits that commonly came in velvet, and they had long hair kept in curl—a style popularized after Frances Hodgson Burnett's *Little Lord Fauntleroy*. Less formal Sailor suit wear was also very popular, particularly the pullover middies patterned after navy shirts. Boys could move to full-length trousers in the 1895 *Montgomery Ward Catalogue* at the age of 9. Everyday wear for boys often consisted of knickers or trousers, a collarless shirt, and a vest, or for rural youth denim overalls became popular by the 1890s. Sweaters also made their appearance in the 1890s and a variety of styles were available. A wide variety of hats, like the popular straw hat or English school hat, were also commonly worn.[20]

Girls' Fashions

Fashions for girls followed the same general trends that influenced women's clothing styles during the Gilded Age. Unlike their mothers' dresses, dresses made for girls rarely sported bustles but did have puffs and panniers that pulled their dresses into a large gather at their lower back. Girls' formal dresses in the 1880s were nearly as heavily ornamented and frilly as their mothers' dresses with overskirts and underskirts often made of organdy, sheer muslin, velvet, linen, silk, or taffeta. Colors for girls' fancy dresses in this decade tended to run toward the same dark colors as adult fashions. Everyday dresses for girls were usually in cotton, gingham, or wool and often covered by heavily starched white, gray, tan, blue, or unbleached muslin aprons or smocks. Sailor suits for girls were also popular with a middy blouse and skirt. Girls' dresses tended to have a large lace collar or smocking around the yoke that set their styles apart from adults. By the 1890s the shirtwaists sporting the enlarged upper arm and the large fluted skirts became very popular styles as did the wash dress. The 1895 *Montgomery Ward Catalogue* sold girls' wash dresses ($.45–$2.50) in gingham, flannel, and calico which mainly came in light prints for 2- to 14-year-olds. Shirtwaists were generally worn only by older girls. Ward's sold chambray shirtwaists

($.60) in misses' sizes for 10- to 16-year-olds, which came in pink, light blue, and dark blue. Girls wore bonnets that followed the styles of their mothers', dark stockings, and generally black kid boots that came just above the ankle and buttoned on the outside for everyday wear. In the 1890s black patent leather Mary Janes were the dress shoes of choice.

Just as with boys' pants, age determined the length and style of dresses for girls. The younger the girl the shorter the dress could be according to refined standards, though below the knee. But as a girl aged her hems lengthened and by puberty corsets were required. In the 1890s girls aged 3 to 5 often appeared in empire waist dresses while older girls, 4 to 14, wore dresses with natural waistlines. Toddler girls were dressed in Reefer jackets with full sleeves. The 1895 *Montgomery Ward Catalogue* sold six different Reefer jackets ($1.10–$2.50) for girls 2 to 4 years old in navy, red, cardinal, tan, and white.[21]

CONCLUSION

The Gilded Age witnessed great changes for the fashion industry. Most significant were the concurrent development of the ready-made clothing industry and the sized pattern industry. Americans could order patterns by mail to fashion their own clothing on the improved sewing machines of the era or order ready-made clothing from companies like Montgomery Ward. Men's formal wear continued to be the universal dark suit throughout the Gilded Age, whereas women's fashions changed considerably. The ornate, heavily layered dresses of the 1870s and 1880s began to change with the introduction of the wash dress in the 1880s. The simplicity of the wash dress was followed in the 1890s by formal styles that were also simpler but fashionable, such as the shirtwaist and fluted skirt. Women's clothing styles of the 1890s were designed for a much more physically active generation. Children's clothing also clearly separated them from adults. Knickers and short dress lengths clearly marked the children of the era. It is fascinating relative to today that Victorian parents felt no need to differentiate the sex of their infants and toddlers, who were dressed in unisex long gowns and dresses.

6

Food

BACKGROUND

The rise of modern mass society in the United States during the Gilded Age had a profound effect on food for the average American. Massive urban centers linked by an ever-growing network of railroads connected Americans like never before in history, and with the invention of refrigerated railroad cars and factories as well as agricultural mechanization there was a new ability to supply out-of-season vegetables and fruits, canned foods, and meats to Americans all over the country. As early as the 1850s, Americans were the best-fed people in the world. Meals tended to be large and heavy with ample meat. The typical American consumed on average a little over 4,000 calories per day. Although food along most transportation routes was of dubious quality before the 1870s, by the 1880s the quality of railroad food rose dramatically as intense competition among the growing number of lines caused many railroad companies to take losses on excellent food in order to draw riders. Travelers were aided further when Fred Harvey built 17 Harvey restaurants on railroad lines providing high-quality, affordable food served by pleasant waitresses in a clean environment.

Even though food was increasingly plentiful there were poor Americans that suffered from hunger and malnutrition in the Gilded Age. Americans from the Northern city slums to Southern sharecroppers to hard-scrabble farmers on the Great Plains often lived on the edge of malnutrition and many went hungry. Scarcity was being replaced by plenty, but in the modern market economy the inability to afford food could cause hunger and malnutrition as easily as famine.

AVERAGE AMERICAN FARE

Meals

The meals Americans ate were all relatively large by modern standards and somewhat different than today. Americans might eat some combination of breakfast, lunch, late tea, supper, and dinner. Breakfast in the nineteenth century followed the ample American model, not the modest continental breakfast of a roll and coffee. A middle-class American might typically eat seasonal fruit, cereal, coffee or tea, eggs, meat or fish, potatoes, some kind of toast or muffin, and waffles, pancakes, or biscuits. Away at a Rochester, New York, boarding school, 13-year-old Fannie Munn Field ate a breakfast of warmed-up veal, potatoes, omelet, graham muffins, peaches, and coffee. Homestead, Pennsylvania, steelworkers ate a similar breakfast of oatmeal and milk, eggs, bacon, coffee, and bread with butter and jelly. Lunch or luncheon was the lighter informal midday meal. For industrial workers it might be a pail lunch eaten during a rushed break. Middle-class women used luncheon as a social event, whereas middle-class men might make it a business function. Late tea was primarily a middle-class event and denoted a lighter, informal evening meal served cold. Supper was much like late tea but centered around a hot meal. Dinner could be taken from noon until late evening and was the formal main meal of the day. Particularly among the industrial working class and the middle class, who worked far from home, dinner became increasingly an evening meal.[1]

Food

The standard American food was heavily influenced by English cooking even in the Gilded Age, with relatively few other foreign influences. The average American in this era would have been working class, though there was great variation in the incomes of mainly native-born workers, who dominated the skilled jobs, and the immigrant workers largely stuck in unskilled positions. Virtually all of their work, however, required hard physical labor, so an average diet that included 4,000 calories a day was not out of step with their needs. Their food was rich and heavy, laden with butter, cream, sugar, and lard. The diet of a skilled worker at the Homestead steel plant was typical. He had oatmeal and milk, eggs, bacon, bread with butter and jelly, and coffee for breakfast. For lunch he consumed a quick meal of soup, bread, and fruit, while the typical dinner was eaten in the evening with meat (most likely beef), beans, potatoes, fruits, beets, and pickles. Like most native-born Americans' diets, the steel workers' meals were relatively bland; Americans shared deep reservations about over-spicing foods and relied primarily on "salt and small amounts of pepper, cloves, cinnamon, mace, ginger, nutmeg, and a few herbs."

Foreign visitors were shocked by the sheer volume of food on an American table. One reason for this plenty was the long-term decline in food prices throughout the Gilded Age. Noted food historian Harvey Levenstein said, "Indeed, in 1898 one dollar could buy 43 percent more rice than in 1872, 35 percent more beans, 49 percent more tea, 51 percent more roasted coffee, 114 percent more sugar, 62 percent more mutton, 25 percent more fresh pork, 60 percent more lard and butter, and 42 percent more milk."[2] Foreign visitors also commented with a note of disdain that Americans tended not to prepare anything well and ate their food with ferocious speed; deliberate dining with fine conversation seemed devalued in a nation with so much. But Americans seemed determined to show their prosperity through the generously laden tables they enjoyed at home, at countless picnics and barbecues, and in restaurants.[3]

Meat

Meat dominated the meals of most Americans and was relatively cheap compared to meat prices in Europe. Typical working Americans could afford to eat meat at two or three meals a day. Whereas pork had been the universal meat throughout all of America before the Civil War, by the Gilded Age inexpensive beef was flooding urban markets and it became the overwhelming favorite. G. H. Hammond invented the refrigerated railroad car in 1871 and by the 1890s entire meatpacking plants were refrigerated. With railroads connecting the Great Plains to cities, refrigeration made it possible for inexpensive beef to reach most regions of the nation. Beef was eaten at every meal, often sliced thinly, fried, and eaten with gravy. Roast beef, corned beef, beef tongue, as well as the fine cuts such as sirloin, porterhouse, tenderloin, and filet were all popular among Americans. Indeed, as working-class incomes rose so too did the consumption of beef. Other types of meat were also widely eaten including lamb, turkey, chicken, duck, goose, and pork. While Americans of English stock sometimes held onto the tradition of beef or goose at Christmas, by the Gilded Age most Americans had made the turkey their meat of choice for the holiday. Employers were already giving away free turkeys to their employees by the 1880s. Wild game was still popular throughout rural areas, particularly duck, deer, goose, turkey, antelope, buffalo, and rabbit, but its importance in American diets was declining markedly.[4]

Oysters and Seafood

Fresh seafood was important in the American diet only on the coasts, with the notable exception of oysters. Average Americans ate little fresh seafood beyond fish if they lived in the interior of the nation, away from the fishing fleets of the East and West Coasts. Turtle soup and lobsters were quite popular, but expensive delicacies. Fresh oysters proved to be the exception and they were universally popular with Americans of all social classes. Middle- and upper-class dinner parties often began with oysters on the half shell, fried oysters, or an oyster soup while working-class Americans enjoyed this repast in oyster bars and saloons where they sold for one penny each on the waterfront. Even on the mining frontier in California, Nevada, Idaho, and Colorado oysters on the half shell were common and popular. Reno, Nevada's Capital Chop House advertised that it kept "Fresh and transplanted oysters always on hand and served at all hours in any style desired." Even if fresh seafood was not readily available for those Americans in the interior, aside from oysters, canned seafood was becoming much more common by the Gilded Age: canned crab, lobster, oysters, salmon, sardines, and innumerable varieties of fish.[5]

Dairy

Dairy production also increased during the Gilded Age thanks to the railroad system, which allowed for daily pickups of fresh milk. Dairy farmers sold 2 billion pounds of milk in 1870 but that figure rose to a staggering 18 billion pounds by 1900. Milk was a popular beverage in the Gilded Age and demand remained high despite concerns over disease carried in the milk. This increase was due not only to better transportation but also to farmers discovering that dairy cows produced more milk if fed fresh, green feed. Also, in 1890, Dr. Stephen Babcock invented a machine that could ascertain the butterfat content of milk, which made it easier for farmers to monitor and control the quality of their product and improve their herds. These improvements also made the production of other dairy products more profitable, such as cheese, cottage cheese, butter, and cream cheese. In addition to milk, butter was by far the most popular dairy product. Butter was used heavily on bread, in baking, and to make sauces for meats, oysters, or fish. By the Gilded Age large quantities of butter were mass produced in factories which improved in speed and quality with the 1880 invention of the cream separator. Many rural Americans, however, continued to produce their own butter, particularly because of the fears of tuberculosis spread through dairy products. Most farm-produced butter, often called "dairy" butter, was packed in round decorative molds that were commonly four inches in diameter.[6]

Vegetables

Most modern Americans have the mistaken belief that their ancestors ate huge quantities of leafy green vegetables and generally ate a much healthier diet than most Americans do today. This conception, however, is far from the truth. Indeed, Gilded Age Americans consumed more meat than vegetables when they could. The vegetables they ate in the largest quantities were primarily potatoes, sweet potatoes, squash, cabbage, dried beans, and rice, with only small sides of yellow or leafy green vegetables. Potatoes were such a staple that they appeared at breakfast, lunch, and the evening meal and came in a dizzying array of preparations: boiled, mashed, fried, stewed, baked, escalloped, and French fried. Raw vegetables were virtually never eaten by the average person, though there were regional exceptions, because most people considered them to contain low levels of poisons. Native-born Americans boiled vegetables for an hour or more under the conception that this would boil out the toxins. *The Nevada Cookbook* (1887), compiled by the good women of Carson City, declared vegetables had to be well cooked because "Rare vegetables are neither good nor wholesome."[7]

Fruit

Fresh fruits also grew in popularity and in availability because of the extension of railroads and the introduction of refrigerated railroad cars. Apples continued to be the most popular fruit in the United States; many Americans hated the dried, wrinkled apples they consumed through the long winter months. The massive expansion of railroad networks, refrigerated cars and factories, and agricultural mechanization brought a large supply of out-of-season fruits into American homes. Strawberries from the Carolinas, the Gulf states, Arkansas, Missouri, and Tennessee made their way to northern markets. A wide array of citrus fruits, like oranges, grapefruits, and lemons, came from orchards in California and Florida. By the Gilded Age oranges were common enough that it became a widespread custom to put one in children's stockings at Christmas. Fruits produced outside of the United States also appeared, like bananas and pineapples. Aside from relatively exotic fruits, a host of well-known fruits were available most of the year: peaches, grapes, cantaloupe, avocado, pears, plums, apricots, cherries, raspberries, and blueberries.[8]

Home Canning

Home canning of vegetables and especially fruits became very popular after John Landis Mason invented the screw-top glass canning jar in 1858. Further refinements in 1869, a top seal, made the product much better. The Ball Brothers soon followed with their Ball jar in 1884. The availability of fresh fruits and vegetables encouraged home canning for use during the winter months and Americans began to can and preserve a much wider variety of vegetables and fruits than ever before. Cookbooks provided a wide assortment of recipes for canning such diverse products as plum marmalade, brandied peaches, tomatoes, corn, and watermelon rind.[9]

Sugar and Desserts

Sugar also became a major part of the average person's diet in the Gilded Age. Sugar underwent a revolution in production which made it cheaper, and which had long-term consequences in the American diet. Greater importation of international sugar, which was surging during the Gilded Age, combined with the mechanization of sugar production, caused sugar prices to fall after the Civil War. Sugar, which had once been thought of as a luxury item only the wealthy could afford in large quantities, became a necessity for the average American. Americans consumed an average of 41 pounds of sugar annually by the early 1870s, which was six times more than in the 1780s. Food preparers catered to the American demand for sugar, putting it into a wide variety of products such as canned spaghetti. Per capita sugar consumption surged to a staggering 68 pounds by 1901. Refined, white granulated sugar was cheap, widely available, and, as consumption figures illustrate, infiltrated much of American food.

A wide variety of sweets and desserts relied on the new abundance of sugar. Penny candies, sheathed in brightly colored wrappers, were widely available and cheap enough for most American children to afford by the 1860s. Ice cream, which had been an exotic and elite treat as late as the 1830s, was common and relatively inexpensive by the 1850s. Ice cream saloons and soda fountains (which appealed to women dedicated to temperance) served ice cream to hungry patrons eager for the combination of flavoring, cream, ice, and sugar for only a penny a glass by the 1880s and street vendors sold the treat for even less. Home ice cream makers were available to the elite in the 1840s but were within the reach of the middle class by 1880. By 1895 almost anyone could afford a small two-quart ice cream maker, which retailed for $1.50 in the *Montgomery Ward Catalogue*.

Chocolate also captured the imagination of Americans in the Gilded Age. The Spaniards were the first to mix sugar with ground cacao into a drink and out of this union would develop solid sweetened chocolate candies. Men like Stephen Whitman aped French methods—the French were the premier bonbon and chocolate candy makers of the early nineteenth century—to produce an American chocolate candy industry in the 1860s. Until the 1890s chocolates were relatively expensive and generally associated with women and male gift giving to their "sweethearts." Chocolate candy makers, such as Milton Hershey, changed those perceptions when they developed a chocolate specifically designed for children's tastes by adding milk. Hershey would go one step further by making his chocolate inexpensive. Hershey penny bars and over 130 chocolate novelties drew a massive number of consumers by 1899.

Sugar also served as the main attraction in a wide array of desserts: hot and cold puddings, tarts, pies, cakes, breads, custard, jellies, and preserves. Indeed, 42 percent of the recipes provided by the *Ladies' Home Journal* from 1884 through 1912 were for desserts. Perhaps the most "modern" dessert of the age was the introduction of granulated gelatins by companies like Knox, Jell-O, Plymouth Rock, Crystal, and Junket. Gelatin had formerly been expensive and an elite dessert. Modern Americans might find this hard to believe but gelatin had cachet in the 1880s and 1890s with the middle class and intricate gelatin molds appeared. Sugar made all of these desserts and sweets desirable, changing America's food consumption to its modern pattern, which meant the consumption of unprecedented amounts of refined sugar.[10]

Beverages

The most common beverages in America were water, coffee, and milk. Temperance advocates encouraged water drinking and virtually every eating establishment in the country served iced water by the Gilded Age. Cocoa, lemonade, as well as hot and iced tea, both green and black, were also popular beverages. Soda fountains sprang up in cities and towns throughout the country as an alternative to saloons, and the new availability of fruits led to a wide variety of flavored sodas that sold for $.02. The most popular flavors were vanilla, strawberry, pineapple, and ginger. Charles Hire also introduced a new drink, root beer, which he deftly maneuvered to be declared the National Temperance drink. Hire's Root Beer sold 3 million bottles in 1893. New cola drinks, like Coca-Cola and Pepsi Cola, appeared in 1886 and 1896, respectively, and were made with a soda water base, cola nut extract, and liberal doses of caffeine. The consumption of hard liquor decreased throughout the Gilded Age, reaching a low mark of 1.2 gallons per capita in 1900. Wine consumption rose slightly from .3 to .4 gallons per capita from 1870 to 1900, primarily because it continued to be expensive and frowned upon by Temperance advocates, though there was great demand for champagne. American beer consumption, however, vastly increased, climbing from 2.7 gallons per capita in 1855 to 15.5 gallons per capita in 1900. While European immigration certainly had much to do with beer's rising popularity, native-born working-class consumption also rose.[11]

Regional Variation

Even among native-born Americans there was regional variation in food choices and preparation. Americans of German ancestry in Cincinnati, St. Louis, and Milwaukee brought their love of beer, spicy sausages, and cabbage, for example, well before the massive influx of immigrants late in the Gilded Age. The South also had a regional diet that continued to focus on salt pork, flour, grits, molasses, and sugar. There were nearly two hogs per capita in southern states compared to one hog for every 10 people in New England. Diets were the scantiest among the poor black and white sharecroppers of the South, where planters often actively circumscribed what their tenants grew in order to maximize profits from plantation stores, though traditional southern greens supplemented relatively poor diets.[12] On the frontier farmers, cowboys, migrants, and miners endured the plain meals of biscuits, bacon, and beans cooked in generous amounts of lard when they had to, but as soon as other food was available they eagerly purchased it. Even in mining regions competition among freight companies was extremely high and they moved food supplies even into the most remote mining camps very quickly. Retail stores also opened very quickly in mining towns, often within a few months. In Nevada City, California, there was one retail food store for every nine miners. Virginia City, Nevada, boasted "thirty grocers, four butchers, nine bakers, and two fruiterers as well as twenty-five saloons, seven boarding houses, and nine restaurants" by 1860 and within a year added 15 to 20 meat markets. One serious distinction between miners and others on the Western frontier was that miners ate out very frequently when they could, perhaps as much as modern Americans. Restaurants popped up quickly in mining towns. The What Cheer House, owned and operated by Johnny Knocke, was a representative inexpensive miner's restaurant. Nearly 100 rooms were available for $.50 a night and meals ran at moderate prices. Stewed beef, potatoes, and bread and butter sold for a reasonable $.05 while the most expensive menu item was the porterhouse steak for $.25. This San Francisco landmark reputedly served nearly 4,000 meals per day. Miners also more readily adopted some foreign foods like French haute cuisine, Chinese cooking (it was very inexpensive), and the Cornish pasty (a round pastry with meat and potatoes cooked inside).[13]

Food Processors and Brand Names

Much of the meat, grains, vegetables, and fruits that were becoming more available to Americans were created by increasingly large food processors. Businesses learned that they could consolidate, create very large business enterprises, and earn enormous profits through large economies of scale (basically a large business that produces on a massive scale and charges less for a product than a small business and still makes large profits). At the same time businesses realized that by creating national brand names they could create buyers and even charge higher prices by guaranteeing consistent quality (see Chapter 3). So, very large

Interior view of the Kneisel and Anderson grocery store, on the south side of 6th (Sixth) Street, Georgetown, Colorado. © Denver Public Library, Western History Collection.

producers emerged, jockeying for market position through brand-name use and advertising. Gustavus Swift and Philip Danforth Armour joined with a few others, for example, to create the "Big Five" in meatpacking, known as the Beef Trust to reformers, which controlled a massive market share and drove out competitors. Washburn-Crosby with its brand name Gold Medal Flour and Pillsbury dominated the flour industry. The American Sugar Refining Company took control of most of the sugar industry with its brand name Domino, and started a successful campaign to convince the public that brown sugar was full of dangerous microbes. New brand names also arose in the processed cereal industry as Americans were introduced to breakfast cereals on a mass scale for the first time. Henry D. Perky's Shredded Wheat, Kellogg's Corn Flakes, Quaker Oats, and Post Grape Nuts and Toasties were some of the most successful cereals, though a host of competitors emerged, starting a revolution in American breakfast eating habits.[14]

Canned Foods

The incredible spread of canned foods during the Gilded Age also transformed American eating habits. Canned foods appeared as early as 1812 when Thomas Kensett built a small factory on the New York City waterfront canning salmon, lobsters, oysters, meats, fruits and vegetables, and quickly switched from expensive glass containers to tin. Others soon followed and by 1855 the Mills B. Espy Company canned cherries, strawberries, peaches, and tomatoes. Gail Borden's *Eagle Brand Condensed Milk* was probably the most famous canned good to appear before the Civil War and heralded the fantastic multiplication of canned goods in the Gilded Age, primarily by large processors. In 1860 only 5 million cans of food were produced annually, but that number grew to 30 million cans by 1870 and exploded to over 120,000 annually. The invention of the pressure cooker in 1874 by A. K. Shriver gave canners control of the heating of canned goods, which allowed them to seal the cans, kill germs, and keep the cans from exploding. Canning factories grew from under 100 in 1870 to almost 1,800 in 1900. Technological improvements transformed can making from a hand process to a machine process that could churn out 2,500 cans an hour in the mid-1880s and 6,000 cans an hour by the mid-1890s. Processors like Heinz, Franco-American, Joseph H. Campbell Preserve Company (Campbell Soup Company), the Norton Brothers Company, and a host of smaller producers canned a stunning variety of fruits, vegetables, soups, milk, seafood, and meats. Canned goods fanned throughout the nation via the ever-expanding railroad lines, bringing exotic foods to isolated regions and breaking the monotony of frontier food. Canned food became so important on the California mining frontier that tin dumps made their first appearance in the 1850s. In canning, like many enterprises in American business at the turn of the century, the trend was toward consolidation and merger. For example, the Norton Brothers Company merged with roughly 60 other firms in 1901 to create the enormous American Can Company. Growers actually experimented with new strains of fruits and vegetables that would meet the demands of industrial canning. Processed foods were becoming a much more important part of the average American's diet during the Gilded Age.[15]

OTHER FOOD TRADITIONS

As nearly 11.3 million immigrants poured into the United States between 1871 and 1900 they brought with them eating and cooking habits far outside the mainstream of traditional Anglo-American cooking. Middle-class reformers attacked immigrant foods because of the traditional Anglo-American dislike for highly spiced foods (particular venom was reserved for garlic) and because of new ideas in nutrition. Scientific nutritionists firmly believed that heavily spiced foods required much more energy to digest and also caused alcohol cravings. Ethnic prejudice ignored the fact that spices often made cheap cuts of meat palatable.

Nutritionists also attacked the practice of making hearty stews, soups, gulyashen, and borschts as dangerous because these mixtures of pasta, meat, and vegetables required excessive energy to digest. They advocated the Anglo-American method of cooking and eating each dish separately which according to the science of the day was more efficiently digested. Nutritionists also criticized as unhealthy the light continental breakfast that many immigrants ate. European immigrants largely ignored these middle-class attempts at reforming their food habits, though different ethnic groups assimilated to American food at varying rates and degrees. In heavily populated ethnic enclaves, specialty stores would often emerge, catering to the Old World food desires of their people. Most ethnic groups readily adopted more meat into their diets when they found prices significantly cheaper in the United States.

Immigrant Foods

Chinese

The Chinese maintained their foodways more rigidly than almost any other immigrant group. Their method of quick sautéing vegetables ran counter to traditional Anglo-American ideas of the appropriate method for cooking vegetables, which was to boil them into mush. The Chinese continued to use their own spices and herbs, and ate virtually no dairy products. Chinese cooks were highly sought after, particularly on the West Coast, but they usually cooked standard American fare. A few Chinese innovations made their way into general American food habits by the 1890s: egg foo yong and chop suey. Exactly where and how these particular dishes were created is a matter of historical controversy and none of the existing explanations appear to be definitive. Few native-born Americans ate at Chinese restaurants with the exception of the miners on the Western frontier.

Germans

German food had survived the dominant Anglo-American cuisine in regions heavily populated by Americans of German descent like several Pennsylvania counties and the cities of Cincinnati, St. Louis, and Milwaukee. Sauerkraut, German potato salad, German fried potatoes, Hamburg steak, sauerbraten, and pretzels were already well known in these enclaves of German-Americans. German stores sold items like sausages, smoked fish, smoked Westphalia ham, knockwurst, and bratwurst.

Poles, Czechs, Ukrainians, Russians, Slovaks

Poles, Czechs, Ukrainians, Russians, and Slovaks did maintain ethnic food habits but assimilated more quickly to American foods, particularly the young, than other groups. Many of their foodways were not terribly different from the German foods already prevalent in certain parts of the nation. Slovaks, though, had very different traditions and found it almost impossible to maintain their elaborate, spicy meals in the mill towns where they often found themselves living and working. Food available in the mill stores was bland and monotonous: meat, white flour, potatoes, and bread. Most of these peoples, however, readily adopted the abundant sweet rolls and relatively inexpensive meats. Ethnic foods like borscht, liver cake, caraway seed, kielbasa, and kolacky, a fruit-filled pastry, continued to survive. Some of these foods eventually entered mainstream food patterns, like kielbasa, which is today better known as Polish sausage.

Hungarians

Hungarians had many of the same problems that confronted the Slovaks, which was to preserve a complex and spicy culinary tradition in the United States. Hungarians typically ate meals five to six times per day though they quickly adjusted to the U.S. standard of three meals per day. Hungarian traditions eventually introduced broad segments of American society to paprika and goulash.

Greeks

Greek food habits were also very different from the Anglo-American tradition. A Greek woman complained that she "almost starved" when she migrated to the United States because of the "painfully tasteless American food, the tough beef and mutton, the vegetables all cooked in water, and potatoes at every meal." Greeks became well known for operating small grocery stores that stocked the items their people desired: wines, sharp cheeses, olive oil, black olives, dried fish, figs, and sardines. The Greeks introduced Americans to lamb dishes, stuffed grape leaves, moussaka, and baklava.

Jews

Jewish cooking was incredibly diverse, but the culinary traditions most Americans associated with Jewish cooking were those of German, Russian, and Polish Jews. Like most other groups they created their own networks of stores, but Jews were particularly pressed to meet their own food needs because of the kosher requirements dictated by their religious beliefs. Kosher butchers and stores quickly emerged and provided kosher meats, garlic pickles, potato and cabbage salads, gefilte fish, lox (smoked salmon), bagels, knishes, pastrami, cheesecake, and sour rye and pumpernickel breads.

Scandinavians

Scandinavians also brought their distinctive eating habits to the regions they settled, particularly Wisconsin, Minnesota, the Dakotas, and the Pacific Northwest. Pickled herring, meatballs, rye bread, and beet salad were all Swedish favorites. The relatively high densities of Scandinavians in these areas helped them maintain large parts of their food traditions.

Italians

The ethnic group that tenaciously clung to its foodways and at the same time had the most profound influence on American food was the Italians. Italian entrepreneurs devised networks to truck farms outside of the cities where they settled to satisfy the demand of Italian immigrants for fresh fruits and vegetables. Italian fruit and vegetable wholesalers and retailers soon became important merchants in the distribution and sale of food in many American cities. Italians became well known for planting fruits and vegetables in window boxes and any spare ground they could find. Italians also demanded olive oil, cheese from their homeland, anchovies, pastas, wines, tomatoes, and Italian sausages. Whereas most other ethnic groups attended the cooking classes sponsored by the numerous settlement houses in America's cities, Italians steadfastly refused to attend classes that taught American cooking, sticking to their own culinary traditions. Italian spaghetti was one of the few ethnic foods to become popular with the general American population, though most native-born Americans cooked the pasta until it was mush and used a watery ketchup sauce.[16]

EATING OUT

Americans in the Gilded Age ate out at restaurants more than ever. As more Americans joined the ranks of the salaried and wage earners, wages rose and a new leisure culture developed, so eating out became much more common. Restaurants, lunch counters, saloons, and bars became important sources of a quick bite, leisurely dinner, and often entertainment.

Inexpensive, Fast Lunch

As more Americans joined the industrial and office work forces, fast, inexpensive lunches that could be purchased came into demand. For middle- and working-class men the saloon's free lunch was ubiquitous across the country and provided ample lunches for the cost of a $.05

beer. Typical saloon lunches consisted of a buffet of bread or crackers, bologna or something like it, sliced tomatoes, salad, pickles, onions, radishes, and maybe a hot stew or soup. The free-lunch spread at the Council Bar in Butte, Montana, was certainly atypical when they heaped 20 feet of their enormous bar with their bountiful free lunch which included bologna, liverwurst, anchovies, summer sausage, pickled tripe, pig's snout, kippered fish, various cheeses, crackers, pickles, whole and sliced beets, radishes, green onions, as well as wheat, white, pumpernickel, and rye breads. These meals were incredible bargains when even inexpensive restaurants charged $.15 for a meal. Not every saloon offered a free meal, but those that did not often provided a "businessman's lunch" for $.10–$.20. For people concerned with the presence of alcohol, numerous fast and relatively inexpensive $.15 restaurants opened that catered to the army of business people, clerks, and retail workers in the downtown business corridors of American cities. These restaurants varied but offered items like sandwiches, salads, and soups. Street vendors also provided large amounts of fast food to urban workers in fabulous variety. For example, one well-organized street vendor business, the Mexican Food Corporation, blanketed New York City with white-clad vendors selling hot tamales.[17]

Ethnic Restaurants

When they were concentrated enough in cities most ethnic groups had restaurateurs open establishments that catered specifically to their food desires. These restaurants ranged from elite, expensive enterprises to moderately priced, down to quite cheap. For example, New York City boasted the elegant Morelli's Italian and Frascati's Spanish restaurants, and San Francisco had the likes of Perini's Italian and Zinkand's German fine restaurants. Medium-priced German, French, Italian, Spanish, Chinese, and Jewish restaurants were in most major cities. New York even boasted a number of English chophouses where tripe, liver and bacon, Welsh rarebit, and pork and mutton pies were on the menu. The restaurants, however, catered mainly to these ethnic groups and not to native-born Americans. Italian spaghetti joints were one of the few ethnic restaurants to attract native-born Americans by the 1890s.[18]

Fine Dining

French Influence

The American elite, unlike most native-born Americans, adopted a foreign culinary style as their preferred food, the French haute cuisine. French restaurants were the most popular fine dining establishments in the country and none was more renowned than Delmonico's, founded in New York City in 1832. French chefs were hired by all of the wealthy, often at exorbitant salaries. The conspicuous consumption of the elite demanded that they illustrate their taste with the finest French foods and incredibly elaborate dinner parties. The eating habits of even the American elite tended toward the heavy side in spite of their sedentary work habits. A typical dinner party menu listed a dizzying array of courses. This menu from General Winfield Scott Hancock's dinner party at Delmonico's in 1880 was typical of the wealthy. The dinner consisted of, in order, raw oysters, two soups, hors d'oeuvres, a fish course, Relevés (a saddle of lamb and filet of beef), entrées (chicken wings with peas and lamb chops with beans and mushroom-stuffed artichokes), Terrapin en casserole á la Maryland, sorbet (to clear the palate), and roast canvasback duck and quail. For dessert there was timbale Madison, an array of ice creams, whipped creams, jellied dishes, banana mouse, and elaborate confectioneries. Fruit, petits fours, coffee, and liqueurs followed the dessert. As you can imagine, the elite tended more toward large sizes than we would find preferable today, but larger sizes were considered attractive in the Gilded Age. Indeed, the icon of beauty in the Gilded Age, the actress Lillian Russell, known popularly as the "American Beauty," weighed over 200 pounds (see Chapter 10).

Almost all things French were good to the new American elite whose vast industrial fortunes and lack of family pedigree made them intent upon showing each other how polished and refined they could be. As has often been the case in American history the rich valued every cultural refinement of Europe over everything American (see Chapters 5, 9, and 10). The elite were the first to adopt French salad, mainly because lettuce was an expensive luxury only the wealthy could afford outside of those rural Americans who grew their own. Lettuce varieties in the nineteenth century wilted quickly and bruised so easily that transport was difficult until the invention of iceberg head lettuce in 1903.

Elite Restaurants

Elite fine dining tended to gravitate toward the elegant French restaurants like Delmonico's. Boston had Young's Hotel and Parker House; New York possessed Hoffman House, Savoy, Waldorf-Astoria, and Imperial; Philadelphia had the Continental; Chicago the Palmer House and Sherman House; New Orleans the St. Charles; and San Francisco the El Dorado House, Marchand's, Café Riche, and West Coast Delmonico's; while Denver boasted six fine restaurants that specialized in French haute cuisine. There were, as previously mentioned, fine dining establishments devoted to other ethnic foods throughout urban America but none were as popular as the French restaurants.

5454 Brown Palace Hotel Cafe, Denver, Col

Brown Palace Hotel Cafe, Denver, Colorado, ca. 1900. © Library of Congress.

Western Fine Dining

In an ironic twist, fine dining on the frontier turned out to be very different than in the more settled parts of the country. Elite restaurants popped up quickly in frontier areas such as Tombstone, Arizona, Virginia City, Nevada, and Georgetown, Colorado. Fine restaurants serving French haute cuisine on the frontier soon came to rely on the business of the average miner. Historian Joseph Conlin convincingly argues that miners were more inclined to spend money on expensive dinners than most working-class Americans, due to their boomtown, get-rich-quick mentality. When precious metal reserves ran out some of the first businesses to close were fine dining establishments. Because of the egalitarian nature of fine restaurants in the West, elite men tended to retreat to private gentlemen's clubs and elite women to private luncheon and dinner parties.[19]

MIDDLE-CLASS DINNER PARTIES

Middle-class Americans eagerly adapted elite forms to their own situations in an attempt to clearly show their refinement and gentility, not only to others but also to themselves. The United States was a rapidly changing, highly mobile society with a volatile boom-and-bust economy, which made the middle class eager to establish clear class boundaries and create unity and coherence among themselves. Increasingly complex etiquette formulas in all facets of life were adopted by the Victorian middle class, and dining became one of the major expressions of their desire to codify appropriate behavior in etiquette manuals and even cookbooks. For a group of people often a generation away from the simpler sort of folks, these complex dining rituals reinforced their own sense of superiority and group solidarity. Dressing for dinner, for example, became an important symbol of middle-class propriety, even in the comforts of one's own home. The symbolic nature of dressing for dinner took precedence over the desire for dining comfort even among their own families.

Mimicking the upper class, the middle class also began to put great emphasis on dinner parties. At more formal parties the hostess would send out engraved invitations by messenger, often listing the menu and the people attending, who were to be, according to the etiquette manuals, all of relatively the same social rank. Women dressed according to the latest fashion, but without arms or necks bared, and men generally were to wear dress coats and trousers. When dinner was to be served the hostess would nod to her husband who escorted the lady of honor from the drawing room to the dining room, followed by the other gentlemen escorting their assigned dinner partners with the older, more socially prestigious going first. The hostess would be seated last, escorted by the gentleman of honor. As guests dined on the multicourse meal the hostess was responsible for maintaining a nice flow of uncontroversial conversation. Etiquette writers warned diners never to comment on the food, eat slowly, take small bites and small portions, never touch the food with a hand, eat with the proper utensil with easy facility, control their emotions, and to stifle all bodily concerns. Most etiquette writers recommended one to two hours for dinner parties.

The ample food was served á la Russe, which meant that the bulk of the food was placed on a sideboard and served in courses. Servants were

THE COOK.

Menus for the Week.

[These Menus are the copyrighted property of The Cook, and must not be republished without due credit being given.]

MONDAY.

Breakfast.

Melons.
Graham Flakes with Cream.
Cold Meats.
Fried Egg Plant, (266). Cucumbers.

Dinner.

Consommé Colbert, (328).
Broiled Bluefish.
Cucumbers.
Breast of Veal, stuffed,
Sorrel, Baked Tomatoes.
Queen Fritters.
Water Cress Salad, (91).
Blanc Mange, (30).
Water Melon, (32).
Cheese, Claret.

TUESDAY.

Breakfast.

Fruit.
Shredded Oats with Cream, (292).
Spanish Omelet, (330).
Veal Toast.

Dinner.

Okra Soup, (331).
Boiled Sheepshead, Cream butter, (332).
Boiled New Potatoes.
Roast Capon.
Young Carrots, Cream sauce.
Stuffed Peppers, (74).
Lettuce Salad, (98).
Minute Pudding, (159).
Cantaloupes.
Cheese, Coffee.

WEDNESDAY.

Breakfast.

Fruit.
Graham Flakes with Cream.
Fried Softshell Crabs, (154).
Tomato Salad, (208).

Dinner.

Vermicelli,
Broiled Weakfish, Butter sauce.
Cucumbers.
Spring Lamb, Mint sauce.
Green Peas, Cauliflower.
Pineapple Fritters, (315).
Tomato Salad.
Raspberry Short Cake, (274).
Camembert Cheese,
Coffee.

THURSDAY.

Breakfast.

Berries.
Cracker Cream Toast.
Cold Roast Lamb.
Broiled Tomatoes, (4).

Dinner.

Sorrel Soup, (333).
Boiled Salmon Trout,
Anchovy Sauce.
Fricassee of Veal with Peas.
Green Corn, String Beans.
Fried Egg Plant, (260).
Romaine Salad, (228).
Peach Dumpling,
Canned Cammebert Cheese,
Coffee.

FRIDAY, (Without Meat).

Breakfast.

Berries with Cream.
Curry of Crayfish, (70).
Tomato Omelet, (229).
Breakfast Gems.

Dinner.

Clams.
Bisque of Clams, (334).
Broiled Sheepshead.
Cucumbers.
Curry of Lobster, (335).
Stuffed Tomatoes, (198).
Lettuce Salad, (95).
Cold Cabinet Pudding, (158).
Water Melon.
Rhine Wine.

FRIDAY, (With Meat).

Breakfast.

Fruit.
Smoked Venison with Egg.
Broiled Young Carrots.
Toasted Muffins.

Dinner.

Consommé Macaroni.
Boiled Striped Bass.
Sauce Bearnaise, (19).
Leg of Mutton.
Green Corn, Young Beets.
Peach Fritters.
Watercress Salad.
Nopolitain Cream.
Macaroons.
Cheese, Claret.

SATURDAY.

Breakfast.

Cantaloupes.
Rice Fritters.
Broiled Spring Chicken.
Hash Cream Potatoes, (226).

Dinner.

Clams.
Veal Broth with Rice.
Fillets of Spanish Mackerel.
Cucumbers.
Fried Frogs Sauce Remoulade.
Cauliflower.
Roast Gosling.
Tomato Mayonnaise, (263).
French Rice Pudding.
Cheese, Fruit, Coffee.

SUNDAY.

Breakfast.

Peaches with Cream.
Spring Lamb Chops.
Broiled Potatoes, (5).
Breakfast Salad.

Dinner.

Clams.
Cream of Cauliflower.
Baked Bluefish.
Swertbreads à la Jardiniere.
Stuffed Artichokes, (91).
Roast Squab on toast.
Escarole Salad, (267).
Cold Custard, (120).
Pineapple Salad, (3).
Cheese, Claret.

☞ THE NUMBERS IN THE MENUS ARE FOR REFERENCE TO THE FORMULAS IN "SEASONABLE RECIPES," ACCORDING TO WHICH DISHES SO MARKED SHOULD BE PREPARED.

Sample menus for middle-class and affluent people, 1885. Published in *The Cook*, a weekly handbook of domestic culinary art for all housekeepers. © Library of Congress.

required for this type of dinner party, and etiquette writers recommended one servant for every three guests for serving and clearing of plates. Middle-class food was definitely showing the influence of French cooking by the 1880s, but it continued to embrace the largely Anglo-American cooking heritage. Etiquette writer Mary Slurwood recommended this "simple" menu for a middle-class dinner party. The dinner included, in order, oysters, soup á la Reine, broiled fish, Filet de Boef aux Champignons or roast beef or mutton, roast partridges, tomato salad, cheese, flavored ices, jellies, fruit, coffee, liqueurs, and a variety of wines (chablis, Rhine wine, champagne, claret, and burgundy or sherry). The middle-class dinner party differed somewhat in the types of food presented, but not at all in the quantity. The much-talked-about servant shortage of the late nineteenth century was a constant concern for middle-class women eager to throw elegant dinner parties.

These dinner parties required fairly elaborate spaces in which these dramas could be played out. Increasingly, dining rooms were necessary symbols of gentility to middle-class Americans. Dining rooms would be equipped with dinner party necessities: often a dining room suite of furniture, the central table, a large sideboard (these are often called buffets today) which was used for storage and to place the food on before it was served to the table, and tasteful chromolithograph prints (see Chapter 4). A wide array of crystal, cut glass, china, and silverware were needed for a party. An 1873 etiquette writer recommended that every family possess crystal, china, cut glass, silver, and earthenware everyday plates in the following proportions: three dozen wine glasses, two dozen champagne glasses, two dozen claret glasses, three dozen goblets, six water carafes, six decanters, one liqueur stand, twelve liqueur glasses, two glass pitchers, one celery glass, one trifle bowl, eight dessert dishes, one fuller dinner service, one common set of earthenware for the kitchen, one common tea service, one good tea service, one breakfast service, and one good dessert service. This list did not even include the required silverware, which in an 1873 guidebook was listed as three dozen forks, two dozen tablespoons, a dozen and a half dessert spoons, two dozen teaspoons, six salt spoons, one cheese knife, four butter knives, one asparagus tong, two sugar tongs, two soup ladles, four sauce ladles, two gravy ladles, two sugar ladles, a fish slice, cheese scoops, and grape scissors. Even kitchen utensils were required in large numbers. In her 1881 cookbook Maria Parloa recommended a minimum of 139 kitchen utensils for a well-stocked kitchen. Many of these items could be quite costly, but by the Gilded Age, mass production brought prices down to reasonable levels. Department stores and mail order catalogs carried all of these items. Even the *Montgomery Ward Catalogue*, geared toward rural and small-town Americans, carried these middle-class dining items. Of course, less expensive aluminum ware and steel flatware were available, but so too was solid silver flatware where a cream ladle cost $3.20 and a soup ladle $14.75. The catalog sold silver tea services ($35.45), crystal berry dishes ($3–$5.25), fruit stands ($1.25), cake baskets ($1.50), crumb pans ($.20–$.80), roughly 23 different china patterns, as well as nine pages of cut glass and crystal glassware. The materials needed for a respectable middle-class dinner party were available to virtually every American within range of the post office.[20]

CONCLUSION

The Gilded Age witnessed transformations in American food patterns. Native-born Americans tended to stick with Anglo-American cuisine (with the notable exceptions of frontier miners and the wealthy) that focused on ample portions of meat with white bread, potatoes, cabbage, and small sides of vegetables. New technologies in transportation and refrigeration brought to consumers fresh vegetables and fruits that were out of season as well as new, exotic fruits. These same technologies brought fresh meat, particularly beef, and caused a marked decline in prices. While the upper class adopted French cuisine and the middle class aspired to such lofty demonstrations of refinement, a wide variety of immigrants from all over Europe and China brought new cooking styles and foods into the United States. Although only Italian food in the form of spaghetti made significant inroads into the typical native-born American's diet in the Gilded Age, almost all of the different ethnic food traditions would eventually add something to standard American cuisine in the twentieth century.

7

Leisure Activities

BACKGROUND

Leisure became increasingly important in Gilded Age America as people found themselves with generally more money and time, particularly in urban areas. Americans threw themselves into a wide range of fads, games, toys, hobbies, and sports. As the American middle class grew, they came to play a prominent role in the new leisure activities, at least more than those Americans trapped in cycles of poverty, but even for those who were less-well-off financially a host of leisure activities were available. As the urban entertainment industry was born sports became professionalized, and drew their players mainly from the ranks of working-class Americans.

FADS

Several fads swept through Gilded Age America and all were tied to the new consumer culture emerging in the period, and tied to leisure. The fads listed here spiked rapidly in popular enthusiasm, experienced a massive initial rush of being the "thing," and then dropped off in popularity rather quickly. There were many minor fads, like trade card collecting (Chapter 3), but the major fads of the era were croquet, roller skating, bicycling, coon songs, and Brownies. It is of little surprise that, in this period so consumed by sports, several of the games revolved around activities related to sporting events. Brownies, however, illustrated the growth of a consumer culture directed toward young people.

Croquet

By far the most popular family lawn sport of the Gilded Age started as an elite game, croquet. The origins of croquet are somewhat clouded, but it had become popular among the British elite by the 1850s. By 1865 two croquet rule books were published in the United States, one of them based on the version of croquet played at the wealthy resort in Newport, Rhode Island. Winslow Homer painted a series of famous canvases of croquet players in 1865 and 1869. Croquet promoters founded the National Croquet Association in 1879 and organized the first national tournament in 1882. Lightweight backyard croquet kits were mass produced by American industry and spread the game into the backyards of the American middle class in the 1860s and 1870s. In the 1895 *Montgomery Ward Catalogue* croquet sets cost only $.68 for the least expensive four-ball version and $3.40 for the most expensive eight-ball version. At the height of the croquet fad, wickets boasted candle sockets for night play. The game was particularly popular among women. By the 1880s the game's faddish popularity began to be diluted by the emergence of lawn tennis.[1]

Roller Skating

In 1863, James Leonard Plimpton, a businessman from Massachusetts, invented a roller skate that could turn by putting a spring on this four-wheeled contraption. It was called a "rocking skate" and was the first one that really let people skate curves and turn. Plimpton opened a skating club in New York where gentlemen enjoyed showing off for the ladies by doing fancy figures, steps, and turns. Within 20 years, roller skating had become a popular pastime for men and women. Entrepreneurs built large skating rinks, like Chicago's famous Casino Rink whose 1884 opening drew thousands of skaters and spectators. When the Royal Rink opened in Muncie, Indiana, in 1885, a thousand people paid $.15 each to skate. Wealthy men in Newport, Rhode Island, played "roller polo," a hockey game which developed into a popular league sport in several Midwestern cities in the 1880s. Muncie had roller polo teams by 1885 and it was so popular it became a high school sport. Roller skate racing and dancing also became popular pastimes. The glory days of this fad ended in the 1890s with the advent of the safety bicycle.[2]

Bicycling

Bicycling took the nation by storm with the introduction of the safety bicycle in 1890, which featured same-sized pneumatic tires driven by a rear wheel sprocket and chain. Prior to 1890 what became known as

White Star, No. 1.

55985 A first class all around Bicycle; up to date in every detail. This wheel will compare in workmanship and quality with other wheels retailing at $75.00 to $85.00. Weight, 27 pounds. Price... ....$45.00

SPECIFICATIONS.

Frame—1895 pattern, deep frame, with long head and wheel base, narrow tread, made from cold drawn seamless steel tubing and steel forgings.

Wheels—28-inch, with wood rims, fitted with 1¾-inch M. & W. pneumatic tires, steel rims furnished, if desired.

Steering Fork—Cold drawn steel tubing, with steel drop forged crown, adjustable nickeled coasters.

Handle Bar—Made of 1⅜ cold drawn seamless steel tubing, drop or upturned pattern, fitted with cork handles, with German silver ferrules.

Bearings—Ball bearings to every part, made from high grade steel, carefully hardened, all dust proof.

Cranks—Round, 6½-inch throw.

Pedals—Dust proof, fitted with large moulded rubbers, rat-trap pedals furnished when so ordered.

Chain—Humber pattern, $\frac{5}{16}$-inch block chain, hardened, rear adjustment.

Gear—Sprocket wheels, detachable, geared to 63 inches.

Saddle—Garford, model M. 2.

Finish—All bright parts finely nickeled, japanned with our own special enamel, which produces the best finish that can be obtained.

Tool Bag—Fitted with wrench, oil can and pump. This wheel will be furnished with an entirely detachable brake, when so ordered.

An advertisement for a bicycle from the 1895 *Montgomery Ward Catalogue.*

ordinary bicycles were popular mainly with young, affluent men. These bicycles sported an oversized front wheel driven directly by pedals and a tiny rear wheel. Solid tires instead of the comfortable air-filled pneumatic tire, massive front wheels, direct pedals, and exorbitant costs made these monstrosities fit for only the very daring and wealthy. Racers, however, did band together and form the League of American Wheelmen in 1880. Bicycling became a true fad in the United States only after the safety bicycle hit stores in 1890. Men and women, young and old could ride the new safety bicycle, and the number of bicycles owned by Americans exploded from 1 million to 10 million from 1893 to 1900. Americans cycled like never before as millions of people hit the roads all across America. Women joined the cycling craze with a fervor that attracted both support and condemnation from cultural authorities in the United States. While arguments raged over whether bicycling was detrimental or beneficial to women's health, women continued to ride. In fact, bicycle riding spurred dress reform as women sought clothing that would allow them to ride comfortably, such as split skirts (see Chapter 5). Indeed, bicycling became an important metaphor for women's changing place in American society. In 1896, Susan B. Anthony wrote, "Let me tell you what I think of bicycling. I think it has done more to emancipate women than anything else in the world. I stand and rejoice every time I see a woman ride by on a wheel. It gives women a feeling of freedom and self-reliance." Prices for bicycles dropped drastically during the 1890s. In the 1895 *Montgomery Ward Catalogue* nine different bicycles were for sale ranging in price from $65 to $14 for a child's bike, as well as "Stylish Bicycle Clothing" which included caps, sweaters, knickers, and women's bloomers. Like most objects in the Gilded Age, bicycles were sold according to age and sex, with bicycles for men, women, boys, and girls. Tricycles were even available for the very young, ranging from $1.35 to $11.75.[3]

Coon Songs

Another fad in this era was the love of coon songs (see Chapter 9). Coon songs were not united so much in musical style as they were defined by their syncopated rhythm, sometimes quite mild, and outrageous racial stereotypes of African Americans. Many Tin Pan Alley hits were in the coon song genre and more than 600 were published in the 1890s. A sad relic of the past, the coon song exemplified institutionalized white American racism and its powerful hold over the imagination of the country.

Brownies

A fad totally unconnected to sports were the Brownie creations of illustrator Palmer Cox (see Chapter 2). Brownies made their first appearance in *St. Nicholas Magazine* in 1883. These delightful little creatures soon became an absolute sensation with children across the country. Cox's creations always seemed to be playing in department stores with the latest fad consumer items like roller skates and bicycles. Cox parlayed his creations in a small marketing empire that made him quite wealthy through a series of books and Brownie games. Indeed, the 1895 *Montgomery Ward Catalogue* carried three Brownie books (*The Brownies at Home*, *The Brownies: Their Book*, and *The Brownies Around the World*) which sold for $1.05 each; three sets of Brownie ink stamps for $.20, $.40, and $.75, respectively; and Brownie ten pins (a bowling game) for $.45. Brownie tie-in products were everywhere in Gilded Age America, culminating in the famous Kodak Brownie camera which appeared in 1900, marketed toward children. This $1 camera sold roughly 250,000 units and capitalized on the Brownie fad. Brownies became a cultural icon that was a generational marker which helped to define the young people during the late Gilded Age. Most children of the Gilded Age would have experienced Brownies in some form and this experience would have defined their generation and collective memories. The Brownie mania may have been the first time a generation of American young people were united by a common consumer item that became a generational cultural icon.[4]

GAMES

Victorian Americans loved games of all kinds. The capability of industrialization combined with chromolithography to cheaply mass produce dramatic color on cardboard created a new game industry that could provide affordable games to Americans. Card games, board games, children's games, parlor games, and bachelor games were all present before the Gilded Age, but all were influenced by the ability of industry to produce in staggering quantities. A new leisure culture was developing in the nation both inside and outside the home.

Card Games

Card games were a favorite in Victorian homes and consumed a great deal of leisure time for adults and children. Adults enjoyed playing popular games like *Euchre*, *Five Hundred*, and *Whist*. *Old Maid*, *Go Fish*, and *Snap* were popular among children. Educational card games such as *Authors*, required young people to learn famous writers and their works. *Authors* proved to be the favorite of Gilded Age middle-class Americans who placed great store on educational games that inculcated refined sensibilities. The 1895 *Montgomery Ward Catalogue* carried 20 different card games including *Authors* ($.10), *Old Maid* ($.10), *Capitol Cities* ($.19), *Math-*

ematiques ($.19), the *Wild Flower Game* ($.40), the *Bible Game* ($.40), and *American History* ($.40).[5]

Board Games

The first board game, the *Travelers Tour through the United States*, appeared in the United States in 1822, but it was during the Gilded Age, with mass production and the brilliantly colored boxes created by chromolithography, that the board game came into mass popularity. Small producers like W. & S. B. Ives, R. Bliss Manufacturing Company, J. H. Singer, W. S. Reed, and H. B. Chaffee created enduring games and played an important role in the industry, but the big four companies that molded the new game industry in the Gilded Age were the McLoughlin Brothers (1858), Milton Bradley (1860), Selchow & Righter (1867), and Parker Brothers (1888). Each had a niche; Milton Bradley made games mainly for children while Parker Brothers created many of its games for adults. Selchow & Righter's most famous and enduring game was *PARCHEESI*, based on the very popular PACHISI from India, which was introduced in 1867. In 1874, Selchow & Righter trademarked PARCHEESI, one of the first trademarked names in the early game industry.

Most of the games mirrored middle-class values and concerns. Some popular board games were heavily didactic and focused on inculcating morality and virtue. *The Mansion of Happiness* was first produced by Ives in 1843 and endured throughout the century even after the company was purchased by Milton Bradley. The rules stated clearly, "Whoever possesses Piety, Honesty, Temperance, Gratitude, Prudence, Truth, Chastity, Sincerity, Humility, Industry, Charity, Humanity, or Generosity is entitled to advance . . . toward the Mansion of Happiness." Milton Bradley's *Checkered Game of Life* (1860) was in the same vein. Some games emphasized the educational refinement so important to middle-class culture, such as reading, literature, geography, and mathematics. A typical game was the *Young Folks Historical Game* (1890) which quizzed players on American history. Other games focused on middle-class values like business enterprise such as *Bulls and Bears: The Great Wall St. Game* (1896), while still others were simple games of chance and skill which reflected that the cultural acceptance of leisure for its own sake was spreading throughout American society. Some popular games echoed current events of the Gilded Age like *Round the World with Nellie Bly* (1890). Still other games capitalized on the immense popularity of sports in the Gilded Age: *Bicycle Race* (1891), the *New Bicycle Game* (1894), *Bowling* (1896), the *Game of Pool* (1898), and *Basketball* (1898). *The Yale Harvard Game* offered young people the opportunity to play and re-play the yearly "foot-ball" game between the heated rivals and cost $.85. Nursery

An advertisement for a board game from the 1895 *Montgomery Ward Catalogue.*

rhyme themes were also very popular such as *Little Goldenlocks and the Three Bears* (1890), *The Game of Jack and the Bean Stalk* (1898), and *The New Game Red Riding Hood and the Wolf* (1887). Checkers, chess, and dominoes were virtually universal in this era, played by adults and children. Board games were wildly popular and readily available in department stores and mail order catalogs. Reasonable prices, between $.40 and $2.75, brought them into many American homes in the 1890s.[6]

Children's Games

Jigsaw Puzzles

Jigsaw puzzles appeared in the 1850s, mass produced by Milton Bradley and Parker Brothers after 1865, and became very popular games. By the mid-1890s even rural Americans could purchase a variety of "cut up puzzles" through mail order catalogs. A puzzle map of the United States in either small ($.45) or large ($.75) and puzzles of the elephant Jumbo, a steamboat, birds, and a fire department were for sale in the *Montgomery Ward Catalogue*.[7]

Marbles

Marbles was another immensely popular game, particularly among boys of the Gilded Age. Mass-produced glass marbles became widely available in the Gilded Age, and Ohio was the center of marble production where large factories produced a million marbles a day. With new highly colored marbles, no longer just clay or stone, the game inspired fierce competition among boys as they battled for each others' marbles. Aggies, or the rare agate marbles, were particularly sought after. Youngsters in the late nineteenth century usually used the term "mibs" instead of marbles and commonly played the "Ring Taw" game. If the match was "in earnest" each boy sought to knock marbles outside of the ring, or taw, and thereby gain those marbles for himself. The game included elaborate rules about changing shooting position and accidents. A typical game might include participants yelling in the language only serious marble shooters understood: "Fen burnings! Roundings! Dubs! Knuckle down tight where you lay!" "Fen burnings" roughly meant defending the chosen mibs (marbles in the ring) which a player had given special significance by breathing on them. "Roundings" or roundsters meant moving around the ring to get a better position to shoot at the mibs when the shooter's taw (shooter marble) made it out of the ring on the previous shot. "Dubs" referred to knocking out two mibs from the ring on a single shot. "Knuckle down tight where you lay" was called out by the players to remind the shooter that he did not have "roundings" and had to shoot (knuckle down) from where his taw stopped on his previous shot. Marbles play encouraged boys to develop the aggressive and competitive qualities so admired among males in the late nineteenth century. They carefully policed every game that was "in earnest" or "for keeps" to ensure there would be no "hunching or fudging" (illegally moving the shooting hand across the line) or "histing" (raising the hand off the ground when shooting). Charles M. Crandall's *Pigs in Clover* was the only board game to capitalize on the immense popularity of marbles and it became the most popular indoor marble game of the era.[8]

Folk Games

Children also played a wide array of games, many of them originating hundreds, sometimes thousands, of years in the past. Singing games abounded, such as Ring around the Rosie, Farmer in the Dell, and Right Elbow In or Hinkumbooby (better known today as the Hokey Pokey). There were also many counting rhymes that were often used to determine teams for games or who went first. The racism of nineteenth-century America is evident in the following rhyme from Salem, Massachusetts:

> One's all, zuzall, titterall, tann,
> Bobtailed vinegar, little Paul ran
> Harum scarum, merchant marum
> Nigger, turnpike, toll-house, out.[9]

There were also a large number of chasing games such as Tag, Hide and Seek, Blind Man's Bluff, Follow the Leader, Capture the Flag, Hare and Hounds, Witch in a Jar, Hawks and Chickens, and Leapfrog. Other favorites were Jack-Stones, also known as Dubbs, and Five-Stones (today known as Jacks and Hop-Scotch). There were also the rough games played mainly by boys like I Conquer, Snap the Whip, and Soak-About where boys competed and losing always brought some sort of physical pain. A typically violent boys' game went by Rap Jacket in the South and Lickety-cut in the North, but both versions entailed boys facing each other and beating one another with beech poles or switches until one surrendered. All-boy games often involved the intense competition that marked male culture in the Gilded Age. Skipping rope was very popular for girls and there was a surprisingly wide variety of different skipping rope games. Winter and snow brought a variety of games to the colder climes including the ever-present snowball fight and sledding. Sledding took on new dimensions when the Flexible Flyer hit the market in 1889 with its steering bar, now standard in runner sleds, which allowed for greater maneuverability. Many of these games were handed from one generation of children to the next and were part of the folk culture that survived in spite of the commodification and industrialization of American life, while others were created by adults and presented in game books like Emma Gray's (1897) *Fun for the Household: A Book of Games*. Gray suggested a wide assortment of games that were variants of classic games or created by her. Many of Gray's games tested knowledge, like *Authors*, which tested children's knowledge of literature, or *Composition*, which tested their writing ability, while others were action-oriented like *Emperor, Running for the Cap*, and *Jig-ity Jig*.[10]

Men's Games

There were several games in the Victorian underworld that definitely were not for children, but instead were oriented toward adult men, many of whom were bachelors. Pool had long been a male favorite, and by the late nineteenth century pool halls littered working-class neighborhoods. Bowling was also just beginning to be adopted as a favorite male recreation in the 1890s. Saloons, largely all-male hangouts in the nineteenth century except for prostitutes, might carry a pool table or two, but cards were the principal recreation, besides drinking, with whist, rummy, and poker being the most popular games. Blood sports, such as rat baiting, where terriers were set upon rats, and cockfighting also continued to find audiences among the all-male culture in urban and rural areas.[11]

TOYS

The toy industry was well established in the United States from the 1830s through the Civil War and U.S. manufacturers were turning out tin, cast iron, wooden, automaton, and rubber toys in quantity. By 1850, New England was the center of U.S. toy making. Manufactured toys became a part of American life before the Civil War, but exploded in popularity in the burgeoning consumer culture of the industrialized Gilded Age. Macy's became the first department store to create a toy department in 1875. Montgomery Ward started to sell toys in its mail order catalog in 1877 and by 1895 devoted 13 pages to toys, not including sporting equipment. The 1900 U.S. Census listed 500 firms manufacturing toys, employing 4,000 workers, and making virtually every imaginable toy. While homemade toys continued to be popular, particularly among less affluent youth, mass-produced toys flooded American society in materials that hand producers who worked in paper and wood could only marvel at, like tin, cast iron, and India rubber. The sheer number and diversity of manufactured toys in the Gilded Age reached massive, modern proportions.[12]

Popular Toys

Tin, Iron, and Rubber Toys

These new materials revolutionized toy making. Tin toys were the first great leap forward in toy technology in the nineteenth century. The Philadelphia Tin Toy Manufactory (1838) churned out tin toys that were lacquered (called "japanned" in the nineteenth century) and highly colored. These toys were actually made not of pure tin but of very thin steel sheet plated with tin, which made it pliable but strong. There is evidence that tin toy making originated in the United States. Cast iron appeared in toy manufacturing in the 1870s and was primarily utilized by American toy makers. Cast iron bell toys became very popular and normally consisted of a platform or wagon with wheels that when rolled caused a figure on top of the platform to strike a bell. Cast iron mechanical banks were also in high demand in popular figures like Santa Claus, athletes, clowns, as well as caricatured Irish, Chinese, and African Americans. These banks sold for close to a dollar in the mid-1890s. Jerome Secor of Ives, Blakeslee, & Secor was credited with creating the first cast iron vehicle, a locomotive, in 1879 or 1880. Rubber also became an important toy material as well, and rubber animals of all types ($.20–$.40) and balls ($.04–$.14) were available by the mid-1890s.[13]

Clockwork, Steam, and Electric Toys

Mirroring the revolutions in transportation in the United States, artificial power sources were also developed to propel toys. Automaton toys actually had a long history in Europe among the wealthy. Clock-powered toys were the first to appear, and George W. Brown introduced the first American-made clockwork toy in 1856. Edward Ives of Ives, Blakeslee, & Secor invented a clockwork tin train with a working whistle in 1874 and it became a much copied and very popular toy. Clockwork dolls, bears, boats, horses, and a myriad of other items appeared, some of the best produced by Ives, Blakeslee, & Secor. Steam-powered toys that actually operated as small steam engines were also popular, though relatively expensive. William N. Weeden of Massachusetts, the most successful manufacturer of steam toys in the United States, made steam engines ($.20 for simple models to $2.50), trains ($3.50), steamboats ($2), and a working fire pumper ($5.50). Weeden entered the market rather late; his engine appeared in 1884 when he advertised in the *Youth's Companion*, but his company soon became the largest steam toy company. Other important steam toy makers were Eugene Beggs, A. Buckman, and J. A. Pierce. Steam-powered toys were in fact working steam engines that could be dangerous and often included attachments like a circular saw, turning lathe, grindstone, and pulley. Electric toys made their debut in the United States in 1883, introduced by the Novelty Electric Company of Philadelphia when it produced an electric train. Battery powered, these electric toys were novelties and would not become popular until the twentieth century.[14]

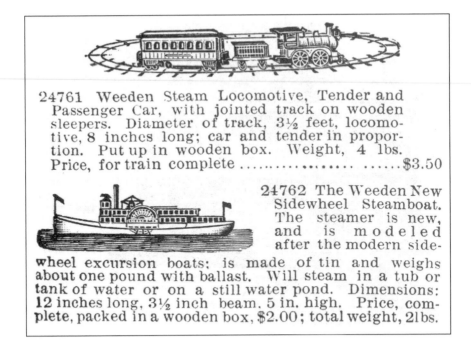

24761 Weeden Steam Locomotive, Tender and Passenger Car, with jointed track on wooden sleepers. Diameter of track, 3½ feet, locomotive, 8 inches long; car and tender in proportion. Put up in wooden box. Weight, 4 lbs. Price, for train complete $3.50

24762 The Weeden New Sidewheel Steamboat. The steamer is new, and is modeled after the modern sidewheel excursion boats; is made of tin and weighs about one pound with ballast. Will steam in a tub or tank of water or on a still water pond. Dimensions: 12 inches long, 3½ inch beam, 5 in. high. Price, complete, packed in a wooden box, $2.00; total weight, 2 lbs.

An advertisement for a toy train and boat from the 1895 *Montgomery Ward Catalogue.*

Crandall's Building Blocks

Charles M. Crandall invented what, according to contemporaries, became a ubiquitous toy in Gilded Age nurseries, Crandall's Building Blocks. Crandall's ingenious interlocking tongue-and-groove blocks were incredibly popular and he introduced an entire series of block sets, most of them painted or covered in ornate chromolithographed paper. Many manufacturers produced alphabet blocks which were a favorite of the education-minded Victorian middle class. Blocks varied widely in price; a dozen plain blocks might sell for $.20 while more elaborate blocks with chromolithographed pictures would go for $.90.[15]

Noisemakers

Noisemaker toys also enjoyed tremendous popularity. In addition to bell toys there were buzzers, a piece of wood or paper strung between a cord that spun and whirred as the strings were pulled and loosened; snappers, a candy wrapped with a paper that snapped loudly when opened; rattletraps, a handle attached to wooden springs that snapped as it was swung in a circle; and whirlers, a string fastened to a stick on one end and a tin can on the other. These noisemakers could be made by children from common materials but also came in factory-manufactured forms. A wide variety of musical instruments were also favorites among American children, particularly bugles, trumpets, and drums. Montgomery Ward sold tin trumpets for as little as $.05 and drums for $.25 in 1895.[16]

Shooting Toys

A wide variety of shooting toys were also popular among American youth in the Gilded Age. All across America boys and girls made their own pea shooters and sling shots, firing all sorts of missiles much to the dismay of animals, teachers, and adults. Homemade and factory-produced bows and arrows were also favored by youth. Toy guns enjoyed high popularity in the Gilded Age, ranging from cork guns to dart guns to air rifles. The Daisy BB gun appeared in 1888 and sold 86,000 rifles; business doubled in 1889. The Daisy air rifle sold for only $.75 in 1895 and continues to be a favorite among young people.[17]

Dolls and Toy Soldiers

Dolls and toy soldiers were also popular among girls and boys, respectively, since toys mirrored the gender division of the Gilded Age. Dolls were made in a wide variety of materials: china, Parian (a variation of china), bisque (unglazed ceramic), rubber, wax, cardboard, papers, and composition (a mixture of plaster of Paris, sawdust, bran, and glue). The 1895 *Montgomery Ward Catalogue* carried a wide variety of dolls that sold for $.20 for paper dolls to $.80 for a standard bisque head doll to $3.50 for the most ornate models. Doll houses and a wide variety of doll clothing, including a doll corset, appeared in the mail order catalog. The most ornate doll houses were made of wood and had china dinner services, imitation food, mantle clocks, tea services, lamps, globes, and all the furniture a prosperous middle-class home would contain. Toy soldiers also came in a wide variety of mediums, first in paper and cardboard, later in wood, and then lead. Cardboard, paper, and wood soldiers were the most popular in the Gilded Age—metal soldiers gained in popularity only in the early twentieth century. Like most toys, the soldiers were very brightly colored. Milton Bradley and Parker Brothers both started making paper soldiers near the turn of the century, and Parker Brothers even employed the famous illustrator Maxfield Parrish, known for his brilliant coloring, to produce its soldiers (see Chapters 3, 12). Wooden soldiers were also popular, though they lacked the detail of their paper counterparts, and sold for $.20 to $.40 per set in the mid-1890s.[18]

Jointed Dolls, Dressed.

25285 Finest bisque heads. solid eyes, flowing hair, teeth, shoes and stockings. Superior quality dolls. Dress made of cotton stuff, trimmed, silk bonnet. Price..................... **$0.50**

25287 Same description; dress of muslin and lace, bonnet trimmed with ribbon. Price...... **1.00**

25288 Same description, dress and bonnet of changeable silk trimmed with ribbons. Price.. **1.15**

25289 Same description: dress, finest muslin. woven through with ribbons. Full silk bonnet with silk strings and balls. Price.............. **1.25**

25290 Same description; dress of fine woolen goods, trimmed with silk ribbons or embroidered. Some hair lace hats, some bonnets. Price........ **2.00**

25291 Same description; dress, fine cashmere trimmed with silk and lace. Full silk bonnet, lace trimmed. Price...... .... **2.25**

25292 Same description; dress, full winter costume of fine woolen goods, trimmed with plush and ribbons. Bonnet to match. Price......... **3 50**

An advertisement for dolls from the 1895 *Montgomery Ward Catalogue.*

Miscellaneous Toys

A host of other toys were popular among children in the Gilded Age. Tops ($.35–$.80), rolling hoops, Jack-in-the-Boxes ($.10–$.25), rocking horses ($.90–$2.25), and wagons ($.75–$7.50) were all very well-liked. Kitchen items, including small working stoves ($.50), irons ($.10–$.35), china and silver teas sets ($.50–$.85), and tin kitchen sets ($.10–$.65) remained widely available favorites. And, many Gilded Age nurseries contained a Noah's Ark play set which sold for $1.75 for the ark and a dozen animals in 1895.[19]

Visual Toys

A final important category was visual toys, which gained widespread popularity for children in the late nineteenth century. There were a number of different optical toys dating back to the early part of the nineteenth century. The Thamotrope, Phenakistoscope, Praxiniscope, Kaleidoscope, and Chromatrope all made their appearance, but the two most influential in the United States were the Zoetrope, introduced by Milton Bradley in 1867, and the Magic Lantern. The Zoetrope was a metal drum pierced by a series of thin slots. A paper strip fit inside the drum and when the drum was spun the figures on the paper strip appeared to move. The Magic Lantern, or Polyopticon, was also very popular. Magic Lanterns worked like overhead projectors, projecting an image from a small slide on the wall using a lamp. Magic Lanterns ($.85–$8) varied in size, projecting pictures from two to almost four feet, and using colored slides from 12 to 4 inches wide, which cost anywhere from $.35 to $7.20 per dozen depending on size and color.[20]

HOBBIES

Although hobbies might be viewed as something that is the opposite of work by the participant, in fact, hobbies often replicate and reinforce the values of the workplace. People in the Gilded Age, like today, enjoyed hobbies because they both compensated for what was missing from their work and celebrated the values of work in the capitalist labor force. Hobbies provided people with the freedom from the coercion of the workplace, where they could determine the tempo and conditions of their activities and completely control what they produced. Hobbies also allowed people to use the skills they had developed at work in productive leisure that they found pleasurable. Hobbies operated as a bridge between the separation of work and leisure that occurred with the emergence of industrial capitalism in the Gilded Age. In an era when middle-class Americans were so concerned about appropriate leisure, hobbies were an important facet of "home-based leisure." It was no accident that before roughly 1880 the term "hobby" had a negative connotation while after that date positive descriptions of the restorative qualities of hobbies appeared throughout the culture. Hobbies, however, not only gave Gilded Age hobbyists a taste of preindustrial labor but also brought the values of the work ethic and market economy into the home.[21]

Collecting

Hobbies can be roughly divided into two categories, collecting and crafts. Collecting was primarily focused on getting a good "deal," by using superior knowledge of the product to find bargains that were worth much more. Collecting relied heavily on the application of knowledge and an acquired expertise, but always in the context of hunting for the hidden bargain. Hunting metaphors were often used by collectors in the Gilded Age. What separated men's collecting from women's collecting was that men historically have collected items that were economically valuable. Men tended to evaluate the monetary worth of their collections. Women, on the other hand, collected differently. They were inclined to accumulate items for sentimental value that were neither ignored nor deprecated by men and somewhat distant from the market values so central to much of male collecting. First, we shall examine collecting hobbies that were considered to have monetary value and then those collections that had purely sentimental and aesthetic worth.[22]

Stamp Collecting

Stamp collecting offers a particularly good example of these themes as hobbyists hunted, traded, and organized rare stamps into collections of monetary value. Certainly, the organization, rationality, competitiveness, and economic motivations of the market economy and workplace are echoed in this hobby. Stamp collecting had been a fad in the 1860s, and though its intense popularity dimmed, it was a well-established hobby by the start of the 1870s. Male hobbyists transformed the nature of stamp collecting by the 1880s. Whereas children and women were among the first stamp collectors, after the 1860s the hobby became dominated by men. Ultimately, what separated the later phase of stamp collecting were attempts to "scientifically" classify and organize stamps into sets. Stamp collectors even coined a "scientific" term for their hobby, philately. Serious philatelists were collectors who appreciated the market value and authenticity of their stamps rather than the aesthetics of the album. While women stamp collectors like Eva Earl promoted women's participation in stamp collecting, the fact that the hobby embraced a market model worked to keep many women out of it. Earl, for example, did not collect in the same manner as men, and admitted cleaning and mending stamps in her collection, which were major offenses to the dominant male notions of scientific authenticity in philately. The identification and organization of the stamps was vital to the dominant philatelist culture of the Gilded Age, but these appeals to scientific collecting did not stop young people, particularly boys, from engaging in this popular hobby as they saw fit.[23]

Manuscript and Coin Collecting

Other popular collecting hobbies in the Gilded Age were much like stamps in their focus on scientific collecting and male domination. Book collectors sought rare manuscripts and compiled collections where the hunt and economic value were stressed. Coin collecting, called numismatics, was another popular hobby. The first annual convention of the American Numismatic Association occurred in 1891 in Chicago.

Antique Collecting

Antique collecting also became quite trendy among Americans in the Gilded Age, but with major differences from the previously mentioned hobbies. Unlike the previous hobbies, large numbers of women engaged in antique collecting alongside men. Collectors scoured the countryside for colonial furniture starting roughly in 1876, as some Americans rejected the dominant, highly ornamented Victorian styles in preference for the simpler colonial styles. By the 1880s furniture manufacturers were making colonial reproductions, but it was still cheaper to search for bargains in the countryside. The idea that there was value in the old dresser or table stowed away in the barn was completely foreign to most farm folk, so there were bargains to be found by ambitious antique hunters. The Columbian Exposition in 1893 generated even more interest with its prominent display of American handicrafts. Antique collecting grew to the point that by mid-decade the first antique dealer devoted to Americana was established in Wethersfield, Connecticut. Much of this collecting was aimed at fine handcrafted furniture, but some collectors, particularly Alexander Drake, also pioneered collecting everyday items like bottles and bird cages. Antique collecting even then had a reputation of fleecing the unwitting, erratic markets, and a somewhat casual acceptance of deceit.[24]

Photograph Collecting

Another Gilded Age hobby that grew to be quite popular was that of collecting photographs, but unlike the aforementioned hobbies this one had little monetary worth. Families commonly collected photographs into books known as cartes-de-visite albums until the mid-1880s when scrapbooks eclipsed them in popularity. Cartes-de-visite albums served as repositories and celebrations of the photographic histories of the family and were normally extremely ornate albums bound in leather, velvet, or inlaid wood. Cartes, small photographs roughly 2⅛ by 3½ inches, were either taken by the family or purchased by the family and placed in the albums. Victorian families prominently displayed cartes-de-visite albums in their parlors. Although individual cartes were affordable, roughly $.10 each, amassing a significant album could be costly. Studio photographers produced cartes and they were the major source of photographs for American families until the introduction of roll film in 1885. Photography emerged full-force in Victorian lives with George Eastman's (1854–1932) invention of the first roll-film camera in 1888, the Kodak. In 1900, Eastman introduced the simplest and cheapest camera yet produced, the Brownie, which sold for $1. Kodak marketed the camera for children and it was named after the Brownie illustrations of Palmer Cox. By 1890 amateur photographers chronicled the photographic history of their families and could now capture action scenes, daily life, and special events quite easily. Unlike other collecting hobbies, acquiring photographs was transformed from collecting to a craft that required skill and the active production of the photographs. Much less formal scrapbooks quickly displaced the formal, expensive cartes-de-visite albums.[25] Regardless of the form, collecting family photographs in albums became a prominent hobby in the Gilded Age, permanently entering American homes.

Button Collecting

Button collecting was a female hobby throughout the Gilded Age. Women primarily collected buttons for sentimental and aesthetic reasons, often making long "charm strings" of 999 buttons. The man the young woman was to marry was to provide the thousandth button. Although buttons might be organized by material, size, and color, there were not the claims of scientific rigor that men brought to their collections. Not until 1939 did books on button collecting begin to transform it into a market-driven hobby and bring men into the field.[26]

Youth Collecting

Young people are natural collectors, going through a collecting phase around the age of ten, and Gilded Age youth were no exception. Young people collected items similar to adults though in much more haphazard ways and often separate from the concerns of adult culture. Boys and girls often mimicked the values of adults, but they also had their own culture that encouraged the collection of bird eggs, cigar tags, wildflowers, marbles, coins, and chromolithographed advertising trade cards. There were gender differences. Although there was indeed collecting that attracted both sexes, cigar tags for example, many collectibles attracted primarily boys or girls. Girls, for example, were the primary collectors of chromolithographed (chromo) advertising trade cards which became a fad in the 1880s, peaked about 1890, and declined by 1900 (see Chapter 3). These trade cards were primarily advertisements for the myriad of new products introduced into the marketplace during the Gilded Age, but it was the novelty of unprecedented vibrant colors created by the chromolithography process that attracted collectors. Many girl hobbyists were also avid collectors of ornate, chromo art from greeting cards, pasting the cut-outs into scrapbooks. Boys, on the other hand, were more inclined to collect marbles or bird eggs. Young Theodore Roosevelt represented boys' interest in collecting natural history specimens in his Roosevelt Museum of Natural History that was housed in his bedroom until the chambermaid forced its removal to the back hall. Theodore collected all kinds of living and dead animals for his museum, much to the dismay of most of his family members, in the name of science. Like adult male collectors he was interested in "the methodical arrangement of classifications, and the patient indexing" and was a skilled taxidermist. Although Theodore Roosevelt was probably not a representative figure even in his youth, his fascination with collecting things from the natural world was typical of boys in the Gilded Age.[27]

Craft Hobbies

Crafts were somewhat different than collecting, serving to reinforce the work ethic rather than simply mirroring the values of the marketplace and the aesthetic drive to create a visually stimulating album. As male productive labor was increasingly separated from the home, many men turned toward crafts. Middle-class women increasingly found that functions that had previously been a necessity for the family, like sewing skills, were no longer needed in the same way and they were transformed into crafts. Crafting was not, and is not, like work in several important ways—the hobbyist controls the production, rarely does the craft for economic support, and takes pleasure in it.

Sewing and Quilting

Sewing offered women a variety of hobbies. Certainly, for large groups of Gilded Age women sewing was a necessity that was needed for the active support of the family, but for middle- and upper-class Americans the mechanization of the process, with the introduction of the sewing machine, patterns, and ready-made clothing, radically altered sewing. For genteel women sewing did become more like a craft that was primarily decorative and did not generally support the family economically. Sewing circles were very popular for women and gave them the opportunity to socialize while still doing "work." Quilting was one of the sewing activities that was transformed from a necessary task for the formation of a household to a hobby. In the 1880s a patchwork quilt became the going fad and women spent hours hunting for new silk patches for their quilts. I am not implying that sewing and quilting were easy, labor-free undertakings, but like all hobbies the labor was under the control of the women; it did not generally support their families economically, and was done mainly for aesthetic reasons.[28]

Embroidery to Needlework

The transformation of sewing from household necessity to hobby is starkly illustrated by the movement from embroidery to needlework. Embroidery had been an elite pastime for several centuries, requiring skill and creativity to perform. As the middle class formed in the late eighteenth and early nineteenth centuries it co-opted and democratized gentry notions of refinement and gentility. Middle-class women adopted the gentry habit of embroidery, which was one of a variety of sewing practices referred to as fancywork. Developed in the early sixteenth century, embroidery consisted of a wide variety of complex stitches and patterns avidly collected by practitioners and displayed on samplers. Embroidery served the function of providing decoration for a home. Victorians loved embroidery and their well-known penchant for heavily decorated rooms led to the widespread use of embroidered items throughout homes in the Gilded Age. Industrialization, however, transformed embroidery from a decorative art to a hobby. German entrepreneurs developed pre-stamped patterns on cloth that were color coded to the thread, so that all women had to do was to stitch the pattern using the colors determined by the pattern's directions. These pre-made patterns went by the name "Berlinwork" or the phrase still commonly used today, "needlepoint." Needlepoint was far more like a hobby than a complex art because it was really quite simple; there was a pre-made pattern which required only one or two stitches (hence today's common term "cross stitch"). Unlike embroidery, needlepoint required little artistic or complex sewing skill to produce a relatively nice piece of work. In a world where decorative objects could be easily purchased for the home, needlepoint illustrated the transformation of embroidery into a hobby.[29]

Decorative Crafts

Victorian women were avid crafters as they sought to decorate their homes with handmade items. Craft books like Florence Hartley's 1859 *The Ladies' Hand Book of Fancy and Ornamental Work* and particularly *Godey's Lady's Book* described how to make a wide variety of craft projects— baskets, card receivers, plaster casts, hair ornaments, and coin purses— as well as woodburning, braiding, lace work, appliqué, tatting, netting, knitting, painting on glass and velvet, and arranging dried flowers, seeds, and shells. Cardboard was the preferred medium for women crafters in the Gilded Age, and they used it to make all types of containers that they covered with a wide variety of materials that included paint, decorative stitching, and vividly colored chromolithographed pictures. Indeed, decalcomanie, invented in 1864, provided pictures that could be directly applied to virtually any object, though vases were a particular favorite.

Boys' Crafts

Like almost everything in the Gilded Age, crafting was split along gender lines as well. For the most part women and girls were actively discouraged from using tools larger than a needle, paintbrush, or crafting knife; large tools were the province of boys and men. Boys in particular were encouraged to develop hobbies using tools, primarily, it seems, to keep them occupied in a useful, nondestructive activity. Boys' tool chests were sold with toys in the 1895 *Montgomery Ward Catalogue* for $.25 to $14. Unlike later periods, middle-class men did not participate in craft hobbies in large numbers. In an era of explosive economic activity, where status and economic security could be tenuous, middle-class men might have been reluctant to participate in craft hobbies that appeared to be too close to working-class occupations.[30]

SPORTS

Sports exploded in popularity in the Gilded Age. As work and home became more separate, leisure activities became more important to Americans. Sporting events emerged as activities that particularly echoed existing values for men: individualism, aggressiveness, and competition. Beginning before the Civil War and continuing until the end of the century, sports began to pervade U.S. society: sports clubs developed, college athletics became big entertainment, baseball was professionalized and became widely popular, a host of new sports were invented, and the modern Olympic Games were revived in 1896. There were of course popular sports before the Gilded Age, like horse racing, harness racing, boxing, gymnastics, rowing, and baseball, but only in the Gilded Age did sports become a prominent part of commodified leisure culture. Modern sports were born in the Gilded Age, defined by athletic games played by skilled amateurs or professionals with clearly defined rules and with masses of spectators.[31]

Sport Culture

The foundations of the new sporting culture of the Gilded Age actually lay in a wave of physical fitness culture that swept through the country starting in the 1860s. The Young Men's Christian Association (YMCA) was the most influential institutional form of sports advocates and by 1894 there were 261 YMCA gyms across the country. Luther Gulick helped to transform the focus of the YMCA away from exercise, like gymnastics, to physical development within the context of competitive games. But central to Gulick's and the YMCA's mission was the belief that the union of directed athletics under Christian patronage would create sound Christian, middle-class manhood. Gulick and other proponents of muscular Christianity, however, helped to lay the foundation for massive, popular professional sports by instilling the ethic of competition and physical culture (see Chapter 2). The craze for physical culture and the new emphasis put on "manly" sport had unintended consequences. This philosophy generated intense interest in competitive sports and when combined with a new leisure culture in urban America, created a situation ripe for the professionalization of sports.[32]

Professional Sports

Baseball

The most important national sport to emerge on the professional level was baseball, setting a standard for organization and play that other professional sports would follow in the twentieth century. Baseball was quickly becoming America's game from the 1840s to the 1860s, well before the aggressive marketing efforts of later generations of baseball advocates. In 1846, Walt Whitman wrote, "I see great things in baseball. It's our game—the American game. It will take our people out-of-doors, fills them with oxygen, give them a larger physical stoicism. Tend to relieve us from being a nervous, dyspeptic set. Repair these losses, and be a blessing to us."

Baseball evolved out of two games brought to North America by English colonists, cricket and the children's game of rounders. Rounders soon evolved into numerous versions of the children's stick-and-ball game called "old cat, one old cat, two old cat, three old cat, goal ball, town ball, barn ball, sting ball, soak ball, stick ball, burn ball, round ball, base, and Base Ball." In 1845, 28 young men organized the New York Knickerbocker Base Ball Club, encouraged by member Alexander Joy Cartwright, a 25-year-old shipping clerk. The Knickerbocker Club and other New York clubs created the modern variation of baseball with a diamond-shaped field, three strikes, an umpire, and nine players on each side. Before the 1870s this type of amateur baseball club dominated the sport. The game continued to evolve with the first base stolen in 1863 and the first curve ball thrown in 1867. The portability of the game meant that Civil War soldiers could play virtually anywhere and its popularity spread during the war. Young and old played baseball all over the country in backyards and vacant city lots, at family gatherings, picnics, and during school recess. Women played the game in spite of disapproval. Young women at Vassar in 1866 and Smith in 1880 organized baseball clubs, but administrative, faculty, and parental pressure forced both to disband because the game was considered too violent for women. Traveling women's teams toured the country, though, and were popular attractions.[33]

Professional players who traveled from city to city for pay became very common by the late 1860s when the Cincinnati Red Stockings, the first all-professional team, organized in 1869 by manager Harry Wright. Financed by a group of investors, Wright put together a group of professional ball players and openly paid them salaries. His well-coached team won all 65 games in 1869 and did not lose a game until half-way through the next season. With their loss the Cincinnati investors withdrew their support and the team disbanded. But in a move that has since become common in professional sports, Harry Wright took his team east to become the Boston Red Stockings. Wright prophesied "Baseball is business now," and he was correct.[34] In 1871 the National Association of Professional Base Ball Players was formed, consisting of nine teams very loosely organized. The National Association was soon eclipsed in 1876 by a cartel of wealthy owners led by William Hulbert. Hulbert spearheaded the organization of the National League of Professional Base Ball Clubs which took virtually total control of the business of professional baseball. Owners tried to attract refined spectators, forbidding alcohol and gambling in the parks and charging a hefty $.50 admittance. The National League lost its monopoly when the American Base Ball Association was formed in 1882. The American Association sold liquor at its ball parks, charged only a quarter for tickets, and generally attracted larger, rowdier crowds than its counterpart.

Baseball was a microcosm of the same forces rending at American society in the Gilded Age. Baseball players, like most wage workers in the Gilded Age, worked in a monopolistic industry where owners controlled the business with an iron fist. Players could be traded, fined, their behavior controlled, and they had no choice of who they played for because of the reserve clause. The reserve clause, which was standard in player contracts, basically gave teams rights to a player unless they decided to release him or trade him to another team. In 1885 the Brotherhood of Professional Base Ball Players, formed and led by Columbia Law School graduate and professional baseball player John Montgomery Ward, fought against the National League's reserve clause and formed their own Player's League. The Player's League gained the support of the American Federation of Labor and its charismatic leader Samuel Gompers. The competition of three professional leagues—the National

League, American Association, and Player's League—was too much and caused the Player's League and American Association to fail. A. G. Spaulding, the dominant figure in the National League and owner of Spaulding Sporting Goods, triumphantly led the National League's charge to absorb the American Association's best teams, bringing their total to 12 teams, and retaining the reserve clause. The power of owners to absolutely control professional baseball remained intact and it remained a monopoly that would continue to strong-arm players for decades to come.

The treatment of African Americans in baseball also echoed the situation of blacks in American society in the Gilded Age. There were successful black professionals playing for a wide variety of teams up until roughly 1887. Mounting hostility from white players who felt blacks should not play with whites caused National League owners to pledge not to hire more black players. Within a short time there were virtually no black athletes playing in the National League. African Americans continued to play baseball in a variety of all-black teams, but they were kept out of Major League Baseball until the mid-twentieth century.

The modern form of Major League Baseball finally coalesced in 1903 with the combination of the American League with the National League. In 1893, Byron Bancroft "Ban" Johnson purchased a minor league on the West Coast and transformed it into a very lucrative operation. In 1899 he renamed the league the American League and in 1900 he moved aggressively into the National League's eastern market. Johnson created four new teams in Eastern cities when the National League dropped four teams. Johnson lured 111 National League players to the American League and by 1902 had a league that rivaled the National League in popularity and quality of baseball. In 1903 the two leagues joined and the first World Series was played. Baseball became a mass spectator sport because of the widespread popularity of athletic culture. In a culture that highly prized athletic prowess, who would not want to see the very best perform? Baseball generated massive amounts of money very early— roughly $10 million per year by the 1880s (see Chapter 11). Baseball pioneered professional sports, setting the pattern of massive revenues, business organization, and control of players that sports like football and basketball would follow decades later.[35]

Boxing

Boxing was the other American athletic contest that grew to the level of a mass sport during the Gilded Age, capitalizing on the growing athletic culture. For decades bare-knuckle prize fighting had been lodged in the urban underworld, controlled by gamblers and shadowy promoters. Richard Kyle Fox, the flamboyant owner of the *National Police Gazette*, helped to resurrect interest in boxing through massive coverage in his periodical beginning in 1880 (see Chapter 8). Fox also did great service to the sport by helping to break its underworld connections by promoting honest bouts with referees. Different weight classes and title belts were just two innovations Fox was responsible for introducing to the sport. The popularity of boxing was definitely aided by the introduction of boxing gloves and the renewed interest of middle- and upper-class men in the "strenuous life" that Theodore Roosevelt promoted. Men like Roosevelt made a fine distinction between bare-knuckle prize fighting, which they saw as brutal and degrading, and the science of boxing which was performed with boxing gloves under the Marquis de Queensberry Rules. In addition to Roosevelt, who boxed in the White House, a wide variety of prominent men promoted boxing at the end of the century: millionaires William K. Vanderbilt and Leonard W. Jerome, Senator Roscoe Conkling, Reverend Henry Ward Beecher, and psychologist G. Stanley Hall. The strength and influence of the sporting culture in the Gilded Age allowed middle- and upper-class men to adopt boxing as a positive sport when just a few decades earlier it had been the province of hustlers, gamblers, and thieves.

Boxing would begin to enter the mainstream of mass sports by the 1890s. In spite of elite proponents of boxing, professional boxing was in fact dominated largely by working-class, Irish-American men. Professional boxing proved to be a method that could secure social mobility for young Irish men, just as it would be for Jews, African Americans, and Latin Americans in the twentieth century. Prize fighting was illegal in most states until the 1890s when the proliferation of boxing clubs and the acceptance of the Marquis de Queensberry rules (gloves, limited three-minute rounds, no wrestling holds, and 10-second rounds) led first to the legalization of bouts in New Orleans. Boxing legend John L. Sullivan represented the Irish-American tough who climbed out of poverty through boxing. Sullivan did fight several highly publicized bare-knuckle contests, but he primarily promoted gloved fights under the Marquis de Queensberry rules. A fighter of Sullivan's ability promoting gloved fights and the new rules helped to establish boxing as a more respected sport. This transformation culminated in the first gloved championship bout under Queensberry rules in 1892, as Sullivan lost to challenger "Gentleman Jim" Corbett for a $50,000 purse in New Orleans. Boxing had moved from the shadowy sporting underworld and the bachelor subculture into a mainstream sport and entertainment.[36]

Cycling

Professional cycling grew out of the enormous popularity of bicycling in the 1890s, and the United States produced several racers that had a major impact on the international racing scene. In 1892 the United States joined with Denmark, the Netherlands, Canada, Belgium, France, Great

Britain, and Germany to form the International Cyclist Association, which became the Union Cycliste Internationale in 1900. Professional racing became so popular in the United States that the National Cycling Association formed in 1898 to regulate the U.S. professional racing circuit. The circuit ran in the United States from May through November and riders mainly raced on banked wooden tracks known as velodromes. Velodromes were typically 333.3 yards so that three laps equaled 1,000 yards, though there were some that varied in length from 200 to 500 yards. By 1895 there were 100 velodromes in the country and several famous venues ran races, such as Madison Square Garden. By 1896, Madison Square Garden commonly sold out all its races. The sport's popularity caused the Garden to experiment with races and it began staging six-day races in 1896. In the age before the safety bicycle George Hendie set the half-mile world record in 1886 and won five straight national championships. Other famous riders included August Zimmerman, who would draw crowds of 30,000 people to watch him race, and Marshall "Major" Taylor, who won several world titles. Taylor set the track record at the famous Newby Oval velodrome in Indianapolis, Indiana, when he was only 15 years old and then was promptly banned from the track because he was African American. After turning pro, Taylor won the national sprint championships in 1898, 1899, and 1900. Taylor went on to become an internationally recognized cyclist and a fairly wealthy athlete in spite of the racism he encountered in the United States.[37]

Amateur Sports

Professional sports benefited from the athletic culture of the Gilded Age, but they were not the only manifestation of this ethos. Amateur sports proliferated tremendously in the clubs of the wealthy, on city vacant lots and town fields, schools, churches, and universities. The valorization of professional athletes would never have reached such a high level if there were not millions of boys and men, girls and women also playing those sports. The sporting culture emerged as part of the growing leisure culture of the United States during the Gilded Age.

Elite Athletic Clubs

Athletics clubs flourished in the United States by the 1850s, and were part of a much larger movement of American men into clubs and fraternal organizations in the nineteenth century. Clubs gave men a sense of belonging and camaraderie in an era of tremendous geographical mobility, urbanization, immigration, and general upheaval and change. Clubs re-created the tight-knit communities of the colonial era in an age that was increasingly anonymous and urban. Wealthy men began to organize sporting clubs in the 1850s as the influence of the elite English sporting movement made its way across the Atlantic. Track and field, football, rowing, cycling, cricket, yachting, lawn tennis, golf, and croquet appeared in hundreds of clubs across the country. New York's elites took the lead in the sporting culture, forming the New York Yacht Club in 1844. The New York Athletic Club (NYAC) was created in 1866 followed soon by other New York clubs like the Staten Island, American, Manhattan, Pastime, University, and Crescent clubs. The NYAC constructed the first cinder track in the United States in the 1870s and promoted national amateur contests in track and field, boxing, swimming, and wrestling. This New York club model spread quickly around the country—there were 150 elite city clubs in 1883. Cities like Baltimore, Chicago, Detroit, St. Louis, New Orleans, Boston, and San Francisco established clubs, some of which rivaled the original New York clubs. The Chicago club built one of the most elaborate and expensive clubhouses of the Gilded Age, costing almost $1 million and standing nine stories tall. The creation of the amateur ideal was exclusionary, celebrating the amateur and condemning those who took pay for sports. Sports became a method by which the rich could show their status to each other and provide vivid displays of conspicuous consumption. Advocates of the amateur ideal derided working-class athletes who accepted pay in athletics, such as was the case in baseball. To maintain the purity of the amateur ethic and govern the athletic contests sponsored by the clubs, elites created the National Association of Amateur Athletes of America (1879) and later the Amateur Athletic Union (1888).

Golf

Elite athletic clubs also brought other sports into vogue in the Gilded Age, especially golf, tennis, and croquet. Victorian women played all three of these new sports. Golf made its way to the United States from Great Britain in 1887 when Scottish émigré John Reid established the St. Andrews Club in Yonkers, New York, the oldest surviving golf club in the nation. The game caught on quickly with the wealthy throughout the United States. Millionaire William K. Vanderbilt hired famous Scottish golfer Willie Dunn to build Shinnecock Hills Golf Club in 1891. Located in Southampton, New York, the first professionally designed golf course in the country was crowned with a magnificent clubhouse designed by the famous architect Stanford White. In 1894 the United States Golf Association (USGA) was founded, going briefly by the name Amateur Golf Association before switching to USGA, to regulate rules and create sanctioned tournaments. In 1895 the United States Open and the United States Amateur were played for the first time. In the same year the U.S. Women's Amateur tournament began with Lucy Brown taking home the honors in a 13-woman field. Women proved to be avid golfers; Charles Dana Gibson's famous illustrations often had his "Gibson Girls" on the links (see Chapter 12). The universities and colleges of the elite also took up the game and the first national collegiate champion, Louis Bayard, Jr., was crowned in 1897. It was also in that year that the first U.S. periodical devoted to the sport, *Golf*, appeared in print.

Tennis

Tennis was another introduced sport that gained widespread popularity in the Gilded Age. Cricket and yachting clubs were the first places that introduced tennis to the American elite, and two lawn tennis courts were built in 1874 in Staten Island, New York, and Nahant, Massachusetts. By 1881 the United States National Lawn Tennis Association had formed in Newport, Rhode Island, and hosted the national tournament until 1913. Women moved quickly into tennis despite playing in "tennis outfits" that still included heavy dresses, bustles, and hats (see Chapter 5). Women's tennis tournaments appeared as early as 1881 and the first women's national championship tournament started in 1887. Like many lawn sports in this era, tennis spread quickly to the middle class and became a popular family sport. By the 1890s entire lawn tennis sets (including net, four rackets, ropes, mallet, pegs, and four balls) sold for as little as $7.67.[38]

Youth Sports

Sports became increasingly integrated into the world of young people in the Gilded Age (see Chapter 2). The growth of a strenuous ethic among men in the late nineteenth century encouraged adults to sponsor athletics for young people. The YMCA was a major source of the massive growth in youth athletics in the United States. YMCA programs encouraged football, swimming, lawn tennis, baseball, basketball, rowing, and volleyball. High school sports had achieved widespread acceptance and were already an important part of school life by the 1890s. Sporting culture became so popular that it sparked a playground movement in American cities in the first two decades of the twentieth century where cities built parks to organize and control athletics for young people. In short, there was a general explosion of athletics among all ages of young people in the Gilded Age.[39]

Collegiate Athletics

College sports had an even higher profile and generated massive team loyalty as well as revenues. College administrators were taking control of the regulation, scheduling, and organization of sports by the 1890s. Collegiate sports were an important addition to college life in the Gilded Age, but they had not been before the Civil War. Rowing, baseball, and football were the most popular sports for men and were played in wide variations by the 1850s, while basketball emerged as the favorite women's sport after its invention in 1891. Rowing was perhaps the oldest collegiate sport, appearing in the elite colleges of the Northeast in the 1840s. The sport grew in popularity after the 1852 Harvard-Yale regatta. Rowing contests became a staple, particularly in the elite colleges. Baseball was also quite popular; the first collegiate contest took place in 1859 when Amherst played Williams. Track and field competitions also appeared in the 1870s and 1880s. But by far, the most popular collegiate sport was football.[40]

Football was popular at both the high school and college levels, and became so prominent that it was one of the largest money-making sources for colleges by the 1890s. Yale's football program generated $100,000 per year by the turn of the century, which was more than the university spent on its programs in law or medicine. What had started as a club sport among young men in the 1870s had developed into a revenue-generating mass sport regulated and organized by university officials. The annual Thanksgiving Day game between the two best college teams, which were generally Yale and Princeton, drew close to 40,000 spectators by the early 1890s.

The game much more closely resembled rugby, with continuous action, before Walter Camp began to transform it with rule changes in 1880. Camp played for the Yale squad from 1876 through 1882, and until 1909 served as the advisor and coach of the team. While in college Camp represented Yale at the annual collegiate rules convention. In 1880 he suggested the scrimmage and in 1882 "the series of downs to gain a set number of yards (initially five), new styles of blocking (or interference, as it was known at the time), and tackles below the waist."[41] Camp's rule suggestions, adopted by the various collegiate football squads, changed the nature of the game. Camp's role at Yale continued from 1876 to 1909, a 33-year span in which Yale lost only 14 games. He went on to be the most dominant figure in collegiate football into the twentieth century, and was instrumental in further rule changes. This form of Gilded Age football might shock modern observers by its brutality and emphasis on sheer physical force as teams fought for five yards, when compared to the complex blocking schemes, passing routes, and zone blitzes of the modern game. Mass formations, like the flying wedge, were so brutal that the rules commission outlawed them, but the level of viciousness in Gilded Age football was shocking even to spectators of the day.[42]

Basketball and Volleyball

Other important sports developed out of the new team-oriented, competitive sports of the YMCA. Basketball began at the Springfield, Mas-

A group of football players at Miami University posing on the field. © Miami University Archives.

sachusetts, International Young Men's Christian Association Training School, a YMCA school that trained the organization's physical education directors. Student and part-time instructor James Naismith invented the game under the guidance of director Luther Gulick. Confronted with a challenging gymnastics class and in-between the warm-weather sports of football and baseball, Naismith developed this competitive team sport and it currently is played much the same way as his players did in Springfield in 1891. The game spread amazingly fast, first through the national web of YMCA branches but then much more widely into the schools, colleges, and universities. Basketball quickly became the most popular team sport among women, particularly on college campuses. Massive numbers of spectators soon crowded YMCA basketball games. The popularity of the sport spread to the sprawling Gilded Age cities. While football fields and baseball diamonds could be difficult to create in crowded residential areas, a basketball court could fit easily onto a corner lot or a small playground. Volleyball appeared a few years later in 1895. William G. Morgan invented volleyball at the Holyoke, Massachusetts, YMCA so that older men would have an indoor sport that was not as strenuous as basketball.[43]

Target Shooting

Target shooting also became a popular pastime among respectable people in the Gilded Age. The Civil War and the mass production of firearms spread the ethos of the gun even in the more settled regions of the eastern United States. Target shooting became popular and one contest between a U.S. team and an Irish team drew 10,000 spectators in 1874.[44]

Fishing

Another popular leisure activity for men and even women in the Gilded Age was fishing. Fishing was closely associated with the other outdoor activities, like hiking, hunting, and camping, that were so popular in the Gilded Age (see Chapter 11). Fishing was not relegated to rural areas, and became very widespread among urban, adult anglers in the East. And while children and women certainly could and did fish, men were the dominant force in organizing and defining this activity. Fishing clubs emerged in the 1830s spreading rod-and-reel fishing, and nearly 100 books on fishing appeared in the Gilded Age. The 1895 *Montgomery Ward Catalogue* carried over 11 pages of fishing rods, reels, lures, tackle boxes, live bait, nets, and a wide variety of fishing accessories that only the most serious of fishermen could have afforded.[45]

Two women and a child fishing, 1886. Courtesy of the Northeastern Nevada Historical Society.

CONCLUSION

The growth of the industrial economy helped to commodify leisure activities and mass-produce new hobby, sporting, and game equipment. More leisure time and money for many Americans helped to fundamentally transform the ways in which Americans experienced their time away from work. Middle-class Americans were on a "quest for suitable leisure" and when traditional folkways no longer sufficed, American industry was happy to produce new activities. In the new leisure culture Americans were more willing and able to purchase entertainment.[46]

8

Literature

BACKGROUND

Reading played a very prominent role in the lives of most Americans in the Gilded Age. Before the explosion of entertainment media in the twentieth century, reading material was the only mass medium and a vital leisure activity. Indeed, for the middle class the "right" literature became a mark of class status, producing a common experience, language, and values. Reading, however, was an important activity for virtually all Americans, and literacy rates reached 93 percent for men and 91 percent for women among native-born whites by 1860.[1]

There was also a much wider selection of reading material and greater availability. The print industry underwent changes that revolutionized print culture through standardization of production, increased efficiency, and large bureaucratic structures, which produced a mass market. While the first half of the nineteenth century had been characterized by a scarcity of published reading material, the second half of the century witnessed a massive growth in printed material. The expansion of distribution networks such as railroads, postal subscription, and mail order catalogs vastly increased the ability of all Americans to receive printed material. Accompanying this was an increase in the amount of printed matter available to Americans in the Gilded Age; the new books published grew by 300 percent between 1880 and 1900. There was a corresponding growth in newspapers, which experienced a 700 percent increase in circulation between 1870 and 1900. Magazine circulation also grew dramatically and stood at 65 million in 1900, which meant there were "three magazines for every four people" in the country. This growth of printed material is not as flashy as the introduction of radio or television, but its impact was just as marked in the United States.[2]

LIBRARIES

Circulating and Subscription Libraries

American readers had access to a wide variety of subscription libraries in the late eighteenth century through the mid-nineteenth century, where members paid a fee to belong to the library. Subscription libraries, also called social libraries by some historians, were susceptible to downturns in the economy because they relied entirely on member fees and donors. Circulating libraries were another form of library that appeared in the United States after the American Revolution, and though prominent for a time were largely gone by 1860. Booksellers primarily formed circulating libraries because of the prohibitive cost of books prior to the Civil War, and they rented books from their stores much like we rent videos or DVDs. Circulation libraries were never as prominent nor as important as subscription libraries, and even these began to lose their central place among the American reading public as mass production made books and magazines less expensive, which fundamentally changed the print culture of the nation. Opportunities for Americans to get books and magazines without purchasing them expanded in the Gilded Age.[3]

Sunday School and School

By the Gilded Age Americans also had access to books through school libraries, Sunday school libraries, and the growing public library establishment. Although several states passed laws creating school libraries—particularly Massachusetts, Rhode Island, Connecticut, Indiana, Ohio, and Illinois—their collections rarely amounted to much beyond textbooks, a few general works, and inspirational literature. Historians know much less about Sunday school libraries. Denominational presses like the Methodist Book Concern, the American Baptist Publication Society, the Presbyterian Board of Publication, and the Lutheran Publication Society, and organizations like the American Bible Society, the American Sunday School Union, and American Tract Society, however, printed such vast amounts of material that the Christian churches of the Gilded Age must have been well stocked. Individual Sunday school libraries could be quite large, such as St. Paul's Sunday school library in New York City, which issued library cards.

Interior view of the Denver Public Library's reading room, ca. 1900. ©
Denver Public Library, Western History Collection.

Public Libraries

The development of the free public library system was by far the most
important event for American readers in the Gilded Age. With the massive economic growth of the nation, intense immigration, and the he-
gemony of middle-class values regarding the importance of education
and reading, the movement to create free public libraries gained support.
As "foreigners" flooded American shores, the desire to educate and
"Americanize" these immigrants encouraged the founding of free public
lending libraries. Libraries came to be seen as essential arbiters of taste
and intellectual refinement as well as important forces of cultural assimilation. Because libraries became a nexus of so many cultural aspirations
they soon attracted the attention of philanthropic benefactors.

Peterborough, New Hampshire, was the first community to create a
permanent free public library in 1833 and a number of New England
towns followed its example in the 1840s. States passed laws allowing for
local taxes to be collected for the development and maintenance of public
libraries, led by the New England states. The founding of the Boston
Public Library in 1852, however, really sparked nationwide emulation

and started the public library movement. The Boston Public Library became the premier library in the country, boasting a staggering 575,000 volumes by the mid-1890s. The expansion of libraries was also given impetus by the founding of the American Library Association (ALA) in 1876, which provided professional librarians with organizational structure and institutional strength. Public library growth, however, was not evenly spread throughout the nation. For example, by 1900, 343 of Massachusetts' 346 townships had public libraries while in 1905 Oregon, Washington, and Idaho combined had only roughly 24 public libraries. Libraries were spreading, though, and in 1876 the federal Bureau of Education published a special report, "Public Libraries in the United States of America: Their History, Condition, and Management," which listed 3,647 public libraries that had at least 300 volumes. As this report shows, most public libraries early in the Gilded Age were quite small, but as time passed the collections grew. By 1903 the nation boasted roughly 1,000 public libraries that had at least 5,000 volumes. One of the most significant reasons for the great library growth in the early twentieth century was certainly millionaire Andrew Carnegie's philanthropic support. Carnegie (1835–1919) began donating money for libraries in the United States in 1889 and by the twentieth century had established the "Carnegie Formula," which required towns to support the library with public taxes. By 1920, Carnegie had given away $56 million to build 2,509 libraries. Not all working-class Americans, however, felt comfortable going to the local public library. Many unions created reading rooms where workers could find reading material free from the middle-class influence of public librarians.[4]

READING CIRCLES

There were also large numbers of book clubs in both urban and rural areas throughout the nineteenth century. The most prominent reading club was the Chautauqua Literary and Scientific Circle (1878) which promoted a home reading list that was designed to last four years. By 1891 there were 180,000 people participating in the Chautauqua book club. From 1878 to 1898, Americans established 10,000 local Chautauqua circles and 75 percent of these circles were in communities of between 500 and 3,500 people. Chautauqua sponsored a wide variety of reading programs such as the Chautauqua Library of English History, the Home College Series, and the Garnet Series. Catholics organized their own reading circles separate from the Protestant Chautauqua groups, and one of the most prominent was the Columbian Reading Union organized by *Catholic World* magazine in 1889. The Columbian Reading Union sent out lists of books and encouraged the formation of local Catholic reading circles. The Chautauqua Literary and Scientific Circle and Columbian Reading Union were two of the larger and more well-organized reading circles, but there were countless local reading groups.[5]

BOOK SELLERS

Gilded Age Americans could buy books from a number of sources: bookstores, subscriptions, door-to-door salesmen, railroad newsboys, and in rural mail order catalogs. Book stores were located primarily in urban areas and were not too plentiful; in 1859 there were 843 locales with bookstores and in 1914 there were only 801. As a result, dry goods stores, department stores, and drug stores often sold books. But one of the most successful methods for selling in the Gilded Age was through subscription. Traveling salesmen, known as book agents, sold subscriptions door-to-door, and when they had sold a certain number they would order the volumes from the publisher. Upon receiving the books the book agent would deliver them and collect payment. Hartford, Connecticut, became the center of the subscription book industry by the 1870s, boasting 12 subscription firms that employed an estimated 50,000 agents. The subscription book industry sold nearly $12 million dollars worth of merchandise annually by the 1890s. Book agents and subscription companies rarely handled fiction (though the works of Mark Twain sold very well by subscription), but instead concentrated on success literature, biography, one-volume encyclopedias, dictionaries, Bibles, devotional literature, history, as well as numerous how-to books on things like gardening, raising livestock, medical care, and correspondence.[6]

By the 1890s another very successful medium of book selling emerged, the rural mail order catalog. The 1895 *Montgomery Ward Catalogue* is a good example of the widespread access to books; it contained a remarkable 39 pages of books that could be ordered and delivered to virtually anywhere in the United States. Indeed, the catalog's Book Department was larger than the Harness and Saddlery Department which stood at 28 pages and not far from the 65 pages of the Hardware Department. It is telling that in a catalog marketed to farmers and other rural Americans books took up more space than harness and saddle equipment. The variety in the *Montgomery Ward Catalogue* was stunning, and included atlases, dictionaries, encyclopedias (30 volumes of the *Encyclopedia Britannica* sold for $48), etiquette manuals, novels, and a wide variety of nonfiction on birds, insects, farming, gardening, canoeing, camping, hunting, trapping, fishing, dogs, cattle, sheep, swine, bees, and poultry. The catalog also illustrated the diversity of taste among Gilded Age Americans. Genteel writers were plentiful, and the catalog carried a large set of Louisa May Alcott's works: *Little Men, Little Women, Eight Cousins,*

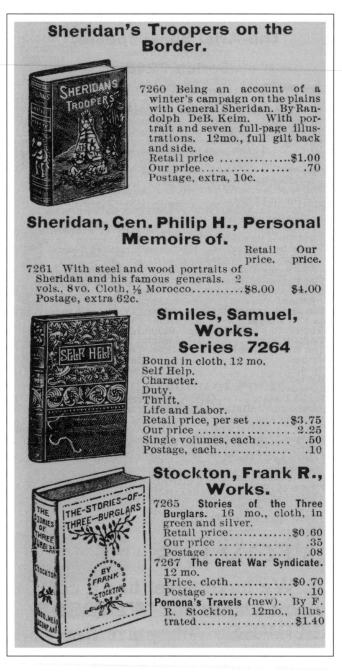

Sheridan's Troopers on the Border.

7260 Being an account of a winter's campaign on the plains with General Sheridan. By Randolph DeB. Keim. With portrait and seven full-page illustrations. 12mo., full gilt back and side.
Retail price $1.00
Our price................. .70
Postage, extra, 10c.

Sheridan, Gen. Philip H., Personal Memoirs of.

	Retail price.	Our price.
7261 With steel and wood portraits of Sheridan and his famous generals. 2 vols., 8vo. Cloth, ½ Morocco	$8.00	$4.00

Postage, extra 62c.

Smiles, Samuel, Works.
Series 7264

Bound in cloth, 12 mo.
Self Help.
Character.
Duty.
Thrift.
Life and Labor.
Retail price, per set $3.75
Our price 2.25
Single volumes, each....... .50
Postage, each.............. .10

Stockton, Frank R., Works.

7265 Stories of the Three Burglars. 16 mo., cloth, in green and silver.
Retail price.............$0.60
Our price .... .35
Postage .... .08
7267 The Great War Syndicate. 12 mo.
Price, cloth.............$0.70
Postage .... .10
Pomona's Travels (new). By F. R. Stockton, 12mo., illustrated....................$1.40

An advertisement for various books from the 1895 *Montgomery Ward Catalogue.*

Jack and Jill, Work, Moods, Life Letters and Journals, Hospital Sketches, Modern Mephistopheles, Rose in Bloom, Jo's Boys, Old Fashioned Girl, and *Under the Lilacs* ($.98 each). On the other end of the spectrum, Ward's offered at least 35 Horatio Alger novels in two different bindings ($.88 and $.52). A sample of the other books available for purchase were *The Arabian Nights;* Frances Hodgson Burnett's *Little Lord Fauntleroy,* the works of James G. Blaine, Emerson's *Essays,* Arthur Conan Doyle's *The White Company* and *Adventures of Sherlock Holmes,* several books by Rudyard Kipling, the works of the ancient Jewish historian Josephus, histories by contemporary historian Francis Parkman, Plutarch, Shakespeare's works, Mark Twain's entire writings, Sir Walter Scott, Frank R. Stockton, seven different Home Library series such as the Modern Library, Mayne Reid, E.D.E.N. Southworth, Dante's *Inferno,* Milton's *Paradise Lost,* Tennyson's *Idylls of the King,* and John Bunyan's *Pilgrim's Progress.*[7]

MIDDLE-CLASS READING

Middle-Class Culture of Reading

Henry Seidel Canby, editor of the *Saturday Review,* noted in his memoirs, *The Age of Confidence,* that reading held a central place in middle-class life in the 1890s:

And hence my reading memories are of absorption in a book, earless, eyeless, motionless for hours, a life between covers more real than outer experience, such an obsession in reading as I believe does not exist now. . . . It [reading] was an extension without break or casualty of our own lives, and flowed back freely to become a part of our mentality.

Canby claimed adults might read Macaulay, Tennyson, Byron, Longfellow, Whittier, Harriet Beecher Stowe, or bound volumes of *Illustrated America.* The typical children's library held bound volumes of *St. Nicholas Magazine* and *Toby Tyler;* works by Sir Walter Scott, Howard Pyle, Frank Stockton, Horatio Alger, Harry Castleman, and Oliver Optic; the Elsie books; *Little Lord Fauntleroy;* and perhaps volumes of the *Five Little Peppers.* As Canby suggested, reading held a special place for middle-class Americans in the Gilded Age that it would not have in the twentieth century. Reading illustrated the gentility and refinement of the reader, serving as a class marker that differentiated respectable folk from rough. Reading was the main form of home entertainment; it created self-improvement and fostered a common literary heritage that united middle-class readers. The incredible popularity of the card game *Authors* illustrated the middle-class emphasis on knowing the "right" authors (see

"Disgusted with life, she retired to the society of books," 1888. © Library of Congress.

Chapter 7). Middle-class families often engaged in literary activities together like playing *Authors*, word games, and reading aloud.[8]

Reading played such an important role in the lives of middle-class Americans that advice book authors became very popular in the Gilded Age. These reading advisors gained their credibility not due to their inherited or social position but instead through academic or professional credentials. These advice book authors suggested history, biography, geography, natural science, and travel literature as the best sources of self-improvement. The novel, however, was in the highest demand in the Gilded Age, dominating the bestseller list and library borrowing. When the reading advisors had to recommend novels they generally suggested the novels of "British writers Charlotte Brontë, Sir Walter Scott (especially his Waverley novels), William M. Thackeray, Dinah Muloch, George Eliot, and Anthony Trollope, and the American writers Louisa May Alcott, Nathaniel Hawthorne, and Harriet Beecher Stowe." There was widespread concern, particularly over what women and children were reading.[9]

Family House Magazines

The family house magazines were the predominant and most powerful disseminators of middle-class, genteel culture in the country from 1865 to 1893. Controlled by the Northeastern elite, *Harper's Monthly*, *Century*, *Scribner's*, and *Atlantic Monthly* set the tone for middle-class culture and values. The owners of these quality monthlies played a key role in their magazines' mission and content, promoting them as uplifting and civilizing agents. *Century*, which had the largest circulation among these quality monthly magazines, sold a peak of 250,000 copies per month by 1885, but like the other quality monthlies, competition from the mass-market magazines caused its circulation to fall to 125,000 by the late 1890s. *Century* editor Richard Gilder was a representative figure among the editors of the quality monthlies. Gilder and the other editors perceived of themselves as stewards of genteel culture. These editors believed they had to protect their readers from being shocked by literature in bad taste, even if they saw value in it. For example, Gilder was quite friendly with Walt Whitman and liked his poetry, even when Whitman's reputation was at its nadir, but refused to publish it for fear it would shock his readers. Gilder also brought in the best illustrators for *Century* and was so successful in attracting writing talent that by the mid-1880s publication in *Century* was a symbol of literary success. Under Gilder local color, historical fiction, and the new realism stories appeared by the 1880s. The quality monthlies carried the best authors of the day and serialized many of the most popular novels of the Gilded Age. English writers like Rudyard Kipling as well as American writers like Mark

Twain, William Dean Howells, Henry James, and Bret Harte all appeared in these quality periodicals. The editors of these magazines sought to improve the moral and artistic standards of their readers and promoted genteel culture as a cure for the overwhelming focus on success and materialism of the Gilded Age.[10]

Success Literature

Members of the lower middle class and those aspiring to middle-class status were also the primary audience of another type of Gilded Age literature, the success manual. In an age when success in the market economy was considered integral to self-made, middle-class manhood, the secrets of success were eagerly sought by young men hoping to "make it" in the tumultuous boom-and-bust economy of the age. Henry Seidel Canby's memoir, *The Age of Confidence*, again captured the allure and power of commerce when he recalled the business spirit of Wilmington, Delaware, in the 1890s:

Business, in the nineties, which was the dominating occupation and chief subject of thought in our community, had no conscious relation to economics . . . no doubts except the doubt of profits, no responsibility to the community except dividends and salaries, no object but money-making. And yet it was much more than an occupation—it was a philosophy, a morality, and an atmosphere.[11]

Success manuals responded to this drive for business success and fostered it. Praising rural values, Protestant morality, individualism, and good character, these success tracts sold in the millions. At least 144 different success manuals appeared between 1870 and 1914. Orison Swett Marden produced 30 pamphlets and books, and his *Pushing to the Front* went through 250 editions. Samuel Smiles' combined U.S. sales for *Self Help* (1860), *Character* (1871), *Thrift* (1875), and *Duty* (1880) were over 1 million. Other popular writers, like William Mathews and Wilbur Crafts, saw their books go through multiple editions very quickly and some of the tracts were sold by different publishing companies at the same time.[12]

Self-Made Ethic

Success writers offered a few simple solutions to the complexities of work in the Gilded Age. Men had to strive for self-reliance and independence, gaining success through their own efforts. Self-made business success was the ultimate goal and self-improvement was a necessity. Success writers relied on simple notions such as the idea that physical vigor equated to business success. Indeed, writers often conflated moral and physical power, and then equated this power with material success.

Orison Marden clearly connected physical vigor and success to true manhood in 1898:

As a rule physical vigor is the condition of a great character. The weak, chestless, calfless, forceless, languid, hesitating, vacillating young man may manage to live a respectable sort of life; but he seldom climbs, is not a leader, rarely gets at the head of anything important.[13]

Most success writers also firmly held that adversity was beneficial to a man's efforts to succeed and that poverty was often the best training ground. Industrialist Andrew Carnegie's famous *Gospel of Wealth* devoted an entire chapter to explaining the "Advantages of Poverty," and claimed that

poor boys . . . become the leaders in every branch of human action . . . the greatest and the best of our race have necessarily been nurtured in the bracing school of poverty—the only school capable of producing the supremely great, the genius.

Only a self-made man, strengthed through adversity, poverty, and manly physical force could truly succeed, or so the success writers claimed.[14]

Success writers provided a simplistic view that sound character and individual hard work could overcome any obstacle and achieve success, even as the world around them was transformed with startling rapidity. The fact that so many millions of these books sold and that the topic was so pervasive illustrates not the efficacy of their solution (which was simplistic and somewhat nostalgic in the burgeoning corporate capitalist economy) but the widespread concern among the middle class over the changing nature of the economy and society in general.

Literary Styles

Writers in the Gilded Age turned away from the sentimental style that had been so powerful in mid-century, and, perhaps shaped by the horrors of the Civil War, began to examine the world around them in a more "realistic" way. Local-color stories that focused on different U.S. regions, the new realism stories, and at the end of the century naturalism, all emerged to shape "high" literature in the Gilded Age.

Local Color

Local-color stories were in essence regional literature in the realist vein that explored the distinctive subcultures of the vast United States through short stories and novels. These efforts to preserve regional cultures were not surprising given the fact that a new mass, industrial culture was forming in this period, exerting a homogenizing force on American society. This regional literature had a realist focus but at times exhibited a streak of nostalgia and romanticism. Local-color fiction innovatively introduced local dialects into American fiction, extolled rural values, often set up a conflict between new ways of doing things and traditional methods, and celebrated the rural community. Bret Harte wrote about the trials of the gold rush camps in *The Luck of the Roaring Camp* (1868). Hamlin Garland became famous for his bleak descriptions of farm life in the upper Midwest in *Under the Lion's Paw* (1891). New England had dominated American writing before the Civil War and continued to produce a number of regional writers. Perhaps the best was Sarah Orne Jewett, who wrote about her native Maine in stories like "A Marsh Island" (1885), "The Country of Pointed Firs" (1896), and "The Foreigner" (1900), which appeared in the quality monthlies, particularly *Atlantic Monthly*. The South had a number of local-color authors: Georgia's Joel Chandler Harris gained fame with his Uncle Remus short stories that appeared in *Century* and *Scribner's Monthly* in the 1880s. Kate Chopin also gained recognition for her writing about her home state of Louisiana in works like the collection of short stories *Bayou Folk* (1894). Mark Twain was a dominant force in the realist movement and in local-color stories with his series of novels about life on the lower Mississippi River: *The Adventures of Tom Sawyer* (1876), *Life on the Mississippi* (1883), and *The Adventures of Huckleberry Finn* (1885).

Realism

Mark Twain, William Dean Howells, and Henry James are generally considered to be the most prominent figures in high literary realism from the 1880s through the early twentieth century. In many ways, realism was the literary attempt to understand and control the forces of change assailing Gilded Age America in a truthful way that was not exaggerated, romantic, or sensationalized. William Dean Howells exerted tremendous influence over high literature in the Gilded Age as assistant editor (1866-1871) and then editor of *Atlantic Monthly* (1871–1881), editorial columnist in *Harper's Monthly* (1886–1892, 1899–1909); as a consulting editor for the first few issues of *Cosmopolitan*; and as generally a very prolific and highly respected literary critic and author. He is perhaps best known today for his novels, *The Rise of Silas Lapham* (1885) and *A Hazard of New Fortunes* (1890), which are broadly critical of the dark side of the capitalist economy of the Gilded Age. Henry James, though not as prolific as Howells nor as popular as Twain, became famous for his novels such as *The Portrait of a Lady* (1881), *The Bostonians* (1886), and particularly *The Turn of the Screw* (1898). Twain remains the most popular of the three and his use of vernacular language was typical of realism.

The Pivotal 1890s

The 1890s was a transitional decade between those giants of the last half of the nineteenth century and the rising literary stars. Many of the most famous writers of the Gilded Age were still active in the 1890s: E. C. Stedman, Francis Parkman, William Dean Howells, Henry James, Charles Dudley Warner, T. B. Aldrich, Mark Twain, F. Marion Crawford, Mrs. Burnett, E. E. Hale, Edward Eggleston, George W. Cable, R. H. Stoddard, Frank Stockton, Joaquin Miller, Bret Harte, Sarah Orne Jewett, Joel Chandler Harris, Sidney Lanier, John Muir, John Burroughs, Thomas Nelson Page, and R. W. Gilder. All of these writers were still alive in 1894 (except for Lanier), were around 60 years old, and were still publishing at least one book per year. However, the 1890s also brought into the literary spotlight the new authors who would break from the genteel realism proposed by Howells. In the 1890s the first major offerings of several rising literary stars appeared in print: James Lane Allen, Kate Chopin, Richard Harding Davis, H. B. Fuller, Hamlin Garland, Mary E. Wilkins, Stephen Crane, Booth Tarkington, John Kendrick Bangs, Alice Brown, Richard Burton, Theodore Dreiser, Ellen Glasgow, James Huneker, Jack London, Bliss Perry, George Santayana, Ernest Seton, O. Henry, and Edith Wharton. Just as the nation was on the cusp of a new century, American literature was on the edge of a new realism promoted by a rising generation of writers.[15]

Naturalism

Many of these younger writers wrote under the philosophy of naturalism, which appeared in the 1890s. Naturalism was a spin-off on realism's focus on a true-to-life, unsentimental view of human existence, but was placed within a pessimistic world that was amoral and indifferent to human presence. The main characters of the naturalistic writers were often lower-class or lower-middle-class men who struggled against the impersonal natural forces while the forces of heredity, environment, or instinct acted to circumscribe their choices and actions. The protagonist's fight for survival was often steeped in violence and passion. Social Darwinism with its emphasis on heredity, racial instincts, amoral natural forces influencing all creatures, and the survival of the fittest had a tremendous influence on this literary style. Although naturalistic writers started producing work in the 1890s, many of the most successful and influential novels were written in the twentieth century. Stephen Crane was an early and successful proponent of naturalism, with his classic novel *The Red Badge of Courage* (1895) and his Whilomville Stories, which were serialized in *Harper's New Monthly Magazine* in the late nineteenth and early twentieth centuries. Jack London wrote a series of novels and short stories in the naturalist genre, and those that are still most widely read today are *Call of the Wild* (1903), *Sea Wolf* (1904), and *White Fang* (1906). Theodore Dreiser wrote *Sister Carrie* (1900), which catapulted him into literary celebrity and launched his career as well as his constant battles with editors to make his novels "suitable" for the reading public. Edith Wharton also produced a great deal of important naturalistic fiction such as *The Touchstone* (1900) and *Ethan Frome* (1911), but she is probably most well known today for *The Age of Innocence* (1920).[16]

Bestsellers

Acclaim by literary critics, however, did not make a bestseller. Like today, bestsellers in the Gilded Age came in many forms, such as success tracts, historical romances, religious novels, dime novels, and adventure stories, to name a few. Novels with religious themes were very popular, like Lew Wallace's *Ben Hur: A Tale of the Christ* (1880), the pro-Catholic *L'Abbé Constantin* by Ludovic Halévy (1882), Charles Sheldon's *In His Steps: What Would Jesus Do* (1897), and Henryk Sienkiewicz's *Quo Vadis?* (1896). Children's novels also sold well, such as Frances Hodgson Burnett's *Little Lord Fauntleroy* (1886); Anna Sewell's *Black Beauty*, which became popular in the United States in 1890; Robert Louis Stevenson's *Treasure Island* (1883) and *Dr. Jekyll and Mr. Hyde* (1885); Margaret Sidney's (Harriet Lothrop) *Five Little Peppers and How They Grew* (1881); and Frank Baum's *The Wizard of Oz* (1900). Other popular books were Bret Harte's collection of short stories, *The Luck of the Roaring Camp and Other Stories* (1870), Edward Eggleston's *The Hoosier School-Master* (1871), Archibald Gunter's *Mr. Barnes of New York* (1887), Hall Caine's *The Deemster* (1888), and Tolstoi's *War and Peace* (1886). Bestsellers in the 1890s included Sir Arthur Conan Doyle's *Adventures of Sherlock Holmes*, James Barrie's *The Little Minister* (1892), Anthony Hopes Hawkins' *The Prisoner of Zenda* (1894), Stephen Crane's *The Red Badge of Courage* (1895), Opie Read's *The Jucklins* (1896), and Edward Noyes Westcott's *David Harum* (1898) and *Eben Holden* (1900). Rudyard Kipling became something of a phenomenon in the 1890s with *Barrack-Room Ballads* (1892), *Plain Tales from the Hills* (1888), and *The Light that Failed* (1894) hitting the bestseller list in that decade, though his more well-known works from the early twentieth century did not sell as well.[17]

Home Libraries Series

The Gilded Age also saw the rise of the Home Libraries Series where publishing companies would promote a series of "great books" that everyone needed to read. These series certainly appealed to middle-class Americans who sought a common cultural literacy and reading advice, but they also appealed to working-class Americans who sought inexpensive fiction. Many of the Home Library Series defied the genteel and sensationalistic labels used in the Gilded Age, perhaps denoting that reading habits were more complex and varied among the social classes than is generally believed. On the forthrightly respectable side of the spectrum was Charles Dudley Warner's *Library of the World's Best Literature* (1897) in 30 volumes. The 1895 *Montgomery Ward Catalogue* sold seven competing Home Library Series such as Modern Library, the 150-book series Library Editions of the New Oxford and Princeton, and the Selected Paper Covered Books Series which sold for as little as $.16 each. Many of these inexpensive paperback books were intended to be portable so that people could carry them on trains and trolleys as traveling and commuting grew in the late nineteenth century. One example was *Frank Leslie's Home Library of Standard Works by the Most Celebrated Authors*. The cheap libraries often reprinted European classics inexpensively because American publishers did not pay royalties until after the United States agreed to abide by an international copyright law in 1891. These inexpensive books certainly made it very easy for virtually anyone to purchase literature.[18]

JUVENILE LITERATURE

Genteel Youth Magazines—*St. Nicholas* and *Youth's Companion*

Particularly important leaders in respectable middle-class magazines were the *Youth's Companion*, with is behemoth circulation of 500,000 in 1900, and what is generally considered the best children's magazine of the era, Scribner's *St. Nicholas Magazine* (1873). *St. Nicholas* benefited from absorbing a number of shorter-lived children's periodicals that came and went in the boom-and-bust economy of the Gilded Age, most notably *Our Young Folks* and *The Children's Hour* in 1873 and the *Little Corporal* and *Schoolday Magazine* in 1875. Others like the *Riverside Magazine for Young People* (1867), *Wide Awake* (1875), and *Pansy* (1874) simply disappeared in the new, competitive market for children's attention.[19]

Youth Consumer Culture

Arguably, no other source illustrates the growth of a consumer ethic and a distinctive youth culture better than *St. Nicholas*. Even though Mary Mapes Dodge (1831-1905), the powerful editor of the magazine for over 30 years, did believe that moral uplift and strong support of the values of the respectable classes was important, she also railed against children's literature that was aimed primarily at the parents. Dry, dusty, and wearisome, the old style needed to be replaced by *St. Nicholas* which would be a "pleasure-ground" where young people could discover "a brand-new, free life of their own for a little while." Although adults produced the literature and Dodge had a free hand in shaping the content of the magazine, young people were the focus as a distinct consumer group. Mapes after all chose the title *St. Nicholas*, which signified to all young people by 1873 the jolly old Santa Claus who was the primary figure of "children's material culture." Eventually, the notions of children as consumers was made explicit when *St. Nicholas* included a "What I Want for Christmas" page that enabled readers to choose Christmas presents from the advertisements in the magazine. Young folks could write down the gifts and their corresponding page numbers on the specially prepared form and give it to their parents. The ties between *St. Nicholas Magazine*, children's consumer culture, and Christmas were established.[20]

Quality Literature

The *Youth's Companion* and *St. Nicholas* were remarkable in the quality of their writers, their size, and in the comprehensive nature of their content. The magazines boasted some of the greatest and most influential writers of the age such as Louisa May Alcott (*Little Women*), Frances Hodgson Burnett (*Little Lord Fauntleroy*), Mark Twain (*The Adventures of Huckleberry Finn*), Rudyard Kipling (*The Jungle Book*), and Howard Pyle (*The Story of King Arthur and His Knights*). In fact, *Little Lord Fauntleroy*, several of *The Jungle Book* stories, and *The Story of King Arthur and His Knights* originally appeared as serial stories in *St. Nicholas*. But it was the incredible array and quality of this literature that set both of these magazines apart from their competition. History, sports, fairy tales, poetry, current events, adventure, success, sentimental, nature, science, and small children's stories could all appear in a single issue. Like the *Youth's Companion*, *St. Nicholas Magazine* survived several decades into the twentieth century, and though the latter's circulation was a more modest 70,000-95,000 it boasted an incredibly loyal readership. The magazine was relatively costly, selling for $.25 an issue, $3 per year, or $5 for the elaborate annual bound copies.[21]

Genteel Values

Both the *Youth's Companion* and *St. Nicholas* operated to create specific roles for young people based upon the gentry values of refinement and respectability that were so dear to the Northeastern elites who owned and operated the great publishing houses of the Gilded Age. Men like G. P. Putnam, Charles Scribner, and James and John Harper consciously viewed themselves as "custodians of morals and culture" and sought to bring their gentry values into their periodicals. Historian R. Gordon Kelly has noted that the high-quality children's magazines produced basically three plot formulas: the ordeal, change of heart, and gentry mission. Although children were cut off from their families in these stories and the young heroes and heroines exhibited self-reliance and bravery, the independence of these young people was always within set limits. The moral structure of the stories was vitally important and any action or violence had to have some higher moral purpose. The editors and owners of these magazines promoted values they believed were vital for all youth, and these values appeared over and over in the massive number of stories that poured out of the Gilded Age publishing houses. Spotless character, intellectual and moral refinement, self-control, and a dedication to public service were all essential ingredients in genteel children's literature.

Our Young Folks, absorbed by *St. Nicholas* in 1873, starkly illustrated the connection between the values of the creators of these magazines and the children themselves when they invited their readers to write essays on the nature of a true gentleman in 1871. Over 400 young people replied with a list of values that appeared in the very stories they read in *Our Young Folks*: integrity, modesty, manners, purity of heart, dedication to service, bravery, justice, generosity, temperance, self-control, and taste.[22]

St. Nicholas editor Mary Mapes Dodge echoed the sentiments of the young people from *Our Young Folks* in her "Jack-in-the-Pulpit" advice column in 1877. Dodge counseled young men:

Avoid all boastings . . . backbiting, abuse, and evil speaking; slang phrases and oaths in conversation, deprecate no man's qualities, . . . avoid giving offense, and if you do offend, have the manliness to apologize; infuse as much elegance as possible into your thoughts as well as your actions; and, as you avoid vulgarities, you will increase the enjoyment of life, and grow in the respect of others.[23]

The adults who created these magazines appear to have been in agreement with the children who read them about the importance of respectable values. The model of the lady and gentleman were standards universally admired by the adults and children who produced and consumed these magazines.

Differences in Boys and Girls

Although there were genteel values that were common for all youth who read these magazines, the standard Victorian way of thinking about gender was that boys and girls, just like men and women, were in fact the exact opposites of each other. Like women, girls lived in a domestic world and were portrayed as less rugged, more emotional, and certainly more mannerly and pious. Louisa May Alcott's "Pansies" (1887), which appeared in *St. Nicholas*, illustrated the ideal values for girls through the young characters of Eva, Carrie, and Alice who were polite, kind, reserved, and respectful. Boys were given much more latitude in behavior and were often expected to misbehave, even in magazines like *Youth's Companion* and *St. Nicholas*, though paragons of virtue, like *Little Lord Fauntleroy*, continued to be popular. But, for boys courage, physical power, and aggressiveness were admired characteristics alongside honesty, integrity, and character. E. A. Bradin's "Hermann, The Defender of Germany" (1873), O. W. Blackwell's, "Pine-Knots Versus Pistols: A True Story of the Revolution" (1894), and Frank Stockton's, "The Buccaneers of Our Coast" (1898) all presented models of heroic, violent manhood for boys.[24]

Youth Form Their Culture

St. Nicholas provides even greater insight into the youth culture of the day. Young people had a serious impact on the magazine and helped to create their own space and culture. The "Letterbox" allowed readers to write to the editors, and young people made their voices heard about which authors and stories they liked. Editor Mary Mapes Dodge gave close attention to the opinions of her readers and actually had her own "Jack-in-the-Pulpit" column for several years where she addressed young people's questions. But by far the most important center of youth culture was the St. Nicholas League which appeared in 1899, encouraging readers to submit their own stories, poems, puzzles, drawings, and photography. Within three years the League had 40,000 members. Membership was free and open to every reader under the age of 18. Contributors could earn gold badges, silver badges, and honorable mention. Here the young readers of *St. Nicholas* created their own space, shaped by them and reflective of their concerns. Although it is obvious that the values of the Victorian middle class, to which most of the young readers belonged, appeared strongly in these youthful works, these young people were carving distinctive space for their own youth culture.

Palmer Cox's Brownies

That these young people created their own independent culture is the subject of much debate, but the strength of youth as a consumer group that could craft its own wants became obvious when Palmer Cox's "Brownies" series burst onto the pages of *St. Nicholas* in 1883 (see Chapters 3 and 7). Children made this series of illustrated drawings featuring chubby little sprites a national phenomenon, and it became a marker of a shared popular youth culture that endorsed play, mischief, and youth-centered consumer goods. Cox often drew his pixie-like mischief makers in stores playing with the latest items popular among young people: "bicycles, ice-skates, roller-skates, baseball equipment, and hot-air balloons." Perhaps the greatest product spin-off of Cox's creation was Eastman Kodak's Brownie camera which appeared in 1900 (see Chapter 7). The camera was specifically designed for and marketed to children, using Cox's Brownies in their advertising, and sold for only $1.[25] Virtually every middle-class child who grew up in the late nineteenth century would have known about Brownies, much like the 1950s generations would remember the Mickey Mouse Club.

WORKING-CLASS READING

Mass literacy transformed literature in the Gilded Age, making it possible for entrepreneurs to create newspapers, story papers, and cheap paperback books that catered explicitly to working-class audiences. There is strong evidence that native- and Irish-born working-class families spent substantial amounts of their incomes on newspapers and books in 1889.[26] Indeed, though children read both story papers and dime novels, they were not the only or even the primary audience (see Chapter 2). The dime novel industry did very well during the Civil War with soldiers and after the conflict sought a following of young, working-class men. The success of the dime novel industry was due mainly to the mass literacy of working-class Americans. The *National Police Gazette* also had an undeniable appeal to working-class Americans as did the newspapers of organized labor. Working-class Americans certainly read other literature, but these sources reflected the values, concerns, and "accents" of working-class culture.

Story Papers

Story papers burst onto the American literary market in the 1850s, providing weekly papers with five to eight stories for roughly five or six cents. Short-lived story papers appeared as early as 1839, but Robert Bonner's creation of the *New York Ledger* in 1855 established the story paper as a solid medium that would endure into the 1890s. The *New York Ledger* had enormous success as an all-fiction story paper, reaching a circulation of 400,000 by the 1860s. A wide array of successful competitors emerged: Street and Smith's *New York Weekly* (1859), Beadle and Adams' *Saturday Journal* (1870), James Elverson's *Saturday Night* (1865), George Munro's *Fireside Companion* (1867), and Norman Munro's *Family Story Paper* (1873). Story serials were carried in the weeklies, written by notable authors like E.D.E.N. Southworth and Ned Buntline (Edward Zane Caroll Judson). The story papers sought to appeal to the entire family by providing a wide selection of genres, including westerns, domestic romances, adventures, and historical romances.

Dime Novels and Cheap Libraries

Following the success of the weeklies, dime novels appeared after Erasmus and Irwin Beadle and Robert Adams formed a publishing house in 1856 that pioneered a new style—a complete, shockingly violent story about 100 pages long and sporting a sensational cover which sold for a dime. A host of dime novel publishers soon formed, mimicking the Beadle formula and producing thousands of these stories for the reading public: George Munro (1863), Norman Munro (1870), Robert De Will (1867), Frank Tousey (1878), and Street and Smith (1889). Although the heroes of the early Beadle dime novels rarely broke with conventional middle-class morality, the stories were packed with grisly violence that went on endlessly in a formulaic, contrived plot designed for maximum mayhem.

Several of these dime novel publishers had apprenticed in the printing trades as young men only to find their professions de-skilled and forever changed by mechanization. Erastus Beadle, Robert Bonner, Frederick Gleason, George Munro, Theophilus Beasley Peterson, and Francis Shubael Smith left their failing printing trades and went into publishing story papers and dime novels. Many of the men who became successful publishing sensational literature were from the ranks of the working class, so it should be no surprise that this literature was imbued with working-class values.

The popularity of dime novels actually rose during economic depressions, which were frequent in the Gilded Age. Cheap libraries, which are today often conflated with dime novels, emerged in 1875 when publishers began to offer these series of 16- or 32-page pamphlets for a nickel. Beadle and Adams issued their Fireside Library, George Munro a Seaside Library, Norman Munro a Riverside Library; Street and Smith offered a number of series such as the Log Cabin Library and Nick Carter Library; and Frank Tousey sold the Five Cent Weekly Library and the New York Detective Library. The cheap libraries were something like the Home Library Series, but the main difference was that the latter actually sold full-size books rather than the 16- or 32-page (comic-book-length) pamphlets. But by the 1880s the overall quality and moral tone of this genre deteriorated markedly.

A host of famous writers, many of them making the leap from story papers, poured out stories for the dime novels, creating new heroes for their largely working-class reading public. Edward Ellis, Mayne Reid, Edward Wheeler, and Samuel S. Hall were all popular, but the king of them all was Edward Zane Caroll Judson, who wrote under the pseudonym Ned Buntline as well as a number of others. Rarely did these writers cross over into the more respectable children's magazines of the age, with the notable exception of William O. Stoddard.[27] By the 1890s, however, the publishing houses exerted more control and many stories were written by hired staff writers who produced them under pseudonyms, like Old Sleuth, owned and controlled by the publishing company.[28] Dime novel writers created the Western and Detective genres,

The cover of one of Beadle's dime novels, *Oonomoo, the Huron*, 1863.
© Library of Congress.

placing older formulaic adventure plots into new situations. Western heroes like Buffalo Bill and detectives such as Nick Carter roared through
their adventures, modeling to their young readers a rugged, independent, and violent manhood. Yet alongside these working-class heroes
and heroines, meting out rough frontier and urban justice, were other
formulations, such as the heroic working girl and the honest mechanic.
Dime novel readers probably did not care what genteel editors or librarians thought. Working-class youth lived in a different world from
middle-class Americans and these stories honestly reflected values that
working Americans admired—integrity, honesty, nobility, physical
toughness, and a capacity for violence.[29]

Working-Class Values

   What set dime novels apart from middle-class literature was their reflection of working-class culture in what Michael Denning calls "mechanic accents."[30] Denning brilliantly illustrates how dime novels
reflected the "accents" of working-class culture by focusing on working-
class heroes and heroines. Dime novels, story papers, and the cheap library paper books all took many of their story lines from the sensational
criminal cases that appeared in popular newspapers, adding to their
popular appeal with timely stories. Several formulas appeared regularly
in dime novels, such as the republican plot of inheritance, the secret
brotherhood of workers, the honest mechanic, proletarian detectives, the
Western hero, and the Cinderella story. Proletarian detectives, unlike
their genteel counterparts like Sherlock Holmes, reflected working-class
culture by solving cases not through logical deduction but instead
through disguise and physical strength. Honest mechanics always won
their strikes and even when they gained a fortune always sided with
their working-class brothers on the picket line. Outlaws were often the
heroes in dime novel Westerns, at least for a time, but instead of reflect-
ing a conflict between law and order these stories more often reflected
the conflict between labor and capital. The outlaws idolized for a time
by dime novels were outlaws like the James Gang who robbed banks
and trains, the symbols of Eastern concentrated wealth and the power
of the capitalist class. The James Gang's great enemies were not lawmen
but Pinkerton Agents, which every labor union member in the United
States knew were hired as strikebreakers by wealthy industrialists. Outlaws like the James Gang struck a populist cord with many working-
class Americans who resented the power of concentrated wealth, which
often took the form of railroad corporations and banks to the average
citizen in the Gilded Age. Laura Jean Libbey was one of the most successful and prolific writers of dime novels about women, but her stories
were the opposite of sentimental fiction. Sentimental heroines never
physically labored, were extremely pious, and were so physically weak

that they were often fainting or dying at the end of the story. Libbey's heroines worked and were proud of their labor; there was virtually no mention of evangelical piety, and these women were portrayed as physically capable and active. Indeed, one of the main plot lines in Libbey's stories was that of an upper-class man—an evil capitalist or millionaire—who tried to seduce and rape the heroine, but instead of fainting the plucky woman showed remarkable ingenuity in fighting against the rapist and escaping his clutches. In the endings of the Libbey novels the poor woman often married a wealthy man, but never lost her working-class sensibility—a classic Cinderella story. Working-class accents were clearly present in this sensationalistic literature.[31]

Working-Class Proponents and Genteel Critics

Although these blood-and-thunder stories often upheld general notions of middle-class morality, they challenged the gentry elite's control of the publishing world and the ability of libraries to influence youthful reading habits. One of the great genteel complaints was that these stories lacked realism, and that the young heroes of these stories were independent to a ridiculous and harmful extent. The very idea that a 14-year-old boy could operate independently like a man was, in the minds of respectable ideologues, ridiculous and harmful to young readers. Writers and editors of respectable middle-class literature often aggressively attacked sensational fiction, as Mary Mapes Dodge illustrates. Librarians were particularly engaged in these conflicts. The influence of librarians grew in the Gilded Age as paternalistic millionaires, notably Andrew Carnegie, established hundreds of libraries in communities across the nation. Although there was a spirited debate among librarians about the inclusion of fiction, virtually all agreed to exclude story papers, dime novels, and cheap libraries from the shelves.

Many librarians and social reformers considered sensational stories to be harmful to the minds of young people and believed they could potentially lead young people into a life of crime. Anthony Comstock, the great Gilded Age vice crusader, focused on the dangers of the dime novel and story paper to young minds in his book *Traps for the Young* (1883). He declared that story papers and dime novels were "Satan's efficient agents to advance his kingdom by destroying the young." Newspapers and commentators often connected Jesse Pomeroy, the infamous child serial killer, and his murders with an alleged insatiable appetite for dime novels (see Youth Crime in Chapter 2). Newspapers reported that Pomeroy's unhealthy connection with Indians in the dime novels he read and their use of torture led the boy to his terrible deeds.[32] Indeed, Comstock devoted an entire chapter in *Traps for the Young* to boys and girls who spiraled into lives of crime after reading dime novels. Sensational stories encouraged young men to run out West or to sea and lured their readers into violence.[33] It is rather unlikely that dime novels or sensational literature actually caused any of these problems. Genteel critics' shrill denunciations of sensational literature revealed more about their fears of working-class youth than the perceived dangers of these stories.

While middle-class critics and librarians fought vehemently against this sensational literature, attacking the violence and unrealistic plots (see Chapter 2), working-class Americans bought dime novels, story papers, and cheap library pamphlets by the millions. Whereas middle-class Americans preferred literary realism, working-class Americans sought sensationalism. When Dorothy Richardson, who had a middle-class background but found herself working in a paper box factory, asked her co-workers if they had read standard middle-class classics like Louisa May Alcott's *Little Women*, Victor Hugo's *Les Miserables*, or Jonathon Swift's *Gulliver's Travels*, they had never heard of these books. In fact, they mocked her for her middle-class accent and her lack of knowledge of prominent dime novelists. When Richardson tried to introduce her co-workers to the wonders of the March family from *Little Women* by describing the plot, they could not understand why anyone would want to read such a story. Their response is enlightening.

When I had finished, Phoebe stopped her cornering and Mrs. Smith looked up from her label-pasting.
   "Why, that's no story at all," the latter declared.
   "Why, no," echoed Phoebe, "that's no story—that's just everyday happenings. I don't see what's the use putting things like that in books. I'll bet any money that lady what wrote it knew all them boys and girls. They just sound like real, live people; and when you was telling about them I could just see them as plain as plain could be—couldn't you Gwendolyn?"
   "Yep," yawned our vis-à-vis, undisguisedly bored.[34]

These working-class women rejected the realism that dominated middle-class literature. Instead of realistic stories they wanted sensational stories set in the present but with out-of-the-ordinary events. As Phoebe asked, why would anyone want to read about real life? Working-class Americans often chose fiction which reflected their values and was at odds with middle-class sensibilities.

The *National Police Gazette*

The *National Police Gazette* was the sensationalistic newspaper equivalent of the dime novel and attracted a large reading public of working-class and lower-middle-class men (see Chapters 1 and 7). Indeed, the *National Police Gazette*, "the content of which represented a combination of the modern-day *Playboy*, *National Enquirer*, and *Sports Illustrated*," promoted sensationalism through its reporting of violent, sadistic, and bizarre crimes, sexual scandals, sports, celebrity gossip, and racy illustrations.[35] After Richard Kyle Fox purchased the newspaper in 1887, he expanded the format to 16 pages printed on distinctive pink paper. Fox added more coverage of crime, sex, and sports, and by the 1880s he had achieved fantastic success. Also by the 1880s the standard format had been developed: a lurid illustration on the cover; page two contained a Fox editorial, short news stories, and theater gossip; page three offered fantastic human interest stories and some crime news; pages four and five contained photographs or illustrations of famous sports stars and actresses; page six held the primary crime story; page seven presented a long article on a featured sport or sporting event; pages eight and nine were all macabre illustrations, often of crime scenes; pages ten and eleven were sporting news; pages twelve and thirteen were more photographs and illustrations; pages fourteen and fifteen could have short sports stories but were primarily classified advertisements. The *Police Gazette* had a circulation of roughly 150,000 per week by the 1880s and 1890s, and special issues could sell as many as 400,000 copies. These figures wildly underestimate its reading public, however, because the *Police Gazette* was ubiquitous at saloons, hotels, liveries, and barber shops.[36]

Sensationalism

The *National Police Gazette*, like dime novels and cheap nickel libraries, gained its widespread popularity because of its sensational content. Gruesome crimes were the most popular, the bloodier and more bizarre the better. Crime columns entitled "Murder Mania" or "Homicide Harvest" appeared. Love crimes involving a romantic love triangle, ghastly murders, lynching, seduction, horrifying abortions, urban vice, and women impersonating men were all news topics covered with some regularity. The crime and sex stories were almost always accompanied by a salacious woodcut illustration of a terrible murder or a voluptuous young woman showing plenty of bare legs, shoulders, breast cleavage, and for a short time in the 1870s, even bare breasts.

Women

Women appeared in the *National Police Gazette* primarily as objects for the male gaze, but they were also constructed as more capable of taking care of themselves than was typical in middle-class literature. Scantily clad women appeared regularly in the illustrations in the weekly, but so too did women who did things typically reserved for men. Women performing all kinds of sporting feats appeared in the newspaper, like Belle Gordon, the *Police Gazette* Champion Lady Bag Puncher. In addition to the prurient illustrations and sporting oddities, however, women also

ROBERT ANDERSON, HANGED AT LOUISVILLE, APRIL 2, FOR WIFE MURDER.

BALLING OFF SIMPSON, THE PAWNBROKER—AN INJURED HUSBAND SATISFIES HIS LACERATED FEELINGS BY SHOOTING THE FRIEND OF THE FINANCIALLY-DISTRESSED IN HIS PLACE OF BUSINESS; NEW YORK CITY.—See Page 3

CHAS. WARDITE, HANGED WITH ANDERSON, FOR COMMITTING RAPE ON A WHITE GIRL.

"Keep cool," observed the scribe, mockingly, "keep cool."

"It's all well enough to talk about keeping cool," resumed the girl, as she plunged down on the trunk again, "but here I am out of home and home for the thirteenth time in two weeks. This is the last house I was booked out of after working myself to death getting 'em ready to move. You ought to see how the skin is knocked off my knees and elbows."

"So," said the reporter. "I oughn't."

"Well," said the girl as she jumped up and straightened out her shirts and gave her hat a blow to set it straight. "Will the press show this matter up? Has a poor girl got any rights that a bloated millionaire is bound to respect?"

"I will state your case," said the reporter, "and let an unbiased public judge. It is not for me to decide." And then he got up from off the trunk, and the lady after borrowing a quarter from him, which he closely folly gave out of his hard earnings, in order that she might get her trunk removed, sat down and yelled to him as he went out of the gate:

"If you meet a nigger or an Irishman send him here to hustle this trunk."

A HORRIBLE HUSBAND.

A Member of the Parliament of Ontario Charged with Adultery and causing the Death of His Wife.

The slander suits of Casaden vs. Campbell and

Casaden vs. Edgecomb, in the Elgin county assizes, St. Thomas, Ont., is attracting a great deal of attention throughout the dominion of Canada. The defendants promised to prove Dr. Casaden, member of the provincial parliament, to an adulterer, forger, and guilty of killing his wife by systematic ill-treatment. The allegations of the defendants are as follows: At the general elections last year Dr. Casaden, of Iona, was returned for West Elgin, in the re-

forgery and adultery and murdering his wife by inches. John Campbell, inspector of weights and measures, was especially explicit in charging Casaden with having seduced a servant girl, the grave of whose child, after death, was marked with a tombstone bearing Casaden's name; with having adulterous connection with two married ladies of good standing, whose names will be kept out of court if possible, besides sundry abuses. Campbell's evi-

...strongly radical constitutionalism in Canada. He was married years ago to an intellectual, handsome, and wealthy lady named Ferguson, whose money was used to give him a medical education in Europe. They did not live happily together. After her money was spent, report said he abused her terribly, if he did not hasten her end by more direct means. She died, and her brother and two brothers-in-law, the three leading men in the reform party in Elgin, hated him bitterly, and did not conceal it. When he was running for parliament they openly accused him of

...demon of this charge was so considerate that, though Casaden had entered a slander suit, when he saw the deposition of defendant he had the claims asking damages for slander to that local strand out of his plea, and thus confessed tacitly to the allegations. He is alleged to have tried to get out of prosecuting the slander suit on any ground, but he had to choose his shirts or be brought up before the bar of parliament and dismissed from the house. Campbell's other charge against Casaden, for which the latter asks damages, are ill-treatment of his wife and a systematic effort to break her heart by forcing on her a

knowledge of his illicit intercourse with other women, and by general brutality. Poison was hinted at when Mrs. Casaden died, but defendants decline to reiterate that portion of the accusation, as proof is now impossible. These shocking allegations about a man of the high position of Casaden, who has been honored in Masonry, is a brilliant orator and successful physician, coming from his own brothers-in-law, electrified the community. The charge of forgery was made, and is defended by Edgecomb, a brother Mason, who is a reputable and wealthy business man. Everybody concerned is of the first respectability. Casaden is about forty years old, and of elegant address.

Red-Hot Luck.

A young lady who read that "it is lucky to pick up a horseshoe" happened in a blacksmith shop the other day, and picked up one. The surprising suddenness and piercing shriek with which she dropped it showed that it was not lucky. The blacksmith had just made the shoe, and it was so hot as a blind furnace.

There is a horse husband somewhere in Kansas by the name of Joseph S. Rutledge, and his wife Nancy A. Rutledge, of Glasgow, Ohio, would like to know his whereabouts.

THE SECOND GRAND PEDESTRIAN MATCH FOR THE CHAMPIONSHIP OF AMERICA AND THE O'LEARY BELT; SIX DAYS, GO-AS-YOU-PLEASE—BEGAN AT MADISON SQUARE GARDEN SUNDAY NIGHT, APRIL 4, ENDING SATURDAY NIGHT, APRIL 10—SCENE DURING THE RACE.—[SKETCHED BY GAZETTE SPECIAL ARTIST.—See Page 3.

appeared as capable of extreme violence, which directly contradicted middle-class notions of feminine weakness and innate morality. The *Gazette* glowingly reported on women who committed heinous crimes of passion and gave great coverage to the urban sex districts. More often, though, female violence was turned against other women. The *Police Gazette* clearly objectified women through sex and violence and created a "soft-core pornography."

Class Antagonism

The *Police Gazette* also had an antagonism toward the privileged that manifested itself in several ways. Like dime novels, it often carried stories of a working-class heroine that physically fought a middle-class or upper-class "swell." In this case, though, this newspaper certainly emphasized the titillating aspects of the attempted rape or sexual conquest as much if not more than the female victory. The *Police Gazette*, however, did seem to delight in working-class women physically dominating the swell. Given this weekly's proclivity toward objectification of women this very well could be a masochistic male fantasy of female domination, but it also appears to be an open class antagonism toward the middle-class and upper-class sporting men who enjoyed the urban night life and commercialized sex industry with working-class prostitutes in American cities. The paper also gave positive coverage to strikes and often presented the wealthy as "alternately heartless or incompetent, vultures or buffoons." Yet, this populist thrust was never a protest of existing conditions nor a call for reform, as much as it was part of a sensational leisure ethic for working-class men.[37]

Organized Labor Literature

Another significant literature for working-class Americans came out of the labor movement. The literature produced by organized labor and radical presses grew dramatically in the Gilded Age, and literally thousands of publications appeared. Newspapers were a very vital part of working-class literature, and had been since the early nineteenth century. Immigrant workers also brought from Europe traditions of organized labor and quickly created their own foreign language presses. The number of foreign language newspapers increased every year from 1885 to 1913, and German language newspapers were the first workers' papers printed in Chicago. August Spies founded the German language *Arbeiter Zeitung* (Worker's Times) in the mid-1880s. This prominent anarchist newspaper, printed on red paper, played a prominent role in the May 1886 strikes in Cincinnati, which had a large German population, as well as in the 1887 Haymarket Incident in Chicago. Another prominent anarchist paper from the 1880s was the *Der Anarchist* out of Chicago, edited by Adolph Fischer and George Engel. The strength of foreign language workers' newspapers was starkly illustrated by the fact that even in 1925 nine of the fifteen daily labor newspapers were in foreign languages. Furthermore, virtually every union in the country, whether it was local or national, produced a publication. The Knights of Labor published first the *Journal of United Labor* and then the *Journal of the Knights of Labor*, the American Federation of Labor produced the *American Federationist*, and the United Mine Workers boasted the *United Mine Worker's Journal*. The more radical labor press generated significant publications in English as well as foreign languages, such as the anarchist newspapers *Liberty*, produced in Boston and New York, and Chicago's the *Alarm*, which was created by Albert Parsons and produced out of the same office as the *Arbeiter Zeitung*. But the most successful of the radical newspapers was the socialist paper *Appeal to Reason*, which began in 1895 and reached a circulation of 750,000 by 1913. Indeed, by 1912 socialists produced over 300 newspapers, with 13 dailies, by themselves. These labor newspapers catered to working-class needs and reflected their values.[38]

Transitional Juvenile Literature

Although the differences between sensational and genteel literature appear to be profound, there was in fact always a transitional literature that mediated between the extremes. Indeed, the differences between respectable and sensational literature would be difficult for many modern readers to even pinpoint. Writers like Oliver Optic (1822–1897), Harry Castlemon (1842–1915), and Horatio Alger (1832–1898) all lived in a transitional netherworld between respectability and the blood-and-thunder dime novels and story papers. By the 1890s, the temper of the nation was changing enough that adventure stories were beginning to be more widely accepted in juvenile novels and even in that bastion of gentility, *St. Nicholas Magazine*, which made it even more difficult to define the differences between sensational and respectable literature. The transitional literature further blurred these distinctions.

Optic, Castlemon, and Alger

Optic, Castlemon, and Alger played a significant role in creating a middle ground in juvenile literature in the Gilded Age and all were quite popular with young audiences. William Taylor Adams, better known by his pseudonym Oliver Optic, pioneered the new juvenile market through his novels and the various juvenile magazines he edited, such as *Oliver Optics Magazine*. Adams created a formula that would eventually come to dominate juvenile fiction, which consisted of action and adventure firmly set within the moral boundaries of the middle class. Adams would inspire a new generation of children's writers and was a mentor to Horatio Alger. Harry Castlemon, the famous pseudonym of Harry A. Fosdick, wrote 58 juvenile novels dedicated to adventure. Horatio Alger, however, was by far the most prodigious of them all, producing over 100 juvenile stories from the end of the Civil War to his death in 1899. Alger's stories concentrated on the rise to respectability of young heroes fighting to make their place in the world. Accordingly, in Alger's fictional universe the only life worth living was one that modeled middle-class morality and behavior as the basis of business and life success.[39] The works of these writers were not exactly like that of dime novels but they were still viewed with some suspicion by the guardians of genteel society. Educators, genteel literary critics, medical advisors, and youth counselors all advised against precocious youth who exhibited the adult values of independence and autonomy too much. So, even though Optic, Castlemon, and Alger espoused middle-class morality, their precocious young heroes broke free from the patriarchal control that supporters of genteel literature thought essential. Neither sensational nor respectable, these authors created a gray world of juvenile literature that would blur the lines of children's literature.

Patten and Stratemeyer

By the 1890s a new wave of juvenile authors was entering the field using the successful formula of Optic, Castlemon, and Alger. These writers responded to the calls for strenuous physicality for boys that was so prominent in the culture of the 1890s (see Sports in Chapter 7), but placed it within the older moral framework. Gilbert Patten (1866–1945), using the pseudonym Burt L. Standish, would use the formula of middle-class morality combined with action and throw in a new element for American fiction, the sports plot. Patten introduced his famous characters, first Frank Merriwell and later his brother Dick, in 1895, and went on to write 208 Merriwell stories all filled to capacity with constant athletic contests that they always won. Edward Stratemeyer (1862–1930) would radically change juvenile series fiction in the early twentieth century when he formed his syndicate of writers, who wrote series like Nancy Drew and the Hardy Boys under established pseudonyms Carolyn Keene and Frank Dixon. Stratemeyer had experience in writing dime novels and Alger-style fiction (actually finishing a book for the aging Alger) and fused the two styles in his Rover Boys series. In 1899 the first three Rover Boys books appeared, introducing Dick, Tom, and Sam Rover who camped, competed in every conceivable sporting contest, fought with villains, and explored Africa.[40] Their adventures carried them all over the country and the world, largely independent of parental supervision and quite capable of defeating even the most dangerous adult enemies with their fists or guns.

St. Nicholas *and Adventure Literature*

This new predominance of adventure literature influenced even *St. Nicholas Magazine*. The magazine cleverly followed this general trend toward greater adventure literature so that it could still claim the moral high ground. *St. Nicholas* incorporated adventure through historical stories about famous American heroes and adventurers in the 1880s and 1890s, and a good example was the thrilling series "Buccaneers of Our Coast" by Frank R. Stockton (1897–1898).[41] Historical stories dominated the magazine until the early twentieth century when adventure fiction became predominant. By the 1920s adventure fiction and general interest nonfiction stories filled the pages of *St. Nicholas*. Combativeness and violence emerged full-force in *St. Nicholas* adventure stories as admired traits of manliness. The decade of the 1890s does not provide a sudden break with the past that is total and dramatic, but does show the beginning of an increasing rise in the popularity of the adventure genre which emphasized middle-class morality combined with a strenuous, violent, manly character. By the early twentieth century the seemingly endless Gilded Age debates over precocious children in literature were fading as middle-class children's literature adopted and adapted the tactics of the dime novel for its own uses.

NEWSPAPERS

Mainstream newspapers were also an extremely significant literature in the Gilded Age. Newspaper circulation grew by 700 percent from 1870 to 1900, illustrating the massive expansion of print in this era. Newspapers, of course, differed widely in content, audience, and quality. Thousands of small-town newspapers were published throughout the United States. Local publishers usually produced an 8- to 10-page paper every week, which was often created by a single owner/editor and concentrated on local issues. Large metropolitan newspapers also multiplied dramatically, from 971 in 1870 to 2,226 by 1900. There was, of course, Adolph Ochs' daily *New York Times* (1851), which focused on business news.

Sensational Dailies and Yellow Journalism

By the 1880s a new style of newspaper emerged. Inspired by the success of the *National Police Gazette* and other sensationalistic weeklies, Joseph Pulitzer pioneered a slightly more respectable though nonetheless sensational style when he revived the *New York World* (1883). When Pulitzer took over the newspaper it had a circulation of 15,770, but through his efforts the *World* exploded to over 153,000 in two years. This new style of newspaper "catered to the immigrant" and "the workingman" but sought a much wider audience than the racy *National Police Gazette*. William Randolph Hearst, who worked as a reporter for the *World* in 1886, followed Pulitzer's style when his wealthy father gave him the *San Francisco Examiner* in 1887, and he then purchased the *New York Journal* in 1895. These dailies copied many of the attributes of the *National Police Gazette* and introduced new items: separate sections to the paper, extensive sports coverage, fashion news, human interest stories and biographies, travel columns, advice columns, local color columns, comics (with color comics introduced in the Sunday edition in 1896 in the form of Richard Outcault's "The Yellow Kid," followed shortly by Rudolph Dirks' "Katzenjammer Kids"), lavish illustrations and photographs, a one-cent price, and massive advertising. By the 1890s syndicated columnists were appearing in large numbers of newspapers every week and the Associated Press and the United Press were the beginnings of wire news services. The large urban dailies often ran 24 to 36 pages and were produced by a multitude of reporters, columnists, copy editors, artists, advertising men, and printers. On a daily basis these newspapers sold well—Hearst's *Journal* had a daily circulation of 310,000 by 1896—and combined newspaper circulation rose from 36 million in 1890 to 57 million in 1905. These mass circulation dailies pioneered what Hearst called a "new style journalism" but soon came to be known as yellow journalism (named after Outcault's comic strip). Yellow journalism adapted the sensationalism of the older weeklies and popularized it for the American public.[42]

CONCLUSION

A magazine revolution began in 1893 when S. S. McClure created *McClure's* and Frank Munsey cut the price of his *Munsey* magazine to $.10, well below his cost to produce it, and made his profits from advertising. These new mass-market magazines significantly changed American literature. They soon outpaced the older, quality monthly magazines. *Munsey's* reached 700,000 in circulation by 1897 and by 1901 had double the circulation of *Harper's Monthly*, *Century*, and *Scribner's* combined. The new mass-market magazines—primarily *McClure's*, *Munsey's*, *Cosmopolitan*, and by the early twentieth century, *The Saturday Evening Post*—were distinguished by their nationwide sales, low prices, massive circulation, and their profits generated mainly from advertising revenue. Between 1890 and 1905 monthly magazine circulation increased to 65 million. The new mass-market magazines were so successful because they combined the content of the middle-class quality monthly magazines with the sensationalism and focus on massive advertising of the daily newspapers. Indeed, these connections became even more pronounced after William Randolph Hearst purchased *Cosmopolitan* in 1905. Magazines followed a similar pattern to juvenile literature. Borrowing from the genteel literary focus of the quality monthlies, the new mass-market magazines carried some of the most well-respected authors of the Gilded Age, who wrote in the realistic and naturalistic styles, such as Louisa May Alcott, Rudyard Kipling, Howard Pyle, Booth Tarkington, Hamlin Garland, and Stephen Crane. On the other hand, the new mass-market magazines adopted some of the tactics of the sensational daily newspapers such as a focus on current issues, stunts, and human interest stories. Even the Progressive journalism in the mass-market magazines from 1903 to 1910 was heavily influenced by the sensationalism of the daily newspapers. As historian Matthew Schneirov notes, the popular magazines "presented a 'dignified' version of the 'sensational newspaper' style." This magazine revolution occurred just as the number of new middle-class occupations—largely clerical workers, salespeople, public service workers, and salaried professionals—expanded from 756,000 in 1870 to 5.9 million by 1910. This new middle class grew faster than any other sector of American society, and provided a massive, national audience for the more dignified and toned-down sensationalism created by the mass-market magazines. While genteel literature and working-class publications continued to prosper throughout the twentieth century, it was the combination of these two styles that came to dominate the mass literary market.[43]

The Gilded Age

9

Music

BACKGROUND

Popular music in the Gilded Age has been described as "pale imitations of European culture and shallow sentimentality." While this may be a fair assessment of the content, the commercialization of pop music certainly heralded the modern music industry, and the continued mixing of African and European musical forms were creating new and important musical styles in the United States. The Gilded Age laid the foundation of twentieth-century popular music through the creation of an organized popular music industry that churned out ballads and formed the basis of both blues and jazz.

Indeed, it is very difficult to separate the widespread popularity of music in the Gilded Age with the commercialization of the music industry. It was the growth of the sheet music industry that spread songs far and wide throughout the country and stimulated interest in music. Even rural mail order catalogs contained a wide variety of sheet music such as popular dance, orchestral, gospel, ballads, minstrel, banjo, guitar, piano, and mandolin. Industrialization also made it possible to mass produce musical instruments cheaply and spread them throughout the nation on the growing railroad networks (see Chapter 11). Pianos and organs increasingly became symbols of genteel status for middle-class Americans and were a physical presence in the parlor that represented refined taste and artistic development. As a result of this demand, which continued to grow into the early twentieth century, piano production soared from 100,000 per year in 1890 to 350,000 per year in 1909, and 1897 marked the introduction of the first pneumatic player piano. Montgomery Ward sold five different organs ($37–$63) in its 1895 catalog and three piano styles for $175, $195, and $210. These were very moderately priced for pianos; manufacturers like Steinway sold their pianos for at least $600. The massive variety of instruments in the *Montgomery Ward Catalogue* vividly demonstrated the demand for musical instruments even in the nation's most rural areas: fourteen accordions ($2–$10), four concertinas ($2.15–$11.25), two flute accordions ($.75–$1.10), thirty-one harmonicas ($.10–$.85), six flutes ($1.65–$16.70), five piccolos ($.55–$4.70), five fifes ($.20–$1.25), two piccolo flageolets ($1.90–$2.80), five flageolets ($.25–$2.60), four clarinets ($11–$28), four mandolins ($5.50–$15), four violoncellos ($8–$17), seven double base viols ($18.46–$43.20), nine guitars ($3.75–$26), seven banjos ($1.75–$18), four zithers and one dulcimer ($3.75–$16), twenty-three violins ($2–$47), three violas ($4.70–$13.85), a kazoo ($.08), parlor bells ($1.35), orchestra bells ($6.50, $9.50), seven tambourines ($.35–$2), five bones sets ($.10–$.35), a cymbalet ($.05), triangles ($.35–$.75), Jew's harps ($.05–$.40), nine different drums ($3–$13.50), five cymbals ($2.50–$6.25), and a wide variety of cornets ($5.15–$26), trombones ($7.20–$16.70), and bugles ($1.30–$3.80). Such diversity in a mail order catalog illustrated the importance of music in the lives of Gilded Age Americans.[1]

POPULAR MUSIC BEFORE TIN PAN ALLEY

Negro Spirituals and Work Songs

Much of the musical development of the Gilded Age was influenced by African-American spirituals and work music, and both developed before the Civil War when the line between secular and religious music was not so well defined. Slave spirituals gained national recognition when former antislavery activists published collections of songs they had heard while working with former slaves just after the Civil War. *Slave Songs of the United States* (1867), compiled by William Francis Allen, Charles Pichard Ware, and Lucy McKim, was the first major effort to document and publish Negro spirituals. Eventually, many spirituals were published, though often with the distinctive features watered down for white audiences. Spirituals and work songs exhibited the "antiphony, rhythmic complexity, repeat phrasing, uninhibited vocals, and bodily movements" that typified African-American folk music.[2] African-American music, particularly emanating from the spiritual and work song, with its syncopated rhythm strongly influenced a wide range of American popular music including minstrel songs, military marches, waltzes, coon songs, ragtime, black gospel music, and blues.[3]

Band Instruments.

It is now time for bands to prepare for the political campaign of 1896. It will be "red hot," and there will be a great demand for music. The new tariff law makes quite a reduction in cost of brass instruments, besides we are getting lower prices from manufacturers on account of placing large advance orders, and a comparison of our present prices with former quotations will show that we have given our customers full benefit.

The German Piston Valve Instruments are made expressly for us by a reliable manufacturer in Germany, and we can recommend them as being equal to any German Piston line on the market.

Our Light Action French Piston Valve Instruments, made by Jules De Vere & Co., Paris, are becoming very popular; our sales have doubled during the past year and so far as we know every instrument has given perfect satisfaction.

On orders of 5 or more band instruments we will be pleased to quote special prices on application.

German Piston Valves.

Water key, music rack and German silver mouthpiece with each instrument.

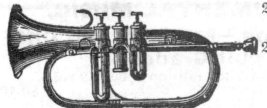

26410 E♭ Cornet, brass,
Each...... $5.10
26411 E♭ Cornet, nickel plated.
Each...... $6.10
Weight, boxed, 6 pounds.

26410-11

26412 B♭ Cornet, brass, same style as No. 26410 . $5.75
26413 B♭ Cornet, nickel plated 6.70
Weight, 7 pounds.

26414 E♭ Alto Valve Trombone, brass.......... $7.20
26415 E♭ Alto Valve Trombone, nickel plated.
Each................. $9.30
Weight, boxed, 8 pounds.

26414–15—E♭ Alto.
26416-B♭ Tenor Valve Trombone, same style as
26414, brass........ . ... $ 9.30
26417 B♭ Tenor Valve Trombone, same style as
26414, nickel plated................ ....11.85
Weight, boxed, 9 pounds.

An advertisement for musical instruments from the 1895
Montgomery Ward Catalogue.

Pop Music

A wide assortment of music was popular in the Gilded Age including waltzes, polkas, marches, hymns, and particularly ballads. Ballads, developing from older hymn and folk song traditions, became the dominant form of popular music. Historian Russel Nye recognized that the standard American ballad consisted of

the thirty-two bar evangelical hymn pattern, built of harmonically related eight-bar phrases divided into introduction, verse, and refrain . . . it used the AABA song form . . . a musical statement, followed by its repetition with variation, followed by a "release" or "bridge" forming a transition to a restatement or conclusion.

As early as mid-century, ballads dominated pop music with their snappy tunes, simple four-chord structure, and catchy lyrics. These songs were designed to be easy to play and sing, since most songs of this era made their money through selling sheet music. Perhaps the best-known balladeer of the nineteenth century was Stephen Foster (1826–1854), who penned "Swanee River," "My Old Kentucky Home," "Oh! Susanna," "Camptown Races," "Jeannie with the Light Brown Hair," and "Beautiful Dreamer." Like so many of Foster's tunes these, penned in the 1840s and 1850s, became American classics, and remained very popular throughout the country during the Gilded Age.[4]

Musical Syncretism

Most popular music in the Gilded Age was actually an interesting mixture of European and African musical forms. A mild form of syncopation gained widespread popularity in American music from early minstrel shows, which were vehicles for African-American music developed in spirituals and work songs. A number of popular songs exhibited this mild syncopation even before the Civil War, such as "Dixie," "The Yellow Rose of Texas," and Stephen Foster's "Camptown Races" and "Oh! Susanna." There was a syncretism in American music that adapted African and European styles, producing something new and different. Widely different musical styles, spanning the spectrum from sentimental ballads to a Sousa military march, from Tin Pan Alley ballads to gospel songs, from coon songs to ragtime, would be the product of this blending of musical traditions.[5]

Hits

The music industry, however, was still relatively unorganized. In the 1870s sheet music hits sold in the thousands while hits by the late 1880s and 1890s would sell in the millions. Before the organization of the industry into Tin Pan Alley, song writers churned out hits much as they had done since the 1840s. Popular hits continued to focus on topical events, like "The Torrents Came Upon Them," which was about the 1884 Johnstown Flood. James Bland, a Howard University graduate, worked in a successful minstrel troupe and produced some of the most memorable hits of the 1870s, particularly "Carry Me Back to Old Virginny" (1878). Western songs appeared which romanticized the West and cowboy life in "The Captain of the Cowboys" and "Home on the Range" (1876). Sentimental favorites like "Silver Threads among the Gold" (1873) remained popular alongside songs that glorified drinking such as the incredibly popular "The Little Brown Jug" (1869) and "There Is a Tavern in the Town" (1891).[6]

Music with a Cause

Many different organizations in the Gilded Age produced music for their causes. Various reform movements turned to music as a political motivator and sought a wider audience for their efforts through music. Indeed, many of these songs were written and performed in a standard folk song tradition. As the music industry expanded, however, a number of these songs became commercial hits and were published in the form of sheet music.

Temperance

M. H. Evans and Emma Pow Smith wrote "When Girls Can Vote" (1890) in support of the efforts of the Women's Christian Temperance Union, the largest women's organization of the Gilded Age. The song attacked male vices.

> Young fellow, don't you come too near
>   With swearing, drinking, smoking;
> For girls don't like the breath of beer,
>   But long to do the voting
> When girls can vote, hurrah, hurrah!
>   Saloons will not here her; (hurrah!)

This song was typical of the anti-drinking movement, connecting the vice with men and saloon culture. With songs like "The Little Brown Jug" appealing to such a wide audience it was little wonder that temperance advocates struck back with their own music.

Populist Songs

Labor unions and farmers' organizations were geographically worlds apart but they were at least united philosophically by their hostility to-

ward concentrated wealth and corporate capitalism, as well as their celebration of manual labor that actually produced something. These
themes appear over and over in union and farmers' songs that called for
united action. Populist songs united both groups in the music, even
though their attempt at political unity through the Populist Party failed
by the late 1890s (see Chapter 1).

Populist songs that appealed to both labor and farmer groups often
attacked concentrated wealth and monopoly. Leopold Vincent produced
the *Alliance and Labor Songster* (1891) which provided a large repertoire
of songs for the movement. Large railroad corporations, which seemed
to control entire states in the Gilded Age, attracted particular venom,
which was exemplified by R. J. Harrison's "The Anti-Monopoly War
Song" (1882). The title alone illustrated that the conflict between laborers
and monopoly capital was more than a small one, it was a war. The
lyrics attested to the song's aggressive attitude, and the closing lines
clearly illustrated its tenor.

> Be the Rail-Roads' robber-spoil,
> Onward! onward to the fray!
> Hurl the monster from your way,
> Let your cry of battle be
> Ruin to Monopoly!

Songs like this sought to unite working people of all kinds through attacks on their common foe, monopoly capitalism. Populist music was an
important part of efforts to organize their movement.

Labor Songs

There were scores of songs, however, sung just by labor unions and
geared only to their concerns and issues. For example, one of the most
prominent goals of organized labor in the Gilded Age was the eight-
hour day, and by 1878 the popular song "Eight Hours" was published
promoting this goal. I. G. Blanchard actually wrote "Eight Hours" in
1866 but his words were not set to music until Jesse H. Jones provided
the music and published the song in 1878. The song relied on the common themes present in much of the organized labor music: the dignity
of labor, exploitation by the wealthy, and a call for reform.

> We mean to make things over.
>   We are tired of toil for naught,
> With but bare enough to live upon,
>   And never an hour for thought;
> We want to feel the sunshine
>   And we want to smell the flowers

We are sure that God has will'd it,
  And we mean to have eight hours.

Other songs like "Drill, Ye Tarriers, Drill" (1888), whose origin is very cloudy, praised the drillers and blasters who built the nation's railroads while Septimus Winner's "Out of Work" (1877) delved into the life of the unemployed urban worker. Songs like these seemed to appeal primarily to the industrial laborer, since an issue like an eight-hour day had little relevance to farmers, but gained wide popularity among a general public where wage labor was quickly becoming the norm.

Farmers' Songs

Like industrial workers, farmers also had songs specifically for themselves. The Grange and Farmer's Alliance (see Chapter 1) both united farmers into organizations that fought against the power of monopoly capitalism during the Gilded Age, and both groups used songs to unify their membership and spread their message. Song writers like George F. Root, who was one of the most prolific and popular song writers of the 1850s and 1860s, produced songs meant to appeal to rural America, and his "The Hand That Holds the Bread" (1874) actually won widespread popularity. Root's song praised the power of farmers and called them to action. The song declared, "Brothers of the plow! The power is with you . . . Oppression stalks abroad, Monopolies abound . . . Awake! then, awake! . . . And heaven gives the power to the hand that holds the bread!" "The Hand That Holds the Bread" appeared in *Grange Melodies*, which was published first in 1881 and reprinted as late as 1904. The songbook covered a wide array of themes involving labor, patriotism, home, funerals, and temperance. Grangers came together with their "Greeting Song;" praised different work in "Laborer," "Maid," "Shepherdess," "Harvester," "Husbandman," and "Matron"; admonished members "Forget Not The Dead"; sentimentalized "The Dear Old Farm"; called for concerted struggle in the "Battle Song"; sang the praise of the United States in "O' Columbia, We Love Thee"; supported temperance in "Hail the March of Prohibition"; and firmly declared "Labor is King." There were even songs "for little Grangers" like "Work," which extolled children, "Don't think there is nothing for children to do because they can't work like a man . . . work, work, work, children, work, there's work for the children to do."[7]

White Gospel Music

Urbanization in the Gilded Age brought millions of people into American cities and towns and precipitated a massive evangelical revival. The urban evangelical revivalists, particularly Dwight L. Moody, sought to use music to bring the "good news" of Christianity to as many Americans as they could beginning in the mid-1870s. Moody employed Ira Sankey as his musical director, and they created sacred music patterned after popular music. Moody and Sankey sought to entertain and evangelize. Fanny Crosby became famous as a gospel lyricist, penning the words to over 9,000 songs. Philip Bliss also gained fame with his gospel music but was killed tragically in a train wreck in 1876. Sankey, however, gathered some of the most well-known songs of Bliss and added them to other gospel songs in *Gospel Hymns* (1876), including the favorites "Beautiful River" and "Sweet By and By." This became a very popular musical style that was outside of Tin Pan Alley in the Gilded Age.[8]

TIN PAN ALLEY

Just as sensationalized mass-market newspapers and magazines were beginning to dominate popular taste in journalism and literature by the 1890s, so too did sensationalized mass-market songs come to prevail in popular music. Tin Pan Alley exemplified the organization of a system to mass produce popular song hits. Thomas Harms (1881) and the Witmark (1885) brothers (Isidore, Julius, and Jay) founded firms that treated music as an industrial product, seeking not to edify nor even to entertain but instead to produce popular hits that would generate massive profits. They pioneered the use of market research and hired in-house composers to write hit songs. Song writers and publishers began to congregate on 28th street to be closer to the popular shows that helped them make their songs big sellers. Writer Monroe Rosenfeld coined the moniker "Tin Pan Alley" because he thought the constant piano playing sounded like the clanging of tin pans. As New York City became the center of musical theater and song publishing, the two interconnected industries drew more song writers to the city. Only after an 1891 copyright law protected European music did Tin Pan Alley and this style of musical production really take form, as American song writers and publishers had to develop original music instead of relying on the theft of European songs.

"After the Ball"

Charles Harris' "After the Ball" (1892) was the first big hit of the decade and stimulated the growth of the Tin Pan Alley system. This song sold 2 million copies in sheet music within a few years and its total sales were as high as 10 million. "After the Ball" was a lovely ballad written to a waltz tune, which was both pleasant listening and excellent dance music. Harris wrote the music in Milwaukee and published it himself, because he felt that Tin Pan Alley publishers had cheated him on earlier song sales. Harris plugged his song using methods that were already pioneered by other Tin Pan Alley publishers. One of the best ways to plug a song was to get singers in musical theater to perform the song during their shows. Harris offered vaudeville star J. Aldrich Libbey $500 and a share of the song's royalty profits, both of which were typical Tin Pan Alley methods, to plug the song. Libbey worked "After the Ball" into his performances on the touring show *A Trip to Chinatown*, which was one of the most popular musicals of the decade and ran for 650 performances in 1892 (see Chapter 12). This exposure helped make the song a runaway hit. Julius Witmark offered $10,000 for the song, but Harris realized its long-term potential. As the touring company traveled through the nation orders for the song began to increase and Harris was soon earning $25,000 per month from the sale of sheet music. Tin Pan Alley sheet music, which in this era normally sold for around $.50, customarily carried the name of the songwriter and a picture of the famous singer who performed it on the cover. "After the Ball" was no exception, sporting a picture of Libbey.[9] The song was so popular that John Philip Sousa's band played it at the 1893 Columbian Exposition, giving it even more massive exposure. Even if only a fraction of the 27 million visitors to the fair (see Chapter 11) heard the song, it would still have had an immense audience. Harris used his royalties to open his own publishing house on Tin Pan Alley in 1903.

"Plugging" a Song

The success of "After the Ball" alerted Tin Pan Alley to the possibilities of massive sales and the fact that a huge audience could be tapped. Song writers and publishers of Tin Pan Alley consciously sought to conform to popular taste and write hits. Publishers plugged their songs by paying not only theater stars but also talented amateurs (there were numerous vaudeville amateur nights) and even street musicians to play them. Harris' offer to Libbey was standard for the era, and famous singers were often given a portion of the royalties of a song for plugging it. Tin Pan Alley publishers made sure that their songs were performed in the vaudeville theaters, touring musical theater, saloons, and beer gardens. In the 1890s it cost Tin Pan Alley publishers roughly $1,300 to promote a song, though only about half ever recouped the outlay and only approximately 1 in 20 was a genuine hit.

Song Writers and Publishers

There was a relatively small group of men who were extremely successful at this pop music production. There were outstanding writers like Paul Dresser (brother of Theodore Dreiser, see Chapter 8), Charles K. Harris, Gussie Davis, Edward Marks, Joseph Shelly, Harry Kennedy,

Charles Graham, and Monroe Rosenfeld penning sheet music hits that were published by the big three publishing firms, Woodward, Witmark, and Stern-Howley-Harrison. Harris had a number of hits on the heels of "After the Ball." Paul Dresser scored 10 hits in 1896, 6 in 1897, 16 in 1898, and tallied at least 5 hit songs every year until he died in 1906. Dresser's "On the Banks of the Wabash" (1899) and "My Gal Sal" (1905) were huge hits. Charles Gussie Davis, the first successful African-American composer on Tin Pan Alley, hit it big with "In the Baggage Coach Ahead" (1896). Million-sellers became much more commonplace in the 1890s, with Charles H. Hoyt's and Percy Gaunt's "The Bowery" (1892); Harry Dacre's "Daisy Bell," which is better known as "A Bicycle Built for Two" (1892); Charles B. Lawlor's and James W. Blake's "The Sidewalks of New York" (1894); John E. Palmer's and Charles B. Ward's "The Band Played On" (1895); Maude Nugent's "Sweet Rosie O'Grady" (1896); James Thornton's "When You Were Sweet Sixteen" (1898); Chauncey Olcott's "My Wild Irish Rose" (1899); and Arthur J. Lamb's and Harry Von Tilzer's "A Bird in a Gilded Cage" (1900) all selling more than a million copies of sheet music. Most of these songs capitalized on romance, love lost, untimely death, daily life, nostalgia, or good times, and were often set to waltz tunes.[10]

Coon Songs

Coon songs were another very popular form of Tin Pan Alley music in the 1880s and 1890s, and became a veritable fad (see Chapter 7). Indeed, throwing some syncopation and African-American racial stereotypes into a song in the 1890s and early twentieth century often led to a Tin Pan Alley hit. The style of coon songs varied dramatically from waltz to ragtime but the content remained based on a common set of racial stereotypes. More than 600 coon songs were published in the 1890s, and some sold spectacularly. Fred Fisher's "If the Man on the Moon were a Coon" sold 3 million copies of sheet music. White and black song writers wrote in the coon song idiom, including the famous white composer George Cohan.

Influence of Minstrelsy

African-American musical traditions had been popular in the United States in the form of the minstrel show since the 1830s. Minstrel troupes continued to travel and entertain extensively after the Civil War, and there were 28 documented traveling all-African-American minstrel groups in the 1870s. Black, white, and even mixed black and white minstrel troupes continued to be very popular entertainment into the 1890s as vaudeville started to form. Remarkably, even black performers like

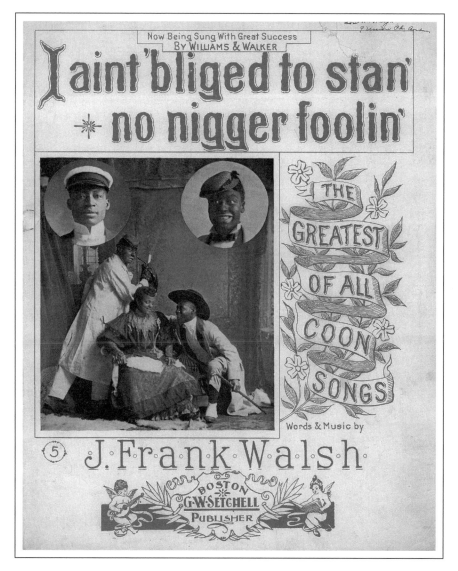

Sheet music cover, 1897. © Duke University Special Collections.

Bert Williams, who became famous in vaudeville, had to appear in black-face for white audiences. Blackface performances remained popular in vaudeville well into the twentieth century, and though many sought to temper the racist depictions within their shows, audiences expected to see the racist stereotypes. In this environment coon songs became all the rage.

Common Elements

Coon songs had common elements. They often employed the syncopated rhythm of African-American music along with "foot-tapping, time-clapping rhythms" that manifested themselves in dances like two-steps, cakewalks, or marches. But these songs also utilized racist stereotypes of African Americans for the entertainment of the white majority. Indeed, as Wilson J. Moses has noted, white stereotypes of blacks tell us a great deal more about whites than they do about blacks. These songs perpetuated stereotypical images of how whites wanted blacks to be: comical, superstitious, lazy, natural dancers, addicted to watermelon and chicken, ultra-sexual, and dangerous. Above all, coon songs were supposed to be happy, funny songs. The racist humor was most evident in the fact that coon songs were often in African-American dialect, which was considered hilarious. Whites imposed on blacks these unfortunately durable stereotypes which lasted well into the twentieth century. The songs also dealt with topics typically taboo in most Tin Pan Alley hits, like sexuality and violence, but they gained acceptance because they were about African Americans and they were couched in "humor." Coon songs best illustrate how popular songs were sensationalized in the 1890s by their focus on sexuality, gambling, and violence in a comic setting. Coon songs pushed the boundaries of sexual explicitness in popular music, and this was tolerated because the descriptions were of African Americans, who, according to the racist ideology of the era, were more sexual than whites. Coon songs like "The Hottest Coon in Dixie," "I Got Mine," "You Don't Have to Marry the Girl," "I Don't Like No Cheap Man," "Pump Away Joseph," and "A Red Hot Member" often characterized the "red hot" coon and his "honey" in bawdy, titillating sexual explicitness that would become more common after the turn of the century. Bully songs were another popular element in the coon genre and normally dealt with a dangerous black man, often a hustler and gambler, wielding a razor, which soon became the ubiquitous symbol of black violence. May Irwin's "Bully Song" (1896), "Leave Your Razors at the Door" (1899), and "I'm the Toughest, Toughest Coon" (1904) were representative of this style. Coon songs, however, channeled this violence into a so-called "acceptable" form, which was a black-on-black violence that was tolerable to the wider white audience. Songs with this type of sexuality, gambling, and violent content with white characters rarely made it in Tin Pan Alley. But when white America projected these values onto blacks and sang about them in "funny" coon songs, gambling, sexuality, and violence were suddenly acceptable in pop music. In an age when Jim Crow segregation, voting restrictions, and the lynching of African Americans were rampant in the United States (see Chapter 1), it appeared that white America wanted to justify these actions against blacks through popular culture. James Dormon claims, "The coon songs were as popular as they were because they provided psychic balms by way of justifying the unjustifiable to white Americans who were as delighted with 'coons' as they were determined to believe in them." Coon songs reaffirmed the necessity of subordinating and controlling African Americans, and they justified segregation, voting restrictions, and even lynching.[11]

Black Parody

While African Americans participated in the writing and performing of these songs, too little research has been done to explore how African-American entertainers dealt with the racism of their era. Simply being able to make a good living as an entertainer or song writer was significant for African Americans in the intensely racist Gilded Age. There is tantalizing evidence that black Americans did not sit idly by as they were stereotyped. In one instance, the *National Police Gazette* sponsored a ragtime piano contest to perform the extremely popular hit "All Coons Look Alike to Me," which was written by African-American composer Ernest Hogan in 1896. The only black finalist, "Duke" Travers, refused to perform the song, stating that he did not know the tune. The song was deemed so offensive by New York City blacks that a white person whistling the tune instigated fights. But even more interesting is David Krasner's work that illustrates how some black performers infused their coon songs with parody and subversive elements that undermined white racist stereotypes. A good example is what looks like a typical coon song from its title, "No Coons Allowed" (1897), which appeared in the all-black theater production *A Trip to Coontown*, but actually parodied and attacked segregation in its lyrics. The song detailed the story of the "dead swell gentleman of color" who sought to take his gal to the best restaurant in town, but when he arrived the sign said "no coons allowed." The gentleman hired a lawyer and went to the courthouse to decry such treatment, but when they tried to enter they saw a sign over the door, "No coons allowed!" The comedy of the song hid the parody from white audiences that black audience members would immediately have recognized, namely the racist system that segregated blacks and ensured that they would never be treated fairly under the law.[12] There is great potential for more study of attempts by black artists and entertainers to subvert racism through parody or infusing their work with a trickster figure.

Ragtime

Ragtime was another musical style that came out of African-American culture. While coon songs certainly negatively stereotyped African Americans, they also provided greater opportunity for African-American musicians, brought syncopated rhythms further into the mainstream, and ultimately made it easier for ragtime to be accepted by white audiences. Indeed, some of the coon song hits were performed in a ragtime singing style. Ragtime came in two relatively distinct forms, one that was primarily for singing and an instrumental version that was composed primarily for pianos.

Piano Ragtime

The emergence of composed ragtime coincided with the growth of the piano industry and sales. The increase in pianos in the United States was both fueled by and helped fuel the popularity of ragtime. In spite of the popularity of this fad in music and its voluminous sales of sheet music, this style was in fact very difficult to play. The piano player had to maintain a steady left-hand bass beat while the right hand played a syncopated treble melody that displaced the accents. The traditional interpretation of the term "ragtime" is that it derived from "ragging" on the piano, but another more recent interpretation by Samuel Floyd maintains that the term came from black musicians who raised rags (handkerchiefs) to indicate it was time to dance. Whatever the provenance of the term, piano ragtime was difficult to play but undeniably had massive popular appeal in the 1890s and early twentieth century.

Ben Harney

Ragtime developed out of African-American folk music that was brewing all sorts of new music in the late nineteenth century. Ragtime piano music was certainly well known among black and a few white musicians before it first appeared in sheet music in 1896. Borrowing syncopated rhythms from minstrel show music was common in a variety of American music, and the ragtime piano players figured out how to "rag" just about any piece of music. White musician Ben Harney learned the ragging style from the black folk musicians in Middlesborough, Kentucky, and learned how to apply it to piano music at least by the early 1890s. Harney wanted to publish "You've Been a Good Old Wagon but You've Done Broke Down" in 1893, but when he tried to put the actual notes down on paper he had a very difficult time translating the music to the notes. Harney worked out the notes with the help of John Biller, and Greenup Music Company published "You've Been a Good Old Wagon" in 1895, which was the earliest published ragtime piano piece. The song was obviously from the African-American folk traditions because several variations of the lyrics survived in folk songs such as "Sugar Babe," "Sweet Thing," and "Crawdad Song." Witmark and Sons picked up "You've Been a Good Old Wagon" in 1896 in Tin Pan Alley. Harney moved to New York City in 1896, became a well-known ragtime musician, and published the book *Ragtime Instructor* (1897) on how to play ragtime piano music. There is little doubt that Harney was a significant figure in ragtime, but his claims to be its originator are undoubtedly exaggerated.

Scott Joplin

Indeed, hundreds of ragtime musicians, including Scott Joplin (1868–1917), swarmed to the Columbian Exposition in 1893 to play on the Midway or more likely in Chicago's saloons and concert halls. The timing clearly illustrates that Joplin, perhaps the most influential of the ragtime composers, and other ragtime musicians obviously had been developing this style for some time before Harney published his first rag in 1895. Other published rags soon followed Harney. In January 1897, William Krell's "Mississippi Rag" appeared in sheet music followed in December by Tom Turpin's "Harlem Rag." Scott Joplin wrote the "Maple Leaf Rag" in 1897 and it was published by 1899, going on to sell over 1 million copies of sheet music. Like Harney's "You've Been a Good Old Wagon," Joplin's hit rag was composed outside of Tin Pan Alley in Sedalia, Missouri. Ragtime was a musical form that developed in several regions throughout the nation, emerging as a composed music in the 1890s from a variety of black and white entertainers. Ragtime remained popular until the middle of the 1910s, and would be an important precursor to the next great wave of popular music to assume a dominant position in American culture—jazz.[13]

BAND MUSIC

Brass bands were very popular before, during, and after the Civil War. Small to large bands appeared in villages, mining camps, and cities all across the country in the Gilded Age. Bands were a ubiquitous part of American life, providing entertainment for parades, picnics, dances, concerts, political campaigns, restaurants, and bars. These bands came in all sizes, shapes, and abilities, including town brass bands, ethnic bands, and the famous African-American brass bands of New Orleans. Industrialization made it possible for instrument companies to lower the cost of their products and the transportation revolution made them widely available. The 1895 *Montgomery Ward Catalogue* offered 11 pages of musical instruments (see Background), such as flutes ($1.65–$16.70), clarinets ($11–$28), violins ($2–$47), trombones ($10.55–$16.70), and cornets

($5.10–$26). Amateur, semi-professional, and professional musicians were an important part of American entertainment.[14]

Patrick Gilmore

The most important and successful band leader just after the Civil War was Patrick Gilmore (1829–1892). Gilmore became famous for his massive concerts like the National Peace Jubilee in Boston, which assembled an orchestra of 500, a band of 1,000, a chorus of 10,000, and a host of famous soloists. The concert lasted five days and presented music that included band music, symphonic music, oratorio, and even singing school children. Gilmore exceeded these efforts for the subsequent World Peace Jubilee (1872) when he gathered 2,000 players and a chorus of 20,000 in a coliseum built for the concert that seated 100,000 people. The World Peace Jubilee went on for 18 days and featured musicians from France, England, and Germany, including Johann Strauss and his Vienna orchestra.

Elite Music Critics

The response to these concerts by agents of high culture illustrated how music would diverge in the Gilded Age. Music critic John Sullivan Dwight attacked Gilmore's efforts as the best that could be done by a man of "common education" and someone who catered to "the popular street taste." Dwight, who was the editor of *Dwight's Journal of Music*, demonstrated a determination by the cultural elite to impose a hierarchy on American musical tastes, separating the art from entertainment. The combination of the entire musical resources of a region for such a massive concert would occur periodically later in the Gilded Age, but the high culture champions of music as art would increasingly come to the conclusion that the masses of Americans could not adequately appreciate their art.

Touring

Gilmore, however, paid scant attention to such critics and created the pattern for a successful band leader with his 22nd Regimental Band in New York, which actually had few connections to the military. Gilmore's band, like the symphonic orchestra of Theodore Thomas, survived through concerts and substantial tours. In the summer and winter the band played concerts in New York venues and toured in the spring and fall. Gilmore's concerts featured popular favorites and classical orchestral songs, usually with a soloist on trombone, baritone horn, saxophone, or most commonly cornet. Several famous cornet players toured with Gilmore, such as Matthew Arbuckle, Jules Levy, Alessandro Liberati, and Herbert L. Clarke. Departing from the mid-century custom of relying entirely on brass, Gilmore reintroduced woodwinds until his band consisted of one-third clarinets, one-third various woodwinds, and one-third brass. Gilmore toured until his death in 1892.[15]

John Philip Sousa

John Philip Sousa (1854–1932) assumed Gilbert's mantle as the most prominent band leader in America when he formed his own band in 1892, the year of Gilbert's death. Sousa had been around music his entire life, apprenticing seven years with the U.S. Marine Band starting at the age of 13 and by 1880, at the age of 25, Sousa had accepted the post of director of the U.S. Marine Band. In 1892, Sousa created his own military band, taking it through constant touring to fairs, expositions, theaters, and opera houses. The members of Sousa's band were polished professionals, dressed neatly in military-style uniforms. Like Gilbert before him, Sousa mixed musical styles at his concerts, throwing together hymns, popular songs, and some syncopated ragtime numbers alongside classical symphonic numbers and his own famous military marches. For example, Sousa played Fred Stone's "Ma Ragtime Baby" (1898) at the Paris World's Fair and won a prize. He was a very prolific composer and produced 12 operettas, 11 suites, 70 songs, and 136 marches. Sousa, like many song writers of this era, made much of his money through sales of his sheet music, and roughly 18,000 bought his music in 1900. Sousa marches became hugely popular, often focusing on patriotic themes such as *The Stars and Stripes Forever* (1897), and, like Stephen Foster before him, his songs would find a permanent place in American music.[16]

ORCHESTRAL MUSIC

Theodore Thomas

Theodore Thomas (1835–1905), a German-born American conductor, grew to be one of the most influential classical musicians of the Gilded Age. His genius lay in that he found an audience for classical music that saw the music as he did—as a high art that sought to edify, not just to entertain. Thomas helped to create the professional symphonic orchestra in the United States and the new profession of full-time symphony orchestra musician during his tenure as a conductor (1865–1890). The Thomas Orchestra, however, had to tour constantly in order to survive in the 1860s and 1870s. Thomas played a pivotal role in "establishing the ritual elements in a symphony orchestra concert" which manifested themselves in a rapt but quiet audience, a formal dress code, and musical performances true to the composer's work. These elements created an aura of prestige around classical music played by symphonic orchestras and it was not long before the wealthy began to patronize these performances just as they did art (see Chapter 12). One of the largest problems for symphonic orchestras in the Gilded Age was that there was not really a great deal of difference between them and the better bands of the era and they often played the same music at their concerts. Indeed, Thomas, like Gilmore and Sousa, often played polkas and waltzes along with music by Liszt and Wagner to appeal to his audiences as he toured. Musical eclecticism was the norm in musical performance until the 1890s. Men like Thomas, however, sought to create a greater distinction between the band and the symphony. It is also important to note that the cultural elite preferred French haute cuisine (see Chapter 6), but in the realm of classical music the major influence in the United States until World War I was German.

Permanent Symphonic Orchestras

Henry Lee Higginson, a prominent Boston banker, charted the future of symphonic orchestras in 1881 when he created the permanent Boston Symphony Orchestra. Higginson ran the orchestra for several years in a rather dictatorial fashion, though he did ensure the viability of the orchestra from his own considerable fortune when receipts did not match outlays. Although no other cities copied Higginson's method, they did aspire to standing orchestras. In 1891, Chicago set the model that other cities soon emulated when 50 donors pledged $1,000 per year for three years to start the Chicago Symphony Orchestra, which lured Thomas away from New York to fulfill his dream of conducting a standing symphony orchestra. The Chicago Symphony consisted of 62 full-time musicians. Philadelphia, St. Louis, Cincinnati, Minneapolis, and Pittsburgh all copied the Chicago example. The advocates of symphonic music as high art increasingly turned to wealthy patrons to support their permanent orchestras and classical music was transformed into an object controlled principally by a cultural elite.[17]

Richard Wagner

These orchestras relied on the works of masters like Mozart, Beethoven, Bach, and Handel, but new classical music also swept through the nation. Indeed, Richard Wagner's (1850–1898) works were so popular that a Wagnerian cult formed, primarily through the efforts of Wagner's friend Anton Seidl, who like Thomas was a German emigre. Seidl had been Wagner's assistant and close friend for seven years before he became a conductor in his own right, and he migrated to the United States in 1884. He soon became renowned for his conducting and support of Wagner's operas, such as *Tristan und Isolde*, *Die Walküre*, *Das Rheingold*, *Siegfried*, and *Götterdämerung*. Seidl took over the New York Philhar-

monic in 1891 when Thomas left for Chicago, and his ability to success-
fully stage summer concerts at Coney Island from 1888 to 1896 amazed
even his critics.[18]

The Second New England School

The Second New England School, also called the Boston Classicists,
were a group of mainly New England composers who composed new
music in the German tradition. These American composers were particularly active from 1890 to 1897 and had a close relationship with Theodore Thomas. Thomas encouraged their efforts and used their music in
his orchestra. John Knowles Paine, Harvard professor of music; George
W. Chadwick, longtime faculty member and then director of the New
England Conservatory of Music; Arthur Foote, organist at the First Unitarian Church; Horatio Parker, Yale professor of music; Martin Loeffler,
assistant concertmaster for the Boston Symphony Orchestra; Edward
MacDowell, Columbia music professor; and Amy Beach (one of the very
few women composers) were all important contributors to this indige-
nous group of classical composers.[19]

DEVELOPING MUSIC

There were several musical forms developing in the late nineteenth
century that would not reach full expression until the twentieth century.
Most of these forms developed in the African-American musical gumbo,
which was producing so many offshoots that it is difficult to untangle
the roots of each because they seem to all lead back to the same place.
Black gospel music, blues, and jazz would all form in the Gilded Age,
emerge fully formed in the first few decades of the twentieth century,
and would become highly influential musical forms.

Black Gospel Music

African-American evangelicals were undoubtedly influenced by white
gospel music, but to this they added their own tradition of the Negro
spiritual. Black gospel music began its development as composers started
setting down the older spirituals in sheet music. In the 1890s black song
writers, most importantly minister Charles Albert Tindley, began to produce music that emphasized the "good news" of Christianity and followed the biblical injunction to make a joyous noise to the Lord. Tindley
was the first to compose in and publish the African-American gospel
style. Some of his most famous songs were "I'll Overcome Some Day"
(1901), which became famous in the Civil Rights Movement as "We Shall

Overcome," "What Are They Doing in Heaven" (1901), and "Stand by Me" (1905), made famous in the 1960s by Ben E. King and the Drifters. Black gospel music, however, was just in its infancy in these years and its greatest refinement and popularity would occur in the coming decades. It is important to note that black and white gospel music were closely related, and there were crossover hits, but racism and distinctive sound differences often kept them separate.[20]

The Blues

While the first published blues music did not appear until W. C. Handy published "The Memphis Blues" in 1912, it does deserve some mention. There is little doubt that African-American singers and musicians developed blues music in the last decades of the nineteenth century, well before Handy became interested in what he termed "primitive" music and published his blues. In fact, elements of the blues appeared in popular music, particularly ragtime. So while the development of the blues as a distinct form did not occur until the early twentieth century, it was brewing in the cauldron of African-American secular music in the Gilded Age.

Jazz

Jazz also was coalescing in the late nineteenth century and was particularly influenced by ragtime. There was considerable confusion about the differences between jazz and ragtime in the early twentieth century, and many musicians referred to them interchangeably. While music critics might disagree with this view, it does demonstrate how fluid these musical lines were in the early twentieth century. Just after World War I, jazz would take America by storm.[21]

CONCLUSION

The Gilded Age possessed a rich musical culture that spanned a wide range of musical styles. Industrialization and the emergence of rural mail order catalogs made musical instruments affordable and available in virtually every part of the nation. Music was a vital part of American culture from the largest cities to the most primitive mining camps. Folk traditions continued alongside the organization of a commercialized music industry. Scholars even began to take notice of music. Harvard University's Francis James Child painstakingly researched and compiled old folk songs and published *English and Scottish Popular Ballads* between 1882 and 1898. In a similar vein, journalist Charles F. Lummis collected over 300 Hispanic folk songs in California and the Southwest starting in 1885. Sheet music continued to be the most lucrative way to make money from published music, but all that would soon change after 1900 with improvements in phonographs and recordings. The modern recording industry was poised to develop and it would permanently alter not only the music industry but also the ways in which Americans experienced music.[22]

10

Performing Arts

BACKGROUND

Performing arts in the Gilded Age expanded to meet the entertainment desires of the American public, but bifurcated in new ways. Elite culture increasingly defined popular entertainment as lowbrow and somewhat vulgar, laying claim to the notion of performance as art in the form of symphonic orchestral music, "legitimate" theater, and opera. Ticket prices for all of these entertainments rose to a level where the average American could not afford to attend. Meanwhile, popular performing arts blossomed in the form of the circus, Wild West shows, popular theater, burlesque, and vaudeville. Performers in these venues rose to national stardom and offered high-quality, affordable entertainment. As per capita income doubled between 1870 and 1900 and the work week shortened, many Americans had more time and money for entertainment. The average American turned toward relatively inexpensive popular entertainments and these would foreshadow the influence of popular culture in the twentieth century.

OPEN-AIR ENTERTAINMENT

Circuses

The circus was already a well-established American tradition by the 1870s and Americans in cities and rural areas, East and West, North and South were intimately familiar with its wonders. As early as the 1850s there were an incredible number of small to large traveling circuses.

While circuses had their share of animal menageries and human oddities, part of their staple was also a rich tradition of performances of all kinds and virtually always included a band.

P. T. Barnum

P. T. Barnum (1810–1891) emerged as one of the most significant circus owners of the Gilded Age, and his shows introduced first the two-ring then the three-ring circus and joined separate elements to create the standard nineteenth-century circus—an animal menagerie, performers, musicians, and the ubiquitous freak show. On April 10, 1871, after disastrous fires in his museums in the 1860s, Barnum opened his first circus, partnered with William Coup and Dan Castello. It was Coup's idea to negotiate with the railroad companies on their tour route which resulted in the first complete circus tour by railroad in 1872. In spite of problems with rail travel, Coup saw its possibilities, and had custom-made railroad cars built specifically to transport the circus. The railroad show advertised its presence with the brightly colored and oddly shaped cars as it traveled through the countryside. Barnum later took credit for this innovation, which was accomplished only at the insistent urging of Coup. Others soon adopted this form of travel so that by 1890 there were 11 other rail circuses: Ringling Brothers Circus, The Great Wallace Show, Sells Brothers Circus, John Robinson Circus, Adam Forepaugh, William Main, Lemon Brothers Circus, Frank A. Robbins Circus, Bob Hunting Circus, W. H. Harris Nickel Plate Show, and the Miles Orton Circus. The massive expansion of railroads in the Gilded Age (see Chapter 11) meant that circuses could travel faster and more easily than ever.

Barnum & Bailey

After 1875, Barnum sold his museum and show properties in order to concentrate on his traveling shows. Barnum joined with the shrewd, young circus promoter James A. Bailey to create Barnum & Bailey, the Greatest Show on Earth (1880). Bailey made his name when he became partial owner of his first circus at the age of 29 and then made a triumphant circus tour through South America and the South Pacific from 1875 to 1877. He brought his incredible organizing talents into the partnership and this, combined with Barnum's knack for promotion (see Chapter 3), made them a formidable pair. The Barnum, Bailey, Hutchinson, and Cooper circus (within a few years Hutchinson and Cooper were bought out) introduced the first three-ring circus in 1881, with its multiple, nonstop action. That year the circus grossed $1.116 million and netted $360,000. Although Bailey left their partnership for two years from 1885 to 1887, when Bailey rejoined the circus Barnum gave him complete control. Their partnership produced one of the most successful circuses of their day.

Circus Performers

Circuses were a major form of entertainment and a viable option for performers in the Gilded Age. In 1889 there were 22 large traveling circuses in the United States, and they all needed a substantial number of performers. The early Ringling Brothers (Al, Otto, Alf, Charley, and John) show, their Carnival of Fun, was not a circus at all but a traveling troupe of entertainers that included music, singing, plate spinning, and comic skits. They eventually merged their show with Yankee Robinson's Great Show in 1884 creating a small circus. Circuses included performers of all kinds, unlike our modern conception of the circus. There were the ubiquitous clowns, a band of musicians, gymnasts, contortionists, trapeze performers, tightrope walkers, and perhaps the most popular acts of the era, the trick equestrian riders. Agnes Lake Hickok was a well-known trick rider. She started her career as a rider, became famous as the owner of the Lake's Hippo-Olympiad & Mammoth Circus until she sold it in 1873, and was even more well known as the spouse of Wild Bill Hickok. She again gained fame as a rider alongside her daughter, Emma, after she sold her circus and toured until 1882. Another well-known performer was the clown Frank "Slivers" Oakley, who worked for Barnum & Bailey, working out a pantomime baseball routine that made him famous at the turn of the century. This incredibly well-known clown even had a ragtime piano song dedicated to him by Harry Cook, called "Slivers' Eccentric Rag" (1909). Slivers was a marquee solo clown act and earned up to $750 per week.

Ringling Brothers and Circus Mergers

Just as the business merger mania was sweeping American businesses, mergers began to alter the circus landscape in the 1890s. Bailey bought the famous Forepaugh Circus in 1890 and the well-known W. W. Cole Circus in 1896. By 1896, Bailey controlled the Barnum & Bailey Circus, Buffalo Bill's Wild West Show, and Forepaugh-Sells Circus. Competition between the Bailey properties and Ringling Brothers intensified: when Bailey brought back the long-neglected and costly 40-horse hitch, Ringling Brothers countered with a 40-piece band mounted on stark white horses. The concentration of circuses would culminate in 1907 when Ringling Brothers purchased Barnum & Bailey after Bailey's untimely death.[1]

Wild West Shows

Buffalo Bill

"Buffalo" Bill Cody and Nate Salsbury developed the Wild West Show in 1883, which helped to romanticize the West through its thrilling Western performances. Cody brought authenticity to the show because of his background as a buffalo hunter, Indian fighter, and Army scout, but his was not a simple image. E.Z.C. Judson (Ned Buntline) introduced Cody as a hero in one of his dime novels in 1869 (see Chapter 8) and Cody soon became a dime novel favorite, appearing in roughly 550 books. Capitalizing on this fame, Cody starred as himself in several stage shows starting in 1872 with *The Scout of the Plains*. Cody, however, was not simply a literary creation; he actually did live a relatively violent, rough life in the West, though the exact extent of his "adventures" is a matter of some debate among historians. Witnesses did verify his famous showdown with the Cheyenne warrior Yellow Hand. After the Battle of Little Bighorn and the defeat of Custer in 1876, Cody quit his performing and secured a job as the scout for the U.S. Cavalry. While on a scouting mission, Cody's group came upon the Cheyenne and Yellow Hand. Yellow Hand and Cody fired their rifles at each other at close range. Cody hit his adversary, quickly closed on his fallen foe, and promptly scalped him. He proudly displayed Yellow Hand's scalp throughout his performing career. While the image of Buffalo Bill was in large part manufactured by Cody, there was always some truth and authenticity at the core of the image. Indeed, Cody always claimed his troupe did not perform, but simply behaved as they routinely did in the West.

Cody and Salsbury

Cody capitalized on his image and his experience as a performer to launch his Wild West Show on the urging of Nate Salsbury, who proposed the concept. Cody started his Wild West Show with W. F. Carver and A. H. Bogardus, though Salsbury refused to join because he thought Carver dishonest. By the end of 1883 they dissolved their partnership and Cody joined Salsbury (who had a real genius for coordinating such a large enterprise) in what would be a long and lucrative association.

Guns and Horses

The Wild West Show had much in common with the circus, but unlike the circus the main parts of this show were guns and horses. Cody's claim notwithstanding, the show relied heavily on staged dramas that were primarily scripted. Guns, horses, and violent performance were the centerpieces of the show. Cowboys, scouts, soldiers, and sometimes Mexican vaqueros fought and defeated Indian attacks on a settler's cabin, an emigrant train, and a stage coach. There were also reenactments of specific battles. These thrilling attacks came at full speed on horseback with pistols and rifles blazing. Charging horses, thrilling actions, and the crack of hundreds of guns made these particularly loud and exciting performances. Cody often led the attack that drove the Indians away from the cabin or coach, and often reenacted his famous rifle duel with Yellow

A reenactment of an Indian attack on white settlers, in Buffalo Bill's Wild West Show, London, England, ca. 1900. © Denver Public Library, Western History Collection.

Hand that ended with a massive fight. Horse races, trick riding, and military horse maneuvers were all prevalent in the show as well. Cowboy Buck Taylor demonstrated cowboy riding skills when he picked up a hat and handkerchief from the ground while galloping at full speed, and female trick riders Della Ferrell and Georgia Duffy wowed audiences with their skills and daring. Indian riders also performed—after 1885 there were always more than 100 Indians in the show. In the 1890s, Cody added many equestrian acts from other parts of the world as well, like mounted soldiers from England, Germany, and the United States in addition to Arabian horsemen, Russian Cossacks, and Argentine gauchos. There were also other cowboy entertainments like "Bucking Bronco," "Bucking Steer," and "Steer Riding," out of which the modern rodeo developed. Audiences, then as now, watched as these men rode seemingly ferocious animals trying to buck, kick, or gore the brave riders clinging desperately to their backs. Guns played a prominent role in the show and promoters billed firearms as an essential Western element that was as important in settling the West as the plow. The shooting acts were very popular, starring famous shooters like Cody, Annie Oakley, and Lillian Smith. Oakley in particular would gain fame in the United States and Europe for her incredible skills. Cody had the only speaking role throughout the show. The performances relied almost entirely on intense action on horseback and the show usually started with a grand review of all the riders, often several hundred, thundering through the grounds. All of this action was set to music by the cowboy band.

The Columbian Exposition

The show grew to be extremely popular and toured constantly. The Wild West Show made several successful tours of Europe. People flocked to the show almost everywhere it went in spite of its relatively high cost, $.50 for adults and $.25 for children. The Wild West Show gained probably its largest and easiest audiences at the 1893 Columbian Exposition. When fair organizers refused to let the show into the fair, Salsbury and Cody set up their show close to the entrance of the Chicago fair and drew an estimated 6 million people. The mixture of horses, guns, violence, and a romantic vision of the West struck a responsive cord with Americans and many Europeans.

Order of Performance

By this time a typical show had developed a relatively consistent performance and an 1895 program was representative. The show started with the "Star-Spangled Banner" and music by the cowboy band. Then hundreds of riders rode through on the Grand Review. Annie Oakley then wowed the crowd with her incredible shooting and slowly accustomed them to the noise of firearms. Horse races followed between the various riders from around the world. A Pony Express staged scene followed that reenacted the famous mail riders. Another reenactment came next—the Indian attack on the emigrant train which culminated in an extremely loud gun battle between the Indians and Buffalo Bill's scouts and cowboys. A series of horse races, trick riding, bull riding, bronco riding, and roping came next. Soldiers then displayed their precision cavalry drills set to music. Another staged attack thrilled audiences as Cody and the cowboys repulsed an Indian attack on the coach. More horse races and riding skills were displayed. Cody himself then showed off his riding and shooting skills. The show ended with a staged buffalo hunt, another staged attack, this time on the settler's cabin, and the final salute. A number of imitation Wild West shows developed in the United States and Europe, and this became a very popular form of open-air performance that lasted well into the twentieth century.[2]

POPULAR THEATER

By the Gilded Age a number of different kinds of theater performances were held in every conceivable venue for a wide range of prices: dollar theaters, concert saloons, variety theaters, 10-20-30 theaters, and dime museums. Unlike theater in the early nineteenth century, audiences were segregated according to price and location of the theater starting in the 1850s. As Americans enjoyed more leisure time and disposable income than before, they turned increasingly to urban amusements, like the theater, where they could see entertainers performing in almost every conceivable venue.

Concert Saloons and Variety Theaters

Concert saloons and variety theaters, different names for basically the same thing, spanned a wide array of establishments that ranged from dingy saloons to large theaters. What united these concerns were the cheap or free shows they presented. As theater grew prohibitively expensive for many by mid-century, concert saloons grew to be one of the most popular forms of urban entertainment. Close to 30,000 people attended concert saloons, beer gardens, and music halls as early as 1866. Some of these venues were dives that had a crude stage off to the side while others were quite elaborate and catered to a sporting crowd that spanned all social classes. The crowd was mainly male except for the performers, waitresses, and prostitutes. In fact, the line between performers, waitresses, and prostitutes was often blurred. Women in concert saloons would solicit several high-priced drinks with promises of increasingly intimate exchange that would eventually move to upstairs rooms. The sex and cheap entertainment were primarily designed to encourage the purchase of alcoholic drinks. Stale beer and smoke were the two dominant odors that permeated these establishments which generally, with the exception of the more elaborate theaters, had a fierce reputation as incredibly rank and dirty.

Performances in this type of atmosphere varied tremendously. Smaller dives would have primarily local talent, but the ornate larger concert saloons could stage performances as elaborate as "legitimate" theater. They staged primarily the variety shows which had become popular in the 1840s, featuring singers and dancers but also presenting virtually every manner of skill. Acts that centered on physical feats were common. Wrestlers and boxers would commonly challenge a man from the audience to a match or bout, and weightlifters were popular as well. Scantily clad women often appeared as weightlifters or boxers, women fighting other women of course (see Chapter 8), again titillating male audiences with their physicality and tight-fitting outfits. Comedy routines with an earthy, ribald humor that revolved around sexual innuendo, known early on as purple acts, were also common. Another ubiquitous act was the troupe of suggestive female dancers, in the French cancan tradition, who strutted, thrust out their hips, and exposed their "drawers" with high leg kicks. Concert saloons of course continued but they lost much of their importance when other cheap amusements emerged in the 1880s and 1890s, such as burlesque, vaudeville, and cheap theater.[3]

Dime Museums

Dime museums offered another early venue of entertainment for those with limited funds in the Gilded Age. These museums normally housed a motley assemblage of human and natural oddities, perhaps a few paintings, some scientific marvels, and a theater. Dime museums were also one of the first venues to try to attract respectable audiences, which in this age meant middle-class women, by introducing afternoon matinees, banning prostitutes, barring liquor and tobacco, and eliminating bawdy acts. Moses Kimball opened one of the first such museums, the Boston Museum in 1841, followed by P. T. Barnum's American Museum in New York in 1848. Like Kimball, Barnum ran mainly reform melodramas like *The Drunkard: Or the Fallen Saved*. Barnum's museum theater was quite large, with seating for 3,000 people. Museum theaters sprang up in cities throughout the nation, and some hired resident acting companies that produced some of the finest actors in the nation.

The typical dime museum show consisted of a parade of the "scientific oddities" like the bearded lady or dog-faced boy and then an array of fairly standard performers. First came the "quick crayon-sketch masters, magicians, illusionists, mind-readers, sword-swallowers, glass-chewers, fire-eaters, and contortionists" followed by "comics, Irish tenors, banjo players, acrobats, dancers, and 'educated animal acts.' " New York City's Bowery, however, housed the cheaper museums that catered to a male audience seeking titillation and they booked acts much like the concert saloons.[4]

Burlesque

Late in the century the variety show entertainment offered in concert saloons began to take very different paths. One path led to respectable performances in vaudeville and the other to the less respectable burlesque circuit. Burlesque continued the brazen sexuality of the concert saloon, capitalizing on the new commercialized sexuality so prominent in American cities. Burlesque formed a circuit of theaters much like vaudeville, though unlike vaudeville the burlesque circuit thrived on sexual innuendo and explicit material. The word burlesque primarily referred to a parody in the 1840s and 1850s, and it was common for shows to burlesque opera or serious plays. Parodies of popular opera and theater continued to be referred to as burlesques and thrived in mainstream theater, but there began to develop a burlesque circuit of theaters that relied on sexually explicit material that was distinct from the earlier form. Starting in the 1860s burlesque began to be associated with "purple acts," which eventually came to be known as "blue acts," that relied on sexual material. By the late 1860s theatrical performances with women dressed in transparent clothing were common. For example, P. T. Barnum imported Lydia Thompson and her troupe of British chorus girls in 1866, and they performed in flesh-colored tights and revealed bare arms. In an era of corsets, multiple layers of full-length skirts, petticoats, hip pads, and bustles that obscured the female body (see Chapter 5), wearing form-fitting tights was extremely titillating. Thompson's troupe starred in a hit show in 1868, *Ixion*, where they dressed in their tights and played men's roles. The show grossed $375,000 in its first year. Mabel Saintley also became famous starring in Mme. Rintz's Female Minstrels in the 1880s. Burlesque's association with intellectual comedy dimmed by the 1880s when burlesque theater managers sought to increase the sexually explicit material by showing as much female flesh as was legal. Burlesque theaters presented shows often in a three-act sequence: first an ensemble of comedians entertained the crowd with jokes and songs, then variety acts appeared, and finally a one-act musical parody. The burlesque circuit would be a fertile breeding ground for comedians who sought to leap into the more successful and respectable vaudeville circuit. These performances were definitely not for the respectable and manifested the commercialization of sex that was becoming so prominent in the Gilded Age. The burlesque circuit would survive in this form until the 1920s when it was transformed into a more debased form that was primarily a medium for strippers.[5]

Vaudeville
Pastor, Albee, and Keith

Vaudeville grew out of the variety theater so popular in the early and mid-nineteenth century. Tony Pastor, a former circus ringmaster and singer, sought to create a clean variety show, free from the taint of sexuality and vulgar comedy so prevalent in the concert saloons. Pastor wanted to alter the perceptions of the variety show as early as 1865 but really began to succeed when he moved to the Fourteenth Street Theater in New York City in 1881. Like the dime museums, Pastor attracted genteel audiences by bringing in women during afternoon matinees and banning peanuts and liquor from his shows. Other entrepreneurs saw the advantages of attracting a respectable crowd, and soon Edward Franklin Albee and Benjamin Franklin Keith began to experiment with live shows. Keith introduced the continuous show format, where performances continued in a cycle without emptying the theater after every show, which became the standard vaudeville pattern. Albee, Keith's manager, suggested they replace the variety show with a shortened, pirated version of *The Mikado* in 1885. Audiences who could not afford the $1.50 for Broadway tickets swarmed to Keith's theater for $.25 tickets. Popular musical theater interspersed with variety shows became a successful format. Dancers, singers, magicians, mind readers, acrobats, contortionists, comedians, one-act playlets, human oddities, sports stars, opera singers, orchestra musicians, jugglers, escape artists, dancing bears, strongmen, musicians of all kinds, and circus acts were just some of the acts constantly playing on vaudeville. Keith and Albee, however, also brought in "gold brick" acts that brought the prestige of stars from symphony orchestras, operas, or Broadway shows to vaudeville. Vaudeville theater owners handsomely paid legitimate theater stars, like Louisa Lane Drew or Ethel Barrymore, to do 15-minute playlets, do a short classical piece, or sing an aria. A typical vaudeville bill listed acts in order of appearance and typically consisted of eight acts: the opening act was normally acrobats or animals, "singing sister" or "dancing brother" acts often went second, next was a one-act play or comedy skit, fourth was a novelty or dance act, fifth was a star act, intermission, sixth was a big act like animal acts or choirs, the next to closing position was for the headliner who was often a singer or comedian, and then a mediocre closing act. Comedians were often hired to emcee the bill and there was always some sort of music which could range from a single piano to a full orchestra. Performers were often on the road for 40 weeks out of the year and performed anywhere from two to five performances a day depending on the circuit.

Cheap Theater

Vaudeville also developed into inexpensive theater. With "legitimate" theater prices growing, vaudeville demonstrated that there was a demand for low-priced entertainment, particularly theater. In the 1890s, New York City's theater seating capacity grew over twofold and the number of touring shows increased from 50 in 1880 to more than 500 in 1900. Much of this growth was coming from the expansion of inexpensive theater. From the vaudeville entrepreneurs like Keith and Albee, Sylvester Poli, and F. F. Proctor came new low-priced playhouses known as 10–20–30 theaters, so called for the tiered ticket prices ranging from $.10 to $.30, that catered to the crowds of urban amusement seekers. While melodrama faded from Broadway, its popularity thrived in the 10–20–30 theaters, that unlike "legitimate" theater often relied on resident stock companies. By the mid-1890s many failing opera houses were transformed into these cheap theaters with resident companies and became fantastically successful. The expansion of theater capacity in New York, Chicago, Denver, and a host of other cities was based not on the growth of legitimate theater but on the expansion of these cheap playhouses. While melodrama, farce, and musical comedy were popular staples in the cheap theaters they also ran Broadway shows that were a year or two old. Elite critics lambasted popular theater as mere entertainment, and not very good entertainment, that denigrated theater as art. Popular theater goers did not care. Popular theater, therefore, was much more an outgrowth of vaudeville than the elite controlled legitimate theater.

Vaudeville Circuits

By the early 1890s vaudeville had emerged as the main variety theater entertainment in the country, and thrived with inexpensive prices ($.10–$.25). Keith and Albee, Sullivan & Consodine, Alexander Pantages, and Marcus Loew were among the entrepreneurs that built chains of theaters throughout the country, creating the vaudeville circuits. In the early twentieth century these circuits became differentiated by price ($.10–$.25) and talent, with the major stars playing the "big time" Orpheum Circuit and earning $450 to $1,000 per week, while "small time" performers played circuits that paid as little as $15 per week. These circuits were massive and demanded travel that could only be accomplished with a well-developed railroad network (see Chapter 11). For example, the Orpheum circuit by the 1910s looked like this: Orpheum Theater–San

Francisco, Orpheum Theater–Los Angeles, Orpheum Theater–Oakland, Orpheum Theater–Kansas City, Orpheum Theater–Omaha, Orpheum Theater–Denver, Orpheum Theater–New Orleans, Orpheum Theater–Memphis, Orpheum Theater–Minneapolis, Orpheum Theater–St. Paul, Orpheum Theater–Winnipeg, Orpheum Theater–Seattle, Orpheum Theater–Portland, Orpheum Theater–Vancouver, Orpheum Theater–Salt Lake City, Orpheum Theater–Lincoln, Orpheum Theater–Duluth, Orpheum Theater–Des Moines, Orpheum Theater–Souix City, Alhambra Orpheum Theater–Ogden, Orpheum Theater–Madison, Clunie Theater–Sacramento, Yosemite Theater–Stockton, Victory Theater–San Jose, White Theater–Fresno, Burns Theater–Colorado Springs, Palace Theater–New York, Palace Theater–Chicago, Majestic Theater–Chicago, Majestic Theater–Milwaukee, Columbia Theater–St. Louis, Majestic Theater–Fort Worth, Majestic Theater–Dallas, Majestic Theater–Houston, and the Majestic Theater–San Antonio. In the early twentieth century the Theater Owners and Bookers Association, called the TOBA circuit, developed an all-black circuit which played to black audiences in the South and major cities like Chicago, Baltimore, Washington D.C., St. Louis, and Kansas City. Harlem's famed Apollo Theater was part of the TOBA circuit. Black vaudeville performers referred to TOBA as "tough on black asses" for the low pay and difficult conditions.

Vaudeville Performers

Most of the great vaudeville performers of the late nineteenth century are largely forgotten today, but they were household names in the Gilded Age. Comedian team Webber and Fields became famous for their "Dutch" comedy routines and their *The Passing Show* (1894) set the standard for musical reviews. Williams and Walker became the most famous of the African-American vaudeville performers, and in a bizarre twist Walker commonly appeared in blackface (see Chapter 9). Sissieretta Jones formed the Black Patti Troubadours in 1896, named after white opera sensation Adeline Patti, and went on to a successful vaudeville career that spanned over 20 years. Lillian Russell rose to fantastic stardom from vaudeville to Broadway singing operetta tunes. May Irwin started as a child performer and went on to be a leading act in vaudeville in the 1880s with her singing and comedy. In the 1890s she moved to a successful Broadway career in musical farces like *The Widow Jones* (1895), *Courted in Court* (1896), *Belle of Bridgeport* (1900), and a number of successful productions in the early twentieth century. She became one of the famous white "coon shouters," singing coon songs in the bully genre like the "Bully Song" introduced in *The Widow Jones* (see Chapter 9).[6]

"LEGITIMATE" THEATER

Dramatic Theater

The Sacralization of Culture

By the Gilded Age the exclusion of the rowdy elements (working-class men and prostitutes) from "legitimate" theater was virtually complete. Theater owners exerted more control over their patrons' behavior and excluded prostitutes and rowdies by building smaller theaters and raising ticket prices. By the 1880s tickets to the theater were $1 to $1.50, which constituted nearly two-thirds of a typical nonfarm worker's daily wages. This began the process that historian Lawrence Levine refers to as the sacralization of culture, where cultural elites transformed theater into an art that sought not so much to entertain as to edify audiences. Legitimate theater was so successful in attracting respectable audiences that by the 1890s the crowds were primarily female. Although women in the 1860s and 1870s were viewed as the main force of culture and civilization, by the 1890s male theater critics saw them as a force of commercialization that threatened theater because they did not have the intellect to truly appreciate it as high art. By 1900 the term "legitimate" theater was used extensively to differentiate it from popular theater, vaudeville, the circus, and burlesque.

Shakespeare

A good example of how this transformation of theater into high culture took place was the way in which the works of Shakespeare were transformed. Before the 1860s, Shakespeare's plays were performed universally throughout American theaters to all manner of audiences, and were the subject of countless parodies. In the Gilded Age, however, with the separation of audiences into different theaters the proponents of high culture began to view Shakespeare as high art, separate from the unwashed masses and truly appreciated only by an educated cultural elite. The cultural elite sought to enshrine Shakespeare, who ironically originally wrote for a broad and largely uneducated audience, as an element of a refined and educated culture. At the same time the increased emphasis on literary instead of oral culture, massive immigration of southern and eastern Europeans for whom Shakespearean English was incredibly dense, and the decline of oratory in American society all contributed to the decline of Shakespeare as part of a common culture. Exacerbating the decline of Shakespeare in the common cultural experience of Americans was the fact that the entertainments that had accompanied the theater before the Civil War—like jugglers, acrobats, and comedians—were segregated from "legitimate" theater and performed in other venues like concert saloons, burlesque, vaudeville, and circuses.

The Transformation of Theater

Theater underwent a great deal of change in the Gilded Age. New York City became the center of theater just as it became the center of the popular music industry. Also, trends in theater changed as realism began to influence acting as much as it influenced literature (see Chapter 8). Combination touring companies completely took over from the old resident stock company in legitimate theater (but not in the cheap playhouses; see Cheap Theater). Before the 1870s stars would take shows to different locales, using actors from the local repertory company to stage the show. The massive expansion of railroads during and after the Civil War (see Chapter 11) allowed for theater stars to take their own combination companies on the road. As early as the 1876–1877 seasons there were almost 100 touring combination companies and a decade later there were 282. Conversely, there were 50 permanent resident stock companies in 1870, four in 1880, and practically none by 1900. Another major change was the emergence of the Theatrical Syndicate (1896) controlled by Sam Nixon, Fred Zimmerman, Charles Frohman, Al Hayman, Marc Klaw, and Abraham Erlanger. Since most touring shows came out of New York City theater, local theaters had to book several touring shows in order to get an entire season. Into this vacuum stepped the syndicate, which offered local theater managers a full season of top shows in return for exclusive contracts with the Syndicate. The Theatrical Syndicate concentrated on gaining control of the major theatrical circuits between the large cities. The Theatrical Syndicate attacked theaters that refused to book exclusively through them by building a syndicate theater close to the competitor and offering shows at low prices until their rival folded. Actors and producers who refused to cooperate would be boycotted by the syndicate. These tactics gained the Theatrical Syndicate far-reaching control of legitimate theater by 1900.

Famous Actors

With Americans thirsting for theater a number of actors rose to fame in the Gilded Age. After the death of the most famous actor of the mid-nineteenth century, Edwin Forrest, a new giant of the stage emerged, Edwin Booth (1833–1893). Booth was perhaps most well known for his 1863 rendition of Hamlet, which ran for 100 shows, a record not surpassed until the twentieth century. Whereas Booth was undoubtedly aided to his rise to fame as the son of the famous actor Junius Brutus Booth, he was just as certainly hurt by the fact that his brother was John Wilkes Booth, assassin of Abraham Lincoln. Edwin took several years off after his brother's deed, but continued as a highly demanded star until his death in 1893. Booth far outlasted most of his contemporaries on the stage and was arguably the greatest tragic actor of his day. Booth was certainly aided by a resurgence in the 1880s when fellow actor Lawrence Barrett joined with him, taking over completely the organizing and management tasks. Edwin Adams, Charles Couldock, and Joseph Haworth were also well-respected tragedians. Augustin Daly (1839–1999) also rose to fame as a writer, producer, and actor who ran his own touring company. Daly became famous for producing stage stars from his troupe including such actors as Clara Morris, Agnes Ethel, Fanny Davenport, and particularly John Drew II and Ada Rehan. Famous comedians of the Gilded Age were Edmund Milton Holland, May Irwin, Nat Goodwin, Francis Wilson, Fritz Williams, William Crane, James Herne, and Sol Smith Russell. By the 1890s and early twentieth century a new generation of serious actors were dominating the stage such as David Belasco, Richard Mansfield, H. H. Sothern, and Otis Skinner. Some actors became so tied to their characters that contemporary audiences thought of the actors as the characters they portrayed. William Gillette's Sherlock Holmes set the standard for the famous detective that influenced virtually every subsequent performance, and James O'Neill gained fame as the Count of Monte Cristo but found it almost impossible to break from the role that made him famous.

Drew/Barrymore Family

Like the Booth family there were other famous acting families in the Gilded Age. The famous actors Louisa Lane Drew and John Drew would produce a veritable troupe of actors. Louisa Lane started as a child actress and gained widespread fame. She married John Drew, a famous Irish actor who had purchased the Arch Street Theater. Upon John's death she managed the theater from 1862 to 1892. Her son John Drew II became a famous actor in his own right and his sons John and Sidney Drew would also go on to fame as actors. Louisa and John Drew's daughter Georgiana Drew also became an acclaimed actress before she married well-known actor Maurice Barrymore. Their children—Lionel, John, and Ethel—went on to significant acting careers on stage and in movies in the twentieth century. John Barrymore is the grandfather of the most current Drew/Barrymore actress to achieve fame, Drew Barrymore.[7]

Musical Theater

The most important influences on American musical theater in the Gilded Age were the musical farces of Harrigan and Hart, operettas, musical revues, and African-American musicals. Vaudeville had a distinct and important influence. Distinctions between the variety show format of vaudeville and Broadway were not as sharp as modern audiences might think, and the lines between them were fluid with many vaudeville stars moving to Broadway and many Broadway stars lured to the top vaudeville circuit. Tony Pastor, one of the creators of vaudeville, "discovered" the talents of Edward Harrigan, Tony Hart, George M. Cohan, and Lillian Russell first in vaudeville before they all became stars on Broadway.

Harrigan and Hart

American musical theater started slowly out of the 1860s. Most historians of music at least nod to the appearance of *The Black Crook* (1866) as an important step in musical theater, though this production was more of a music spectacular than a recognizable musical. What *The Black Crook* did do was run for 475 shows and totaled gross box-office receipts of more than $1 million, making it the first bona fide Broadway hit. More important to the development of the form of the musical were the farces of Harrigan and Hart. Edward Harrigan and Tony Hart specialized in New York Bowery humor that offered humorous portrayals of the Bowery's inhabitants. They developed their act in New York's variety theaters. Harrigan provided the lyrics and David Braham, Harrigan's father-in-law, composed the music. By 1873 their act was called *The Mulligan Guard* and was much more developed than a simple musical sketch but was not quite a musical. They became so successful that they launched a 40-minute musical comedic sketch titled *The Mulligan Guard Picnic* (1878) on Broadway. This began a seven-year run of musical farces that relied heavily on thick ethnic dialect, slapstick, dancing, puns, and parody. The emphasis on realistic local dialect echoed the realism and local color so prominent in literature (see Chapter 8). *The Mulligan Guard's Ball* (1879), *The Mulligan Guard Surprise* (1880), *Cordelia's Aspirations* (1883), and *Dan's Tribulations* (1884) were all shows that were part of the saga of Dan and Cordelia Mulligan and Dan's marching band. These musical farces relied on outrageous humor but also touched real ethnic and racial tensions between urban blacks, Irish immigrants, and German immigrants. Harrigan and Hart were stars and widely known; Rudyard Kipling's novel *Kim* (1901) even quoted *The Mulligan Guard*. The successful duo ended their collaboration in 1885, but their efforts in musical theater dampened melodrama and brought greater realism, which had an enduring influence on American musical theater.[8]

Gilbert and Sullivan

Operetta also had a major influence on American musical theater in the Gilded Age, particularly the work of the British team Gilbert and Sullivan. Operetta, also called comic opera or light opera, was the middling ground between the farcical musical and the opera. Like musical farces but unlike opera, operetta relied on speaking parts for its characters to move the plot. Yet, operetta relied on an emotional tone similar to opera and normally used trained opera singers. As a result the composition of operetta music and the singing was often of higher quality than the standard musical farce. William S. Gilbert's lyrics and Arthur Sullivan's music transformed musical theater by creating operettas where the music blended perfectly with the coherent and witty plots. Gilbert was gifted in writing silly and yet satirical lyrics that were at once pithy and poignant. Gilbert and Sullivan were already famous in England for *Trial by Jury* (1875) and *The Sorcerer* (1877) when their first huge trans-Atlantic hit, *H.M.S. Pinafore* (1878), made them overnight sensations on Broadway. American producers pirated the operetta because no international copyright agreement was in place, and staged unauthorized performances in the United States to great acclaim, well before Gilbert and Sullivan brought their production to New York in 1879. The show sold out the 1,000 seats of San Francisco's Tivoli Theater for 63 consecutive nights. To stop the pilfering of their work Gilbert and Sullivan opened their next show, *The Pirates of Penzance* (1880), concurrently in the United States and Great Britain. The duo followed with *Patience* (1881), *Iolanthe* (1882), *Princess Ida* (1884), and the stunningly popular *The Mikado* (1885). The complete development of Gilbert and Sullivan operettas made American musical theater look primitive indeed. Gilbert and Sullivan operettas had great characters, "well-knit comic plots, songs that grow naturally out of comic or romantic situations on the stage, well-crafted lyrics that make their points deftly, and memorable tunes."[9] Gilbert and Sullivan would have a tremendous influence on the development of American musicals, helping to set high standards of form, lyrics, tune, and coherence.[10]

1890s Musicals

Under the influence of the sophistication of Gilbert and Sullivan productions American musicals and operettas grew more complex and substantial. American operetta abounded on Broadway in the 1890s. Reginald De Koven and Harry Smith's *The Begum* (1887) and *Robin Hood* (1891), John Philip Sousa's *El Capitan* (1896), and Victor Herbert's *Prince Ananias* (1894), *Babes in Toyland* (1903), and *Naughty Marietta* (1910) signalled that American operetta had come into its own. At the same time the musical farce tradition of Harrigan and Hart continued to be very popular draws on Broadway. *A Trip to Chinatown* (1891) was one of the biggest hits of the decade (see Chapter 9). *The Belle of New York* (1897), which made Edna May a star, also proved to be very successful and was one of the first U.S. musicals to do well in Great Britain. This vernacular style culminated in the early twentieth century in George M. Cohan's productions like *The Governor's Son* (1901), *Little Johnny Jones* (1904), and *George Washington, Jr.* (1906).[11]

African-American Musicals

Like so much in the Gilded Age, African Americans were part of the popular culture and their distinctive syncopated musical styles became popular in the general culture; yet they remained apart. Traveling minstrel shows continued to be popular though many of these were slowly transformed into musical comedy troupes that sought to distance themselves from the romanticization of the Old South. Most of the African-American shows until 1897 were revues that featured a wide variety of songs and styles until Bob Cole and Billy Johnson produced *A Trip to Coontown*. George Walker and Bert Williams, who moved seamlessly from vaudeville to theater and back again, also added significantly to musical theater. They first appeared in the musical *The Gold Bug* (1896) where they performed the cakewalk, a syncopated dance that came out of plantation slave life, which became a national fad. After becoming one of the leading acts in vaudeville they turned again to musical theater. Walker and Williams wrote *In Dahomey* (1903) with poet Paul Laurence Dunbar and composer Will Marion Cook. The musical became a hit on Broadway and in London. Walker, Williams, and Cook went on to make *Abyssinia* (1906) and *Bandanna Land* (1908). Vaudeville star Sissieretta Jones also staged several musical comedies in the early twentieth century. While these shows gained widespread acclaim and there is little doubt that syncopated African-American music had a broad impact on the nation (see Chapter 9), black performers became extremely rare on Broadway after 1915. Cole, Walker, Williams, and Cook self-consciously sought to create black-controlled productions that not only avoided the destructive stereotypes of African Americans so prevalent in the culture, but also parodied, mocked, and satirized those terrible stereotypes. Images of the happy Sambo, the ultra-sexual black woman, and the dangerous "bully" Negro plagued African Americans in this era of coon songs, Jim Crow segregation, and the lynch mob. Black theater, at least, could quietly mock and undermine these stock characters. Since segregation denied blacks admittance into most theaters, a circuit of theaters that served African Americans emerged in the early twentieth century.[12]

Opera

Opera had been popular in the United States for all of the nineteenth century, and before the Gilded Age had enjoyed a widespread popularity among all classes of Americans. At mid-century scores of English and Italian touring opera companies traveled throughout the United States. But, like legitimate theater, elites began to take control of opera in the

Gilded Age, redefining it as an elite art and not a popular entertainment. Elite opera houses like the Academy of Music and later the Metropolitan Opera House, both in New York City, catered to the rich. After the 1892 fire destroyed the Met it was rebuilt with the Diamond Horseshoe—the 35 box seats of the wealthy shareholders who lorded over the opera. In the middle of the U was J. P. Morgan and spread out along this array of dazzling wealth were 11 other boxes held by Morgan associates, 11 boxes possessed by the Vanderbilts, and 5 boxes controlled by the old New York knickerbocker crowd like the Astors. As the elite began to lay claim to opera they asserted the artistic supremacy of operas performed in the language in which they were composed, which meant not English. Italian, French, and German opera were art and only the cultivated and educated elite could appreciate the art and drama of true opera in its native language. Opera translated and performed in English was for popular entertainment only and did not have the power to edify audiences. Like so many European artistic accomplishments, opera became just another masterpiece to be purchased and displayed by the fabulously wealthy Americans of the Gilded Age who desperately sought the cultural status afforded by Old World art.

Performers

Several American opera singers rose to star status. Christine Nilsson gained fame in the typical fashion by touring in Europe and then the United States. Emma Abbott, on the other hand, never liked Europe and she gained fame in the United States through her constant touring with her opera company. The greatest of all was Adeline Patti who became the most sought-after opera performer of the Gilded Age. Patti was a star in Europe for 20 years before she arrived in 1881 for her first American tour. She was a sensation in Italy where this diva doubled then tripled her fees to the delight of the newspapers. Opera, though, changed over the course of the Gilded Age from an entertainment that was widely popular and available to most Americans to an elite-controlled "art" that became increasingly viewed by smaller numbers of Americans as it was edged out by popular theater, vaudeville, and the English language operettas.[13]

FILM

Film also appeared for the first time in the Gilded Age. In 1894 investors opened parlors with Thomas Edison's kinetoscopes, charging $.25 for admittance and to watch the short films in five different machines. These early film entrepreneurs found it impossible to make a return on their investment—the upscale crowds that could afford the high cost (remember hours of vaudeville entertainment could be had for as little as ten cents) simply did not come into the parlors. Biograph came out with its competing mutoscope in 1897 but the market was simply not with upscale crowds. The large array of film projectors, however, did become widely used after 1896 in lecture halls and in vaudeville acts. Film would become a favorite in the vaudeville play bill after Benjamin Franklin Keith first used a film in one of his theaters in 1896. Entrepreneurs also quickly discovered that sporting men and boys were interested in the short films and in the late 1890s penny arcades were opening in cities throughout the country. The machines appeared in barber shops, drug stores, hotels, boardwalks, midways, ferry and rail terminals, and even theater lobbies. For a penny a viewer could watch waves crashing on the shore or the titillating shorts like *Little Egypt*, *How Girls Undress*, *How Girls Go to Bed*, or *The Birth of the Pearl*. By the early twentieth century the penny arcades were moving into immigrant neighborhoods and some of the largest boasted 100 peep show machines. In 1904, Harry Davis opened the first nickelodeon in Pittsburgh. The nickelodeon was a nickel theater which projected the short film on a screen and the audience watched from theater seating. There was an explosion of nickel theaters. In New York alone the number of theaters showing movies rose from 50 in 1900 to 400 by 1908. Movie industry pioneers developed the modern movie theater and feature films by 1915. Film in the Gilded Age, however, was still largely a curiosity and film makers had not yet realized how important performance could be to the medium.[14]

CONCLUSION

As elite culture took control of certain forms of performing arts—legitimate theater and Shakespeare, opera, and symphonic music—they became increasingly marginalized in the lives of average Americans. Whereas Shakespeare and opera were widely shared cultural experiences for many Americans before the Civil War, by the Gilded Age these had become the bastions of high culture. As a result, most Americans eschewed these performing arts in favor of those that more accurately reflected their lives and income like cheap theater, vaudeville, burlesque, the circus, or Wild West shows. The Gilded Age was a foreshadowing of the growing importance and power of popular culture and the promise of what would be in the twentieth century.

11

Travel

BACKGROUND

The massive expansion of railroads and the introduction of streetcars dramatically improved travel within cities and throughout the nation. These new travel possibilities allowed for the massive expansion of a new vacation and tourism industry in the Gilded Age that radically increased the ability of Americans to take vacations. As railroads spread their web throughout the nation and cities improved their transportation systems it was increasingly easier and cheaper for Americans to travel across the continent. Even as travel grew easier, rising incomes and expectations of leisure pushed Americans toward tourism and vacations in unprecedented numbers.

PUBLIC TRANSPORTATION

Railroads

Expansion

The massive expansion of railroads and their central importance in transportation and freight made them the major symbol of American progress in the Gilded Age. Railroad expansion in the West preceded large-scale settlement of the region. Of the 12 states admitted into the United States after the Civil War to 1912, only Nebraska had under 1,000 miles of railroad track upon admission. Railroads solved the enormous problem of distance in the American West, allowing large numbers of migrants to travel relatively easily and quickly into the vast western territories. Illustrating the importance of westward migration, very few of the lines ran north and south; most ran east and west. The completion of the transcontinental railroad in 1869, when the Union Pacific and Central Pacific lines met in Promontory, Utah, united the nation literally and metaphorically. The ability to unite East and West by 1,800 miles of rail became a national symbol of American ingenuity, technological superiority, and material progress. By the early 1880s railways pushed four other transcontinental lines into the Pacific Northwest and southern California. Even as these connections were being made, eastern lines were also dramatically expanding, giving the nation 193,346 miles of rail. Standardized rail gauge, electrical signals, manual mechanical interlocking, the railroad companies' adoption of standardized time zones, and new inventions like George Westinghouse's air brake and Eli Janney's automatic coupler, made railway travel much safer and faster.

Passenger Numbers

Passenger traffic on railroad lines grew dramatically in the last third of the nineteenth century, and become safer, more luxurious, and faster than ever. Americans flocked to the 1,224 railroad companies, which by 1900 carried 576,831,000 passengers per year when the entire population of the United States was only 76 million. Railroads were definitely becoming faster, and in 1893 a train broke the 100-mile-per-hour barrier. Not only were trains safer but also smoother and quieter with the invention of the paper wheel by Richard Allen (1869), which used compressed paper at the center of the car wheels. The paper center absorbed the shock and sound from the wheels, making the ride smoother and quieter. Passenger trains eventually developed a wide variety of cars, including the smoking car, available for different fares.

Coach Cars

Passenger traffic varied tremendously by railroad line and in cost. Raised-roof coach cars gave riders much more room and ventilation than the early passenger cars, though there was considerable difference in accommodations and price between the common cars and the parlor cars traveled by the well-to-do. Long-distance passengers seeking lower fares often traveled in the wooden coach chair-cars.[1] The famous author Robert Louis Stevenson traveled from the East to the West Coast on the coach chair-cars in 1892 and found that the trip alternated between pleasant and terrible. When he tried to get on the cars in New Jersey he found the passengers were locked out and they were forced to stand in the rain for some time. Food was often unavailable for long stretches (30 hours at one point), the coach chair-cars were at times extremely cold, he was forced to change trains because to cross the country he had to go to a

An Elko (Nevada) hotel. Courtesy of the Northeastern Nevada Historical Society.

different railroad line, and at times he suffered from incredible thirst. Even when the train stopped Stevenson often found it difficult to get food quickly enough before the train pulled away from the station. Stevenson did note that the food was fairly good and cheaper than Pullman food prices. Short-distance travelers found the standard chair-cars comfortable, but, as Stevenson found, cost-conscious long-distance travelers faced difficult sleeping conditions. In cold weather riders huddled around the two stoves, one at each end of the car, in attempts to stay warm, and lounged uncomfortably in hot weather because windows often had to stay shut to keep out the dust. But for the cost-conscious the coach fare, which from Omaha to San Francisco cost $33.20 in 1869, was an affordable way to travel quickly across the continent. Surely it was easier, safer, and much more convenient than overland travel in a Conestoga wagon. Scores of guidebooks were produced to give advice about train travel, such as *The Pacific Tourist* (1876) by Henry T. Williams, and it was a topic that magazines constantly covered as well because of its revolutionary effect on travel in the Gilded Age.[2]

Immigrant Cars

Third-class cars, known also as immigrant cars after their main occupants, were even more dismal. Stevenson traveled the last leg of his trip not in the typical chair-car, but in an "immigrant train." He entered the bachelor's car, which was stuck between the women and children's car and the Chinese car. He described the car as a "long, narrow wooden box, like a flat-roofed Noah's ark" with a stove at one end and a restroom at the other. There was a middle passage with benches lining each side that were "too short for anything but a young child. Where there is scarce elbow-room for two to sit, there will not be space enough for one to lie." On this train, railroad employees rented boards and cushions to immigrants for $2.50 which could be placed from bench to bench. The seats then could be turned to face each other, forming a bed. This was only possible when the train was not crowded. Stevenson also found that the equality he found so prevalent in the country did not really extend down to the immigrant third-class passengers. When there were holdups the third-class cars were always first to be delayed. Also, when the immigrant train pulled away from the station conductors often did not yell the customary "all aboard," so third-class passengers had to pay close attention to their train or be left. American attitudes toward the immigrants varied from hostile to patronizing. One rich rail traveler described the immigrants as "wild and strange as denizens of another world." Stevenson also found the food provided at stations to be "palatable" and inexpensive. But, the constant delays made it impossible to predict when they would stop, so there could be very long gaps between meals. These delays made the newsboys (also known as a butch, train butch, or news butch) who were present on virtually all trains, even more vital for third-class travelers because they sold fruit, candy, books, newspapers, dime novels, cigars, soap, tin washing dishes, towels, coffee, tea, sugar, pitchers, dried fruits, nuts, and canned foods. Accounts from those who traveled the immigrant cars, however, related how many families brought large stocks of food to make the trip less expensive. Stevenson was so relieved upon entering California, close to his destination in San Francisco, that he wrote, "Few People have praised God more happily than I did." By the 1880s several railroad lines had improved immigrant train service, including plain sleeping cabins and direct service to the coast without delays.[3]

First-Class Cars

First-class travel was a far different experience. Parlor cars allowed for very comfortable travel for customers who could pay the higher fare, often featuring reclining chairs. But it was the addition of sleeping cars that revolutionized long-distance travel for American rail passengers. Many firms competed in the sleeping car sector like the Rip Van Winkle Line, Woodruff Sleeping and Parlor Coach Company, Monarch Parlor-Sleeping Car Company, and the Wagner Palace Car Company, but by the end of the century the Pullman Company had developed a near monopoly on sleeping cars. Pullman boasted 4,138 cars traveling 184,000 miles of rail and carrying 14,969,000 passengers in 1905. George Pullman improved on his prewar designs, introducing the "Pioneer" which contained expensive carpets and upholstery, mirrors, and hand-carved wood. Pullman soon introduced complimentary bed linen in his sleeping cars and dining cars that served excellent food. Pullman created his own company town, named after himself, where his company produced the most luxurious parlor, sleeping, and dining cars of the Gilded Age (see Chapter 4). Pullman's famous hotel car featured a sleeper cabin with an attached drawing room. By 1887 several railroad lines had installed electric lights in their cars. Typical first-class travelers did not get their own cars but instead rented a berth in a section of the Pullman. Travel guides recommended to readers that they travel with a companion so that they could take up an entire section of the car and would not have to sleep in a berth next to a stranger. Round trip travel from coast to coast started at $300 for basic first-class accommodations.

Pullman also custom-made hundreds of cars for the richest men in the country who often owned multicar trains; personal Pullman cars became an important symbol of status and allowed for comfortable travel for the rich. These elite cars were called "varnish" for their luxurious wood paneling. Florence Leslie, the spouse of the very wealthy publisher Frank Leslie, traveled in one of Pullman's elite model hotel cars in 1877. She found it quite luxurious, equipped with a kitchen, storeroom, and an

African-American cook who prepared meals that she described as Delmonican, after the famous New York City restaurant that specialized in French haute cuisine (see Chapter 6). Her greatest inconvenience was an eight-hour delay because of an accident farther up the line. The car Leslie enjoyed, though they were all somewhat different, was probably much like the typical private car which usually contained a bathroom with a bronze tub, a kitchen, saloon, an eight-person dining table, and bedrooms. Pullman's elite cars were unique works of art. J. P. Morgan chartered a special multicar train which possessed a barber's car with a domed Tiffany skylight, while the Budweisers had a tap with cold beer in each car.

Luxury lines offered a wide variety of amenities to their customers. They typically possessed not only parlor cars for day travel and sleeping cars but also specialized cars such as club, library, dining, observation, saloon, chapel, and music cars. Pullman's company introduced the flexible vestibule which made it possible for passengers to travel to the different types of cars in safety and comfort. Certain lines also carried cars just for women traveling without male escort. Luxurious depots began to appear like Union Station (1894) in St. Louis, which served 18 railroads, and Boston's South Station (1898). Luxury lines also offered fairly fast travel; in 1876 a special train traversed the 3,317 miles between New York City and San Francisco in three and a half days. By the turn of the century, railroads had transformed travel and freight in the United States, dramatically speeding travel to the West.[4]

Free Riders

Men who hopped trains for free rides were on the opposite end of the spectrum from the luxury of the Pullman cars and even far removed from what comforts there were in the immigrant car. Historian David Courtwright refers to this group as a "floating army" of at least a half million men who were primarily itinerant industrial and agricultural laborers. Nineteenth-century Americans knew these men as tramps. Most Gilded Age tramps were only temporary riders on the rails, moving from job to job, but there was a core of permanent, homeless migrants. The wheat harvest in particular was a time of high tramp traffic as men poured into the wheat states. Flippin' (jumping a train for a free ride) was extremely dangerous. Tramps, however, came from male-dominated subcultures that valued the courage, daring, and skill that flippin' took. They also ordinarily labored in dangerous jobs like mining, logging, construction, and agriculture which made them accustomed to the risks of flippin'. Tramps normally tried to force the doors of a freight car, rode on top of the cars, or rode underneath the trains on the rods, suspended just above the track. Tramping was very common in the Gilded Age and prominent men like Supreme Court Justice William O. Douglas and writer Jack London spent time riding the rails.[5]

Stagecoaches

Although railroads were certainly the most dynamic force transforming travel in the Gilded Age, stagecoach lines still played a prominent role in transportation in the West. In remote regions where railroads did not reach, stagecoaches played a major function in moving people from the main railroad lines into the hinterland. The oval Concord coach was one of the most popular, though Troy, Celerity, and numerous wagons also served as coaches in the rural areas. Most stagecoach lines quickly disappeared with the appearance of railroad trunk lines, though in rural mining districts stage lines continued to run into the early years of the twentieth century.[6]

Steamboats

By the end of the Civil War waterway traffic, which had opened the American West up the Missouri and Minnesota Rivers, was starting a precipitous decline, initiated by the success of the railroads. As early as 1876 railroads shipped 80 percent of grain to eastern port cities. The great steamboats of pre–Civil War America could not find enough freight. By 1883 one Minnesota River steamboat owner complained in a letter, "Times out there have been very hard and it is almost impossible to make collections and to meet even running expenses." Although the riverboats in Minnesota continued to run with significant passenger numbers into the 1880s, their days were numbered. By 1900 virtually all passenger traffic on steamboats had ceased, though the riverboats managed to hold a portion of freight. It was clear that the age of the steamboat had passed.[7]

Hackney Carriages

An important mode of public transportation in the Gilded Age, which has received shamefully little coverage from historians, was that of the hired carriage. Hired carriages came in a variety of sizes in the Gilded Age and were generally referred to as a hackney carriage or simply as a hack. Originally, the term "hackney" referred to the typical riding or carriage horse, then came to designate a horse for hire, and ultimately came to refer to any carriage for hire. The larger size hacks tended to be broughams, which were nicely suited for this purpose (see Heavy Carriages). Smaller, two-wheeled carriages for hire were called cabriolets, possessing a folding top, seating for two, and an apron that covered customers from foot to waist. By 1830 people commonly referred to the cabriolet simply as a cab. The hansom cab became by far the most famous of these vehicles, appearing in the United States by the late 1880s from England. Drivers sat on an elevated seat behind the occupants. Hack fares tended to be quite high, particularly in New York City where they started at $1 (in an age when the average worker might earn $2–$3 per day) and rose according to the number of passengers and distance of the ride.[8] When compared to other means of public transportation, which usually ran from $.03 to $.10, the hackney carriage was a luxury only the wealthy could afford.

Mass Transit

Horse Omnibus and Horse Rail

Mass transit revolutionized travel in and to American cities, allowing for the rapid geographic expansion of cities. The introduction of horse-drawn omnibuses and later horse railways from the 1830s through the 1850s dramatically changed American cities. Historians estimate that in 1860 the Metropolitan Railroad Corporation alone transported 6.5 million passengers per year in Boston. The horse railway spread to most cities with more than 50,000 people transported by 1880. Horse railways in New York City charged five to seven cents. Edward Winslow Martin described these railways in 1868 as dirty and always crowded. For more genteel riders he suggested the omnibus, which seated from 12 to 14 passengers and charged 10 cents. The high cost kept "the rougher and dirtier portion of the community" from choosing omnibuses.

Horse-powered transit, however, caused problems. First, horse railways were very slow, managing only five to eight miles per hour, and could not cover the distances needed in a metropolis. Second, cities desired cleaner modes of transportation; the roughly 175,000 horses operating daily in New York City each produced close to 24 pounds of manure and quarts of urine every day. Finally, overworked horses lived only on average two and a half years, and 15,000 dead horses littered New York City's streets every year.

Elevated Railroad and Cable Cars

Larger cities were forced to develop other systems and New York City pioneered the first elevated railroad line in 1870. Although elevated railroads were extremely expensive, noisy, and dirty, they were faster and could cover tremendous territory, so cities like Kansas City, Brooklyn, and Chicago followed New York's lead. Another alternative was the cable car, invented by Andrew Smith Hallidie, which employed a stationary steam engine to run a cable that powered the cars. Cable cars proved to be smooth, fast, and efficient, particularly in the erratic hills of San Francisco. And though several large cities installed cable car systems—Chicago, Philadelphia, and New York—the high cost of installing them and their frequent costly breakdowns ensured that this system never spread to more than 15 cities.

Electric Trolley and Subway

The revolutionary change in city transportation came with the application of electric power. In 1884, Frank Julian Sprague signed a contract with Richmond, Virginia, to create an electric trolley. His invention proved so successful that horse railways, which still made up 69.7 percent of total urban track in 1890, were destroyed by the invention of this relatively quiet, efficient system that could travel cleaner, farther, and faster than horse lines. By 1895 there were 850 trolley lines operating in U.S. cities charging an average of $.05 and flying along at 20 miles an hour. Sprague also successfully electrified elevated railroads, which quickly led to the creation of subways. Boston finished construction on one mile of subway line in 1897 and many other cities followed in the early twentieth century. These developments in transportation, when combined with new techniques in bridge building, helped American cities to expand rapidly and cohesively. Streetcar systems, cable lines, electric surface lines, and elevated rapid transit all paved the way for the massive physical expansion of cities and made it possible for people to travel quickly and cheaply. Virtually no place in or outside of the city was inaccessible, opening the way for large-scale travel to leisure activities.[9]

PERSONAL TRANSPORTATION

Carriage Travel

Historians of the Gilded Age were so enamored of the modern technological transportation systems of the era—namely, the railroad, electric trolley, and subway—that they virtually ignored the most important form of personal travel, which was still the horse. All sorts of carriages and buggies crowded American roads, particularly congesting city streets. As early as mid-century, travel down New York City streets was precarious and filled with hackney cabs, private carriages, horse omnibuses, and horse railways. Edward Winslow Martin described New York City traffic on Broadway as "thronged with vehicles of every description. Often times these vehicles crowd the streets to such an extent that they become 'jammed.' "[10] Carriage, wagon, and transit traffic was so heavy and so poorly managed that by mid-century traffic jams were commonplace in the great cities of the United States. Most individuals did not own Pullman cars or automobiles, but instead relied on horse-and-carriage travel. The country possessed a dizzying array of buggies, carriages, and wagons.

Buggies

There were a wide variety of imported and domestic buggies, which were light coaches generally possessing four wheels, a top, seating for one or two people, and were drawn by one or two horses. Buggies tended to be mid-sized carriage types, though there was tremendous variety and little standardization in names. The 1895 *Montgomery Ward Catalogue* carried several styles of buggies, such as the rectangular models like the Indiana Piano Box ($45.75) and Texas Ranger ($64–$83), as well as gracefully curved phaetons ($70–$95). The *Montgomery Ward Catalogue* added that its phaeton was particularly "popular with ladies, elderly persons, and physicians." Buggy tops were distinctive, and tended to be open on the sides and the front but closed in the rear.

Two-Wheeled Carriages

There were also a large number of light-bodied two-wheeled carriages, which were known under a wide variety of names. The calash was one popular style that bore a removable folding hood and ran on relatively low wheels. This style was also commonly called a cart ($39.50–$45) and strongly resembled most buggies but ran on two wheels instead of four. Americans also developed the sulky, which was a very light, two-wheeled vehicle that seated only one person. Sulkies, also called road carts, were built for speed and ranged in price in the *Montgomery Ward Catalogue* from $9 to $29.

Heavy Carriages

There were a tremendous number of heavier carriages in a diverse array of styles. There was a style known as an open buggy or a wagon, which somewhat obviously looked almost identical to the buggy styles but without tops. They varied dramatically in price in the 1890s and early twentieth century, from $22 to $50. The barouche was another large, four-wheeled carriage designed with a folding cover that only extended over the two rear seats. A driver sat in the forward seat, exposed to the elements, while the occupants sat under the cover facing each other. The barouche cover had no sides and this carriage was generally a fair weather vehicle. The elite barouche models in New York sold for a staggering $1,550 or more in the late 1860s and were far out of the price range of most Americans. Another elite style was the brougham, which was a closed carriage on a boxy frame and came in one- and two-seat models that could carry two and four passengers, respectively. The driver sat outside of the enclosed carriage. The brougham was priced

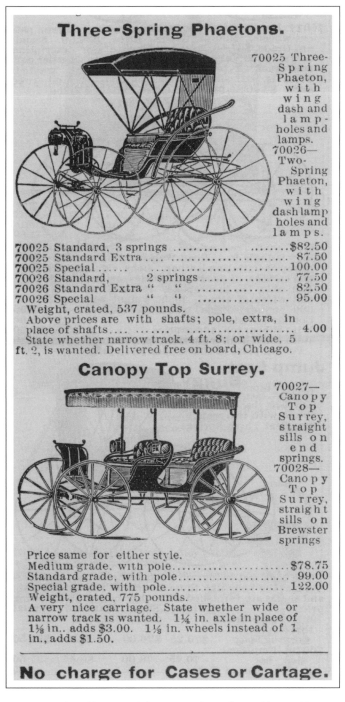

Three-Spring Phaetons.

70025 Three-Spring Phaeton, with wing dash and lamp-holes and lamps.
70026—Two-Spring Phaeton, with wing dash lamp holes and lamps.

70025 Standard, 3 springs $82.50
70025 Standard Extra 87.50
70025 Special 100.00
70026 Standard, 2 springs.................. 77.50
70026 Standard Extra " " 82.50
70026 Special " " 95.00
Weight, crated, 537 pounds.
Above prices are with shafts; pole, extra, in
place of shafts.... .... 4.00
State whether narrow track, 4 ft. 8; or wide, 5
ft. 2, is wanted. Delivered free on board, Chicago.

Canopy Top Surrey.

70027—Canopy Top Surrey, straight sills on end springs.
70028—Canopy Top Surrey, straight sills on Brewster springs

Price same for either style.
Medium grade, with pole......................$78.75
Standard grade, with pole..................... 99.00
Special grade, with pole......... ....122.00
Weight, crated, 775 pounds.
A very nice carriage. State whether wide or
narrow track is wanted. 1¼ in. axle in place of
1⅛ in.. adds $3.00. 1⅛ in. wheels instead of 1
in., adds $1.50.

No charge for Cases or Cartage.

An advertisement for a carriage from the 1895
Montgomery Ward Catalogue.

A Sunday outing in Colorado. © Denver Public Library, Western
History Collection.

very close to the barouche and beyond the means of most Americans.
The rockaway was another popular large carriage style, with two or
three bench seats capable of seating six to nine people. The roof was
open at the sides but extended over the driver. The most popular family
vehicle of the age, however, was the surrey, which appeared in the 1880s
and by 1900 sold 1 million units. The surrey was a four-wheeled carriage
with a canopy, often fringed, a boxy body, and two forward-facing bench
seats. Surreys could be purchased for roughly $80 to $122 in 1895, but
prices fell by 1902 to a point where they were available by mail order
for as little as $39.85.[11]

Horseless Carriages

Automobiles, often called horseless carriages in the nineteenth century,
made their appearance in the waning years of the Gilded Age, but their
greatest impact would not be felt until the twentieth century. While J.
Frank and Charles Duryea are often credited with inventing the first
automobile in the United States, historian Richard Scharchburg claims,

Harry M. Rhoads, behind the steering wheel, poses in a convertible with passenger in front of Westminster University. © Denver Public Library, Western History Collection.

"If you were to ask me who invented the automobile, I would have to say everybody." Scharchburg notes that the complexity of the automobile made its invention an ongoing process of evolution. Certainly, the Duryea motorized buggy (1893) was important but so too was Ransom Eli Olds' steam-powered carriage (1879), and Elwood Haynes' automobile (1894). Over 100 different horseless carriages were sold in the United States by 1900, but they remained only the province of the elite because of their high cost. It is not difficult to understand why early automobiles were called horseless carriages, since they looked almost identical to the buggies and phaetons that were their contemporaries. Ransom Olds transformed the automobile industry in 1901 when his company produced the Oldsmobile Runabout with interchangeable parts and priced it at $650. While out of the price range of the average American industrial worker, $650 was within the means of many buggy owners. By 1904, Olds Motor Works was selling 5,000 Runabouts per year.[12]

VACATIONS

The wide variety of modes of transportation available in the Gilded Age made it possible for Americans to "travel" extensively purely for leisure. Travel could now be entertaining, relatively safe, and even quite comfortable by the standards of the day instead of arduous, dangerous, and exhausting. Travel tourism and vacations had largely been the province of the gentry class prior to the Civil War, and it was only in the Gilded Age that middle-class Americans "invented" vacations for the masses. While average working-class Americans still found prolonged vacations difficult, if not impossible, they often participated in travel leisure with day trips to boardwalks, beaches, resorts, campgrounds, parks, and amusement parks. The idea that commodified leisure was acceptable and desirable for everyone spread quickly throughout the United States, particularly as large urban amusements developed. All Americans enjoyed the leisure travel opportunities afforded by the expansion of inexpensive transportation.

Leisure Ideology

The middle class fundamentally changed the nature of mainstream American culture by defining leisure as a socially constructive force that was necessary for modern people to relax from the exhausting pace of the modern world. The transformation of American cities and the growth of new urban amusements certainly pushed the development of a leisure-oriented culture, but so too did liberal American ministers. By the 1830s, Unitarian minister William Ellery Channing advocated leisure and he was joined by other liberal ministers by mid-century. Henry Ward Beecher was the most famous advocate for middle- and upper-class relaxation. By the 1850s writers began to use the term "vacation" in numerous newspaper and magazines stories, which played an important role in spreading the new leisure doctrine. Railroads also played a significant role, publishing travel brochures to travel spots to drum up business for their lines. Many railroads built special lines directly to resorts in an effort to capitalize on the new tourist trade that would attract hundreds of thousands in the last 50 years of the century. The development of telephones and the traveler's cheque (1891) by American Express also aided in the drive toward travel vacations. Perhaps most important in addition to the desire for vacations was that middle-class Americans increasingly had more leisure time—many white-collar workers earned a week or two of vacation time every year—and disposable income. While not every middle-class family could afford an annual vacation, the idea that vacations were a sign of middle-class status became increasingly prominent.[13]

Resorts and Summer Cottages

Resorts developed very rapidly after the 1850s, expanding widely beyond the elite springs and resorts like Newport, Rhode Island, Saratoga Springs, New York, and the numerous hot springs in western Virginia. Within a short period of time resorts had spread to every section of the nation, from New York's Adirondack mountains to Florida's coast to Colorado's Rocky mountains. In the Northeast resorts like the Mansfield House in Stowe, Vermont, Lake George in upstate New York, Watch Hill in Rhode Island, and Cape Cod were developed. Not to be outdone the South saw the rise of Virginia's Coyner Springs, Yellow Sulphur, Locust Grove, and Cobb's Island; Georgia's Tallulah; White Cliff Springs in Tennessee; and Cloudland House on Roane Mountain, North Carolina. Henry Flagler, co-founder of Standard Oil with John D. Rockefeller, built a railroad on the east coast of Florida and then spread resorts along it at St. Augustine, Daytona, Miami, and Palm Beach. In the Midwest, Michigan's Mackinac Island topped the resorts but there were others like Versailles Springs, Illinois, and numerous hotels on Wisconsin's southern lakes. In the West, Lake Tahoe became a small resort location while Colorado Springs developed into a major vacation destination. African Americans increasingly found they were not welcome at resorts because of the rise of Jim Crow segregation laws (see Chapter 1), so black entrepreneurs founded resorts to service the leisure and vacation needs of African Americans at Cape May, Atlantic City, Silcot Springs in Virginia, Harpers Ferry in West Virginia, and Arundel-on-the-Bay outside of Washington, D.C.[14]

Amenities and Cost

These resorts varied in size, amenities, and cost. Fashionable resorts drew middle-class to very wealthy vacationers. Saratoga Springs, Cape May, and Atlantic City attracted tens of thousands every summer and boasted a large number of restaurants, ice cream parlors, billiard rooms, bathing houses, shooting ranges, tennis courts, golf courses, swimming pools, and barber shops. White Sulphur Springs' main hotel was enormous, 400 feet long, boasting one of the largest ballrooms in the country, and a huge dining room capable of seating 1,200 guests. Mackinac Island's Grand Hotel possessed a veranda that ran completely around the hotel, 880 feet, so that residents could watch the sun rise over Lake Huron and set over Lake Michigan. Prices at fashionable hotels like the Grand Union Hotel at Saratoga went for $28 per week including meals in 1874 and the Blue Mountain Lake resort in the Adirondacks charged $25 per week including meals in 1882. A room in the Grand Hotel on Mackinac Island charged $3–$5 a night with meals in 1887, but by 1890 a single guest paid $35 a week for the most desirable room (a front room with a bath) and a double room went for $54 per week. Families who committed a month or a season to a resort, however, could also get reduced rates. Correspondence to resorts makes it clear that many middle-class vacationers hoped to pay only $10 a week per person, half for children and servants, for seasonal rates at even fashionable resorts. Innumerable unfashionable resorts sprang up on lakes, the coast, and in mountains throughout the nation as well, costing from $10 to $20 per week with meals.[15]

Professional Conventions

Resort vacations came within the reach of many middle-class Americans because increasingly in the Gilded Age the annual meetings of professional associations met at resort hotels. The ability to bring in thousands of people to a convention allowed the professional associations to get blocks of rooms at very inexpensive rates. Such conventions allowed for the expansion of vacations among the professionals of the middle class.[16]

Resort Activities

Regardless of whether the resort was fashionable or unfashionable, terms used in the Gilded Age, they were all normally quite crowded and offered the same activities. Most vacation hotels and resorts boasted a wide array of activities and sports: bowling, card games, dancing, billiards, lawn tennis, roller skating rinks, bicycles, horseback riding, boxing, and bathing (swimming). Even women participated in strenuous and competitive activities like bowling, tennis, golf, hiking, and some sports normally reserved for men, like billiards. As the century progressed women and men increasingly swam together, which was a forbidden activity earlier in the century. Women swimming in bathing suits considered scanty in their day (stockings and mid-calf-length dresses; see Chapter 5) became widely accepted even though the water made the suits cling immodestly to their bodies. In a culture where women wore ankle-length gowns with long sleeves and high collars, corsets, and petticoats, it must have been quite a change to see women in a single layer of wet clothing. Men also could gather in all-male areas where resorts catered to card playing and gambling.

Women

Vacations at resorts attracted more women than men, and perhaps the best explanation for this is that men had to work and often commuted to resorts on weekends and women were granted more liberties. Summer resorts afforded women the opportunity to engage in activities and behaviors normally frowned upon by polite society. Women, for example, engaged in sporting activities and bathing which called self-conscious

A day at the Washington Park beach, Denver, Colorado. © Denver Public Library, Western History Collection.

attention to their bodies. Flirting was another favorite occupation at resorts for both men and women. Indeed, resorts provided one of the few places in the era where middle-class men and women could intermingle freely. Resort vacations allowed women to participate in physical activities that middle-class ideology normally denied them and to show off their bodies in a way acceptable only on the beach. Unlike at other times in their lives where middle-class women minimized public attention to themselves, at summer resorts they consciously put themselves on display at the beach and in the ballroom. Vacations allowed women significant freedoms from the Victorian conventions that otherwise governed their lives and allowed them to experiment in new modes of leisure and physical activity.[17]

Summer Cottages

Renting summer cottages was another very popular vacation. Critics of fashionable summer resorts were numerous, even though these vacation spots attracted hundreds of thousands of people, because of the fears of sexual danger, gambling, and overall concerns with too much focus on "fashionable" society. While these concerns largely evaporated in the early twentieth century, in the Gilded Age resort critics suggested that a better alternative to the resort was the rental of a summer cottage. The rental of cottages on the beach or in the mountains for the summer allowed for a vacation away from the temptations of the resort. Many New York City families left the city for the summer, going out to Long Island, South Oyster Bay, or Freeport where they rented summer cottages or rooms in boarding houses on the beach for the summer. The nearness of the beaches and proliferation of railroad lines often allowed men to commute daily to and from work. This type of vacation was also available to African Americans who found places where they could rent cottages on lakes and in rural areas. These cottages often cost as much as an unfashionable hotel ($10–$20 per week) or as little as $6 per week depending on the location and the amenities. Luxurious summer "cottages" for the upper class at Newport cost $2,000–$3,000 for the season, which was more than the yearly income of many middle-class families.[18]

Self-Improvement Vacations

Self-improvement vacations were another type that critics of summer resorts thought were better for the moral fiber of Americans. Self-improvement vacations did not offer the usual temptations and the concerns over idleness were dispelled by their emphasis on moral and intellectual development. A number of religious denominations created summer camps that became very popular vacation destinations. The Lake Chautauqua events also sparked a new wave of self-improvement vacations that came to be known simply as Chautauqua events.

Religious Camps

Religious camps were one persuasion of the self-improvement vacation. There were almost 100 scenic campgrounds established by different religious denominations, though Methodists were the first and most prolific creators of religious camps. These resorts appealed to middle-class vacationers who wanted a vacation in a religious setting that strictly prohibited drinking, dancing, card playing, and Sunday bathing. Many of the religious resorts started as camp meeting locations but developed into vacation spots by the 1870s. This transformation from camp meeting to religious resort was most evident at Wesleyan Grove on Martha's Vineyard. Methodists created a camp meeting on the island in 1835 and by 1857 there were 250 tents on 12 to 15 acres. In 1860 the Methodist Camp-Meeting Association was formed to manage the camp as it quickly expanded over the next five years into a number of small cottages. Wesleyan Grove on Martha's Vineyard was a small city of cottages by the 1860s. Ocean Grove, on the New Jersey coast 50 miles from New York City, was another camp resort which by 1879 had 700 semi-permanent tents with wooden floors that rented for $2.50 a week. By the 1880s,

20,000 to 30,000 people vacationed at Ocean Grove every summer and the religious camp attracted conference meetings of Christian reform groups like the Women's Christian Temperance Union. Ocean Grove's revivals were complemented by an auditorium (1894) that seated nearly 10,000 people. Compared to resorts or renting cottages the religious camps provided a very inexpensive vacation alternative. These camps popped up throughout the country, like Camp Labor in New Jersey, the camp at Sing Sing, New York, Ocean Grove Retreat near Monterey, California, and Lake Bluff outside of Chicago on Lake Michigan.

While most of these religious resorts were Methodist, there were notable exceptions. The Quaker twin brothers Albert and Alfred Smiley founded a famous religious resort, the Mohonk Mountain House in the Shawangunk Mountains of New York. The Smileys ran Mohonk along strict Quaker guidelines—no liquor, card playing, dancing, or carriages coming or going on the Sabbath. Despite, or because of, these restrictions Mohonk flourished, and was often noted as an attractive destination for women vacationing on their own. James Adam Bradley founded another prominent religious camp, Asbury Park, on 500 acres of land right next to Ocean Grove. Bradley's middle-class camp resort was a milder and nondenominational counterpart to the strict Methodist Ocean Grove, but nonetheless Asbury Park observed Sabbath and temperance restrictions. Instead of abstinence Asbury Park stressed moderation and moral guidance in dancing, theater, and card playing by straining out these activities that were sinful connections to gambling, alcohol use, and sexual licentiousness. Bradley hit upon an incredibly successful formula; Asbury Park attracted between 30,000 and 50,000 vacationers every summer.

Chautauqua

One of the most popular self-improvement vacations was at Lake Chautauqua in New York. Methodist minister John Vincent and manufacturer Lewis Miller founded the resort in 1874 as a place that would bring together piety, leisure, and the middle-class urge for intellectual refinement, sparking one of the most sought-after self-improvement vacations of the Gilded Age. Initially, they intended the camp to be a training ground for Sunday school teachers, but due to the program's popularity Vincent and Miller soon expanded the curriculum to include secular academic studies such as language (Hebrew, Greek, Latin, French, German, and Asian languages), pedagogical studies, philosophy, literature, science, and history. Chautauqua became a phenomenon, drawing 500 to 600 people from 26 states in its very first two-week session in 1874. The *New York Times* estimated that 60,000 to 100,000 people attended Lake Chautauqua events every year by the mid-1880s and by then there were also 30 Chautauqua imitators spread throughout the nation. Indeed, the term "chautauqua" came not to designate simply the camp in New York but instead referred to this type of self-improvement vacation in general. Nebraska boasted its chautauqua in Crete, Michigan had Bay View, and Florida provided the Florida Chautauqua in the western panhandle. Booker T. Washington formed an African-American chautauqua in 1893 at his Tuskegee Institute, and other black-sponsored chautauquas occurred in Normal, Alabama, Mountain Lake Park in Maryland, and at Winona Lake just outside of Warsaw, Indiana. Atlantic City was the site of the Jewish Chautauqua Society which met there every summer. These vacations offered family-friendly atmospheres that catered to the morality and values of middle-class Americans. A week at a chautauqua meant they could enjoy a vacation free from the drinking, gambling, and ostentatious displays of the resorts, and filled with intellectual stimulation.

Inexpensive Cost

Chautauqua vacations were also relatively inexpensive, costing $3 per week in the 1870s and $6–$8 per week in the 1880s in addition to the $1 entrance fee. While most visitors initially stayed in tents at Lake Chautauqua, soon, just like the transformation of the religious camps, cottages began to appear, some of them very elaborately constructed and costing over $1,000. In 1884, Lake Chautauqua went further with the construction of the Athenaeum Hotel which provided fairly luxurious amenities for $2 to $4.50 a day for a room and meals.[19]

Tourism

Tourism also grew dramatically in the last 50 years of the century, particularly among the middle class. As travel grew easier with the physical expansion of railroads and roads, people not only traveled more for professional meetings, visiting, and business, which allowed for much sightseeing along the way, but also simply for travel vacations. Indeed, tourist sites grew in importance throughout the nineteenth century as symbols of American power, grandeur, and progress. Tourist sites of national renown helped to forge a common American identity through common symbolism and a shared experience to countless millions of Americans.

Niagara Falls

Niagara Falls was one of the first important tourist destinations in the country. The massive falls on the U.S.–Canadian border just outside of Buffalo, New York, inspired awe with their size and natural majesty. As the Transcendentalists began the romantic attachment to the wilderness, Americans started to view the wilds as intrinsically valuable. These feel-

People socializing at Chautauqua, New York, with Lake Chautauqua in the background, 1908. © Library of Congress.

ings for wild places grew throughout the remainder of the century as industrialization and urbanization made many people feel like there was a pressing need for places unspoiled by human hands. As early as the 1830s Americans were taking the "grand tour" from New York City to Buffalo and Niagara Falls, across the border into Canada to visit Montreal and Quebec, and then back through New England.

Other Popular Sites

Tourism expanded after the Civil War as middle-class Americans visited all kinds of sites. Mammoth Cave in Kentucky was a popular tourist attraction which was metaphorically associated with the underworld as well as great cathedrals. The cave struck both horror and awe in the brave tourists who ventured into its truly massive darkness. Historic sites were another type of popular attraction. Bunker Hill, Gettysburg, Mount Vernon, and the various birthplaces of famous individuals were popular sites. Places of work became prominent tourist attractions as well, such as mines, steel mills, prisons, and stockyards. Mauch Chunk, a town in eastern Pennsylvania on the edge of the great anthracite coal fields, particularly attracted attention for its natural beauty and technological marvels. A gravity railroad ran tourist cars up a steep incline throughout the Gilded Age. Mauch Chunk seemed the perfect meeting of technology and picturesque nature.

Travel Agencies

After the Civil War the travel agency industry developed to help tourists deal with the complexities of travel vacations so that they could easily and affordably get to the vacation sites. British travel agent Thomas Cook expanded his services to the United States, taking Thomas Jenkins as his partner, and set up an office in New York City. Before long an argument broke up the partnership, but John Cook, Thomas Cook's son, took control and significantly expanded the operation. Others soon followed, like Walter Raymond and Irving Whitcomb, who formed the Raymond and Whitcomb Travel Agency in 1879, and the Lamm's Tourist Offices in Jacksonville, Florida and Niagara Falls, opened by T. J. Lamm in 1884.

Western Vacations

With the completion of the transcontinental lines train travel to the West opened up after 1869 and many tourists went West. Guidebooks were available for tourists and tour companies quickly created Western tours. Travel amenities could be quite luxurious on the elegant sleeper cars (see First-Class Cars). Furthermore, thousands of people traveled West to see the natural wonders at Yosemite and Yellowstone. This type of travel, however, came at a price. The cost of these tours was quite high and therefore relegated primarily to the upper reaches of the middle class and the elite. While a week at a summer resort cost $10 to $30 per week and a Raymond and Whitcomb six-day trip from Boston to Niagara Falls to Saratoga went for $40, the Raymond and Whitcomb grand trip to Yellowstone for 25 days cost a staggering $275! A middle-class tourist could travel to Europe for $275.

World's Fairs

World's fairs were also popular tourist destinations, with roughly 100 million people attending the 12 U.S. expositions between the 1876 Centennial Exposition in Philadelphia and the 1916 Panama-California International Exposition in San Diego. Like other prominent attractions, the world's fairs held great symbolic importance. The huge exhibition halls affirmed America's growing technological superiority, unrivaled manufacturing might, agricultural strength, cultural pride, and overall American prosperity and development. President William McKinley declared, "Expositions are the timekeepers of progress," at the 1901 Pan-American Exposition (ironically, he was assassinated shortly thereafter). On the darker side these world's fairs also strongly impressed upon white Americans their racial and cultural superiority over the nonwhite races of the world. The 1893 Columbian Exposition's Midway and the 1904 Louisiana Purchase Exposition's Filipino, American Indian, and Alaskan Eskimo villages, for example, offered startling juxtapositions between Anglo-American cultural and technological superiority and the primitive living conditions and tribal customs of savages. These images were meant to convey to white Americans feelings of self-congratulatory cultural superiority. Americans were undoubtedly attracted to these marvels; Chicago's Columbian Exposition attracted 27 million people. Tobacco farmer Franklin H. Williams traveled from his Massachusetts home to the Centennial Exposition for nine days and spent $13.50. Two decades later at the 1893 Columbian Exposition in Chicago a prudent tourist could spend a week at the fair for $25 while extravagant first-class tour packages were available from travel agencies for about $100.[20]

African-American Tourism

Prosperous African Americans also traveled in the Gilded Age, in spite of the segregation laws of many states. Indeed, *Plessy v. Ferguson*, the "separate but equal" Supreme Court decision that made segregation legal, began because whites were annoyed that prosperous blacks were using the railroads for weekend trips and they pressured the railroad companies to enforce the state's segregation laws (see Chapter 1). When they were segregated into Jim Crow cars, the blacks sued and lost. Such were the perils of travel for African Americans, and yet they continued

1893 Columbian Exposition, Chicago, Illinois. Courtesy of The Francis Loeb Library, Harvard Design School.

to be tourists. Blacks planned extensively and often spent extra money to avoid problems.[21]

Wilderness Vacations

Wilderness vacations were an interesting mix of travel tourism and romantic appreciation of the wilderness. Starting in the late 1860s there was a definitive drive in the United States by many prominent men for wilderness vacations. Men like minister Thomas Wentworth Higginson, minister William Henry Harrison Murray, Theodore Roosevelt, and a host of others feared American manhood—by which they meant white, middle- and upper-class manhood—was declining into effeminacy. Sedentary office jobs in cities, while necessary for the civilization, were draining the strenuous values from men. These men helped to spawn the movement known as muscular Christianity (see Chapters 2 and 7) and offered a host of solutions to solve the ills of manhood. Wilderness vacations was one of their suggestions. Newspapers and magazines extolled the "restorative possibilities of camping." Specialty nature magazines like *Forest and Stream* (1873), *Outing* (1885), *Field and Stream* (1897), and *Outdoor Life* (1897) particularly advocated the outdoor leisure. William Henry Harrison Murray became the earliest driving force for the wilderness vacation when he published his book *Adventures in the Wilderness* (1869), which promoted the Adirondacks as a vacation spot and held that the wilderness was therapeutic for modern people.

Through these efforts wilderness vacations did become a popular leisure activity, particularly in the National Parks. Yosemite, Grand Canyon, Glacier, Mount Ranier, and Yellowstone Parks drew large numbers of dedicated tourists. Yosemite, though only 180 miles from San Francisco, remained isolated from European-Americans until the 1850s and then rapidly became a tourist destination due to relentless promotion in newspapers and magazines and truly breathtaking natural wonders. Naturalists also quickly acted to preserve the wilderness in Yosemite and control economic development of the valley. The great geysers, sulphur springs, mud volcanoes, mountains, and wild animals also made Yellowstone a prime vacation and tourist spot. Railroad access made it possible to get close to Yellowstone, the Grand Canyon, and Yosemite, though relatively arduous travel was required to get into the parks.

Of course these vacations differed widely. There was luxurious camping at several Adirondack campgrounds, such as the Anson Phelps Stokes campground which rented summer homes to "campers." In the Adirondacks, several large resorts were nestled in the wilderness, like the Smileys' Mohonk. As camping grew in popularity in the Gilded Age, campers often would use resorts and hotels as bases for camping trips

Trolley stop (Colorado Springs and Interurban Railway) in Manitou
Springs, Colorado, with Soda Springs drinking fountain, center
foreground, ca. 1900. © Denver Public Library, Western
History Collection.

into the wilderness. Twelve-year old Theodore Roosevelt and his family
camped throughout the Adirondacks using the famous Paul Smith hotel
as their base. Other camps that rented cabins and provided toilets, cook-
house, and guides sprang up in Maine. Countless Americans also took
to primitive camping, pitching tents in the woods to enjoy hiking and
fishing. Campers advocated these vacations as morally and physically
superior to resort vacations. Camping was the antidote to the ills of modern, sedentary urban life.[22]

Day Trips

Not every American could afford extended vacations at resorts, camping trips, chautauquas, or tours, but most Americans could afford an
occasional day trip. Day trips were increasingly possible for working-
class and lower-middle-class people on tight budgets because of the extension of rail and trolley service. Many of the camps provided day trips.

Religious camps like Ocean Grove advertised "A Salt Water Day." A New Yorker could take the train to Ocean Grove round trip for $1.85, eat breakfast for $.50 and dinner for $.75, and rent a bathing suit, rowboat, or a bathhouse for small fees. Summer resorts also encouraged day trips for bathing, picnicking, and boating. Day trips were popular forms of weekend entertainment. Many of the people who went to the world's fairs were local visitors who took the train or trolley to the expositions, often making multiple visits. Baseball parks also served as significant day trip destinations (see Chapter 7). These parks were often built at the intersection of multiple trolley lines which brought tens of thousands of people to the parks: Forbes Field in Pittsburgh was at a confluence of 16 lines and Ebbets Field in Brooklyn had 9 lines which connected to 32 others. Trolley service was so prevalent that Brooklyn named its club the "trolley dodgers." Transportation innovations also brought more people to city parks for picnics and play, like New York's massive Central Park. Boardwalks developed around many resorts and beaches that were within an easy ride to nearby cities—like Coney Island in New York, Cedar Point in Ohio, and Lake Quinsigamond in Massachusetts—where strips of thrilling, inexpensive games and amusements, open air shows, concession stands, ice cream parlors, and soda fountains sprang up. The innovation of the amusement park also attracted massive numbers of day trip vacationers. In 1897, George Tilyou started the process at Coney Island when he enclosed a number of boardwalk attractions into Steeplechase Park and charged admission at the gate. The boardwalks and later amusement parks attracted tens of thousands of people for day trips.[23]

CONCLUSION

By 1900, Americans could comfortably and quickly travel from coast to coast or speed across city streets at 20 miles an hour in an electric trolley. These types of transportation innovations made it possible for the mass vacation industry to develop as more and more Americans turned toward leisure to escape the dreariness of work. Rising incomes and more vacation time made it possible for millions of Americans to engage in tourism, take extended vacations, and indulge in day trips. Travel and expanded leisure opportunities were intimately connected. And yet, for all of this progress, if a traveler was not going by public transportation, then the only option was to take some sort of carriage. Trains, trolleys, and subways were transforming travel, and yet the average family would have owned a horse and surrey in the 1890s to meet their personal travel needs.

12

Visual Arts

BACKGROUND

The visual arts also responded to the industrialization and urbanization of the United States, and American artists sought to create an art that rivaled the great traditions of the ancient world. What emerged came to be called the American Renaissance as sculptors, architects, and painters collectively attempted to illustrate the growing wealth and power of the United States in monumental art and architecture that freely borrowed from Renaissance models. Just as the Renaissance Italians had the de Medici, Sforza, Gonzaga, d'Este, and Montefeltro families, the American Renaissance had the Rockefeller, Carnegie, Morgan, and particularly the Vanderbilt families to patronize art and architecture. The American elite built enormous palatial residences and purchased European art. The Vanderbilt family alone built 17 mansions from 1876 to 1917 and filled them to bursting with European art. Perhaps the most spectacular mansion was George W. Vanderbilt's French Revival style Biltmore House in Asheville, North Carolina, which held 255 rooms and was designed by the famous architect Richard Morris Hunt (see Chapter 4). The American rich purchased Renaissance art and brought it to the United States; however, they also supported budding American artists like painter John Singer Sargent (1856–1925) and sculptors Augustus Saint-Gaudens (1848–1907) and Daniel Chester French (1850–1931).[1]

Popular art also experienced massive growth and profoundly affected the nation. The incredible expansion of newspapers and magazines (see Chapter 8) drove the need for illustrators. High-quality illustrations were everywhere in the Gilded Age. Bastions of high culture were challenged by the emergence of popular magazines which needed high-quality illustrations and chromolithography. Famous illustrators like Charles Dana Gibson and Howard Pyle brought art into the public realm in popular magazines that millions of Americans purchased every week. The quality house magazines—*Century*, *Scribner's*, *Harper's*—all employed top-quality illustrators. In addition to the original work of illustrators, chromolithography made cheap color reprints of famous paintings available to all middle-class and upper-working-class Americans. High culture and art were spreading throughout America as never before and were available to the masses in ways not possible at mid-century. As in theater and opera, cultural elites sought to make distinctions between "high" art and "popular" art and they used these distinctions to create an elitist culture. And yet, for the masses of Americans the ability of inexpensive magazines to provide high-quality illustrations and the use of chromolithography to reproduce "high" art in prints narrowed the division between high culture and popular culture.

"HIGH" ART

I use the terms "high" art and "popular" art with some reservations and the firm belief that art is more a continuum than neat boxes. Gilded Age Americans did make distinctions about art and they used these kinds of labels, so it is a useful way of categorizing the different kinds of artistic production. The cultural elite used high art much like they did almost all cultural products of the Gilded Age, which was to use it as a badge of elite culture that demarcated clear social distinctions.

Art Schools

As if in response to the greater demand for artists in the United States, art schools were founded at an amazing rate during the Gilded Age. In 1875 alone 10 art schools were founded, and others were formed in Chicago (1867 and 1879), San Francisco (1874), New York (1875), Providence (1878), Saint Louis (1879), and Boston (1879). By 1882 there were 39 art schools, 14 art programs at universities, and 15 decorative art societies in the United States. The Society of American Artists was founded in New York City in 1877. Many Americans, however, continued to study abroad such as John Singer Sargent, Thomas Eakins, and Augustus Saint-Gaudens who were all educated at the prestigious French Ecole des Beaux-Arts. Sargent, though a citizen and claimed by the United States, actually lived his entire life abroad. Others trained in Europe but returned to the United States, such as William Merritt Chase, who studied in Munich and Venice but returned to the United States to teach in the New York Art Students League in 1878.[2]

American art not only found patrons but dignified structures in which to show the world American art when philanthropists established large museums. Boston's Museum of Fine Arts, New York City's Metropolitan Museum, the Art Institute of Chicago, and Philadelphia's Museum of Art all appeared in the Gilded Age in monumental buildings to house and exhibit America's wealth and culture.[3]

Sculpture

Like painting, architecture, and illustration, by mid-century sculptors too began to train in much more disciplined, regularized settings than ever before. The two most celebrated sculptors of the Gilded Age, Augustus Saint-Gaudens and Daniel Chester French, followed this model, studying at the prestigious and influential Ecole des Beaux-Arts in Paris where they learned from Classical, Renaissance, and Baroque models. Both men would gain fame designing and executing public monuments that celebrated the power of the new industrial America, but harkened back to Classical models that made none-too-subtle connections to republican and imperial Rome. Each man would deal with themes that centered on the end of the Civil War and the rise of American power, and that celebrated primarily white, male power through heroic figures.

Augustus Saint-Gaudens

Saint-Gaudens worked on several awesome monuments of distinctly American origin that commemorated the Civil War. He started with a sculpture of Admiral Farragut, famed for his famous quip "damn the torpedos, full steam ahead" during the attack on New Orleans. The sculptor created a new form by placing the strong, heroic figure of Farragut on a wave-shaped pedestal carved in bas-relief. Certainly one of the most impressive American sculptures of any day is Saint-Gaudens' Robert Gould Shaw Memorial which he worked on with architect Stanford White from 1884 to 1897. The sculpture commemorated the black 54th Massachusetts which fought in the Civil War under the leadership of Colonel Robert Gould Shaw, who died along with a significant number of his troops in an assault on Ft. Wagner in 1863. Although the 54th penetrated the fort it was pushed back and suffered terrible casualties, including the young white colonel. In spite of the loss, this moment was critical for it proved to a doubting white public that black soldiers would and could fight with distinction in a war that was at least partially based on issues of their freedom; black troops would go on to play a significant role in the Union victory. Saint-Gaudens commemorated these efforts in this magnificent bronze, where Shaw, seated on a horse, leads marching

Rock Creek cemetery, "Grief" Memorial, Washington, D.C. Courtesy of The Francis Loeb Library, Harvard Design School.

black troops, leaning forward as if straining for battle, to that fateful engagement at Fort Wagner. Although an entirely American subject of incredible symbolic importance, the sculpture certainly owes a debt to the Renaissance elements: the sarcophagus frieze and hero on horseback.

Saint-Gaudens finished his Civil War efforts with the remarkable statue of General William Tecumseh Sherman (1892–1903) in New York's Central Park. Gilded in gold, Sherman grimly sits atop his charger, modeled after the warhorses of the great Renaissance sculptors, while his mount trods on the pinecones that symbolize the state of Georgia and Sherman's relentless March to the Sea which devastated a 60-mile-wide swath through the state at the close of the Civil War. Nike, the winged goddess of Victory, marches ahead of Sherman. Funded by the Chamber of Commerce and the wealthy of New York City, the monument, gilded in gold, certainly illustrated the growing power of the North and New York City in particular.

But perhaps Saint-Gaudens' most interesting sculpture had nothing to do with heroic men, but instead memorialized a woman who had committed suicide. Marion Hooper Adams, the spouse of Boston brahman Henry Adams, descendent of Presidents John Adams and John Quincy Adams, committed suicide by ingesting poison in 1885. Inspired by a Japanese bronze, Adams entrusted the monument to his wife to Saint-Gaudens and architect Stanford White. The result was a masterpiece of private grief and spirituality. The bronze statue Saint-Gaudens produced was that of a tranquil woman seated with her right hand gently resting on her cheek and covered head-to-toe in a flowing garment. The result is startling. It is a monument that is at once haunting and yet incredibly sensitive, spiritual, and thoughtful. Adams referred to it as his "Japanese Buddha."[4]

Daniel Chester French

Daniel Chester French was the other great sculptor of the age and he too gained fame with his classical, heroic statues. French was largely self-trained until the 1880s when he studied in Florence and Paris. One of his most famous early statues commemorated the Revolutionary War in Concord, Massachusetts. He produced *The Minuteman* in 1875; a seven-foot-tall bronze Revolutionary War soldier. French made connections to the Roman republic and civic virtue by placing a plow next to this American everyman. The plow's symbolism was telling for it represented Cincinnatus, the Roman farmer who put down his plow to take up the generalship of Rome. After leading the army to victory Cincinnatus rejected his power and went back to his plow and farm—the perfect example of civic duty in a democracy. The plow symbolized American democracy and the efforts of the average American in the fight for freedom and nationhood. From here French gained commissions for a statue of John Harvard for Harvard University in 1884, the ornate bronze doors of the Boston Public Library in 1897, and *Alma Mater* for Columbia in 1903. Another memorable French product was *The Angel of Death and the Sculptor*, which he completed in bronze in 1892 and then in marble in 1926. The piece depicts a beautiful female angel of death coming for a sculptor as he works. French is most well known today, however, for his massive, brooding Lincoln statue in the Lincoln Memorial which exudes power and strength (1922). French also produced what might be his best sculpture in 1919, *Memory*, which turns toward an idealized female nude sitting languorously while she gazes at her reflection in a mirror.[5]

Other Sculptors

Other extremely talented sculptors worked in the Gilded Age alongside French and Saint-Gaudens. Edmonia Lewis gained fame during the 1860s but her Chippewa and African-American heritage brought more curiosity about her than her art. In 1867 she did a bust of Colonel Robert Gould Shaw and *Forever Free*, which depicted a standing man and praying slave woman on her knees, both gazing toward the heavens in the glory of their freedom. Lewis moved to Italy where her heritage attracted less attention than her work but virtually disappeared after the 1880s. John Quincy Adams Ward, a prominent sculptor since the 1850s, continued to have success and won the commission for the James Garfield Memorial (1887). Paul Wayland Bartlett gained early fame with his *The Bear Tamer* (1887) in bronze, which depicted a Native American and a bear cub. He would go on to design bronze figures of Michelangelo and Columbus for the Library of Congress rotunda, an equestrian statue of Lafayette for the Louvre, and *Peaceful Democracy* for the House of Representatives. Another talented sculptor, Frederick William MacMonnies, also worked in bronze, producing *Nathan Hale* (1890), *Pan of Rohallion* (1890), his colossal *The Triumph of Columbia* for the Columbia Exposition (1893), and the *Bacchante* (1893) which shocked Boston and created a sensation surrounding the roughly 16-inch bronze female nude. In addition, George Grey Barnard produced some remarkable work, most significantly his marble *Struggle of the Two Natures in Man* (1894). Western themes emerged in the bronze work of Frederic Remington, Cyrus Dallin, Solon Hannibal Borglum, and Herman Atkins MacNeil. Finally, Bessie Potter Vonnoh, influenced by Art Nouveau and impressionism, worked on small, personal themes, such as her work *The Young Mother* (1896). Hazy outlines and curves characterize this sitting mother, gazing intently into the face of her swaddled infant, as sinuous lines of her dress and the baby's blanket drape across them.[6]

Painting

American painting flourished during the Gilded Age as it had at mid-century, but for the most part painters were no longer as interested in conveying a realistic, romanticized nature as faithfully as possible. Instead they were much more focused on the art itself. The nude became a central figure in American painting for the first time as American artists either trained in Europe or looked to European trends which looked back to Classical, Renaissance, and Baroque models.

Realist Painters

Realist painters seemed to dominate the American scene, with a few notable exceptions. Winslow Homer (1836–1910) exerted a strong influence on American painters and his work exhibited a strong sense of drama, particularly the later works; his realism probably derived from his years as a successful illustrator. One of his best earlier works, though scathingly attacked by high-culture, snobbish critics, is *Snap the Whip* (1872) which portrays nine boys at play in a meadow during recess from the rural one-room schoolhouse in the background. The fun and childish abandon of the moment is intimately captured on the canvas. Homer's later work is certainly more dramatic, particularly *The Life Line* (1884) which shows a male rescuer sliding on a lifeline clutching an unconscious woman as they career over the vicious waves of the sea from one ship to another, both of which are off the canvas. Leaving the ships out of the frame focuses the painting sharply on the harrowing ride and the elemental power of the waves. Homer did not just work in oils but was also highly skilled with watercolors.

Arguably the most famous realist was Thomas Eakins (1844–1916), who also studied at the Ecole des Beaux-Arts in Paris. Eakins also often chose topics that did not fit well with the art establishment's views on proper art topics, gravitating toward those that were relatively mundane. He liked to choose sporting topics and was fascinated with all-male culture. While he was never a virulent misogynist, Eakins clearly was disturbed by the fears of effeminization of middle-class men that was so strong among his contemporaries like Theodore Roosevelt, and he supported the gender division of American society. *The Gross Clinic* (1875) illustrates his distaste for women moving outside of their sphere and caused quite a scandal with its intensely realistic portrayal of a medical school dissection. While male students eagerly dissect the cadaver, the lone female student throws a hand over her eyes in obvious horror. *The Swimming Hole* (1885) is a brilliant painting of five nude young men at a swimming hole with Eakins himself swimming toward them in the bottom left corner. Such a mundane topic is writ large by the almost classical poses the young men assume in the painting. Eakins also became intensely interested in photography and was quite accomplished, using photos to enhance the realism of his paintings.[7]

American Artists Abroad

Other artists were more influenced by European styles, particularly French Impressionism. John Singer Sargent (1856–1925) was heavily indebted to Impressionists such as Degas and his close personal friend Claude Monet. His portraiture typically exhibited bold brush work and bold colors as well as a technical brilliance, though critics believed he showed an uncaring, clinical detachment about his subjects. After Paris received his *Madame X* (1884) with scorn over its overt sexuality and lack of moral uplift, Sargent focused on less scandalous portraits. Today's audiences would laugh at the fact that this painting of a woman with her head turned to be looking off to her left in a strapless low-cut black gown could cause such a scandal, but audiences were much more attuned to these subtleties in the Gilded Age. Sargent's painting of them signaled to people in the Gilded Age that he placed aesthetics above morality in his art. Sargent lived most of his life abroad and gained fame from painting society's elite in England and later the United States, becoming the most famous portrait painter of his day.[8]

Cecilia Beaux painted in a style much like Sargent and was clearly influenced by Impressionism. She was often unfavorably compared to him, though in all fairness Gilded Age critics demeaned her art more on the basis of her sex than her skills. William Merritt Chase believed her to be their generation's greatest female painter. *Mr. And Mrs. Anson Phelps Stokes* (1898) and *Mrs. Larz Anderson* (1900) both brilliantly illustrated her virtuosity and ability to allow something of the inner person to shine through her work.[9]

James McNeill Whistler (1843–1903) and Henry Ossawa Tanner (1859–1937) were two more American artists who lived and worked abroad, though for different reasons. In fact, Whistler only lived six years of his entire life in the United States and was heavily influenced by European and Japanese styles. He is most well known for his painting that is usually referred to as "Whistler's Mother" (1874), but he did fascinating and abstract work such as *Nocturne in Black and Gold: The Falling Rocket* (1874). Tanner lived abroad because as an African-American artist he found France much more accepting of his heritage than the United States. Tanner started his studies in Philadelphia at the Pennsylvania Academy where he studied with Thomas Eakins, but vicious racism against him by other painters was difficult for him. After 1891, Paris would become Tanner's main home where he gained no small acclaim; the French government acquired his *Resurrection of Lazarus* (1897).[10]

American Impressionism

American Impressionists can be a difficult group to pin down because the number of people who were influenced by this style in both color and brush work was large, but many did not fully embrace the style. Difficulty also comes from the fact that several important painters turned to Impressionism mid-way through their careers, such as William Merritt Chase (1849–1916) and Julian Alden Weir (1852–1919). Chase gained great fame with his Impressionist work such as *Idle Hours* (1894), which is a coastal scene painted in the vibrant blues and greens typical of Impressionist painters. Chase, though, never eschewed his Royal Academy training from Munich, Germany, and at times would bring out his darker colors and impasto style which relied on the heavy layering and buildup of paint. Julian Alden Weir was already a very well-known painter and teacher at the Art Students League before he turned to Impressionism in the 1890s. Weir's *The Red Bridge* (1895) firmly placed him among America's best Impressionists and he became a leader of the movement in the United States by the end of the century.[11]

In 1898 a group of American Impressionists called "The Ten" was formed, and they broke from the Society of American Artists which amounted to a tacit rejection of the artistic standards of the critics and juries selected by the Society. The Ten were Thomas E. Dewing, Edward E. Simmons, Julien Alden Weir, John Henry Twachtman, Joseph R. De Camp, Willard L. Metcalf, Childe Hassam, Frank Benson, Robert Reid, and Edmund C. Tarbell. Chase joined in 1902 after Twachtman's death. Several members of The Ten turned to more abstract styles in the twentieth century and by their rejection of the mainstream art structure, definitely foreshadowed the Armory Show (1913) in New York City where modern art burst onto the American scene.[12]

Ironically, Mary Cassatt (1844–1926) was probably America's most accomplished Impressionist painter, but she did not participate in American Impressionism because she lived and worked in France where she was part of the original French Impressionist movement starting in 1877. Cassatt turned to Impressionism decades earlier than The Ten and studied with originators of the style like Manet and Degas, whose influence on her was profound. Like other Impressionists she favored everyday scenes of life, but her most well-known works often focused on women. *At the Opera* (1879), *Mary Cassatt* (1877–1878), *The Bath* (1891–1892), and *The Boating Party* (1893–1894), all focus the viewer's gaze on the female subjects and in the latter two on their child as well.[13]

Mural Painting

Mural painting also deserves mention because after the 1893 Columbia Exposition it entered the mainstream of American art, though the American taste for murals had been growing since the 1880s. In 1895 the National Society of Mural Painters organized to promote mural painting. The famed illustrator Edwin Austin Abbey, Edwin Howland Bashfield, and renowned classicist painter Kenyon Cox were all in great demand as mural painters. One example of the many murals these artists painted is Abbey's *The Quest for the Holy Grail* (1895–1901) in the Boston Public Library, while Bashfield and Cox painted murals for the Library of Congress.[14]

Stained Glass

Stained glass emerged as a major artistic medium in the United States in the 1880s and was primarily the product of the works of John La Farge (1835–1910) and Louis Comfort Tiffany (1848–1933). Both men rejected the mass-produced, clear colored glass available on the market in favor of glasses their companies produced that captured different tones and textures of color within the glass and were opalescent. La Farge did thousands of stained glass windows but one of his most well known is *Peonies Blown in the Wind* (1878–1879). Tiffany gained fame for his Favrile glass, which possessed an iridescent sheen. He used this glass in his glass mosaics such as the famous *Peacock Mosaic* (1890–1891), windows like *Landscape with Peacock and Peonies* (1900–1910), vases, and his now-famous Tiffany Lamps. Tiffany began making his famous lamps with their beautiful stained glass lampshades by 1883 (just four years after Edison invented the light bulb) which brilliantly utilized the incandescent light bulb to produce sparkling colors shining through the stained glass.[15]

POPULAR ART

Illustrators

High and Popular Art Crossover

During the Gilded Age the demand for illustration grew dramatically with the rapid increase in the number of popular magazines leading to the Golden Age of Illustration which lasted from the 1890s to the 1920s. Many talented artists turned to illustration to support themselves and a handful gained great acclaim and wealth. The American Renaissance, which affected so much of the arts in the late Gilded Age, heavily influenced commercial art and allowed, even encouraged, crossover between commercial and fine art. Sculptors, architects, painters, stained-glass artists, and muralists all worked together to create the expansive new public role for art in the new age of American power and prosperity. It is little wonder that some illustrators could straddle the world of commercial, popular art and fine arts in the heady days of the infancy of American international power. The distinction between commercial art and fine art, however, continued and most illustrators with ambitions for fine art had to juggle the demands of the art world and their income from illustration. Some illustrators, most notably Maxfield Parrish, managed to blend the two better than others. Many of the famous illustrators in this last part of the nineteenth century studied with famous painters of the era and also traveled to Europe where they were heavily influenced by European trends in illustration and fine art.

Harper's Weekly *and the Civil War*

The need for good illustrators grew with the emergence of large-circulation magazines in the nineteenth century, and the Civil War particularly created a niche for artists who could represent the conflict to a public eager for news. *Harper's Weekly* in particular hired a whole generation of illustrators to depict the Civil War, thanks mainly to the magazine's art director Charles Parsons. From 1863 until 1889, Parsons worked to nurture young talent for *Harper's* and helped to develop such young artists as Howard Pyle, Frederic Remington, Charles Dana Gibson, and Edwin Austin Abbey. The famous illustrators of the 1860s and 1870s, however, were Felix Octavious Carr Darling, Charles Parsons, Frances Palmer of Currier and Ives, Winslow Homer (who would go on to great fame as a painter and left illustration behind after 1887), Milton Burns, and Mary Hallock Foote. As magazines gained larger audiences in the 1880s and 1890s and as advertising became more important to American businesses the demands for skilled commercial artists grew dramatically.[16]

Technological Improvements

Even as circulations grew and the demand for artists increased, technological progress was making it possible to more accurately reproduce illustrations in a much higher quality. By the middle of the century wood engraving was well established in the United States—basically an illustration or painting was traced onto a block of wood and then carved. This wood block would then be "stereotyped," which meant a process by which a mold was made of the carved wooden block and then a metal cast was taken. This metal plate would then be used in the printing process. The entire wood engraving process meant that any artist's work had to be copied by a sculptor who carved it into wood, thereby mediating between the artist's original and the skills and vision of the sculptor. This process was slightly improved with photography which allowed a picture of the illustration to be placed on the wooden block and traced by the sculptor. Frederick Eugene Ives' invention of the halftone process in 1881 brought the great technological leap forward, allowing the original illustration to be printed in the text. The halftone process involved photographing the original illustration through a screen which broke it up into small dots. Commercial artists could now work in virtually any medium (charcoal, pen and ink, oils, or watercolors) and have their work printed directly into a magazine. Halftones also allowed for the introduction of color through a much less expensive process than chromolithography, but it was still costly enough to keep the routine use of color rare. Magazines normally used full color only on their covers in the 1890s. Ironically, the halftone process and mass advertising, respectively, made illustrations cheaper and increased the illustration budgets of magazines which led to a vast increase in the use of high-quality illustrations and the Golden Age of Illustration. Not until 1901 would color photolithography make the widespread and inexpensive use of color readily available for American magazines.[17]

The Big Three Illustrators: Pyle, Remington, Gibson

In the 1880s a new cadre of talented illustrators emerged and a few would become celebrities in their own right, often commanding large salaries from $15,000 to $50,000 a year. The three greatest names of the 1880s and 1890s were undoubtedly Howard Pyle, Frederic Remington, and Charles Dana Gibson.

Howard Pyle (1853–1911) leads the list as one of America's most well-known and accomplished Gilded Age illustrators with nearly 3,000 illustrations appearing in magazines along with the 20 illustrated books that he authored. Pyle studied art with a Belgian painter, Adolph van der Wielen, in Philadelphia and later at the famous Art Students League in New York. Spanish impressionism would heavily influence his work after 1895. Pyle, like so many others, worked for Charles Parsons at *Harper's* and learned much while working with the cadre of artists in New York. Pyle loved historical topics and most of his work had historical themes that were extremely well researched. But what set Pyle off from other artists was his ability to paint action and drama. Paintings and illustrations by Pyle virtually leapt off the page and his famous pirates seemed as if they were in action and not simply a picture. In an era when adventure played such a role in the collective imagination of American society and Theodore Roosevelt encouraged the "Strenuous Life," Howard Pyle's paintings resonated with the public (see Chapters 2 and 7). Pyle broke from the norms of illustration of his day as well when he wrote and illustrated his own books. Pyle's first illustrated novel was *The Merry Adventures of Robin Hood* (1883). Students were also one of Pyle's most enduring contributions. He taught illustration at the Drexel Institute of Art, Science, and Technology in Philadelphia from 1894 to 1900, and then opened his own private school in his home of

Wilmington, Delaware. Over 100 young artists studied with Pyle, and around him formed a particular style of art known as the famous Brandywine School of American Illustration. Pyle was particularly good at helping female artists to get started in the world of illustration. Some of his protégés went on to great fame such as N. C. Wyeth, Violet Oakley, Jessie Wilcox Smith, and Stanley Arthurs.[18]

Frederic Remington (1861–1909) also burst onto the commercial art scene in the 1880s, going on to become the most well-known artist of the American West in the Gilded Age. This Yale graduate, who was well known in college for his athletic prowess, produced over 2,800 illustrations, numerous paintings, as well as 21 bronze statues from 1895 to 1909. Like many artists of his day, Remington's life as fine artist and commercial artist grew in tandem. Even as he gained financial stability from illustrations he produced paintings that he exhibited starting in 1887, winning several awards for his work. Remington's work with bronze sculpture was remarkable and his 1895 *The Bronco Buster* remains today his most popular sculpture. This sculpture shows a ferocious bronco wildly rearing on its hind legs, all muscle and sinew, while the cowboy grimly grips the reins with one hand and swings his short quirt overhead. Museums purchased his statuettes even during his lifetime.

What made Remington so popular was that the mythology surrounding the Old West was growing in the United States even as that West disappeared. The frontier closed in the 1890s and law and order came as civilization encroached on once lawless territories. Industrialization, urbanization, and the spread of railroads seemed to be interconnecting and homogenizing the world at an alarming pace. In the machine age of great cities the idea of a frontier where rough justice prevailed and tough, courageous pioneers tamed a wild land appealed to the romantic, adventurous spirit of the day. Dime novels, Buffalo Bill's Wild West Show, magazines, and even fine art sought to capture the West that was, at least the mythical West that was (see Chapters 2, 8, 10). Frederic Remington played a dramatic and key role in documenting the rapidly disappearing West in the minds of his audience, but in reality his images were very much filtered through a nostalgic and romantic lens. Remington became good friends with writer Owen Wister, who wrote the first true Western novel, *The Virginian*, in 1902, and illustrated several of Wister's western stories for *Harper's Monthly*. In 1888 he illustrated Theodore Roosevelt's *Ranch Life and the Hunting Trail* and in the early 1890s the historian Francis Parkman eagerly sought out Remington to illustrate his book *The Oregon Trail* (1892). Remington would have no peer until Charles Russell, the Montana painter and illustrator, emerged as a major figure in the early twentieth century.

Charles Parsons, art director for *Harper's*, discovered Remington and gave the budding artist his most steady work with *Harper's Weekly* and

Harper's Monthly. Working for Parsons he honed his forceful, realistic style that seemed to be able to capture motion and action as readily as Pyle. He became good friends with fellow *Harper's* illustrators Howard Pyle, Charles Dana Gibson, and E. W. Kemble. Remington trained at the Art Students League in New York City where he studied under the famous American impressionist Julian Alden Weir. Remington would soon be in tremendous demand not only with *Harper's* but also with *St. Nicholas Magazine, Scribner's Magazine, Century, Cosmopolitan,* and *Outing.* By the late 1890s, Remington's focus turned more to painting. He moved to Connecticut and studied with several important American impressionists such as Childe Hassam, Robert Reid, Edmund Tarbell, and his old teacher and new neighbor Julian Alden Weir. Ironically, Remington finally broke from commercial art in 1909 when his contract with *Collier's* expired, but he enjoyed his new-found freedom for less than a year when in December he died unexpectedly from complications involving a ruptured appendix.[19]

Charles Dana Gibson's (1867–1944) fame was as great as either Pyle's or Remington's. Gibson's salary rose throughout the Gilded Age from $600 to $800 per month in 1890 to nearly $2,000 per month by mid-decade, and by the early twentieth century he earned the highest salary of any illustrator of his day, a whopping $65,000 per year. Gibson's fame, unlike Pyle and Remington, came not from illustrating action scenes of pirates or cowboys but instead from his ability to render earnest beauty and humor in the form of his Gibson Girl, one of the most recognized images of the Gilded Age.

Gibson manifested early artistic ability and attended the Art Students League in New York City where he studied under painting masters Kenyon Cox, William Merritt Chase, and Thomas Eakins. But like so many other American artists his style was tremendously influenced by a trip to Europe where he met the distinguished British illustrator George DuMaurier and studied briefly in Paris. He too wished to paint more by the early 1900s and studied painting for several years, honing his ability throughout his lifetime.

Gibson had no problem finding work and by the 1890s his illustrations appeared in the influential magazines *Century, Harper's Weekly,* and *Scribner's Magazine,* as well as in several books. But it was his Gibson Girl that catapulted him to instant celebrity. Gibson somehow managed to capture the spirit of his age as few artists or musicians did and his feminine creation resonated strongly with millions of Americans. Gibson provided seven different images of his Gibson Girl that allowed him to illustrate different feelings and moods: Beauty, Boy-Girl, Flirt, Sentimental, Convinced, Ambitious, and Well-Balanced. With these single American young women Gibson could comment on American society and its foibles through his "gentle sarcasm." Unlike Pyle's Brandywine School, which painted women in maternal, traditional roles, Gibson was part of the American Beauty illustrators who drew single, modern women on the move. Gibson's young ladies wore the most stylish clothes, freed from the restraints of Victorian excessive petticoats, and participated in the most up-to-date activities like golf, tennis, and bicycling (see Chapter 8). While Gibson's deft hand could draw figures conveying nuanced emotion, his young women often gazed off the page like almost untouchable, ideal beauties. What was remarkable about Gibson was his perceptive ability to satirize his own upper-crust social class while at the same time endearing these people to his illustrations. Even though Gibson poked fun at the middle class and upper crust, women still followed the clothing and hairstyles of his creations.

By the early twentieth century Gibson sought to develop his painting and leave illustration. Although financial circumstances forced him to return to illustration, he found that as time passed he no longer had that incredible resonance with what the public wanted as he had had in the 1890s. However, he continued to illustrate and produce well-received paintings until his death in 1944.[20]

Other Illustrators

There were also other famous illustrators that deserve mention. Edwin Austin Abbey studied art at the Pennsylvania Academy of the Fine Arts, which seemed to produce so many great artists in the Gilded Age, but gained his experience working for *Harper's Monthly* alongside A. B. Frost and Howard Pyle. In an age when full-color illustrations were relatively rare, much of his work was done in watercolors and oils and appeared in full color by the 1890s. He gained lasting fame for his Shakespearian illustrations which are still considered to be among the best ever done. A. B. Frost became the country's most famous illustrator of rural America. E. W. Kemble was another who became famous for his drawings of African Americans which today are striking for their dichotomous appearance: half seem to possess great sensitivity to the difficulties of African-American life and the other half appear to portray the egregious African-American stereotypes so common in the Gilded Age (see Chapters 9 and 10). Jessie Wilcox Smith, a Pyle student at Drexel, became the foremost illustrator of children by the late nineteenth and early twentieth centuries, and her work heavily relied on Gilded Age idealized and sentimental notions of childhood. Edward Penfield also gained fame for his posters and magazine illustrations.[21] Hundreds of illustrators found prosperous work in the Gilded Age but few matched the tremendous critical and economic successes of Pyle, Remington, and Gibson.

Maxfield Parrish—Transition to the Twentieth Century

The most obvious transitional figure between the Gilded Age and the twentieth century illustration was Maxfield Parrish (1870–1966). Although he was a popular illustrator by 1900 and published in most of the elite magazines, his greatest success and fame would come in the twentieth century. Parrish managed to create for himself a career in both commercial and fine art. His work bridged fine art and popular art because he gained popularity for his paintings, prints, and calendars not through gallery shows, but through mass marketing. Parrish was certainly one of the artists who benefited from the impulses of the American Renaissance—he lived in the artist colony in Cornish, Connecticut, which drew Augustus Saint-Gaudens, Paul Manship, Daniel Chester French, and Charles Platt as residents or guests for extended periods. Like Pyle, Remington, and Gibson, Parrish relied on romanticism and nostalgia in his work, which often did go back to an idealized Medieval era, but his incredible use of color and glazes, particularly in the backgrounds, definitely set him outside the boundaries of the stark realism of the three older illustrators. His style was by no means abstract, but his highly idealized landscapes were quite different from those of the other illustrators. Parrish's brilliant colors, particularly his vibrant blues, called "Parrish blue," gave his paintings an other-worldly feel that was definitely modern in its orientation and distinct from the styles of the other Gilded Age illustrators.[22]

Chromolithographic Prints

What democratized art in the Gilded Age and made it available to most Americans was the chromolithographic process invented in Europe and brought to the United States. Lithography was invented in the late eighteenth century and chromolithography by the mid-nineteenth century. Special greasy crayons were used to draw on a prepared limestone. The stone would then be wet with water and a greasy paint applied to the stone, adhering only to the drawing, and then would be used to print the image. Color could be duplicated by using multiple stones; one stone was required for each color. This of course made the process difficult because the poster or page had to be exactly aligned for each printing. By the 1860s a remarkable array of colors were available, which, combined with the falling costs of paper and printing, created a market where inexpensive colored lithographic copies of art were widely disseminated throughout the nation. In the 1860s close to 60 companies produced lithographs and employed 800 people, but this exploded to 700 businesses employing 8,000 workers by 1890. Louis Prang was undoubtedly the most famous lithographer of the late nineteenth century,

mainly because of his successful self-promotion, but he did not invent
the process nor was he the originator of the term "chromo" for chromolithographs. High-end chromos would run $20, though the average
print cost about $2–$3, and virtually all famous paintings were reproduced for American consumers. The paintings of Mary Cassatt, Julien
Alden Weir, James Whistler, and Thomas Eakins were all available. The
Currier and Ives shop in New York was famous for providing high-
quality chromos, which as a medium of art became omnipresent. Art
historian Robert Taft holds that the 1896 chromolithograph of Cassilly
Adam's *Custer's Last Fight*, commissioned by the Anheuser-Bush Company and sent to thousands of saloons, was the most popular piece of
art in America. Chromolithography changed affordable, popular visual
arts dramatically by adding vibrant color to everyday items like greeting
cards, advertisements, stationery, campaign buttons, and of course art
prints. Yet even as chromolithography grew in popularity, the connois-
seurs of high culture, like E. L. Godkin, attacked it as a debased art form
and "pseudo-culture." By the 1890s chromo had taken on pejorative
meanings and it was used to designate something fake or cheap. At the
1876 Centennial Exposition chromo prints were placed with the "fine"
arts, but at the Columbian Exposition in 1893 they were displayed as
"industrial" and "commercial" art. And yet, in spite of this high cultural
prejudice chromo prints remained exceptionally popular, decorating
many middle-class homes (see Chapter 4).[23]

Photography

The newest and most scientific art to develop in the Gilded Age was
that of photography. Photography literally burst onto the American
scene during the Gilded Age as flexible roll film and inexpensive hand
cameras were developed (see Chapter 7). Photographers, however,
quickly realized its potential as an art form as well. Picking up from
Mathew Brady's Photographic Corps from the Civil War, other photographers put their cameras to artistic use. During the 1860s and 1870s
photographers spread over the American West to document the frontier
region. Carleton E. Watkins, Timothy O'Sullivan, and William Henry
Jackson captured the panoramic view of the West that most people had
only seen in landscape paintings. Jackson was particularly talented and
used large 20-by-24-inch glass plates which allowed him to capture
breathtaking panoramic views such as *The Grand Canyon of Yellowstone*
(1871). Jackson inspired much of the twentieth century's landscape photography, particularly that of Ansel Adams. Photography also helped in
motion studies. Photographer Eadweard Muybridge collaborated with
painter Thomas Eakins to study the motion of people and animals
through the use of photographs. Eakins was quite an accomplished pho-

tographer in his own right and his photographs exhibited his ability to artistically frame a photograph so that it possessed its own aesthetics. Jacob Riis also added to the mystique of photographs by including them in *How the Other Half Lives* (1890) which chronicled the lives of the desperately poor in New York City (see Chapters 2 and 4). But by far the most influential and important photographer as artist was Alfred Stieglitz (1864–1946), who demanded that photography be treated as an art form. He produced photographs that had aesthetic, artistic values. Stieglitz spread his ideas to a broad public as editor of *The American Amateur Photographer* magazine and would continue to be a major force in artistic photography well into the twentieth century.[24]

CONCLUSION

American art during the Gilded Age reflected the growing economic and political power of the United States. There also was greater exchange between the United States and Europe as many artists studied abroad and brought European styles back to the United States. And even though there is little doubt that elite patronage was important to artists, high and popular arts seemed to blur during this era. Mass-market magazines demanded high-quality illustrations that lured some of the nation's most talented artists into commercial art even as chromolithography made high art accessible to millions of Americans. Further complicating the clear distinctions between "high" and "popular" art was the fact that many of the most famous illustrators studied art with some of the most famous painters of the Gilded Age, and there were several illustrators who went on to become famous painters or who straddled both the illustration and painting worlds. The Vanderbilts may have commissioned an original painting but chromolithography could make it available to the average American for $2. While folk art had always been important to average Americans, high art and its aesthetics now made its way into American homes in ways heretofore impossible. Industrial mass production brought high art to the masses and made it popular.

Cost of Products, 1890–1899

Telegraph rates between New York City and San Francisco, 1895, 10 words or less, $1

Wholesale price of brick, 1895, $5.31/1,000

Wholesale price of coal, 1895, $2.98/ton

Median sales price of new homes, 1890, $3,250

Fire insurance for two wood frame houses in Columbia, SC, 1899, $4.75/yr.

Bricklayers in Massachusetts income, 1896, 50 hours/week, $3.87/day

Seamus Cavanah, manager of salmon cannery, salary, 1896, $5,500/yr.

Roger and Vivian Fairmont net worth, 1897, $37 million

Postal rate for first-class mail, 1895, $.02

Vaudeville ticket, 1890s, $.10–$.25

Opera ticket, 1890s, $1–$7

Broadway theater ticket, 1890s, $1.50

Three months of dance lessons in San Francisco, $10

Grand Hotel double room on Mackinac Island, 1890, $54/week

Summer cottage, 1890s, $10–$20/week

Raymond and Whitcomb travel agency 25-day trip to Yellowstone, 1890s, $275

Tuition at the University of the City of New York Law School, 1896, $200 for two years

Large, ornate family Bible, 1895, $3.45

Robinson Crusoe by Daniel Defoe, 1895, $1.05

Library Editions of New Oxford and Princeton Series of 150 great books, 1895, $.50/each

Tattered Tom series books by Horatio Alger, 1895, $.88

BonBons, 1896, $.60

Lang's Readymade chocolate icing, 1893, $.20

Vernard's Eagle Chocolate, 1895, $.20/lb.

Cleveland's Baking Powder, 1893, $.15

Chapman's Grocer's Coffee, 1898, 11 lbs./$1

Watermelon, 1898, $.10

Whole chicken, 1898, $.15

Fresh pork, 1898, $.06/lb.

Ham and bacon, 1898, $.10/lb.

Corn meal, 1898, $.12/peck

Eggs, 1898, $.12/dozen

Lard, 1898, $.08/lb.

Milk, 1898, $.06/quart

Starch, 1898, $.05/lb.

Wheat flour, 1898, 12-lb. bag, $.35

Sugar, 1898, $.06/lb.

Cans of corned and roast beef, 1896, $.10/lb.

Can of Leibig Company's beef extract, 1896, $.10

Canned goods generally sold for $.10

Extra fine cream cheese, 1896, $.15/lb.

Perfection flour, 1896, $2.50 half-barrel, $4.75 barrel

Hershey's Chocolate penny bar, $.01

Salada Ceylon Tea, 1898, $.50/lb.

Molasses, 1896, $.10/gal.

Smoked herring, 1896, $.15/box

Florida palm tree, 1896, $.20

Anti-Skeet mosquito pesticide, 1896, six wafers in a box, $.10

Six rose plants, 1896, $.25

Sweet pea seeds, 1896, ten packets, $.10

Meat cutter, 1895, $2

Three-tine hay fork, 1895, $.30

Five-hoe grain drill, 1895, $14

Circular sawing machine, 1895, $16

Kemp's manure spreader, 1895, $85

Wind mill, 1895, $24.40

Wood plane, 1895, $.80

Hammer, 1895, $.28

Axe, 1895, $.60

2-inch screws, 1895, $.06/dozen

Kerosene, 1895, 52-gallon barrel, $.10/gal.

Wallpaper, 1896, $.10/roll

Paint, 1895, $1.15/gal.

3-inch paint brush, 1895, $.28

Axle grease, 1895, 1-lb. box, $.05

12-gauge shotgun, 1895, $35

Winchester rifle model 1892, 1895, $11.86

Colt double-action 38-caliber pistol, 1895, $10

Baseball glove, 1895, $1.50

Baseball, 1895, league quality $1, playground quality $.25

Boxing gloves, 1895, $4.75

Wooden fishing rod, 10½ feet long, 1895, $.10

Fishing reel, 1895, $1.50

Large tackle box, 1895, $1.88

Oak upholstered parlor suite (arm chair, rocker, divan, two parlor chairs), 1895, $33.70

Iron bed frame, 1895, $4.75

English stone porcelain chamber set (washbowl, pitcher, chamber pot and cover, water pitcher, drinking mug, brush vase, soap dish), 1895, $3.15

3-drawer dresser with beveled mirror, 1895, $5.70

Sideboard, 1895, $13.45

Infant cradle, 1895, $3.50

Lemonoide Polish, 1896, $.50

Linoleum, laid, 1896, $.80/yard

Dr. Rose's Obesity Powders, 1890, $.58

Dr. Williams Pink Pills for Pale People, 1890, $.50

Morgan's Cod Liver Oil and Horehound Drops, 1898, $.05

Electric Bitters, 1898, $.50

Rikers Expectorant, 1895, $.60

Cook's Cough Cure, 1895, $.20/bottle

Lablanche face powder, 1896, $.50

Modene hair remover, 1896, $1

Wrinkleine lotion, 1896, $1

Nail trimmer, 1899, $.25

Forest Fringe Violet perfume, 1896, $1

Shaving soap, 1895, $.04/cake

Campbell's Safe Complexion Wafers face cleaner, 1896, $1

Dr. Sheffield's Creme Dentifrice, 1898, $.25

Copco Bath Soap, 1896, $.05

Mrs. Hannah Cobb's Improved Laundry Soap, 1895, 100 12-oz. bars per box, $3.35/box

Borax, 1895, $.17/1-lb. package

Toilet paper, 1895, $.06/roll

Texas rawhide saddle, 1895, $7.75

The Winton Motor Carriage, 1899, $1,000

Indiana Piano Box buggy, 1895, $45.75

Surrey, 1895, $99

White Star No. 1 bicycle, 1895, $45

Baby carriage, 1895, $3.70

Boys' wagon, 1895, $.75

Autoharp, 1896, $7.50

Banjo, 1895, $2.75

Violin, 1895, $4.45

Harmonica, 1895, $.10

Piano, 1895, $350

Cornet, 1895, $5.10

Waterman's fountain pen, 1896, $4

Travel trunk, 1895, $4

Metcalf writing paper, 1893, $.75

Ladies' umbrella, 1895, $.65

Gentleman's umbrella, 1895, $.50

Ladies' Home Journal, 1893, $.10/issue, $1/yr.

Wall Street Journal, 1890, $5/yr.

New York World, 1895, $.01/newspaper

New York Times, 1898, $.01

New York telephone charges, direct line, 1895, $90

New York to Boston boat fare, 1895, $2

Cook Tours Nile Steamers, cruise ship New York to Egypt, 1895, $675–$1,225

Ravenna pattern china, 1895, 7 8-inch plates, $1.17

Plain white English stone china, 1895, 100 pieces, $8.75

6-quart tin coffee pot, 1895, $.18

Iron tea kettle, 1895, $.28

Windsor 5-pint sauce pan, 1895, $.28

Steel teaspoons, 1895, $.32/dozen

Silver teaspoons, 1895, $6.60/dozen

Corn popper, 1895, $.08

Potato masher, 1895, $.08

Ladies' pearl-handled knife, 1895, $.34

Singer sewing machine, 1895, $13.50

Laundry wringer, 1895, $2

Iron, 1895, $.55

Mosley Improved Water Heater No. 3, 1895, $15

Refrigerator (actually an ice chest), 1895, $10.34

Grand Windsor stove, 1895, $24.30

Bronze metal hanging lamp, 1895, $3

Ornate wooden clock, 1895, $3.90

Merritt typewriters, 1895, $11

Hand camera, 1895, $13.50

Microscope, 1895, $4

Ladies' 14K gold pocket watch, 1895, $25

Alpaca wool cloth, 1895, $.08/½ yard

English tweed cotton cloth, 1895, $.07/¼ yard

Wool brocade with Jacquard design, 1895, $.35/yard

Outing flannel, 1895, $.04/¾ yard

Black Bengaline silk, 21 inches wide, 1895, $1.50/yard

Linen napkins, 1895, $.60/dozen

Bleached damask towel, 1895, $.27/each, $3.12/dozen

Linen glass doilies, 1895, $.20/dozen

Ladies' dress pattern, 1896, $.30

Ladies' shoes, 1895, $2.50

Ladies' cotton hose, 1895, $.10/each, $1.10/dozen

Ladies' night dress, 1895, $.70

Ladies' shirt waist, 1895, $.85/each, $9.75/dozen

Ladies' ready-made dress, 1895, $.59/each, $6.65/dozen

Ladies' Newport suit, 1895, $5.95

Ladies' ready-made dress skirt, 1895, $2.75

Wash dress for 8-year-old girl, 1895, $.55

Ladies' spring cape, 1895, $2.35

Ladies' jacket, 1895, $3

Ladies' Mackintosh coat, 1895, $2

Men's shoes, 1895, $4

Men's fancy dress shirt, 1895, $1

Men's wool underwear with fleece lining, 1895, $2

Men's sack suit, 1895, $3

Men's full-dress suit, 1895, $33

Men's wool trousers, 1895, $3

Men's jeans, 1895, $1

Men's fancy vest, 1895, $.80

Men's Mackintosh coat, 1895, $3.75

Infant cloak, 1895, $2.75

Infant robe, 1895, $.85

Children's reefer jacket, 1895, $1.10

Boys' suit with knickers, 1895, $.75/cotton, $1.90/wool

Boys' and youth's suit with long pants, 1895, $2.50

Children's Zouave suit, 1895, $2

Boys' shirt, 1895, $.30

Boys' summer underwear, 1895, $.25

Cowboy hat, 1895, $1

Men's fedora, 1895, $.75

Boys' straw hat, 1895, $.20

Authors card game, 1895, $.10

The Game of Travel board game, 1895, $.85

Doll with bisque head, 1895, $.50

Magic lantern, 1895, $1.15

Wooden soldiers, 1895, $2.10/dozen

Steam train, 1895, $3.50

Marbles, 1895, bag of 100 assorted sizes, $.20

Wooden top, 1895, $.35/dozen

Notes

CHAPTER 1

1. Robert G. Barrows, "Urban America," in *The Gilded Age: Essays on the Origins of Modern America*, ed. Charles W. Calhoun (Wilmington, Del.: Scholarly Resources, 1996), 92–93; U.S. Bureau of the Census, *Historical Statistics of the United States: Colonial Times to 1970*, 2 vols. (Washington, D.C.: GPO, 1975): 1: 11–12, 22–37.

2. *Historical Statistics of the United States*, 1: 106; Roger Daniels, "The Immigrant Experience in the Gilded Age," in *The Gilded Age: Essays on the Origins of Modern America*, ed. Charles W. Calhoun (Wilmington, Del.: Scholarly Resources, 1996), 63–89; Raymond A. Mohl, *The New City: Urban America in the Industrial Age, 1860–1920* (Arlington Heights, Ill.: Harlan Davidson, 1985), 22–25; Charles N. Glaab and A. Theodore Brown, *A History of Urban America*, 3rd ed. (New York: Macmillan, 1983), 135–36, 139–40; Barrows, "Urban America," 97–98.

3. Mohl, *The New City*, 21–22; Glaab and Brown, *A History of Urban America*, 138–39; Barrows, "Urban America," 96–97.

4. Glaab and Brown, *A History of Urban America*, 112–33.

5. *Historical Statistics of the United States*, 1: 22–37; Mohl, *The New City*, 8–13; Glaab and Brown, *A History of Urban America*, 112–15; Howard P. Chudacoff, *The Evolution of American Urban Society* (Englewood Cliffs, N.J.: Prentice Hall, 1975), 56; Barrows, "Urban America," 94–95.

6. Glaab and Brown, *A History of Urban America*, 152–76; Mohl, *The New City*, 35–39; Sean Dennis Cashman, *America in the Gilded Age: From the Death of Lincoln to the Rise of Theodore Roosevelt*, 3rd ed. (New York: New York University Press, 1994), 142; Chudacoff, *The Evolution of American Urban Society*, 64–88.

7. John D'Emilio and Estelle Freedman, *Intimate Matters: A History of Sexuality in America*, 2nd ed. (Chicago: University of Chicago Press, 1997), 199; Paul Boyer, *Urban Masses and Moral Order in America, 1820–1920* (Cambridge, Mass.: Harvard University Press, 1978).

8. Gilbert Fite, *The Farmers' Frontier, 1865–1900* (New York: Holt, Rinehart and Winston, 1966), 15–33.

9. Rodman Paul, *The Far West and the Great Plains in Transition, 1859–1900* (New York: Harper & Row, 1988), 183–219.

10. Fite, *The Farmers' Frontier*; Paul, *The Far West*, 221–50.

11. Paul, *The Far West*, 234–35; Fite, *The Farmers' Frontier*, 131; Cashman, *America in the Gilded Age*, 288.

12. Lawrence Goodwyn, *Democratic Promise: The Populist Movement in America* (New York: Oxford University Press, 1976); Worth Robert Miller, "Farmers and Third-Party Politics," in *The Gilded Age: Essays on the Origins of Modern America*, ed. Charles W. Calhoun (Wilmington, Del.: Scholarly Resources, 1996), 235–60; Cashman, *America in the Gilded Age*, 313–37.

13. Michael Bellesiles, *Arming America: The Origins of a National Gun Culture* (New York: Alfred A. Knopf, 2000), 428–44.

14. Lawrence M. Friedman, *Crime and Punishment in American History* (New York: Basic Books, 1993), 3–4, 104–6, 134–39, 149.

15. David Courtwright, *Violent Land: Single Men and Social Disorder from the Frontier to the Inner City* (Cambridge, Mass.: Harvard University Press, 1996), 45, 81, 96–97, 175–78.

16. Glaab and Brown, *A History of Urban America*, 89, 146–47; James McPherson, *Ordeal by Fire: The Civil War and Reconstruction* (New York: Alfred A. Knopf, 1982), 614; Courtwright, *Violent Land*, 163; Friedman, *Crime and Punishment*, 95–96, 98–100, 135, 137, 156–57.

17. Elliott J. Gorn, "The Wicked World: The National Police Gazette and Gilded Age America," *Media Studies Journal* 6 (Winter 1992): 16; Howard P. Chudacoff, *The Age of the Bachelor: Creating an American Subculture* (Princeton, N.J.: Princeton University Press, 1999), 188–95; D'Emilio and Freedman, *Intimate Matters*, 180–83; Cynthia Eagle Russett, *Sexual Science: The Victorian Construction of Womanhood* (Cambridge, Mass.: Harvard University Press, 1989), 49–51, 70–73.

18. Mohl, *The New City*, 83–107; Glaab and Brown, *A History of Urban America*, 206–28; Cashman, *America in the Gilded Age*, 150–64.

19. McPherson, *Ordeal by Fire*, 545.

20. Eric Foner, *Reconstruction: America's Unfinished Revolution, 1863–1877* (New York: Harper & Row, 1988), 110–18, 281–307; Eric Foner, *Freedom's Lawmakers: A Directory of Black Officeholders during Reconstruction* (New York: Oxford University Press, 1993), xi–xxxv; McPherson, *Ordeal by Fire*, 535, 555–60, 613.

21. Foner, *Reconstruction*, 261–65, 425–59; McPherson, *Ordeal by Fire*, 519–20, 543–45.

22. Carl Degler, *The Other South: Southern Dissenters in the Nineteenth Century* (Gainesville: University of Florida Press, 2000), 208–9.

23. Foner, *Reconstruction*, 564–612; McPherson, *Ordeal by Fire*, 617–19; Cashman, *America in the Gilded Age*, 237–43; Leslie H. Fishel, Jr., "The African-American Experience," in *The Gilded Age: Essays on the Origins of Modern America*, ed. Charles W. Calhoun (Wilmington, Del.: Scholarly Resources, 1996), 142–44, 146; Robert Zangrando, *The NAACP Crusade Against Lynching, 1909–1950* (Philadelphia: Temple University Press, 1970), 5–7; James Allen et al., *Without Sanctuary: Lynching Photography in America* (Santa Fe, N.M.: Twin Palms, 2000), 8–35.

24. Francis Paul Prucha, *The Great Father: The United States Government and the American Indians* (Lincoln: University of Nebraska Press, 1984), 412–606, 659–715; Patricia Nelson Limerick, *The Legacy of Conquest: The Unbroken Past of the American West* (New York: W. W. Norton, 1987), 179–221; Dee Brown, *Bury My Heart at Wounded Knee: An Indian History of the American West* (New York: Owl, 1991).

25. Stuart Creighton Miller, *"Benevolent Assimilation": The American Conquest of the Philippines, 1899–1903* (New Haven, Conn.: Yale University Press, 1982); Joseph Fry, "Phases of Empire: Late Nineteenth-Century U.S. Foreign Relations," in *The Gilded Age: Essays on the Origins of Modern America*, ed. Charles W. Calhoun (Wilmington, Del.: Scholarly Resources, 1996), 261–88.

CHAPTER 2

1. David I. Macleod, *The Age of the Child: Children in America, 1890–1920* (New York: Twayne, 1998), 52–59.

2. Department of Education, *Digest of Education Statistics, 1996* (Washington, D.C.: GPO, 1996), table 38; Macleod, *The Age of the Child*, 71–73, 76.

3. Elliot J. Gorn, ed., *The McGuffey Readers: Selections from the 1879 Edition* (Boston/New York: Bedford/St. Martin's, 1998), 1–36.

4. Ibid., table 38.

5. Joseph Kett, *Rites of Passage: Adolescence in America, 1790 to the Present* (New York: Basic Books, 1977), 135–89.

6. Thomas J. Schlereth, *Victorian America: Transformations in Everyday Life* (New York: HarperPerennial, 1992), 249–53; Hugh Hawkins, *Between Harvard and America: The Educational Leadership of Charles W. Eliot* (New York: Oxford University Press, 1972), 108–30.

7. *Digest of Education Statistics*, table 168; Nancy Woloch, *Women and the American Experience*, 3rd ed. (Boston: McGraw-Hill, 2000), 281–88.

8. Orison Marden, *The Secret of Achievement* (New York: Thomas Y. Crowell, 1898), 233; Orison Marden, *Choosing a Career* (New York: Thomas Y. Crowell, 1905), 55; William Mathews, *Getting On in the World* (Chicago: Scott, Foresman, 1873), 53; Mathew H. Smith, *Great Fortunes; How They Are Made* (Reading, Pa.: Roe Brothers, 1883), 48; Orison Marden, *Character; The Grandest Thing in the World* (New York: Thomas Y. Crowell, 1899), 45.

9. Benjamin G. Rader, *American Sports: From the Age of Folk Games to the Age of Spectators* (Englewood Cliffs, N.J.: Prentice-Hall, 1983), 151–56; Kett, *Rites of Passage*, 189–211; Clifford Putney, *Muscular Christianity: Manhood and Sports in Protestant America, 1880–1920* (Cambridge, Mass.: Harvard University Press, 2001), 1–71, 99–126.

10. Rader, *American Sports*, 157–64.

11. Sherrie A. Inness, " 'It Is Pluck but Is It Sense?' Athletic Student Culture in Progressive Era Girls' College Fiction," *Journal of Popular Culture* 27 (Summer 1993): 99–118; Elliott J. Gorn and Warren Goldstein, *A Brief History of American Sports* (New York: Hill and Wang, 1993), 132.

12. Macleod, *The Age of the Child*, 101–20.

13. Harold Schechter, *Fiend: The Shocking True Story of America's Youngest Serial Killer* (New York: Pocket Books, 2000), 154.

14. Jacob Riis, *How the Other Half Lives* (New York: Dover, 1971), 171–78; James

Haskins, *Street Gangs: Yesterday and Today* (New York: Hastings House, 1974), 27–57.

15. David Nasaw, *Going Out: The Rise and Fall of Public Amusements* (New York: Basic Books, 1993), 10–18, 19–46, 83.

16. John D'Emilio and Estelle B. Freedman, *Intimate Matters: A History of Sexuality in America*, 2nd ed. (Chicago: University of Chicago Press, 1997), 194–201.

17. Quoted from Susan Gannon and Ruth Anne Thompson, *Mary Mapes Dodge* (New York: Twayne, 1992), 119.

CHAPTER 3

1. James D. Norris, *Advertising and the Transformation of American Society, 1865–1920* (Westport, Conn.: Greenwood Press, 1990), 40; Alan Trachtenberg, *The Incorporation of America: Culture & Society in the Gilded Age* (New York: Hill & Wang, 1982), 136.

2. Quoted from Stephen Fox, *The Mirror Makers: A History of American Advertising and Its Creators* (New York: Vintage, 1984), 14–15.

3. Fox, *The Mirror Makers*, 14; Norris, *Advertising and the Transformation of American Society*, 25.

4. Edd Applegate, *Personalities and Products: A Historical Perspective on Advertising in America* (Westport, Conn.: Greenwood Press, 1998), 41–52.

5. Charles Goodrum and Helen Dalrymple, *Advertising in America: The First 200 Years* (New York: Harry N. Abrams, 1990), 20; Applegate, *Personalities and Products*, 57–60.

6. P. T. Barnum, *Barnum's Own Story: The Autobiography of P. T. Barnum* (New York: Dover, 1961), 102.

7. For a listing and searchable database of trademarks, see United States Patent and Trademark Office, <http://www.uspto.gov/main/trademarks.htm> (26 June 2002).

8. Goodrum and Dalrymple, *Advertising in America*, 23; Norris, *Advertising and the Transformation of American Society*, 19.

9. Goodrum and Dalrymple, *Advertising in America*, 24–29; Fox, *The Mirror Makers*, 16–19.

10. Norris, *Advertising and the Transformation of American Society*, 19–25.

11. David Blanke, *Sowing the American Dream: How Consumer Culture Took Root in the Rural Midwest* (Athens: Ohio University Press, 2000), 184–99; William Leach, *Land of Desire: Merchants, Power, and the Rise of a New American Culture* (New York: Vintage, 1993), 44–45.

12. Boris Emmet, *Montgomery Ward & Co. Catalogue and Buyers' Guide, No. 57, Spring and Summer, 1895* (New York: Dover, 1969), xiii, 1–2, 3–34, 38–76, 217–20, 311–16, 352–417, 449–69, 487, 559–61.

13. Blanke, *Sowing the American Dream*, 186–87, 211; Thomas J. Schlereth, *Victorian America: Transformations in Everyday Life, 1876–1915* (New York: Harper-Perennial, 1992), 153–57.

14. Leach, *Land of Desire*, 23, 20–26, 113; Applegate, *Personalities and Products*, 94–95.

15. Schlereth, *Victorian America*, 161; Applegate, *Personalities and Products*, 92–95; Norris, *Advertising and the Transformation of American Society*, 17.

16. Leach, *Land of Desire*, 55–64; Norris, *Advertising and the Transformation of American Society*, 17–18.

17. Fox, *The Mirror Makers*, 26.

18. Ibid., 27–28; Norris, *Advertising and the Transformation of American Society*, 17.

19. Norris, *Advertising and the Transformation of American Society*, 20.

20. Fox, *The Mirror Makers*, 45.

21. Ibid., 40–77; Schlereth, *Victorian America*, 158–59.

22. Fox, *The Mirror Makers*, 38–39; Norris, *Advertising and the Transformation of American Society*, 44; Applegate, *Personalities and Products*, 50–51.

23. Leach, *Land of Desire*, 44–45, 50–54.

24. Frank Luther Mott, *A History of American Magazines*, 5 vols. (Cambridge, Mass.: Harvard University Press, 1957), 5: 20–34; Norris, *Advertising and the Transformation of American Society*, 31.

25. Mott, *A History of American Magazines*, 5: 3–14; Norris, *Advertising and the Transformation of American Society*, 36–41; Matthew Schneirov, *The Dream of a New Social Order: Popular Magazines in America, 1893–1914* (New York: Columbia University Press, 1994), 67, 75–76, 87–92, 175–78.

CHAPTER 4

1. Sean Dennis Cashman, *America in the Gilded Age: From the Death of Lincoln to the Rise of Theodore Roosevelt*, 3rd ed. (New York: New York University Press, 1994), 186–89; Wayne Craven, *American Art: History and Culture* (New York: Harry N. Abrams, 1994), 302–13; Charles N. Glaab and A. Theodore Brown, *A History of Urban America*, 3rd ed. (New York: Macmillan, 1983), 154–57; Henry-Russell Hitchcock and William Seale, *Temples of Democracy: The State Capitols of the U.S.A.* (New York: Harcourt Brace Jovanovich, 1976); Blake F. McKelvey, *The Urbanization of America, 1860–1915* (New Brunswick, N.J.: Rutgers University Press, 1963), 121–25; Daniel Mendelowitz, *A History of American Art*, 2nd ed. (New York: Holt, Rinehart and Winston, 1970), 245–64; Dell Upton, *Architecture in the United States* (New York: Oxford University Press, 1998), 71–78, 207–16, 247–55.

2. Glaab and Brown, *A History of Urban America*, 258–61; Gwendolyn Wright, *Building the American Dream: A Social History of Housing in America* (New York: Pantheon Books, 1981), 177–92.

3. Wright, *Building the American Dream*, 114–34, 186–87; Glaab and Brown, *A History of Urban America*, 166–69.

4. Wright, *Building the American Dream*, 135–51.

5. Michael Doucet and John Weaver, *Housing the North American City* (Buffalo, N.Y.: McGill–Queen's University Press, 1991), 201.

6. Doucet and Weaver, *Housing the North American City*, 204–5; Wright, *Building the American Dream*, 100.

7. Wright, *Building the American Dream*, 102; Doucet and Weaver, *Housing the North American City*, 207–21; Scott Derks, ed., *The Value of a Dollar: Prices and Incomes in the United States, 1860–1999* (Lakeville, Conn.: Grey House Publishing, 1999), 486.

8. Derks, *The Value of a Dollar*, 490; Kenneth Ames, "Meaning in Artifacts: Hall Furnishings in Victorian America," in *Material Culture Studies in America*, ed. Thomas J. Schlereth (Nashville, Tenn.: The American Association for State and Local History, 1989), 206–21; Thomas J. Schlereth, *Victorian America: Transformations in Everyday Life, 1876–1915* (New York: HarperPerennial, 1991), 119–23; Linda E. Smeins, *Building an American Identity: Pattern Books and Communities, 1870–1900* (Walnut Creek, Calif.: Altamira, 1999), 218; Wright, *Building the American Dream*, 111.

9. Wright, *Building the American Dream*, 111–12.

10. Louise L. Stevenson, *The Victorian Homefront: American Thought and Culture, 1860–1880* (New York: Twayne, 1991), 1–2.

11. Stevenson, *The Victorian Homefront*, 1–29; Wright, *Building the American Dream*, 109–11; Schlereth, *Victorian America*, 116–23.

12. Schlereth, *Victorian America*, 127–30; Thomas J. Schlereth, "Conduits and Conduct: Home Utilities in Victorian America, 1876–1915," in *American Home Life, 1880–1930: A Social History of Spaces and Services*, ed. Jessica H. Foy and Thomas J. Schlereth (Knoxville: University of Tennessee Press, 1992), 225–26, 234–35; Merritt Ierley, "The Bathroom: An Epic," *American Heritage* 50 (May 1999): 76; Wright, *Building the American Dream*, 102.

13. John A. Jakle, *City Lights: Illuminating the American Night* (Baltimore, Md.: Johns Hopkins University Press, 2001), 19–37; Richard J. Hooker, *Food and Drink in America: A History* (New York: Bobbs-Merrill, 1981), 211–12; Schlereth, *Victorian America*, 99, 112–16; Schlereth, "Conduits and Conduct," 227–34; Wright, *Building the American Dream*, 102.

14. Smeins, *Building an American Identity*, 264; Wright, *Building the American Dream*, 106.

15. Craven, *American Art*, 280–86, 293–94; Rachel Carley, *The Visual Dictionary of American Domestic Architecture* (New York: Henry Holt and Company, 1994), 134–45, 149–50, 154–62; Smeins, *Building an American Identity*, 213, 227, 230.

16. Carley, *The Visual Dictionary*, 150–53; Smeins, *Building an American Identity*, 264–66.

17. Craven, *American Art*, 299–301; Carley, *The Visual Dictionary*, 166–69.

18. Craven, *American Art*, 287–98; Carley, *The Visual Dictionary*, 163–65, 188–92, 176–201; Smeins, *Building an American Identity*, 236–38.

19. Smeins, *Building an American Identity*, 35; Doucet and Weaver, *Housing the North American City*, 234.

20. Sally McMurry, *Families and Farmhouses in Nineteenth Century America* (New York: Oxford University Press, 1988), 3–9, 87–134, 252; Schlereth, *Victorian America*, 88–91; Wright, *Building the American Dream*, 73–89.

CHAPTER 5

1. Barbara A. Schreier, "Introduction," in *Men and Women: Dressing the Part*, ed. Claudia Brush Kidwell and Valerie Steele (Washington D.C.: Smithsonian Institution Press, 1989), 2–4.

2. Joan L. Severa, *Dressed for the Photographer: Ordinary Americans and Fashion, 1840–1900* (Kent, Ohio: The Kent State University Press, 1995), 185, 203, 293–94, 300, 375, 455, 474.

3. Severa, *Dressed for the Photographer*, 90–91, 190–91, 293, 296–97, 372–73; Lee Hall, *Common Threads: A Parade of American Clothing* (New York: Bulfinch Press, 1992), 75–77.

4. Boris Emmet, *Montgomery Ward & Co. Catalogue and Buyers' Guide, No. 57, Spring and Summer, 1895* (New York: Dover, 1969), 266–69, 273–78, 279–82, 304–5, 514–17; Douglas Gorsline, *What People Wore: A Visual History of Dress from Ancient Times to Twentieth-Century America* (New York: Viking Press, 1952), 191–202; Norah Waugh, *The Cut of Men's Clothes, 1600–1900* (New York: Theatre Arts Books, 1964), 112–21, plates 27–29.

5. Severa, *Dressed for the Photographer*, 314, 387, 471–72; Valerie Steele, "Appearance and Identity," in *Men and Women: Dressing the Part*, ed. Claudia Brush Kidwell and Valerie Steele (Washington, D.C.: Smithsonian Institution Press, 1989), 16; Carole Turbin, "Collars and Consumers: Changing Images of American Manliness and Business," in *Beauty and Business: Commerce, Gender, and Culture in Modern America*, ed. Philip Scranton (New York: Routledge, 2001), 87–92; Anne Hollander, *Sex and Suits: The Evolution of Modern Dress* (New York: Kodansha International, 1994), 103–11; Hall, *Common Threads*, 54–55, 58, 250–53.

6. Severa, *Dressed for the Photographer*, 355, 423, 441, 492, 493, 497, 500, 525, 527, 532, 537; Gorsline, *What People Wore*, 205–38; Hall, *Common Threads*, 53, 62, 102–3, 107.

7. Hall, *Common Threads*, 115–19.

8. Ibid., 105–6.

9. Emmet, *Montgomery Ward Catalogue*, 269–70, 273–78, 280, 282–84, 518–23.

10. Ibid., 482–83, 486–88, 518–19, 556; Barbara A. Schreier, "Sporting Wear," in *Men and Women: Dressing the Part*, ed. Claudia Brush Kidwell and Valerie Steele (Washington, D.C.: Smithsonian Institution Press, 1989), 92–123; Waugh, *The Cut of Men's Clothes*, plate 26; Hall, *Common Threads*, 50, 59, 227–29, 233.

11. Thorstein Veblen, *The Theory of the Leisure Class* (New York: Penguin, 1979), 167–87; Hall, *Common Threads*, 126; Schreier, "Introduction," 5.

12. Severa, *Dressed for the Photographer*, 300–313; Stella Blum, *Victorian Fashions and Costumes from Harpers Bazaar: 1867–1898* (New York: Dover Publications, 1974), 77; Gorsline, *What People Wore*, 181–92.

13. Blum, *Victorian Fashions and Costumes*, 149; Severa, *Dressed for the Photographer*, 372–87; Gorsline, *What People Wore*, 193–202.

14. Hall, *Common Threads*, 57, 103, 111; Severa, *Dressed for the Photographer*, 299, 317, 346–47, 370, 372–73, 377–79, 383, 390, 404–5, 412, 422, 423, 436–37, 438–39, 488, 500–501, 506–7, 517, 536.

15. Severa, *Dressed for the Photographer*, 454–71; Blum, *Victorian Fashions and Costumes*, 227–92; Hall, *Common Threads*, 54–55, 57, 85, 143, 255; Emmet, *Montgomery Ward Catalogue*, 34–37, 287–88, 292–95, 508–12.

16. Blum, *Victorian Fashions and Costume*, 109, 246–47, 256–57, 276, 280; Emmet, *Montgomery Ward Catalogue*, 283–86, 299–301, 308–11; Hall, *Common Threads*, 127; Severa, *Dressed for the Photographer*, 308–10, 382–84, 462–64.

17. Severa, *Dressed for the Photographer*, 466–67; Schreier, "Sporting Wear," 91–120; Blum, *Victorian Fashions and Costumes*, 127, 128, 149, 179, 197, 211, 231, 244–45, 253, 258, 266–73, 280; Hall, *Common Threads*, 51, 59, 79–85, 220–25, 232–33; Cleveland Amory, *Sears, Roebuck and Co. Catalogue, 1902 Edition* (New York: Bounty Books, 1969), 341; Emmet, *Montgomery Ward Catalogue*, 282–85.

18. Emmet, *Montgomery Ward Catalogue*, 272.

19. Anthony Rotundo, *American Manhood: Transformations in Masculinity from the Revolution to the Modern Era* (New York: Basic Books, 1993), 33; Estelle Ansley Worrell, *Children's Costume in America, 1607–1910* (New York: Scribner's, 1980), 132, 135, 155, 159, 185, 187; Hall, *Common Threads*, 152, 165, 167–68, 175, 177, 179, 188–99, 315, 388, 473; Severa, *Dressed for the Photographer*, 315, 388, 473; Emmet, *Montgomery Ward Catalogue*, 286–87; Blum, *Victorian Fashions and Costumes*, 168–69, 215, 242, 250, 254–55.

20. Emmet, *Montgomery Ward Catalogue*, 266, 271–72, 273–78, 280–81, 283, 286–87, 291, 295, 302–3; Worrell, *Children's Costume in America*, 152, 164, 165, 167–68, 169, 170, 174, 175, 177, 179, 182, 187; Severa, *Dressed for the Photographer*, 315–16, 389, 473.

21. Severa, *Dressed for the Photographer*, 314, 388–90, 400, 408, 416, 420, 431, 432, 446, 472–74, 482, 489, 490, 494, 498, 502, 506, 508, 518; Worrell, *Children's Costume in America*, 126, 127, 133, 139, 141, 152–53, 157, 161, 169, 170– 71, 175; Emmet, *Montgomery Ward Catalogue*, 36–37, 295, 301–2, 306–7; Blum, *Victorian Fashions and Costumes*, 87, 101, 116–17, 130–31, 142–43, 154, 156–57, 168–69, 179, 214–15, 222–23, 242, 250–51, 254–55.

CHAPTER 6

1. Harvey A. Levenstein, *Revolution at the Table: The Transformation of the American Diet* (New York: Oxford University Press, 1988), 15, 17, 21, 23, 101; Richard J. Hooker, *Food and Drink in America: A History* (New York: Bobbs-Merrill, 1981), 218, 245, 267–69; Susan Williams, *Savory Suppers & Fashionable Feasts: Dining in Victorian America* (New York: Pantheon Books, 1985), 27, 47, 145–46, 148–49, 159, 165, 168, 186, 191; Joseph Conlin, *Bacon, Beans, and Galantines: Food and Foodways on the Western Mining Frontier* (Reno: University of Nevada Press, 1986), 6–12.

2. Levenstein, *Revolution at the Table*, 32.

3. Ibid., 3–4, 7–8, 101; Hooker, *Food and Drink in America*, 117.

4. Levenstein, *Revolution at the Table*, 21, 23–24, 26, 220–22; Hooker, *Food and Drink in America*, 100–102; Williams, *Savory Suppers & Fashionable Feasts*, 198–99; Phillip Snyder, *December 25th: The Joys of Christmas Past* (New York: Dodd, Mead & Company, 1985), 30–41.

5. Levenstein, *Revolution at the Table*, 12; Hooker, *Food and Drink in America*, 223–27, 256; Williams, *Savory Suppers & Fashionable Feasts*, 180, 181, 184, 193, 201; Conlin, *Bacon, Beans, and Galantines*, 119.

6. Levenstein, *Revolution at the Table*, 26, 31; Hooker, *Food and Drink in America*, 227–28; Williams, *Savory Suppers & Fashionable Feasts*, 117–22.

7. Levenstein, *Revolution at the Table*, 5, 23–25; Hooker, *Food and Drink in America*, 228–31; Williams, *Savory Suppers & Fashionable Feasts*, 169; The Woman's Art and Industrial Association of Nevada, *The Nevada Cook Book* (Carson City, Nev.: Appeal Steam Print, 1887), 48.

8. Hooker, *Food and Drink in America*, 232; Williams, *Savory Suppers & Fashionable Feasts*, 93, 105–7.

9. *The Nevada Cookbook*, 111–24; Williams, *Savory Suppers & Fashionable Feasts*, 276–79.

10. Wendy A. Woloson, *Refined Tastes: Sugar, Confectionery, and Consumers in Nineteenth-Century America* (Baltimore, Md.: Johns Hopkins University Press, 2002), 5–7, 27–31, 36–65, 82–108, 112, 116–54, 187–226; Boris Emmet, *Montgomery Ward & Co. Catalogue and Buyers' Guide, No. 57, Spring and Summer, 1895* (New York: Dover, 1969), 396; Levenstein, *Revolution at the Table*, 6; Hooker, *Food and Drink in America*, 247–51; Williams, *Savory Suppers & Fashionable Feasts*, 122–23, 170.

11. Andrew Barr, *Drink: A Social History of America* (New York: Carroll & Graf Publishers, 1999), 56–58, 62–70, 100–101; Hooker, *Food and Drink in America*, 273–82; Williams, *Savory Suppers & Fashionable Feasts*, 126–37; W. J. Rorabaugh, "Beer, Lemonade, and Propriety in the Gilded Age," in *Dining in America, 1850–1900*, ed. Kathryn Grover (Amherst: University of Massachusetts Press, 1987), 3–23.

12. Levenstein, *Revolution at the Table*, 24–28; Hooker, *Food and Drink in America*, 222; Conlin, *Bacon, Beans, and Galantines*, 10–12.

13. Conlin, *Bacon, Beans, and Galantines*, 29, 105–9, 138, 140–45, 153, 167, 182, 190–92.

14. Levenstein, *Revolution at the Table*, 30–43; Hooker, *Food and Drink in America*, 212–15.

15. Levenstein, *Revolution at the Table*, 36–38; Hooker, *Food and Drink in America*, 214–15; Williams, *Savory Suppers & Fashionable Feasts*, 96–98; Conlin, *Bacon, Beans, and Galantines*, 17–18; Ruth Schwartz Cowan, *More Work for Mother: The Ironies of Household Technology from the Open Hearth to the Microwave* (New York: Basic Books, 1983), 72–73.

16. Harvey Levenstein, "The American Response to Italian Food, 1880–1930," in *Food in the USA: A Reader*, ed. Carole M. Counihan (New York: Routledge, 2002), 75–90; Levenstein, *Revolution at the Table*, 102–7; Hooker, *Food and Drink in America*, 252–67, 284–95; Conlin, *Bacon, Beans, and Galantines*, 182–95.

17. Jon M. Kingsdale, " 'The Poor Man's Social Club': Social Functions of the Urban Working-Class Saloon," in *The Making of Urban America*, ed. Raymond A. Mohl (Wilmington, Del.: Scholarly Resources, 1988), 125–26; Conlin, *Bacon, Beans, and Galantines*, 174–80; Hooker, *Food and Drink in America*, 259–67; Rorabaugh, "Beer, Lemonade, and Propriety," 31.

18. Levenstein, "The American Response to Italian Food," 75–90; Levenstein, *Revolution at the Table*, 102–7; Hooker, *Food and Drink in America*, 252–67, 284–95; Conlin, *Bacon, Beans, and Galantines*, 182–95.

19. Levenstein, *Revolution at the Table*, 10–22; Hooker, *Food and Drink in America*, 236–37, 252–64; Conlin, *Bacon, Beans, and Galantines*, 123–35, 148–52.

20. Levenstein, *Revolution at the Table*, 18–22, 60–63; Williams, *Savory Suppers & Fashionable Feasts*, 5–158; David Miller, "Technology and the Ideal: Production Quality and Kitchen Reform in Nineteenth-Century America," in *Dining in America, 1850–1900*, ed. Kathryn Grover (Amherst: University of Massachusetts Press, 1987), 47–84; John F. Kasson, "Rituals of Dining: Table Manners in Victorian America," in *Dining in America, 1850–1900*, ed. Kathryn Grover (Amherst: University of Massachusetts Press, 1987), 114–41; Clifford E. Clark, Jr., "The Vision of the Dining Room: Plan Book Dreams and Middle-Class Realities," in *Dining*

in America, 1850–1900, ed. Kathryn Grover (Amherst: University of Massachusetts Press, 1987), 142–72; Emmet, *Montgomery Ward Catalogue,* 187–97, 426–39, 526–46.

CHAPTER 7

1. Benjamin Rader, *American Sports: From the Age of the Folk Games to the Age of the Spectators* (Englewood Cliffs, N.J.: Prentice-Hall, 1983), 46–68; Elliott J. Gorn and Warren Goldstein, *A Brief History of American Sports* (New York: Hill and Wang, 1993), 133–38; Boris Emmet, *Montgomery Ward & Co. Catalogue and Buyers' Guide, No. 57, Spring and Summer, 1895* (New York: Dover, 1969), 486.

2. Dwight W. Hoover, "Roller-skating toward Industrialism," in *Hard at Play: Leisure in America, 1840–1940,* ed. Kathryn Grover (Amherst: University of Massachusetts Press, 1992), 61–76.

3. Robert A. Smith, *The Social History of the Bicycle: Its Early Life and Times in America* (New York: American Heritage, 1972); Ellen Gruber Garvey, "Reframing the Bicycle: Advertising-Supported Magazines and Scorching Women," *American Quarterly* 47 (March 1995): 66–101; Emmet, *Montgomery Ward Catalogue,* 555–58, 562.

4. Emmet, *Montgomery Ward Catalogue,* 68, 224, 236; Angela Sorby, "A Visit from *St. Nicholas*: The Poetics of Peer Culture, 1872–1900," *American Studies* 39 (Spring 1998): 59–74.

5. Emmet, *Montgomery Ward Catalogue,* 236–37.

6. Bruce Whitehill, *Games: American Boxed Games and Their Makers, 1822–1992* (Radnor, Pa.: Wallace-Homestead, 1992), 1–14, 80, 101–7, 112; Emmet, *Montgomery Ward Catalogue,* 234–35.

7. Emmet, *Montgomery Ward Catalogue,* 237.

8. Andrew McClary, *Toys with Nine Lives: A Social History of American Toys* (North Haven, Conn.: Linnet Books, 1997), 107–19; Richard O'Brien, *The Story of American Toys: From Puritans to the Present* (New York: Abbeville Press, 1990), 28, 61; Emmet, *Montgomery Ward Catalogue,* 225; William Wells Newell, *Games and Songs of American Children* (New York: Dover, 1963), 185–86.

9. Newell, *Games and Songs,* 198.

10. Ibid., 127, 129, 131, 155, 158, 160, 162, 163, 188, 190, 198–99; Anthony Rotundo, *American Manhood: Transformations in Masculinity from the Revolution to the Modern Era* (New York: Basic, 1993), 36, 39, 44–46; Bernard Mergen, "Children's Play in American Autobiographies, 1820–1914," in *Hard at Play: Leisure in America, 1840–1940,* ed. Kathryn Grover (Amherst: University of Massachusetts Press, 1992), 169; Emma J. Gray, *Fun for the Household: A Book of Games* (New York: The Christian Herald, 1897); James Wilder and Robyn Hansen, "A Glossary of Outdoor Games," in *Hard at Play: Leisure in America, 1840–1940,* ed. Kathryn Glover (Amherst: University of Massachusetts Press, 1992), 227–49.

11. Gorn and Goldstein, *A Brief History of American Sports,* 55–57; Howard P. Chudacoff, *The Age of the Bachelor: Creation and American Subculture* (Princeton, N.J.: Princeton University Press, 1999), 115–24, 155.

12. McClary, *Toys with Nine Lives*; O'Brien, *The Story of American Toys,* 11–23, 51–54; Emmet, *Montgomery Ward Catalogue,* 224–37.

13. McClary, *Toys with Nine Lives*, 22–23, 25–26, 136; O'Brien, *The Story of American Toys*, 16, 38–45; Antonia Fraser, *A History of Toys* (New York: Spring Books, 1972), 202; Emmet, *Montgomery Ward Catalogue*, 228.

14. Fraser, *A History of Toys*, 152–56; McClary, *Toys with Nine Lives*, 23; O'Brien, *The Story of American Toys*, 18, 35–38, 45–46, 54; Emmet, *Montgomery Ward Catalogue*, 225–26.

15. McClary, *Toys with Nine Lives*, 218–20, 229; O'Brien, *The Story of American Toys*, 25–29; Emmet, *Montgomery Ward Catalogue*, 231.

16. McClary, *Toys with Nine Lives*, 135–63; O'Brien, *The Story of American Toys*, 39; Emmet, *Montgomery Ward Catalogue*, 230.

17. McClary, *Toys with Nine Lives*, 198, 201, 204–9; O'Brien, *The Story of American Toys*, 54–56; Emmet, *Montgomery Ward Catalogue*, 462.

18. McClary, *Toys with Nine Lives*, 176–95; O'Brien, *The Story of American Toys*, 61–64; Fraser, *A History of Toys*, 118–20, 146, 149–51, 160–73.

19. McClary, *Toys with Nine Lives*, 18, 164-75; O'Brien, *The Story of American Toys*, 93–106, 164–75; Emmet, *Montgomery Ward Catalogue*, 224–37, 562–63.

20. Fraser, *A History of Toys*, 122–32; O'Brien, *The Story of American Toys*, 41; Emmet, *Montgomery Ward Catalogue*, 230.

21. Steven M. Gelber, *Hobbies: Leisure and the Culture of Work in America* (New York: Columbia University Press, 1999), 1–20, 23, 26, 30, 32–33.

22. Ibid., 78–79, 81–82, 102–6, 112–14.

23. Ibid., 114–28.

24. Ibid., 129–52.

25. Louise Stevenson, *The Victorian Homefront: American Thought and Culture, 1860–1880* (New York: Twayne, 1991), 15, 22, 28.

26. Ibid., 104–5.

27. Gelber, *Hobbies*, 95–97, 116; Ellen Gruber Garvey, *The Adman in the Parlor: Magazines and the Gendering of Consumer Culture, 1880s to 1910s* (New York: Oxford University Press, 1996), 16–50; Edmund Morris, *The Rise of Theodore Roosevelt* (New York: Modern Library, 2001), 18–19; David McCullough, *Mornings on Horseback* (New York: Simon & Schuster, 1981), 114–22.

28. Gelber, *Hobbies*, 155–63.

29. Ibid., 163–66.

30. Ibid., 168–76, 180–88; Emmet, *Montgomery Ward Catalogue*, 224.

31. Rader, *American Sports*, 47; Gorn and Goldstein, *A Brief History of American Sports*, 47–97.

32. Rader, *American Sports*, 146–54; Gorn and Goldstein, *A Brief History of American Sports*, 98–114.

33. Geoffrey C. Ward and Ken Burns, *Baseball: An Illustrated History* (New York: Alfred A. Knopf, 1994), 3, 4–20.

34. Ibid., 23.

35. Ward and Burns, *Baseball*; Paul Zingg, "Diamond in the Rough: Baseball and the Study of American Sports History," *The History Teacher* 19 (May 1986): 385–403; Warren Goldstein, *Playing for Keeps: A History of Early Baseball* (Ithaca, N.Y.: Cornell University Press, 1989).

36. Rader, *American Sports*, 97–104; Gorn and Goldstein, *A Brief History of American Sports*, 110, 114–24.

37. Marshall W. "Major" Taylor, *The Fastest Bicycle Rider in the World* (Brattle-

boro, Vt.: Green-Stephen, 1972); Andrew Ritchie, *Major Taylor: The Extraordinary Career of a Champion Bicycle Racer* (San Francisco: Bicycle Books, 1988).

38. Emmet, *Montgomery Ward Catalogue*, 485.

39. Rader, *American Sports*, 146–64; Gorn and Goldstein, *A Brief History of American Sports*, 98–105.

40. Rader, *American Sports*, 70–75; Gorn and Goldstein, *A Brief History of American Sports*, 88–89, 129–32.

41. Gorn and Goldstein, *A Brief History of American Sports*, 155.

42. Robert Leckie, *The Story of Football: A Lavishly Illustrated History of America's Exciting Gridiron Sport* (New York: Random House, 1965), 1–40; Rader, *American Sports*, 75–86; Gorn and Goldstein, *A Brief History of American Sports*, 153–69.

43. Rader, *American Sports*, 152–53; Gorn and Goldstein, *A Brief History of American Sports*, 173–77.

44. Russell S. Gilmore, "Another Branch of Manly Sport: American Rifle Games, 1840–1900," in *Hard at Play: Leisure in America, 1840–1940*, ed. Kathryn Grover (Amherst: University of Massachusetts Press, 1992), 93–111.

45. Colleen J. Sheehy, "American Angling: The Rise of Urbanism and the Romance of the Rod and Reel," in *Hard at Play: Leisure in America, 1840–1940*, ed. Kathryn Grover (Amherst: University of Massachusetts Press, 1992), 77–92; Emmet, *Montgomery Ward Catalogue*, 489–501.

46. Katherine C. Grier, "Are We Having Fun Yet?" in *Hard at Play: Leisure in America, 1840–1940*, ed. Kathryn Grover (Amherst: University of Massachusetts Press, 1992), 3.

CHAPTER 8

1. Louise L. Stevenson, *The Victorian Homefront: American Thought and Culture, 1860–1880* (New York: Twayne, 1991), 30, 33–34.

2. Barbara Sicherman, "Reading and Middle-Class Identity in Victorian America: Cultural Consumption, Conspicuous and Otherwise," in *Reading Acts: U.S. Readers' Interactions with Literature, 1800–1950*, ed. Barbara Ryan and Amy M. Thomas (Knoxville: University of Tennessee Press, 2002), 140–41; Matthew Schneirov, *The Dream of a New Social Order: Popular Magazines in America, 1893–1914* (New York: Columbia University Press, 1994), 5, 60.

3. Mary Kupiec Cayton, "Print and Publishing," in *The Encyclopedia of American Social History*, ed. Mary Kupiec Cayton, Elliott J. Gorn, and Peter W. Williams (New York: Charles Scribner's Sons, 1993), 2433–35; Elmer D. Johnson and Michael H. Harris, *History of Libraries in the Western World*, 3rd ed. (Metuchen, N.J.: The Scarecrow Press, 1976), 180–223.

4. Johnson and Harris, *History of Libraries*, 265–324; Cheryl Gunselman, "Pioneering Free Library Service for the City, 1864–1902: The Library Association of Portland and the Portland Public Library," *Oregon Historical Quarterly* 103 (Fall 2002): 320–25; Abigail A. Van Slyck, *Free to All: Carnegie Libraries and American Culture, 1890–1920* (Chicago: University of Chicago Press, 1995), 25–26, 174–215; Edward S. Holden, "Great Public Libraries," *Overland Monthly and Out West Magazine* 30 (August 1897): 117; Bureau of Education, *Public Libraries in the United States: Their History, Condition, and Management* (Washington, D.C.: Government

Printing Office, 1876), 1010; Thomas McMillan, "The Growth of Catholic Reading Circles," *Catholic World* 54 (November 1891): 709.

5. Linda M. Kruger, "Home Libraries: Special Spaces, Reading Places," in *American Home Life, 1880–1930: A Social History of Spaces and Services*, ed. Jessica H. Foy and Thomas J. Schlereth (Knoxville: University of Tennessee Press, 1992), 96–97; McMillan, "The Growth of Catholic Reading Circles," 709–13; Frank Luther Mott, *Golden Multitudes: The Story of Best Sellers in the United States* (New York: Macmillan, 1947), 184.

6. Judy Hilkey, *Character Is Capital: Success Manuals and Manhood in the Gilded Age* (Chapel Hill: University of North Carolina Press, 1997), 15–20.

7. Boris Emmet, *Montgomery Ward & Co. Catalogue and Buyers' Guide, No. 57, Spring and Summer, 1895* (New York: Dover, 1969), 38–77, 311–39, 352–417.

8. Henry Seidel Canby, *The Age of Confidence* (New York: Farrar & Rhinehart, 1934), 208; Sicherman, "Reading and Middle-Class Identity," 141–49; Stevenson, *The Victorian Homefront*, 33–34.

9. Stevenson, *The Victorian Homefront*, 30–36.

10. Schneirov, *The Dream of a New Social Order*, 27–72.

11. Canby, *The Age of Confidence*, 232–33.

12. Hilkey, *Character Is Capital*, 1–27.

13. Orison Swett Marden, *The Secret of Achievement* (New York: Thomas Y. Crowell, 1898), 233.

14. Andrew Carnegie, *The Gospel of Wealth and Other Timely Essays* (Garden City, N.Y.: Doubleday, Doran & Company, 1906), 64.

15. Fred Lewis Pattee, *The New American Literature, 1890–1930* (New York: Cooper Square Publishers, 1968), 8–10.

16. Donald Pizer, *Realism and Naturalism in Nineteenth-Century American Literature* (Carbondale: Southern Illinois University Press, 1984), 10–11.

17. Mott, *Golden Multitudes*, 160–205.

18. Stevenson, *The Victorian Homefront*, 34; Sicherman, "Reading and Middle-Class Identity," 141; Michael Denning, *Mechanic Accents: Dime Novels and Working-Class Culture in America* (New York: Verso, 1998), 39; Kruger, "Home Libraries," 96; Joan Shelley Rubin, *The Making of Middle Brow Culture* (Chapel Hill: University of North Carolina Press, 1992), 18.

19. R. Gordon Kelly, *Mother Was a Lady: Self and Society in Selected American Children's Periodicals, 1865–1890* (Westport, Conn.: Greenwood Press, 1974), 3–31.

20. Angela Sorby, "A Visit from St. Nicholas: The Poetics of Peer Culture, 1872–1900," *American Studies* 39 (Spring 1998): 59–74; Lawrence B. Fuller, "Mary Mapes Dodge and *St. Nicholas*: The Development of a Philosophy and Practice of Publishing for Young People," paper delivered to the Annual Meeting of the National Council of Teachers of English, Detroit, Mich., November 16–21, 1984.

21. Frank Luther Mott, *A History of American Magazines*, 5 vols. (Cambridge, Mass.: Harvard University Press, 1930–1968), 3: 500–506.

22. Kelly, *Mother Was a Lady*, 38, 61, 67, 79, 84.

23. "Jack-in-the-Pulpit," *St. Nicholas* 5 (November 1877): 156.

24. Louisa May Alcott, "Pansies," *St. Nicholas* 15 (November 1887): 12–19; E. A. Bradin, "Hermann, The Defender of Germany," *St. Nicholas* 1 (November 1873): 22–23; O. W. Blackwell, "Pine-Knots Versus Pistols: A True Story of the Revolution," *St. Nicholas* 20 (October 1894): 935–36; Frank Stockton, "The Buccaneers

of Our Coast," *St. Nicholas* 25 (November/February/May 1897–1898): 4–14, 279–87, 549–58.

25. Sorby, "A Visit from *St. Nicholas*," 68; Thomas J. Schlereth, *Victorian America: Transformations in Everyday Life, 1876–1915* (New York: HarperPerennial, 1992), 198.

26. John Modell, "Patterns of Consumption, Acculturation, and Family Income Strategies in Late Nineteenth-Century America," in *Family and Population in Nineteenth-Century America,* ed. Tamara K. Hareven and Maris A. Vinovskis (Princeton, N.J.: Princeton University Press, 1978), 214.

27. Both Stoddard and Reid also wrote for *St. Nicholas.* William O. Stoddard, "The White Cave," *St. Nicholas* 20 (November/January 1892–1893): 5, 225.

28. Denning, *Mechanic Accents,* 11–23.

29. Ibid., 10–16.

30. Ibid., 5, 58–60, 79–83.

31. Ibid., 85–200.

32. Harold Schechter, *Fiend: The Shocking True Story of America's Youngest Serial Killer* (New York: Pocket Books, 2000), 96–97.

33. Denning, *Mechanic Accents,* 47–54.

34. Dorothy Richardson, *The Long Day: The Story of a New York Working Girl as Told by Herself* (New York: Century, 1906), 86.

35. Howard P. Chudacoff, *The Age of the Bachelor: Creating an American Subculture* (Princeton, N.J.: Princeton University Press, 1999), 210.

36. Ibid., 187–91, 197, 198–201, 203–4, 204–5; Elliott J. Gorn, "The Wicked World: The National Police Gazette and Gilded-Age America," *Media Studies Journal* 6 (Winter 1992): 3–11; Elliott J. Gorn and Warren Goldstein, *A Brief History of American Sports* (New York: Hill and Wang, 1993), 115–23; Benjamin G. Rader, *American Sports: From the Age of Folk Games to the Age of Spectators* (Englewood Cliffs, N.J.: Prentice-Hall, 1983), 99–100, 102.

37. Timothy J. Gifoyle, *City of Eros: New York City, Prostitution, and the Commercialization of Sex, 1790–1920* (New York: W. W. Norton, 1992), 92–116, 119–20, 133–34, 167, 171, 236–39; Chudacoff, *The Age of the Bachelor,* 198–99, 206–7; Gorn, "The Wicked World," 9–10.

38. Jon Bekken, " 'No Weapon So Powerful': Working-Class Newspapers in the United States," *Journal of Communication Inquiry* 12 (Summer 1988): 104–19; Jon Bekken, "The Working-Class Press at the Turn of the Century," in *Ruthless Criticism: New Perspectives in U.S. Communication History,* ed. William S. Solomon and Robert W. McChesney (Minneapolis: University of Minnesota Press, 1993), 151–75; Joseph R. Conlin, ed., *The American Radical Press, 1880–1960,* 2 vols. (Westport, Conn.: Greenwood Press, 1974), 6.

39. Russell Nye, *The Unembarrassed Muse: The Popular Arts in America* (New York: Dial Press, 1970), 61–71.

40. Ibid., 72–83.

41. Stockton, "The Buccaneers of Our Coast."

42. Ben Procter, *William Randolph Hearst: The Early Years, 1863–1910* (New York: Oxford University Press, 1998), 40–45, 73–74, 99–114; Schlereth, *Victorian America,* 182–86; Carl F. Kaestle et al., "Literacy and Diversity," in *Literacy in the United States: Readers and Reading Since 1880,* ed. Carl F. Kaestle et al. (New Haven, Conn.: Yale University Press, 1993), 528, 531; Cayton, "Print and Publish-

ing," 2438–39; Schneirov, *The Dream of a New Social Order*, 5, 60; Gorn, "The Wicked World," 4–5.

43. Schneirov, *The Dream of a New Social Order*, 4–5, 11–13, 60, 75–102, 204.

CHAPTER 9

1. Richard Crawford, *America's Musical Life: A History* (New York: W. W. Norton, 2001), 233–39, 441–43; Ted Gioia, *The History of Jazz* (New York: Oxford University Press, 1997), 22–23; Russel Nye, *The Unembarrassed Muse: The Popular Arts in America* (New York: Dial Press, 1970), 314; Boris Emmet, *Montgomery Ward & Co. Catalogue and Buyers' Guide, No. 57, Spring and Summer, 1895* (New York: Dover, 1969), 238–49.

2. Waldo E. Martin, Jr., "African American Music," in *Encyclopedia of American Social History*, ed. Mary Kupiec Cayton, Elliott J. Gorn, and Peter W. Williams (New York: Charles Scribner's Sons, 1993), 1763–64.

3. Crawford, *America's Musical Life*, 416–23; Daniel Kingman, *American Music: A Panorama*, 2nd ed. (New York: Schirmer Books, 1990), 27–49.

4. Kingman, *American Music*, 318–21; Nye, *The Unembarrassed Muse*, 312; Crawford, *America's Musical Life*, 244–48.

5. Kingman, *American Music*, 319–20, 359; Gioia, *The History of Jazz*, 5–8, 24; Martin, "African American Music," 1757–74.

6. Crawford, *America's Musical Life*, 429–35, 441–52; Kingman, *American Music*, 326–27.

7. William Brooks, *"The Hand That Holds The Bread": Progress and Protest in the Gilded Age: Songs from the Civil War to the Columbian Exposition* (New York: New World Records, 1978), 1–8; James L. Orr, *Grange Melodies* (Philadelphia: George S. Ferguson Co., 1904), 3, 7, 8–18, 26–27, 31, 34, 63, 135, 184–89; Crawford, *America's Musical Life*, 449–52.

8. Crawford, *America's Musical Life*, 444–52; Kingman, *American Music*, 148–56.

9. Digital Scriptorium, Rare Book, Manuscript, and Special Collections Library, Duke University, Historic American Sheet Music, 1890–1899, Chas. K. Harris, "After the Ball" (Boston: Oliver Ditson Company, 1892), Music #353.

10. Nye, *The Unembarrassed Muse*, 314–16; Crawford, *America's Musical Life*, 441–43, 471–87; Kingman, *American Music*, 327–32; Michael Campbell, *And the Beat Goes On* (New York: Schirmer Books, 1996), 59–62; Digital Scriptorium, Duke University, Historic American Sheet Music, 1890–1899, Maude Nugent, "Sweet Rosie O'Grady" (New York: Jos. W. Stern, 1896), Music B-251.

11. James H. Dormon, "Shaping the Popular Image of Post-Reconstruction American Blacks: The 'Coon Song' Phenomenon in the Gilded Age," *American Quarterly* 40 (December 1988): 450–71; J. Stanley Lemons, "Black Stereotypes as Reflected in Popular Culture, 1880–1920," *American Quarterly* 29 (Spring 1977): 106–10; Wilson J. Moses, "The Lost World of the Negro, 1895–1919: Black Literary and Intellectual Life before the 'Renaissance,'" *Black American Literature Forum* 21 (Spring–Summer 1987): 64; Crawford, *America's Musical Life*, 487–90; Kingman, *American Music*, 277–78; Nye, *The Unembarrassed Muse*, 317–18.

12. Lemons, "Black Stereotypes," 107–8; David Krasner, "Parody and Double Consciousness in the Language of Early Black Musical Theatre," *African American*

Review 29 (Summer 1995): 317–23; David Krasner, *Resistance, Parody, and Double Consciousness in African-American Theater, 1895–1910* (New York: St. Martin's Press, 1997).

13. Dorman, "Shaping the Popular Image," 467; Samuel A. Floyd, *The Power of Black Music: Interpreting Its History from Africa to the United States* (New York: Oxford University Press, 1995), 70; William H. Tallmadge, "Ben Harney: The Middleborough Years, 1890–93," *American Music* 13 (Summer 1995): 167–95; Crawford, *America's Musical Life*, 489, 539–46; Kingman, *American Music*, 332–33, 353–69; Gioia, *A History of Jazz*, 20–27; Nye, *The Unembarrassed Muse*, 318–19; Campbell, *And the Beat Goes On*, 80–89.

14. Crawford, *America's Musical Life*, 454–55; Kingman, *American Music*, 368–69; Emmet, *Montgomery Ward Catalogue*, 238–49.

15. Crawford, *America's Musical Life*, 287–92; Kingman, *American Music*, 332–36.

16. Crawford, *America's Musical Life*, 453–68; Kingman, *American Music*, 336–37; Campbell, *And the Beat Goes On*, 81; Digital Scriptorium, Duke University, Historic American Sheet Music, 1890–1899, John Rastus Topp, "The Shuffling Coon; Buck & Wing Dance" (New York: Jos. W. Stern, 1897), Music B-405.

17. Crawford, *America's Musical Life*, 307–13; Kingman, *American Music*, 431–33; Joseph Horowitz, *Wagner Nights: An American History* (Berkeley: University of California Press, 1994), 34–72; Lawrence W. Levine, *Highbrow/Lowbrow: The Emergence of Cultural Hierarchy in America* (Cambridge, Mass.: Harvard University Press, 1988), 104–46.

18. Horowitz, *Wagner Nights*, 73–343.

19. Crawford, *America's Musical Life*, 351–86; Kingman, *American Music*, 435–38.

20. Crawford, *America's Musical Life*, 444–52; Kingman, *American Music*, 148–56; Martin, "African American Music," 1757–74.

21. Crawford, *America's Musical Life*, 536, 557–63; Kingman, *American Music*, 42–49, 277, 364; Gioia, *The History of Jazz*, 13; Nye, *The Unembarrassed Muse*, 323–24.

22. Crawford, *America's Musical Life*, 435–41, 468–70; Nye, *The Unembarrassed Muse*, 322–23.

CHAPTER 10

1. John Culhane, *The American Circus: An Illustrated History* (New York: Henry Holt, 1990), 28, 32, 73–93, 95–107, 125–42, 145–71, 196–97; Early Chaplin May, *The Circus from Rome to Ringling* (New York: Dover, 1963), 111–27, 129–69.

2. Joy S. Kasson, *Buffalo Bill's Wild West: Celebrity, Memory, and Popular History* (New York: Hill and Wang, 2000); Paul Reddin, *Wild West Shows* (Urbana: University of Illinois Press, 1999), 53–157; Culhane, *The American Circus*, 109–23.

3. Howard P. Chudacoff, *The Age of the Bachelor: Creating an American Subculture* (Princeton, N.J.: Princeton University Press, 1999), 131–34; David Nasaw, *Going Out: The Rise and Fall of Public Amusements* (New York: Basic, 1993), 13–14; Timothy J. Gilfoyle, *City of Eros: New York City, Prostitution, and the Commercial-*

ization of Sex, 1790–1920 (New York: W. W. Norton, 1992), 127–30; Richard Butsch, "Bowery B'hoys and Matinee Ladies: The Re-Gendering of Nineteenth-Century American Theater Audiences," *American Quarterly* 46 (September 1994): 392; Oscar G. Brockett, *History of the Theatre* (Boston: Allyn and Bacon, 1968), 508.

4. Butsch, "Bowery B'hoys and Matinee Ladies," 383–93; Nasaw, *Going Out*, 14–18.

5. John Kenrick, "Variety 101: Burlesque," *Musicals101.com: The Cyber Encyclopedia of Musical Theater, TV, and Film*, <http://www.musicals101.com/variety101.htm> (26 May 2003); Daniel Kingman, *American Music: A Panorama*, 2nd ed. (New York: Schirmer Books, 1990), 282; Chudacoff, *The Age of the Bachelor*, 131–34; Nasaw, *Going Out*, 13–14; Gilfoyle, *City of Eros*, 127–30; Brockett, *History of the Theatre*, 508.

6. Lawrence W. Levine, *Highbrow/Lowbrow: The Emergence of Cultural Hierarchy in America* (Cambridge, Mass.: Harvard University Press, 1988), 77–79; Nasaw, *Going Out*, 19–46; Amy Henderson and Dwight Blocker Bowers, *Red, Hot & Blue: A Smithsonian Salute to the American Musical* (Washington, D.C.: The National Portrait Gallery and The National Museum of American History in association with the Smithsonian Institution Press, 1996), 10–33; Langston Hughes and Milton Meltzer, *Black Magic: A Pictorial History of the Negro in American Entertainment* (Englewood Cliffs, N.J.: Prentice-Hall, 1970), 46–72; Kingman, *American Music*, 286; John Kenrick, "A History of the Musical: Vaudeville," *Musicals101.com: The Cyber Encyclopedia of Musical Theater, TV, and Film*, <http://www.musicals101.com/vaude1.htm> (26 May 2003).

7. Butsch, "Bowery B'hoys and Matinee Ladies," 393–98; Levine, *Highbrow/Lowbrow*, 13–81; Brockett, *History of the Theatre*, 494–516; Garff B. Wilson, *A History of American Acting* (Bloomington: Indiana University Press, 1966), 71–237.

8. Kingman, *American Music*, 282–85, 287–89; Henderson and Bowers, *Red Hot & Blue*, 8–14.

9. Kingman, *American Music*, 283.

10. Ibid., 283–84; Richard Crawford, *American Musical Life: A History* (New York: W. W. Norton, 2001), 527–33; John Dizikes, *Opera in America: A Cultural History* (New Haven, Conn.: Yale University Press, 1993), 202–11, 282.

11. Henderson and Bowers, *Red Hot & Blue*, 33–36; Kingman, *American Music*, 284–85; John Kenrick, "History of the Musical Stage, 1890–1900: Farces & Burlesque," *Musicals101.com: The Cyber Encyclopedia of Musical Theater, TV, and Film*, <http://www.musicals101.com/1890_1900.htm> (26 May 2003).

12. Henderson and Bowers, *Red Hot & Blue*, 19–26; David Krasner, "Parody and Double Consciousness in the Language of Early Black Musical Theatre," *African American Review* 29 (Summer 1995): 317–23; Kingman, *American Music*, 285–87.

13. Dizikes, *Opera in America*, 178–320; Levine, *Highbrow/Lowbrow*, 85–104; Joseph Horowitz, *Wagner Nights: An American History* (Berkeley: University of California Press, 1994), 73–180.

14. Nasaw, *Going Out*, 129–73; Lary May, *Screening Out the Past: The Birth of Mass Culture and the Motion Picture Industry* (Chicago: University of Chicago Press, 1983), 25–28, 35–39; Eileen Bowser, *The Transformation of Cinema* (Berkeley: University of California Press, 1990), 1–20.

CHAPTER 11

1. Russell Bourne, *Americans on the Move: A History of Waterways, Railways, and Highways* (Golden, Colo.: Fulcrum Publishing, 1995), 84–102; H. Roger Grant, ed., *We Took the Train* (Dekalb, Ill.: Northern Illinois Press, 1990), xi–xiv, 33.

2. Grant, *We Took the Train*, 44–52.

3. Bourne, *Americans on the Move*, 107; Grant, *We Took the Train*, 35, 53–58; Oscar Osburn Winther, *The Transportation Frontier: Trans-Mississippi West, 1865–1890* (New York: Holt, Rinehart and Winston, 1964), 124–25.

4. Cindy S. Aron, *Working at Play: A History of Vacations in the United States* (New York: Oxford University Press, 1999), 142; Bourne, *Americans on the Move*, 102; Grant, *We Took the Train*, xv–xvii, xxiv; Alexis Gregory, *Families of Fortune: Life in the Gilded Age* (New York: Rizzoli International Publications, 1993), 164–65; Oliver Jensen, *The American Heritage History of Railroads in America* (New York: American Heritage Publishing, 1975), 222–37; John F. Stover, *American Railroads* (Chicago: University of Chicago Press, 1961), 64–180, 224; Winther, *The Transportation Frontier*, 120–33.

5. David T. Courtwright, *Violent Land: Single Men and Social Disorder from the Frontier to the Inner City* (Cambridge, Mass.: Harvard University Press, 1996), 170–97; Stover, *American Railroads*, 125.

6. Winther, *The Transportation Frontier*, 59–73; Joseph R. Conlin, *Bacon, Beans, and Galantines* (Reno: University of Nevada Press, 1986), 87–109.

7. Winther, *The Transportation Frontier*, 75–79; Stover, *American Railroads*, 172–73.

8. Charles Bernard, *The City of New York: A Complete Guide* (New York: Taintor Brothers, 1876), 70; *The Stranger's New Guide Through Boston and Vicinity* (Boston: A. Williams & Company, 1869), 7.

9. Bourne, *Americans on the Move*, 109–11; Charles N. Glaab and A. Theodore Brown, *A History of Urban America*, 3rd ed. (New York: Macmillan, 1983), 152–76; Raymond A. Mohl, *The New City: Urban America in the Industrial Age, 1860–1920* (Arlington Heights, Ill.: Harlan Davidson, 1985), 35–39; Sean Dennis Cashman, *America in the Gilded Age: From the Death of Lincoln to the Rise of Theodore Roosevelt*, 3rd ed. (New York: New York University Press, 1994), 142; Howard P. Chudacoff, *The Evolution of American Urban Society* (Englewood Cliffs, N.J.: Prentice Hall, 1975), 64–88; Edward Winslow Martin, *The Secrets of the Great City: A Work Descriptive of the Virtues and the Vices, the Mysteries, Miseries and Crimes of New York City* (Philadelphia: Jones, Brothers, & Co., 1968), 45, 117–22; Frank Coffey and Joseph Layden, *America on Wheels, The First 100 Years: 1896–1996* (Los Angeles: General Publishing Group, 1996), 17–20.

10. Martin, *The Secrets of the Great City*, 42.

11. Boris Emmet, *Montgomery Ward & Co. Catalogue and Buyers' Guide, No. 57, Spring and Summer, 1895* (New York: Dover, 1969), 579–81; Cleveland Amory, *The Sears, Roebuck Catalogue, 1902 Edition* (New York: Bounty Books, 1969), 362–81; Centennial Exhibition, *Draftbook of Centennial Carriages* (New York: Hub Publishing, 1876), 29–31.

12. Bourne, *Americans on the Move*, 112–13; Coffey and Layden, *America on Wheels*, 13–25.

13. Aron, *Working at Play*, 4, 15–32, 33, 47, 48, 50–53, 58, 70, 88–89; Matthew Schneirov, *The Dream of a New Social Order: Popular Magazines in America, 1893–1914* (New York: Columbia University Press, 1994), 94–124.

14. Aron, *Working at Play*, 50–55; Gregory, *Families of Fortune*, 120; Mark S. Foster, "In the Face of 'Jim Crow': Prosperous Blacks and Vacations, Travel, and Outdoor Leisure, 1890–1945," *Journal of Negro History* 84 (Spring 1999): 136–39.

15. Aron, *Working at Play*, 62, 71–72; Thomas J. Schlereth, *Victorian America: Transformations in Everyday Life, 1876–1914* (New York: HarperPerennial, 1992), 214.

16. Aron, *Working at Play*, 66–67.

17. Ibid., 53, 72–76, 79–86, 90.

18. Ibid., 60–64, 93–97; Foster, "In the Face of 'Jim Crow,' " 135–36.

19. Aron, *Working at Play*, 101–26; Glenn Uminowicz, "Recreation in Christian America: Ocean Grove and Asbury Park, New Jersey, 1869–1914," in *Hard at Play: Leisure in America, 1840–1940*, ed. Kathryn Grover (Amherst: University of Massachusetts Press, 1992), 8–38.

20. Aron, *Working at Play*, 127–55; John F. Sears, *Sacred Places: American Tourist Attractions in the Nineteenth Century* (New York: Oxford University Press, 1989), 3–121; David Nasaw, *Going Out: The Rise and Fall of Public Amusements* (New York: Basic Books, 1993), 62–79.

21. Foster, "In the Face of 'Jim Crow,' " 130–35.

22. Aron, *Working at Play*, 156–77; Clifford Putney, *Muscular Christianity: Manhood and Sports in Protestant America, 1880–1920* (Cambridge, Mass.: Harvard University Press, 2001), 1–44; David Straus, "Toward a Consumer Culture: 'Adirondack Murray' and the Wilderness Vacation," *American Quarterly* 39 (Summer 1987): 270–86; Sears, *Sacred Places*, 122–81.

23. Nasaw, *Going Out*, 80–103; Schlereth, *Victorian America*, 215.

CHAPTER 12

1. David Bjelajac, *American Art: A Cultural History* (New York: Harry N. Abrams, 2001), 227–28, 232; Robert Hughes, *American Visions: The Epic History of Art in America* (New York: Alfred A. Knopf, 1997), 210–16.

2. Sean Dennis Cashman, *America in the Gilded Age: From the Death of Lincoln to the Rise of Theodore Roosevelt*, 3rd ed. (New York: New York University Press, 1994), 193; Joshua Taylor, *The Fine Arts in America* (Chicago: University of Chicago Press, 1979), 120–28.

3. Bjelajac, *American Art*, 227–28.

4. Hughes, *American Visions*, 207–10, 244–46; Bjelajac, *American Art*, 262–64; Daniel M. Mendelowitz, *A History of American Art* (New York: Holt, Rinehart, and Winston, 1960), 328–33; Donald Martin Reynolds, *Masters of American Sculpture: The Figurative Tradition from the American Renaissance to the Millennium* (New York: Abbeville Press, 1993), 133–42, 187–89; Taylor, *The Fine Arts in America*, 126–28.

5. Bjelajac, *American Art*, 260–61; Mendelowitz, *A History of American Art*, 333–36; Hughes, *American Visions*, 228; Reynolds, *Masters of American Sculpture*, 94–103, 123–25, 233–34.

6. Wayne Craven, *American Art: History and Culture* (New York: Harry N. Abrams, 1994), 377–90.

7. Bjelajac, *American Art*, 250–58; Craven, *American Art: History and Culture*, 338–41; Hughes, *American Visions*, 286–300, 316.

8. Bjelajac, *American Art*, 267–68; Sarah Burns, *Inventing the Modern Artist: Art & Culture in Gilded Age America* (New Haven, Conn.: Yale University Press, 1996), 173–81; Craven, *American Art: History and Culture*, 345–46; Hughes, *American Visions*, 250–55.

9. Burns, *Inventing the Modern Artist*, 172–86; Craven, *American Art: History and Culture*, 352.

10. Bjelajac, *American Art*, 264–65, 274–78; Craven, *American Art: History and Culture*, 346–47; Hughes, *American Visions*, 237–42.

11. Bjelajac, *American Art*, 279–80; Craven, *American Art: History and Culture*, 349–51.

12. Bjelajac, *American Art*, 2281–82; Craven, *American Art: History and Culture*, 351–54.

13. Bjelajac, *American Art*, 266–67; Craven, *American Art: History and Culture*, 347–48.

14. Craven, *American Art: History and Culture*, 358–60.

15. Ibid., 324–27; Hughes, *American Visions*, 246–48.

16. Burns, *Inventing the Modern Artist*, 321; Steven E. Smith, Catherine A. Hastedt, and Donald H. Dyal, eds., *American Book and Magazine Illustrators to 1920, Dictionary of Literary Biography*, vol. 188 (Washington, D.C.: Bruccoli, Clark, Layman, 1998), xvi; David Tatham, "Winslow Homer," in *American Book and Magazine Illustrators to 1920, Dictionary of Literary Biography*, vol. 188 (Washington, D.C.: Bruccoli, Clark, Layman, 1998), 164; Walt Reed, *The Illustrator in America, 1860–2000* (New York: Watson-Guptill, 2001), 12–43.

17. Reed, *The Illustrator in America*, 45, 69; Smith, Hastedt, and Dyal, *American Book and Magazine Illustrators*, xiv–xv.

18. Elizabeth H. Hawkes, "Howard Pyle," in *American Book and Magazine Illustrators to 1920, Dictionary of Literary Biography*, vol. 188 (Washington, D.C.: Bruccoli, Clark, Layman, 1998), 274–85; Susan Hamburger, "Jessie Wilcox Smith," in *American Book and Magazine Illustrators to 1920, Dictionary of Literary Biography*, vol. 188 (Washington, D.C.: Bruccoli, Clark, Layman, 1998), 339–41.

19. Melissa J. Webster, "Frederic Remington," in *American Book and Magazine Illustrators to 1920, Dictionary of Literary Biography*, vol. 188 (Washington, D.C.: Bruccoli, Clark, Layman, 1998), 286–98.

20. Burns, *Inventing the Modern Artist*, 320–21; Catherine A. Hastedt, "Charles Dana Gibson," in *American Book and Magazine Illustrators to 1920, Dictionary of Literary Biography*, vol. 188 (Washington, D.C.: Bruccoli, Clark, Layman, 1998), 129–86.

21. Reed, *The Illustrator in America*, 46, 53, 77, 122; Ken Kempcke, "Edwin Austin Abbey," in *American Book and Magazine Illustrators to 1920, Dictionary of Literary Biography*, vol. 188 (Washington, D.C.: Bruccoli, Clark, Layman, 1998), 3–32.

22. Michael Scott Joseph, "Maxfield Parrish," in *American Book and Magazine Illustrators to 1920, Dictionary of Literary Biography*, vol. 188 (Washington, D.C.: Bruccoli, Clark, Layman, 1998), 230–42; Sylvia Yount, *Maxfield Parrish, 1870–1966* (New York: Harry N. Abrams, 1999), 10–17, 22, 28, 42, 47–54, 136–38.

23. Peter C. Marzio, *The Democratic Art: Chromolithography, 1840–1900, Pictures for a 19th-Century America* (Boston: David R. Godine, 1979), 3–17, 64–93, 94–115, 116–29, 176–200; Lawrence W. Levine, *Highbrow/Lowbrow: The Emergence of Cultural Hierarchy in America* (Cambridge, Mass.: Harvard University Press, 1988), 160–61; Thomas J. Schlereth, *Victorian America: Transformations in Everyday Life, 1876–1915* (New York: HarperPerennial, 1992), 194–95. Marzio's book is absolutely necessary for researching chromolithography and contains some of the only specific and accurate information on this topic.

24. Craven, *American Art: History and Culture*, 367–76; Hughes, *American Visions*, 321–22, 348–52; Beaumont Newhall, *The History of Photography: From 1839 to the Present Day* (New York: Museum of Modern Art, 1964), 67–109.

Further Reading

Allmendinger, David F., Jr. *Paupers and Scholars: The Transformation of Student Life in Nineteenth-Century New England*. New York: St. Martin's Press, 1975.

Anderson, James D. *The Education of Blacks in the South, 1860–1935*. Chapel Hill: University of North Carolina Press, 1990.

Angelo, Richard. "The Social Transformation of American Higher Education." In *The Transformation of Higher Learning, 1860–1930: Expansion, Diversification, Social Opening, and Professionalization in England, Germany, Russia, and the United States*, ed. Konrad H. Jarausch. Chicago: University of Chicago Press, 1983.

Argersinger, Peter H. *The Limits of Agrarian Radicalism: Western Populism and American Politics*. Lawrence: University Press of Kansas, 1995.

Asbury, Herbert. *The Gangs of New York: An Informal History of the Underworld*. New York: Alfred A. Knopf, 1927.

Barron, Hal S. *Mixed Harvest: The Second Great Transformation in the Rural North, 1870–1930*. Chapel Hill: University of North Carolina Press, 1997.

Barth, Gunther. *City People: The Rise of Modern City Culture in Nineteenth-Century America*. New York: Oxford University Press, 1980.

Batterberry, Michael. *Mirror, Mirror: A Social History of Fashion*. New York: Holt, Rinehart and Winston, 1977.

Bierley, Paul E. *John Philip Sousa: American Phenomenon*. New York: Appleton-Century-Crofts, 1973.

Billman, Carol. *The Secret of the Stratemeyer Syndicate: Nancy Drew, The Hardy Boys, and the Million Dollar Fiction Factory*. New York: Ungar, 1986.

Bledstein, Burton. *The Culture of Professionalism: The Middle Class and the Development of Higher Education in America*. New York: W. W. Norton, 1978.

Blight, David. *Frederick Douglass' Civil War: Keeping Faith in Jubilee*. Baton Rouge: Louisiana State University Press, 1989.

Boskin, Joseph. *Sambo: The Rise & Demise of an American Jester*. New York: Oxford University Press, 1986.

Brian, Denis. *Pulitzer: A Life*. New York: John Wiley, 2001.

Brundage, W. Fitzhugh. *Lynching in the New South: Georgia and Virginia, 1880–1930*. Urbana: University of Illinois Press, 1993.

Burke, Colin B. "The Expansion of American Higher Education." In *The Transformation of Higher Learning, 1860–1930: Expansion, Diversification, Social Opening, and Professionalization in England, Germany, Russia, and the United States*, ed. Konrad H. Jarausch. Chicago: University of Chicago Press, 1983.

Callow, Alexander B., Jr., ed. *The City Boss in America*. New York: Oxford University Press, 1976.

Caspar, Scott E. *Constructing American Lives & Culture in Nineteenth-Century America*. Chapel Hill: University of North Carolina Press, 1999.

Caspar, Scott E., Joanne Chaison, and Jeffrey D. Groves, eds. *Perspectives on American Book History: Artifacts and Commentary*. Amherst: University of Massachusetts Press, 2002.

Cawelti, John G. *Apostles of the Self-Made Man: Changing Concepts of Success in America*. Chicago: University of Chicago Press, 1965.

Chambers, Thomas A. *Drinking the Waters: Creating an American Leisure Class at Nineteenth-Century Mineral Springs*. Washington, D.C.: Smithsonian Institution Press, 2001.

Chenoune, Farid. *A History of Men's Fashion*. Paris: Flammarion, 1993.

Cikovsky, Nicolai Jr., and Franklin Kelly. *Winslow Homer*. New Haven, Conn.: Yale University Press, 1995.

Cronon, William. *Nature's Metropolis: Chicago and the Great West*. New York: W. W. Norton, 1991.

DiMelgio, John E. *Vaudeville U.S.A.* Bowling Green, Ohio: Bowling Green University Popular Press, 1973.

Earle, Edward W. *Points of View, The Stereograph in America: A Cultural History*. Rochester, N.Y.: Visual Studies Workshop Press, 1979.

Elson, Ruth Miller. *Guardians of Tradition: American School Books of the Nineteenth Century*. Lincoln: University of Nebraska Press, 1964.

Erisman, Fred. "St. Nicholas." In *Children's Periodicals of the United States*, ed. R. Gordon Kelly. Westport, Conn.: Greenwood Press, 1984.

Fernandez, Nancy Page. "Innovations for Home Dressmaking and the Popularization of Stylish Dress." *Journal of American Culture* 17 (Fall 1994): 23–34.

Furia, Philip. *The Poets of Tin Pan Alley: A History of America's Great Lyricists*. New York: Oxford University Press, 1992.

Gabaccia, Donna R. *We Are What We Eat: Ethnic Food and the Making of Americans*. Cambridge, Mass: Harvard University Press, 1998.

Gannon, Susan, and Ruth Anne Thompson. *Mary Mapes Dodge*. New York: Twayne, 1992.

Garrison, Dee. *Apostles of Culture: The Public Librarian and American Society, 1876–1920*. New York: Free Press, 1979.

Goodwin, Doris Kearns. *Wait Till Next Year: Summer Afternoons with My Father and Baseball*. New York: Simon & Schuster, 1998.

Gorn, Elliott J. *The Manly Art: Bare-Knuckle Prize Fighting in America*. Ithaca, N.Y.: Cornell University Press, 1986.

Greenwich, Paul, ed. *Art Nouveau, 1890–1920*. New York: Harry N. Abrams, 2000.

Greer, Scott, ed. *Ethnics, Machines, and the American Urban Future*. Cambridge, Mass: Schenkman Publishing, 1981.

Hall, Charles J. *A Nineteenth-Century Musical Chronicle: Events, 1800–1899*. Westport, Conn.: Greenwood Press, 1989.

Hamm, Charles. *Yesterdays: Popular Song in America*. New York: Norton, 1979.

Harder, Kelsie. *The Vocabulary of Marble Playing*. Gainesville, Fla.: American Dialect Society, 1955.

Heinze, Andrew R. *Adapting to Abundance: Jewish Immigrants, Mass Consumption, and the Search for American Identity*. New York: Columbia University Press, 1990.

Hoerder, Dirk, and Christiane Harzig, eds. *The Immigrant Labor Press in North America, 1840s–1970s*. 3 vols. Westport, Conn.: Greenwood Press, 1987.

Hoganson, Kristin. *Fighting for American Manhood: How Gender Politics Provoked the Spanish-American and Philippine-American Wars*. New Haven, Conn.: Yale University Press, 1998.

Hollon, W. Eugene. *Frontier Violence: Another Look*. New York: Oxford University Press, 1974.

Homer, William Innes. *Thomas Eakins: His Life and Art*. New York: Abbeville Press, 1992.

Horowitz, Helen Lefkowitz. *Campus Life: Undergraduate Cultures from the End of the Eighteenth Century to the Present*. Chicago: University of Chicago Press, 1990.

Hoxie, Frederick E. *A Final Promise: The Campaign to Assimilate the Indians, 1880–1920*. Lincoln: University of Nebraska Press, 1984.

Hoy, Suellen. *Chasing Dirt: The American Pursuit of Cleanliness*. New York: Oxford University Press, 1995.

Inness, Sherrie A., ed. *Kitchen Culture in America: Popular Representations of Food, Gender, and Race*. Philadelphia: University of Pennsylvania Press, 2001.

Jackson, Kenneth T. *The Crabgrass Frontier: The Suburbanization of the United States*. New York: Oxford University Press, 1985.

Johnson, Deidre. *Edward Stratemeyer and the Stratemeyer Syndicate*. New York: Wayne, 1993.

Jones, Gavin. *Strange Talk: The Politics of Dialect Literature in Gilded Age America*. Berkeley: University of California Press, 1999.

Keck, George R., and Sherril V. Martin, eds. *Feel the Spirit: Studies in Nineteenth-Century Afro-American Music*. Westport, Conn.: Greenwood Press, 1988.

Kensinger, Faye Riter. *Children of the Series and How They Grew; or, A Century of Heroines and Heroes, Romantic, Comic, Moral*. Bowling Green, Ohio: Bowling Green University Press, 1987.

Krug, Edward A. *The Shaping of the American High School*. New York: Harper & Row, 1973.

Kuper, Hilda. "Costume and Identity." *Comparative Studies in Society and History* 15 (June 1973): 348–67.

Laurie, Joe, Jr. *Vaudeville: From the Honky-Tonks to the Palace*. Port Washington, N.Y.: Kennikat Press, 1972.

Lears, T. J. Jackson. *Fables of Abundance: A Cultural History of Advertising in America*. New York: Basic Books, 1995.

Lester, Robin. *Stagg's University: The Rise, Decline, and Fall of Big-Time Football at Chicago*. Urbana: University of Illinois Press, 1995.

Levine, Lawrence W. *Black Culture and Black Consciousness: Afro-American Folk Thought from Slavery to Freedom*. New York: Oxford University Press, 1977.

Linkman, Audrey. *The Victorians: Photographic Portraits*. New York: Tauris Parke Books, 1993.

Mandelbaum, Seymour. *Boss Tweed's New York*. New York: John Wiley, 1965.

Mathews, Nancy Mowll. *Mary Cassatt*. New York: Harry N. Abrams, 1987.

McCallum, John Dennis. *College Football, U.S.A., 1869–1973: Official Book of the National Football Foundation*. Greenwich, Conn.: Hall of Fame Publishing, 1973.

McKlevey, Blake. *The Urbanization of America, 1860–1915*. New Brunswick, N.J.: Rutgers University Press, 1963.

Melton, Jeffrey Alan. *Mark Twain, Travel Books, and Tourism: The Tide of a Great Popular Movement*. Tuscaloosa: University of Alabama Press, 2002.

Melville, Tom. *Early Baseball and the Rise of the National League*. Jefferson, N.C.: McFarland, 2001.

Miller, Zane. *Boss Cox's Cincinnati: Urban Politics in the Progressive Era*. New York: Oxford University Press, 1968.

Mohl, Raymond, ed. *The Making of Urban America*. Wilmington, Del.: Scholarly Resources, 1988.

Moses, L. G. *Wild West Shows and the Images of American Indians, 1883–1933*. Albuquerque: University of New Mexico Press, 1996.

Mott, Frank Luther. *A History of American Magazines*. 5 vols. Cambridge, Mass.: Harvard University Press, 1930–1968.

Nackenoff, Carol. *The Fictional Republic: Horatio Alger and American Political Discourse*. New York: Oxford University Press, 1994.

Nasaw, David. *Schooled to Order: A Social History of Public Schooling in the United States*. New York: Oxford University Press, 1979.

Newsom, Jon, ed. *Perspectives on John Philip Sousa*. Washington, D.C.: GPO, 1983.

Ormond, Richard, and Elaine Kilmurray. *John Singer Sargent: Complete Paintings*. New Haven, Conn.: Yale University Press, 1998.

Perrot, Philippe. *Fashioning the Bourgeoisie: A History of Clothing in the Nineteenth Century*. Princeton, N.J.: Princeton University Press, 1994.

Peterson, Robert. *Only the Ball Was White: A History of Legendary Black Players and All-Black Professional Teams*. New York: Random House, 1999.

Peterson, Theodore. *Magazines in the Twentieth Century*. 2nd ed. Chicago: University of Illinois Press, 1975.

Ponce de Leon, Charles L. *Self-Exposure: Human Interest Journalism and the Emergence of Celebrity in America, 1890–1940*. Chapel Hill: University of North Carolina Press, 2002.

Prucha, Francis Paul. *The Great Father: The United States Government and the American Indians*. 2 vols. Lincoln: University of Nebraska Press, 1984.

Remise, Jac, and Jean Fondin. *The Golden Age of Toys*. Greenwich, Conn.: New York Graphic Society, 1967.

Riess, Steven A. *City Games: The Evolution of American Urban Society and the Rise of Sports*. Urbana: University of Illinois Press, 1989.

Roach, Mary Ellen, and Joanne Bubotz Eicher, eds. *Dress, Adornment, and the Social Order*. New York: John Wiley & Sons, 1965.

Rose, Mark. *Cities of Light and Heat: Domesticating Gas and Electricity in Urban America*. University Park: Pennsylvania State University Press, 1995.

Rudolph, Frederick. *Curriculum: A History of the American Undergraduate Course of Study Since 1636*. New York: Jossey-Bass, 1990.

Sante, Luc. *Low Life: Lures and Snares of Old New York*. New York: Farrar, Straus, Giroux, 1991.

Saxton, Alexander. "Problems of Class and Race in the Origins of the Mass Circulation Press." *American Quarterly* 36 (Summer 1984): 211–34.

Scharnhorst, Gary, and Jack Bales. *The Lost Life of Horatio Alger, Jr*. Bloomington: Indiana University Press, 1985.

Schlesinger, Arthur M. *The Rise of the City, 1878–1898*. New York: Macmillan, 1933.

Schofield, Ann, ed. *Sealskin and Shoddy: Working Women in American Labor Press Fiction, 1870–1920*. Westport, Conn.: Greenwood Press, 1988.

Schorman, Rob. "Ready or Not: Custom-Made Ideals and Ready-Made Clothes in Late 19th-Century America." *Journal of American Culture* 19 (Winter 1996): 111–21.

———. "Remember the Maine, Boys and the Price of this Suit." *Historian* 61 (Fall 1998): 119–35.

Sichel, Marion. *History of Children's Costume*. London: Batsford Academic and Educational, 1983.

Simpson, Jeffrey. *Chautauqua: An American Utopia*. New York: Harry N. Abrams in association with the Chautauqua Institution, 1999.

Slatkin, Wendy. *The Voices of Women Artists*. Englewood Cliffs, N.J.: Prentice Hall, 1993.

Slotkin, Richard. *Gunfighter Nation: The Myth of the Frontier in Twentieth-Century America*. New York: Atheneum, 1992.

Snyder, Robert W. *The Voice of the City: Vaudeville and Popular Culture in New York*. New York: Oxford University Press, 1989.

Solomon, Barbara Miller. *In the Company of Educated Women: A History of Women and Higher Education in America*. New Haven, Conn.: Yale University Press, 1990.

Southern, Eileen. *The Music of Black Americans: A History*. New York: W. W. Norton, 1997.

Sterngass, Jon. *First Resorts: Pursuing Pleasure at Saratoga Springs, Newport, & Coney Island*. Baltimore, Md.: Johns Hopkins University Press, 2001.

Strasser, Susan. *Satisfaction Guaranteed: The Making of the American Mass Market*. New York: Pantheon Books, 1989.

Streitmatter, Rodger. "Origins of the American Labor Press." *Journalism History* 25 (Autumn 1999): 99–107.

Sullivan, Dolores. *William Holmes McGuffey: Schoolmaster to the Nation*. Rutherford, N.J.: Fairleigh Dickinson University Press, 1994.

Tannahill, Reay. *Food in History*. New York: Stein and Day, 1973.

Tapia, John E. *Circuit Chautauqua: From Rural Education to Popular Entertainment in Early Twentieth Century America*. Jefferson, N.C.: McFarland, 1997.

Tawa, Nicholas E. *A Sound of Strangers: Musical Culture, Acculturation, and the Post–Civil War Ethnic American*. Metuchen, N.J.: Scarecrow Press, 1982.

Tebbel, John, and Mary Ellen Zuckerman. *The Magazine in America, 1741–1990*. New York: Oxford University Press, 1991.

Volpe, Tod M., and Beth Cathers. *Treasures of the American Arts and Crafts Movement, 1890–1920*. New York: Harry N. Abrams, 1987.

Warner, Sam Bass, Jr. *Streetcar Suburbs: The Process of Growth in Boston, 1870–1900*. 2nd ed. Cambridge, Mass.: Harvard University Press, 1973.

Weiss, Ellen. *City in the Woods: The Life and Design of an American Camp Meeting on Martha's Vineyard*. New York: Oxford University Press, 1987.

Weiss, Richard. *The American Myth of Success: From Horatio Alger to Norman Vincent Peale*. New York: Basic Books, 1969.

Welch, Richard. *Response to Imperialism: The United States and the Philippine-American War, 1899–1902*. Chapel Hill: University of North Carolina Press, 1979.

Wyllie, Irvin G. *The Self-Made Man in America: The Myth of Rags to Riches*. New Brunswick, N.J.: Rutgers University Press, 1954.

Index

About the Author

JOEL SHROCK earned his Ph.D. from Miami University and is currently an Instructor of History at the Indiana Academy for Science, Mathematics, and Humanities. He has authored an article on race and rape in silent film and co-authored another on student protest of the Vietnam War, which appears in the Greenwood Press volume of essays *The Vietnam War on Campus: Other Voices, More Distant Drums*. He is currently completing a manuscript on popular children's literature in the Gilded Age.